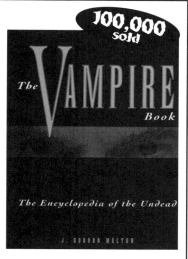
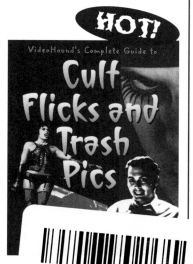

ALSO FROM VISIBLE INK PRESS

The Vampire Book:
The Encyclopedia of the Undead

VideoHound's Complete Guide to Cult Flicks and Trash Pics

VideoHound's Video Premieres

VideoHound's Sci-Fi Experience:
Your Quantum Guide to the Video Universe

VideoHound's Golden Movie Retriever 1997

VideoHound's Family Movie Guide, Second Edition

The VideoHound & All-Movie Guide StarGazer

VideoHound's Movie LaughLines:
Quips, Quotes and Clever Comebacks

VideoHound's Idiot's Delight:
The 100 Dumbest Movies of All Time

Toxic Fame:
Celebrities Speak on Stardom

VideoHound's
VAMPIRES
on VIDEO

VideoHound'[s]
Vampires
on Video

Compiled in Cooperation with
J. Gordon Melton
and the
Transylvanian
Society of
Dracula

Detroit   New York   Toronto   London

VideoHound's®
VAMPIRES
on VIDEO

Copyright © 1997 by J. Gordon Melton

Published by Visible Ink Press®. a division of Gale Research
835 Penobscot Bldg.
Detroit. MI 48226-4094

Visible Ink Press and VideoHound are trademarks of Gale Research

ost Visible Ink Press books are available at special quantity discounts when purchased in
lk by corporations. organizations. or groups. Customized printings. special imprints. mes-
ges. and excerpts can be produced to meet your needs. For more information. contact Spe-
l Markets Manager. Gale Research. 835 Penobscot Bldg.. Detroit. MI 48226-4094.

lton. J. Gordon
    Videohound's vampires on video / J. Gordon Melton
       p.   cm. — (Videohound)
    Includes indexes.
    ISBN 1-57859-002-7 (pbk.)
       1. Vampire films—Catalogs. 2. Vampire films—History and criticism. 3. Video record-
ings—Catalogs.   I. Title.   II. Series: Videohound (Series)
PN1995.9.V3M46   1997
016.79143'675—dc21   97-4010
                                                                          CIP

ISBN 1-57859-002-7
Printed in the United States of America

credits

DIRECTOR/WRITER
J. Gordon Melton

ASSOCIATE DIRECTOR
James Craddock

SECOND UNIT DIRECTOR
Michelle Banks

CAST OF CHARACTERS
Carol Schwartz
Brad Morgan
Terri Schell
Devra Sladics
Beth Fhaner
Christine Tomassini
Christopher Scanlon
Judy Galens
Dean Dauphinais
Michelle Banks
Jim Olenski
Marty Connors

SUPPORTING CAST
Maria Franklin
Beverly Jendrowski
Arlene Kevonian
Ken Benson
Louise Gagne
Ian Goodhall
Sandy Jaszczak
Wayne Fong
Jeffrey Muhr
NeilYee

RESEARCH QUEEN
Christine Tomassini

ART DIRECTION
Mary Krzewinski

COMPUTER GENIUS
Wayne Fong

PRODUCERS
Marty Connors
Julia Furtaw
Terri Schell

PRODUCTION
Mary Beth Trimper
Dorothy Maki
Evi Seoud
Shanna Heilveil

POST-PRODUCTION
Marco Di Vita/The Graphix Group

SPIN DOCTORS
Susan Stefani
Cyndi Naughton
Lauri Taylor
Jenny Sweetland
Betsy Revegno
Kim Intindola

PHOTOGRAPHS
The Kobal Collection

PHOTO EDITING
Michelle Banks
Pam Hayes
Barb Yarrow

CAPTIONS
Michelle Banks
Jim Craddock

TECHNICAL ADVISOR
Jim Olenski

ADDITIONAL RESEARCH
Thomas Video/Clawson, MI

contents

Vampires A to Z

with sidebars, photos & quotes

1

about the author

J. GORDON MELTON is one of the world's most recognized authorities on vampires and is the author of The Vampire Book: The Encyclopedia of the Undead (Gale/Visible Ink, 1994). Well-known as a leading religious scholar and author (The Encyclopedia of American Religions, New Age Encyclopedia), Melton's love for vampires dates back to his college days, when the infamous Hammer Films' Dracula movies (with Christopher Lee) changed the way vampire movies were made. Since those early days, he has accumulated an impressive collection of vampire videos, books, paraphernalia, even comic books.

Melton is also the founder and president of the American chapter of the Transylvanian Society of Dracula, which was founded in Romania in the late 1980s after the fall of tyrannical leader Nicolae Ceausescu. Northern Romania is also known as Transylvania and is the home of Prince Vlad Tepes, the historical figure who is acknowledged to be the "real" Dracula. The Society was founded to help increase tourism in Transylvania and to bridge the gap between vampire fans in Eastern Europe and those in the West. It is different from other vampire fan clubs in that it focuses on the historical, cultural, and literary aspects of the vampire myth. Each year, the Society sponsors an annual symposium for Westerners to meet and talk with Romanian scholars about Dracula, Slavic vampire lore, and contemporary vampire myths. In 1995, the group launched the *Transylvanian Journal: Dracula and Vampire Studies*, which is the first scholarly journal to study vampires. Melton himself traveled to Romania in 1993 and was lucky enough to view the premiere of Francis Ford Coppola's *Dracula* with a Romanian audience.

Through his work in the Society, Melton has been instrumental in organizing **Dracula 97**, a celebration honoring the 100th anniversary of the publication of Bram Stoker's Dracula. For information on that celebration, he can be contacted: c/o Transylvanian Society of Dracula, P.O. Box 91611, Santa Barbara, CA 93190-1611.

acknowledgments

This volume has been compiled from the extensive collection of books and videos of the American Chapter of the Transylvanian Society of Dracula, but there are also several people who were extremely helpful in the completion of this project. Since the founding of the chapter, I have come into contact with a network of people, especially the editors of the many fanzines, who are continually generating material on vampires in general and vampire films in particular. Of these, I particularly want to single out Robert J. Harvey, who generously shared all of his data on vampire movies and pointed out a number of movies I had missed. I am also grateful for the ongoing assistance of Robert Eighteen-Bisang, one of the most knowledgeable Dracula experts working today, and two long-time associates: Jeanne Youngson of the Count Dracula Fan Club, and Martin V. Riccardo of Vampire Studies in Chicago.

introduction

The year 1997 marks the 100th anniversary of the publication of Bram Stoker's novel Dracula. This fact, along with the approach of a new millennium, has caused a new level of interest in vampires in the last few years. This interest has led Dr. J. Gordon Melton to compile this follow-up to the hugely successful Vampire Book (Gale/Visible Ink Press, 1994). This time Dr. Melton focuses on the screen versions of Dracula (and the various other vampires out there), exploring how movies have shaped, and in some cases drastically changed, vampire mythology. In this introduction, Dr. Melton will share some of the insights and information gathered while creating this book. Dr. Melton, the floor is yours.

It could be said that movies have done more to determine popular belief about vampires than novels. In Stoker's novel, Dracula walked around in daylight. Yet we tend to think of vampires as purely nocturnal creatures. Fangs are a key component of the perceived vampire physiology, but folkloric vampires, not to mention Bela Lugosi and the vampires of the 1930s and 1940s, had no fangs. These are just a few of the changes Hollywood has wrought on the vampire legend.

The vampire was right there when the very first movies were being made. Most people who watch television have, for example, seen the 1902 classic science fiction movie *Le Voyage dans la Lune* (A Trip to the Moon) made by Georges Mélies, but few are aware that in 1896, a year before Stoker's *Dracula* appeared, Mélies made the first horror movie, *Le Manoir du Diable* (The Devil's Castle), which also happened to be the first vampire movie. Like *Le Voyage dans la Lune*, it was a very short feature, only two minutes long. A demon transforms into a large vampire bat and attacks the protagonist who finally defeats him with a crucifix.

Over the next generation, movies explored many genres in all walks of life, looking for new story lines, improving techniques, and developing special effects. But the vampire always returned, in part because he (or she) was one of the most powerful metaphors for the uneven power relationships between humans, especially between men and women. Additionally, the vampire movie gave birth to one of the most enduring images in movies, the vamp or femme fatale. The image was established by American actress Theda Bara, who flaunted her vampishness in both her films and personal appearances. Many of the silent movies with the word "vampire" in the title are actually vamp movies. Later on, the power of the vampire was used to illustrate class differences and the disparity between the wealthy and impoverished.

The novel *Dracula*, of course, had a profound effect upon dramatists, who immediately saw its cinematic qualities. It appears that at least two film versions were made prior to the 1922 unauthorized version by F. W. Murnau, released under the name *Nosferatu*. At the time, *Nosferatu* was not an influential picture, as it was suppressed following a successful lawsuit by Bram Stoker's widow. Thus it was that Bela Lugosi's *Dracula*, made nine years later, became such a landmark. Not only was it a rather good horror picture, it was the first major vampire production with a sound track.

In the 1940s, the shock of the original horror classics had worn off, in part due to the variance in the quality of sequels, as well as the effect of the real-life horrors of World War II. This period saw the return of the classic monsters, this time as targets of spoofs. In the new comedic setting, they were the foils for some of the popular comedians of the day, most notably (and successfully) Abbott and Costello. But even these films made contributions to the vampire mythology. One popular movie, *Abbott and Costello Meet Frankenstein*, strengthened the belief in the power of sunlight to kill a vampire.

In the post-war era, vampire movies were integral to the horror film industry's challenge of the censorship laws enacted by different countries. Vampire movies, increasingly characterized by heightened doses of sex and violence, tested the boundaries of acceptability. Some of the worst movies ever made originally found an audience in the 1960s or 1970s simply because of the liberal amount of skin that was shown, or the level of violence pictured in the scenes during which the vampire either attacked someone or was killed.

In the 1980s and 1990s, vampires have staked their claim to a large chunk of the multiplex and video rental markets. With a few straight-to-video and extra-low-budget exceptions, the new breed of vampire movie has generally provided interesting twists on conventional vampire ideas, quality film making, and enough snazzy special effects and blood to satisfy the increasingly hard-to-impress movie going audience.

In contrast, *Plan 9 from Outer Space* has always had the reputation of being as bad as commercial movies could be. However, *Plan 9* turned out to be a delightfully entertaining cinematic event compared to some of the truly awful movies screened during the preparation of this book. In saying that, I would emphasize my authentic appreciation for low-budget flicks. Some of them show more than a spark of creativity and almost all of them have an interesting twist or do something outrageous or disturbing that more mainstream movies would avoid. However, when you get a low-budget product that combines a boring story, poor camera work, bad lighting, and actors who don't know what they're doing, even the most dedicated vampire fan can lose interest quickly. I had to sit there and take it, all for the sake of warning our readers which movies make "trash pics" a welcome entertainment relief. In fact, word tends to get out on these types of movies rather quickly, and titles are often changed to protect the profitability of such stinkers, thereby suckering fans into watching the same dreck they already knew was not fit for human consumption. This is where I immediately ran into a problem. Many movies have been released under a variety of names, a few as many as eight or ten. On occasion different movies were issued under the same name. I am entirely convinced that you can almost rate a movie based solely on how many alternate titles it has.

National origin plays as big a part as quality in the name change game. As might be expected, the same movie will often have a different title in the United Kingdom and North America, in part because the U.S. and England have had different censorship regulations at different times. Also, British and American releases of the same film frequently differ, due to the amount of material that the censors cut. On several occasions directors prepared several cuts, which were released under different titles in different countries, or shot scenes with actors in various degrees of undress, in order to obtain specific ratings to appeal to different audiences in the same country. The problem was accentuated as movies were translated either into or from French, German, Spanish, Italian, or other languages. So I came up with a master list of alternative vampire movie titles and have cross indexed it to the more common title under which we have reviewed it. Thus the reader can consult the list of alternate titles if they don't find their favorite movie listed in the "Vampires A to Z" section, which forms the main body of this work.

Vampires have always been viewed as a fairly solitary species. Vampire aficionados, on the other hand, seem to be a very social group, gathering in many settings to discuss vampire-inspired music, literature, fashion, and culture; participate in role-playing games; attend costume parties; or just share in a mutual understanding of what is sometimes viewed as an unusual pastime. For this reason, I've included a section called "Vampire Connections." This section provides addresses for vampire and vampire film-related web sites, many with links and e-mail addresses. It also includes contact information for vampire-related fan clubs and resource centers, as well as various vampire publications.

The manner in which I reviewed the movies was a bit different for this volume. While overall quality and watchability played their usual key roles, plot, characterization, and dialogue had to be viewed in a somewhat different light. Since most of these films were adapted, or drew their inspiration from, a finite set of literary works, some repetition (and a certain reliance on cliche) was inevitable. Atmosphere took a more prominent place in the hierarchy of desirable traits. Visual style and sensuality could often excuse shortcomings in a script, or lapses in direction. If a film has historical significance, or if it added (or changed) an element of the vampire myth, it gets more attention than a mainstream genre piece. Another important key was how the vampire was treated. How much screen time did he or she get? Was that time used effectively? Was the vampire appropriately menacing? Sexy? Mysterious? Sympathetic if that was the intent? Was the vampire's attack cursory, or did it excite? Hopefully, this book will answer these questions to your satisfaction.

Many related topics just didn't fit within the confines of a single entry. For this reason, the main review section includes sidebars exploring important actors, directors, producers, characters, and milestones in the genre. These are intended to provide added context for the movies reviewed and enhance your enjoyment of the movies (and the book). Photos, tag lines, and quotes provide a diversion from the "burden" of figuring out which movie to watch. Knowing what's available is only half the battle. It helps to know what's worth the time, and it's nice to know why and how it came to be. And in the end, the main point is to entertain in an informative way.

additional
sources

Some of the movies reviewed in this book may be difficult to find using conventional devices such as the neighborhood video rental chain. Many independent and mail-order video outlets specialize in rare or hard-to-find movies. We have included a small list of such outlets to assist you in your search.

Thomas Video
122 S. Main St
Clawson, MI 48017
(810)280-2833

Video Vision
Attn: Chris Hendlin
4603 Bloomington, Ave.
Minneapolis, MN 55407
(612)728-0000

Luminous Film & Video
PO Box 1047, Dept. AC
Medford, NY 11763
(516)289-1644
LFVW@aol.com

House of Monsters
2038 N. Clark St., No. 348
Chicago, Il 60614
fax: (312)929-7205

Video Vault
(800)VAULT66
located in Alexandria, VA

A Million and One World—Wide Videos
PO Box 349
Orchard Hill, GA 30266
(800)849-7309; (770)227-7309
Fax: (800)849-0873; (770)227-0873

Video Oyster
145 W. 12th St.
New York, NY 10011
fax: (212)989-3533
E-mail: video@VideoOyster.com

China West Video
PO Box 291655, Dept. 8
Los Angeles, CA 90029

Facets Video
(800)331-6197
located in Chicago, IL

Movies Unlimited
(800)4-MOVIES
Located in Philadelphia, PA

Alphabetization

Titles are arranged on a word-by-word basis, including articles and prepositions. Leading articles (A, An, The) are ignored in English-language titles; the equivalent foreign articles are not ignored; thus *The Astro-Zombies* appears in the As, but *Les Charlots contra Dracula* appears in the Ls. Some other points to keep in mind:

Common abbreviations in titles file as if they were spelled out, so *Dr. Terror's House of Horrors* will be alphabetized as "Doctor Terror's House of Horrors."

Movies with numbers (such as *The 7 Brothers Meet Dracula*) are alphabetized as if the number was spelled out—so the Hammer Films/Shaw Brothers collaboration would appear in the Ss, as if it were "The Seven Brothers Meet Dracula."

Sample Review

Each review contains up to 18 tidbits of information, as enumerated below. Please realize that we made up a bit of info in this review, because we couldn't find one single movie that contained every single element that might appear in a review. If anyone out there finds that singular entry, please let us know.

---

❶

The Addiction

❷ A low-budget exploration of vampirism purposely shot in black and white. Kathleen Conklin (Lily Taylor), a coed majoring in philosophy at New York University, encounters a vampire on a dark side street of the Big Apple. She takes to her new life philosophically and proceeds to treat students, professors, and street people alike—as her next drink of blood. As Conklin moves from one victim to the next, the story becomes an exploration of the power of addiction and the damnation it brings. While not a unique theme in vampire literature and cinema, it is handled in a fresh and effective manner here. **❸ AKA:** I Drink, Therefore I Am. **❹**

❺ 1995 **❻** (R) **❼** 82m/B **❽** **❾** GB **❿** [Denis Hahn, Fernando Sulichin] **⓫** **Lily Taylor, Christopher Walken**, Annabella Sciorra, Edie Falco, Paul Calderone, Fredro Srar, Kathryn Erbe, Michael Imperioli; **⓬ D:** Abel Ferrara; **⓭ W:** Nicholas St. John; **⓮ C:** Owen Roizman; **⓯ M:** Joe Delia. **⓰** Academy Awards '96: Best Scary Cameo (Walken); Nominations: Independent Spirit Awards '96: Best Actress (Taylor), Best Film. **⓱ VHS** PGV **⓲**

---

1. Title (see also Alternate Titles below, and the "Alternate Titles Index")

2. Description/review

3. Alternate titles (we made this one up)

4. One-to-four-bone rating (or Woof!), four bones being the ultimate praise.

5. Year released

6. MPAA rating

7. Length in minutes

8. Black and White (B) or Color (C)

9. Country in which produced (if other than the U.S.) [we faked this one to]

10. Producer(s) or producing company

11. Cast, including cameos and voiceovers (V). Bolded cast member(s) portrayed the vampire(s)

12. Director(s)

13. Writer(s)

14. Cinematographer(s) (we took some liberties with this one)

15. Music

16. Awards, including nominations (we made up this award, the nominations are real)

17. Format, including VHS, Beta, and Laservideo/disk (LV)

18. Distributor code(s) (see also "Distributor List" and "Distributor Guide")

foreword

The first vampire movie I ever saw was F.W. Murnau's *Nosferatu: Eine Symphonie des Grauens*. I was working at the Museum of Modern Art, which was, in the early 1950's, one of the few places in New York City that showed silent movies. As a film buff, I was in cinematic heaven. We had 20-minute tea breaks and I would slip down the back stairs to the theatre and watch about fifteen minutes of whatever movie was playing that week. The next afternoon I'd stagger my time and do the same. And so on. On my day off, I'd go in and see the whole movie. Is that dedication or what?

Nosferatu in particular took me by complete surprise. Max Schreck scared the hell out of me. No matter how often I've seen the film since, I still remember the instant I beheld the bald baddie for the first time. I am, in fact, convinced that exposure to *Nosferatu* and subsequent movie vampires contributed in large part to the founding of the **International Count Dracula Fan Club**, as well as the **Bram Stoker Memorial Association**, dedicated to the man who was and is, in large part, responsible for the popularity of today's vampire.

I first met Dr. Melton in Ireland some years ago when we were both lecturing at the annual Bram Stoker Summer School. We have since had numerous chats about the various aspects of the Undead mystique and I continue to be amazed at his vast, in-depth knowledge of the genre.

VideoHound's Vampires on Video is yet another fine example of Dr. Melton's expertise, and I consider the book to be one of our Research Library's most important and valuable possessions.

Jeanne Keyes Youngson
President & Founder
The International Count Dracula Fan Club
The Bram Stoker Memorial Association

January 15, 1997

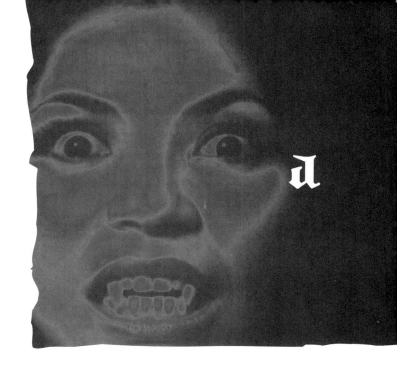

Abbott and Costello Meet Frankenstein

Universal Studios, which in the 1930s was largely responsible for the growth of the horror film genre, changed its focus in the late 1940s and began turning out comedic parodies of its classic horror films. In this farce, Bud Abbott and Lou Costello play baggage clerks charged with delivering a crate to a wax museum, unaware that it contains the remains of Dracula and Frankenstein. (Reprising his role as Dracula was Bela Lugosi, who won the role over the objections of many executives at Universal who wanted John Carradine to play the vampire.) Dracula comes back to life, of course, and immediately tries to revive Frankenstein, who unfortunately needs a new brain. Enter Costello as the brain donor candidate, setting the stage for numerous belly laughs. Lon Chaney makes a brief appearance to warn Lou and Bud of Dracula's machinations. While this film essentially held horror movies up to ridicule, the movie did serve to strengthen the modern vampire myth through its effective scene showing the death of Dracula, who is consumed by the first rays of the rising sun. The success of this movie again staved off the threatened bankruptcy of Universal, just as Lugosi's *Dracula* had done in 1931. *AKA: Meet the Ghosts; Abbott and Costello Meet the Ghosts; Abbott et Costello contre Frankenstein* (French); *Deux Nigauds contre Frankenstein* (French); and *Abbott et Costello et les Monstres* (Belgium). 𝄞𝄞𝄞

1949 83m/B [Universal] **Bela Lugosi**, Bud Abbott, Lou Costello, Lon Chaney Jr., Glenn Strange, Lenore Aubert, Jane Randolph; **D:** Charles T. Barton; **W:** Robert Lees, Frederic Rinaldo, John Grant; **V:** Vincent Price. **VHS, Beta, LV** *MCA*

The Addams Family

The Addams Family television series has had amazing staying power in syndication in spite of the fact that the show was only on for two years in the mid 1960s. This big budget 1990s revival was at the forefront of the

The Addams Family: "No. ma'am. we're not collecting for the Red Cross. but we are collecting something." A bewildered Morticia (Anjelica Huston) and Uncle Fester (Christopher Lloyd) look on from the *Addams Family*.

recent trend towards recycling old television series into feature films. The movie features an entirely new cast, led by Angelica Huston playing the vampish Morticia Addams. The thin plot (which is really just an excuse to explore the bizarre lifestyles of family members for whom the macabre is the mundane), centers on the attempt to steal the considerable Addams family fortune by a man posing as dear old Uncle Fester. The Addams Family was based on characters created by Charles Addams in his *New Yorker* cartoons. A sequel, *Addams Family Values*, appeared two years later. ♫♫

1991 (PG-13) 102m/C [Scott Rudin, Graham Place] Anjelica Huston, Raul Julia, Christopher Lloyd, Dan Hedaya, Elizabeth Wilson, Judith Malina, Carel Struycken, Dana Ivey, Paul Benedict, Christina Ricci, Jimmy Workman, Christopher Hart, John Franklin; *Cameos:* Marc Shaiman; *D:* Barry Sonnenfeld; *W:* Caroline Thompson, Larry Thompson; *C:* Owen Roizman; *M:* Marc Shaiman. Golden Raspberry Awards '91: Worst Song ("Addams Groove"); Nominations: Academy Awards '91: Best Costume Design. **VHS, Beta, LV** *PAR*

Addams Family Values

The cast of the 1991 movie was reassembled for a new round of the unique Addams Family view of life and undeath. As in the first movie, Uncle Fester is at the center of the plot. It seems that Pubert, the newest member of the family, needs a nanny. Of course, the bizarre Addams can't hire a normal nanny and instead end up with a golddigging murderer (Joan Cusack) who is out to marry Uncle Fester and then kill him to gain access to his fortune. In the process, she puts family loyalty to the test by creating a rift between Fester and Gomez. While poking fun at traditional "family values," the story effectively affirms family unity amid the traditional dark humor that fans demand from America's creepiest family. 🦇🦇🦇

1993 (PG-13) 93m/C [Scott Rudin] Anjelica Huston, Raul Julia, Christopher Lloyd, Joan Cusack, Carol Kane, Christina Ricci, Jimmy Workman, Kaitlyn Hooper, Kristen Hooper, Carel Struycken, David Krumholtz, Christopher Hart, Dana Ivey, Peter MacNicol, Christine Baranski, Mercedes McNab; **D:** Barry Sonnenfeld; **W:** Paul Rudnick; **M:** Marc Shaiman. Golden Raspberry Awards '93: Worst Song ("WHOOMP! There It Is"); Nominations: Academy Awards '93: Best Art Direction/Set Decoration; Golden Globe Awards '94: Best Actress—Musical/Comedy (Huston). **VHS, Beta, LV** *PAR*

Addicted to Murder

Joel Winter (Mick McCleery) is a wounded soul. Abused as a child, he has become an adult who is unable to build a positive relationship to women—in fact, he kills them. Everything changes when he meets Angie (Sasha Graham), a vampire. She draws Joel into her world and tries to convince him that he is really like her—a predator and creature of the night. She begins to transform him into a vampire, but the change awakens his lost humanity and he realizes how horrible his life has been. This just doesn't work for Angie, who frames the remorseful Joel for a murder he did not commit. Her actions drive Joel over the edge and force him to fully complete the change into a vampire. A hunter once again, Joel puts his new powers to good use. He recognizes that the vampires are evil and uses his own vampiric power to kill them. 🦇🦇

1995m/C Sasha Graham, Laura McLaughlin, Mick McCleery; **D:** Kevin J. Lindenmuth.

The Addiction

A low-budget exploration of vampirism purposely shot in black and white. Kathleen Conklin (Lily Taylor), a coed majoring in philosophy at New York University, encounters a vampire on a dark side street of the Big Apple. She takes to her new life philosophically and proceeds to treat students, professors, and street people alike—as her next drink of blood. As Conklin moves from one victim to the next, the story becomes an exploration of the power of addiction and the damnation it brings. While not a unique theme in vampire literature and cinema, it is handled in a fresh and effective manner here. 🦇🦇🦇

1995 (R) 82m/B [Denis Hann, Fernando Sulichin] Lili Taylor, Christopher Walken, Annabella Sciorra, Edie Falco, Paul Calderone, Fredro Star, Kathryn Erbe, Michael Imperioli; **D:** Abel Ferrara; **W:** Nicholas St. John; **M:** Joe Delia. Nominations: Independent Spirit Awards '96: Best Actress (Taylor), Best Film. **VHS** *PGV*

Alabama's Ghost

One of the few vampire movies made for the African American community, Frederic Hobbs wrote, produced, and directed this story of a vampire rock group that has to fight off a ghostly attack. A far cry from the best examples of the "blaxploitation" films of the '70s. 🦇🦇

1972 (PG) 96m/C [Vistar Int'l Productions] Christopher Brooks, E. Kerrigan Prescott; **D:** Fredric Hobbs. **VHS, Beta** *LIV*

Alien Massacre

Movie anthology consisting of five short features, two of which—"Count Alucard" and "King Vampire"—are vampire stories. In "Count Alucard," Dracula encounters a werewolf. In "King Vampire," a vampire is turned loose on nineteenth-century London

1967 90m/C [Dorad Corporation, Borealis Ent.] Lon Chaney Jr., John Carradine, Rochelle Hudson, Roger Gentry, Mitch Evans; **D:** David L. Hewitt. **VHS, Beta** ACA, MRV

Alraune

Though largely unknown outside of the German-speaking world, Hanns Heinz Ewers best-selling 1913 gothic novel "Alraune" inspired five film adaptations, the first four of which were silent films. This sound version retells the story of an eccentric, if not certifiably mad, scientist. First he collects the semen of a recently deceased man who had been executed by hanging, then he artificially inseminates a prostitute, who gives birth to Alraune. Alraune grows up as a monstrous creature—a cold, unfeeling woman who feeds on the blood of her lovers and then kills them, taking their souls. 🐺🐺

1952 ?m/C **Hildegarde Knef**, Erich von Stroheim, Karl-Heinz Boehm, Julia Koschka; **D:** Arthur Maria Rabenalt.

Anak Pontianak

In this fourth of the Malaysian vampire series, former star Maria Menado sits one out, but other creatures of traditional Malaysian folklore, including the bodiless vampire-like *polong*, put in appearances. **AKA:** Son of the Vampire; Curse of the Vampire. 🐺🐺

1958 ?m/B [Shaw Brothers] Haj Hattar, Dyang Sofia, Hasimah; **D:** Ramon Estella.

Andy Warhol's Dracula

In this highly rated satirical comedy, Dracula has a problem—he will die unless he can find the blood of a virgin. Unable to find any in his native Transylvania, he travels to Catholic Italy in search of the seemingly rare virginal female. He moves in with a rich family with four "virginal" daughters only to discover that Mario the gardener (played by Joe Dallesandro) has really been having his way

Andy Warhol's Dracula: "Don't Go Breakin' My Heart, no really!" yells a fallen Udo Kier as Dracula.

This movie represents a low point in the careers of both John Carradine and Lon Chaney, Jr. It was probably the high point for most of the rest of the cast. *Dr. Terror's Gallery* has no ties to, and in fact contrasts sharply with, the very fine anthology *Dr. Terror's House of Horror*. **AKA:** The Witch's Clock, Alien Massacre. Dr. Terror's Gallery of Horrors; Return from the Past; The Blood Suckers; Gallery of Horror. 🐺🐺

with two of them and that they won't be wearing white. Dracula is forced to go after the 14-year-old daughter, but he is again foiled by Mario, who gets there first. In the end, Mario and Dracula meet in a final confrontation. **AKA:** Blood for Dracula; Young Dracula. 🦷🦷🦷

1974 (R) 106m/C *IT FR* [Bryanston Pictures] **Udo Kier,** Arno Juergling, Maxine McKendry, Joe Dallesandro, Vittorio De Sica; **Cameos:** Roman Polanski; **D:** Paul Morrissey; **W:** Paul Morrissey. **VHS, Beta** *TRI, GEM, INJ*

Anemia

The middle-aged leader of the Italian Communist Party becomes a vampire after he reads the memoirs left behind by his grandfather, a somewhat shadowy figure. Political satire wins out over horror. 🦷🦷

1986 ?m/C [RAI Radiotelevisione Italiana] **Hanns Zischler,** Gerard Landry, Gioia Maria Scila; **D:** Alberto Abruzzese, Achille Pisanti.

Anne Rice: Birth of the Vampire

Just in time for the big-screen release of Rice's novel "Interview with a Vampire," comes this BBC documentary on the best-selling author of "The Vampire Chronicles." Documents Rice's childhood in New Orleans and interviews with family, friends, and the author, along with short readings from her novels. 🦷🦷

1994 45m/C VHS *FXV*

The Arrival

Science fiction and horror mix in this story of alien invasion. An alien meteor lands on Earth, carrying a never-before-seen vampiric entity. It possesses an old man, transforming him into a serial killer hungry for female blood. As with Dracula, the killer grows younger each time he feeds. He is opposed by an FBI agent (John Saxon). In spite of its moments, *The Arrival* falls short of its potential. 🦷

1990 (R) 107m/C [Ron Matonak] John Saxon, Joseph Culp, Robert Sampson, Michael J. Pollard; **Cameos:** David Schmoeller; **D:** David Schmoeller; **W:** David Schmoeller; **M:** Richard Band. **VHS, LV** *PSM*

The Astro-Zombies

Horror and vampire fans wonder what John Carradine could have been thinking when he signed up for this throw-back to the low-budget horror films of the 1950s. He plays Dr. DiMarco, a mad scientist who spends all of his time trying to produce a super race of astro-zombies (or is it space vampires?). To construct these Frankenstein-like, strange hybrid creatures, he needs a steady supply of dead bodies. This of course alerts the proper authorities to his nefarious plot, and the FBI, various spies, and agents of the Chinese government all gather to crash the doctor's monster party. Simply a terrible film, easily in the "Worse than Plan 9 from Outer Space" category. **Woof!**

1967 83m/C [T.V. Mikels Film Productions] Tura Satana, Wendell Corey, John Carradine, Tom Pace, Joan Patrick, Rafael Campos; **D:** Ted V. Mikels; **W:** Ted V. Mikels, Wayne Rogers. **VHS, Beta** *NO*

Atom Age Vampire

The post-atomic age caused a rethinking of many long-established concepts, including those regarding vampires. As this movie certainly showed, the traditional definition of a vampire could be stretched to fit modern circumstances. Suzanne Loret, having lost her beauty in an accident, turns to one of the seemingly ever-present mad scientists for help. The scientist, who has gained his expertise from treating Japanese victims of the atomic bomb, falls madly in love with her and decides on a radical method of treatment. He kills several women and uses their blood to rejuvenate Loret. The treatment works, but unfortunately it turns her into a

Attack of the Giant Leeches: "Hey baby, what a big mouth you have, wait a minute." An unwilling victim tries to escape the clutches of a giant Leech.

creature who craves regular infusions of blood. Originally released as *L Erde di Satana*, it enjoyed only moderate success in the theaters but has recently been released on video with English dubbing. ♪

1961 71m/B *IT* [Mario Bava, Lion Films, Topaz Film Corporation] Alberto Lupo, Susanne Loret, Sergio Fantoni; *D:* Albert Magnoli. **VHS, Beta** *SNC, NOS, VYY*

Attack of the Giant Leeches

Leeches, like mosquitoes, are identified for obvious reasons with vampires. Giant intelligent leeches latch onto humans as their new food supply and menace their neighboring swamp dwellers. One annoyed resident feeds them his wife and girlfriend. Poor even by Roger Corman low-budget standards.

AKA: The Giant Leeches; She Demons of the Swamp. **Woof!**

1959 62m/B [American International Pictures (A.I.P.)] Ken Clark, Yvette Vickers, Gene Roth, Bruno Ve Sota, Michael Emmet; *D:* Bernard L. Kowalski; *W:* Leo Gordon; *C:* John M. Nickolaus Jr. **VHS** *VYY, SNC, NOS*

Attack of the Mutant Roadkill and the Vampyer Zombies from Beyond the Grave

An ultra low-budget independent effort that is just plain fun—if you're in the mood to

watch a bunch of amateurs have a good time with a far-out story. The plot: A scientist finally discovers a secret formula for which he has been searching. Unfortunately, he knocks his concoction over while celebrating, killing him and sending the formula flowing down the drain into the sewer system. Coincidentally, a city worker just happens to be disposing of all the recent animal road-kills at the same time, tossing the carcasses into the sewer. The formula, of course, brings the animals back to life (along with several residents of the local cemetery), and together the mutant creatures go on a bloodsucking and flesh eating rampage. The movie gets a star for its lack of pretentiousness—it's really nothing more than a home movie made by a group of seriously demented people with a camera, a sense of humor, and too much time on their hands. 🦴🦴

1993 ?m/C

The Awful Dr. Orlof

The "awful" in the title refers as much to the film as to the title character (Howard Vernon). Director Jesus Franco's debut gives a taste of what was to come later in his oeuvre. Borrowing a plot from *The Corpse Vanishes* (1942) and *Atom Age Vampire* (1960), a mad scientist steals human blood to treat his daughter's face, which has been horribly disfigured. Family values of another kind are explored as his brother Marius (Richard Valle), a blind zombie-like creature, becomes involved. After a few surgical mishaps, Orlof finds the perfect donor. The only problem is she's the girlfriend of a cop (Conrado San Martin). French version (with English subtitles and more explicit gore) is also available. 🩸

1962 86m/B [Marius Lasoeur] Howard Vernon, Diana Lorys, Frank Wolff, Riccardo Valle, Conrado San Martin; **D:** Jess (Jesus) Franco; **M:** Jose Pagan, Antonio Ramirez Angel. **VHS** *SMW, VSM, TPV*

"You can't kill what's dead. Eternity's a long time. Get used to it."

—Peina (Christopher Walken) advises Kathleen (Lili Taylor) in *The Addiction* (1995).

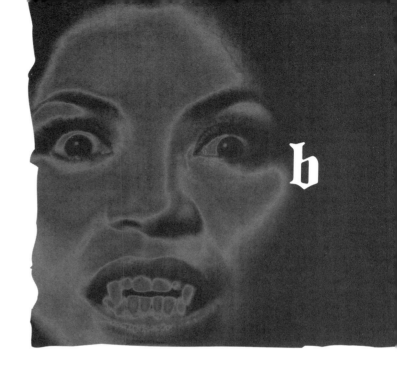

The Bad Flower

Not only can you not keep a good vampire down, but you also can't keep Dracula confined to Transylvania and London, as this South Korean film illustrates. Several years after the success of the *Horror of Dracula* (with Christopher Lee), Hammer Studios sold the rights to the Jimmy Sangster screenplay to a South Korean film company, where it was rewritten by Yongmin Lee. This ninth remake of the Dracula story not only follows the plot of *Horror of Dracula*, but actually incorporates footage from it into the final version. The film was moderately successful in Korea, but few Westerners have ever seen it. *AKA:* Ahkea KKots. 🦴🦴

1961 ?m/C [Sunglim] **Yechoon Lee**, Chimi Kim; *D:* Yongmin Lee.

The Bad Sister

A young Scottish woman living in London is haunted by her mysterious past, including her mother's death under obscure circumstances. Her search for her past continually brings her up against the reality of vampirism in her family in this slow-paced and somewhat boring character study. A made-for-TV movie based on the novel by Emma Tennent. 🦴🦴

1983 ?m/C Isabel Dean, Kevin McNally, Dawn Archibald, Matyclock Gibbs; *D:* Laura Mulvey, Peter Wolfen.

Bandh Darwaza

Hammer-inspired epic from India centers on the story of a demonic vampire who is resurrected and proceeds to wreak havoc on the members of the family responsible for having originally sent him to his grave. For almost three hours the monster attempts to gain revenge himself, leading to plenty of martial arts action and more than adequate doses of blood and gore. After an impressive opening scene, the film slows down and has a lengthy trek to the climax. 🦴🦴

1990 ?m/C Hashmat Khan, Manjeet Kular, Kunita, Satish Kaul; *D:* Tulsi Ramay, Shyam Ramsey.

Barry McKenzie Holds His Own

Barry McKenzie was originally a character in a comic strip in the Australian magazine, *Private Eye*, but the character realized its greatest success as the subject of a series of comedic movies. In this second Barry McKenzie flick, Transylvanian vampire nobleman Eric Count Plasma kidnaps McKenzie's aunt (who he mistakenly believes to be the Queen of England) as part of an elaborate plot to promote tourism in his homeland. McKenzie, of course, organizes a rescue party. Much of the humor in the movie comes from references to Australians love of beer—Plasma encounters a cross made from beer cans, a kung-fu fighter is disabled by well-shaken beer cans that are fired at him, and there are several incidents of drunken vomiting. Even the presence of Donald Pleasence and a talented group of British comic actors cannot save the film from its mediocre writing or forgive its strained attempts to gain laughs with tasteless humor. 🗡🗡

1974 93m/C AU [Satori Entertainment Corporation] Barry Humphries, Barry Crocker, Donald Pleasence; **D:** Bruce Beresford; **W:** Barry Humphries, Bruce Beresford. **VHS, Beta** *NO*

The Bat People

Bitten by a bat while exploring a desert cave, biologist John Beck turns into a bat monster, a fact that really doesn't do a lot for his new bride. Michael Pataki, as a cop caught up in the chaos caused by the Beck, has a memorable scene in which he goes to drastic lengths to avoid a swarm of attacking bats. Good special effects fail to make up for stilted acting and mediocre writing. *AKA:* It Lives By Night. 🗡

1974 **(R)** 95m/C [American International Pictures (A.I.P.)] Stewart Moss, Marianne McAndrew, Michael Pataki, Paul Carr; **D:** Jerry Jameson. **VHS, Beta** *HBO*

Batman Dracula

Never-completed film made by underground artist Andy Warhol during his film experimentation period in 1964. Like most of Warhol's film creations, it lacks a conventional narrative structure. Warhol tried to convey his message through visual images (there was no dialogue). All of his films of this period tended to show stylized people in very stylized settings. Dracula (Jack Smith) wore a costume with elements of Batman's duds, so the movie was informally referred to as *Batman Dracula*. Warhol used a psychological concept of vampirism as the case of a person making unreasonable demands upon others. Warhol's movies were primarily shown to New York audiences where, for a brief period, they enjoyed a following in the arty community and made some contributions to film theory. As this film was never finished, it enjoyed a somewhat smaller audience. 🗡🗡

1964 ?m/B [Filmmaker's Cooperative] **Jack Smith**, Baby Jane Holzer, Beverly Grant, Ivy Nicholson; **D:** Andy Warhol.

Batman Fights Dracula

The international spread of modern super heroes and villains is amply demonstrated in this Philippine effort that pits a vampire-like caped crusader against an evil vampire. 🗡🗡

1967 ?m/C [Lea/Fidelis] **Dante Rivero**, Jing Abalos, Vivian Lorrain, Ramon D'Salva; **D:** Leody M. Diaz.

Beast of Morocco

Noted archeologist Paul Carver (William Sylvester) travels to Morocco to work out his grief following the accidental death of his

11

**Billy the Kid
Versus Dracula:** "A
hundred pounds my
butt, this woman
weighs a ton,"
thinks a strained
Dracula (John
Carradine).

family. Possessed of a death wish, he encounters the temptations of a beautiful princess (Alizia Gir) who leads the Phantoms of the Night, a group of supernatural creatures who exist to steal souls. **AKA:** Hand of Night. ♫♫

1966 88m/C *GB* William Sylvester, **Alizia Gur,** Terence de Marney. **VHS** *SNC*

Because the Dawn

Marie is a Manhattan vampire thirsting for acceptance and blood, not necessarily in that order. Apparently a renaissance woman, she sings the blues, poses for a picture, and rides through Times Square in a horse drawn carriage. Ariel is a fashion photographer at-

tracted to the beguiling vampire. Attraction escalates into obsession, and before long she is on the streets of Manhattan trying to locate the elusive creature of the night. Atmosphere is accentuated by the music of Sting. Independent effort clocks in at a scant 40 minutes. ♫♫♫

1988 40m/C [Amy Goldstein] Sandy Gary, Gregory St. John; **D:** Amy Goldstein. **VHS, Beta** *WMM*

Bela Lugosi Scrapbook

Early compilation of film trailers includes Lugosi's Dracula/vampire movies, outtakes, bloopers, and film clips. ♫♫

197? 60m/B [Discount Video, U-I] Bela Lugosi. **VHS, Beta** *DVT, RXM*

Best of Barnabas

Vampire Barnabas Collins saved the original *Dark Shadows* afternoon soap opera from cancellation back in the 1960s and turned it into the top-rated daytime show. This recent video highlights Barnabas career, loves, and biting remarks with a half-hour of some of his most memorable scenes. 🦷🦷

1990 ?m/C [Dan Curtis Productions] **Jonathan Frid**, Lara Parker, David Selby, Kathryn Leigh Scott.

The Best of Dark Shadows

Led by vampire Barnabas Collins, *Dark Shadows* was America's favorite Gothic television family. In a half-hour of video clips, the family and the assorted characters with whom they interacted are spotlighted. 🦷🦷

196? 30m/C [Dan Curtis Productions] **Jonathan Frid**, Joan Bennett, David Selby, Lara Parker, Kate Jackson, Mitchell Ryan, Alexandra Moltke, Louis Edmonds, Mark Allen. **VHS, Beta** *MPI, TPV*

The Best of Dark Shadows 2

A sequel to *The Best of Dark Shadows*, this second video includes more action from the original *Dark Shadows* television series, which still has a large following of loyal fans. 🦷🦷

199? ?m/C Jonathan Frid, Lara Parker, John Karlen; **D:** Dan Curtis. *MTH*

Beverly Hills Vamp

A low-budget, soft-core excuse to show off the bodies of scream queen superstar Michelle Bauer and her two vampire co-workers at Madame Cassandra's Beverly Hills bordello. The unimportant plot centers on a small group of film-making wannabees who come to Hollywood dead set on making it in the movie industry, and making it with some fabled California ladies of the night. Robert Quarry, who starred in the title role of the Count Yorga films, makes a cameo appearance as a wheelchair-bound priest. 🦷🦷

1988 (R) 88m/C [Vidmark Entertainment] Britt Ekland, Eddie Deezen, Debra Lamb; **D:** Fred Olen Ray. **VHS, Beta** *VMK*

Billy the Kid and the Green Blaze Vampire

Author Gary Raisor wrote a most entertaining and horrific novel about a pool playing vampire. In contrast, Alan Clarke has directed an ineffective video of questionable entertainment value about a snooker champ who also is a vampire. Luckily for Raisor, the movie has nothing to do with the novel. As the plot unfolds, a challenger forces the vampire (Alun Armstrong) to a climactic match which will decide who is best. The only redeeming plot twist occurs near the end when the vampire, whom the audience is led to believe is a pseudo-vampire, begins to demonstrate some supernatural abilities. However, by this time the average viewer has already lost interest in both the vampire and his opponent. 🦷

1985 ?m/C [ITC Entertainment Group, Zenith] **Alun Armstrong**, Phil Daniels, Bruce Payne, Eve Ferret; **D:** Alan Clarke.

Billy the Kid Versus Dracula

John Carradine, who made two of the most memorable Dracula movies in the 1940s, (*House of Frankenstein* and *House of Dracula*) had everything going against him in this revival of his former role. Carradine had aged considerably by the time this film was made, and while his voice remained strong, his body lacked agility. Additionally, the vampire and western genres do not easily

Black Sunday:
"Hey dear lady,
would you wake
up and help save
my life." Katia
(Barbara Steele)
sleeps like a log as
two men fight
beside her.

mix, and Carradine's formal dress seems out of place in the Old West. Finally, a weak plot also conpired against the legendary actor. It seems that Dracula is masquerading as the uncle of a ranch owner named Betty. Before he can put the bite on this niece, he is done in by the famous (and in this film, reformed) outlaw Billy the Kid, who had been masquerading as the ranch foreman while he planned how to make his own romantic move on Betty. Director Beaudine gets credit for trying to save the movie with some atmospheric special effects. ✐

1966 95m/C [Carroll Case, Circle Films, Embassy] **John Carradine**, Chuck Courtney, Melinda Plowman, Walter Janovitz, Harry Carey Jr., Roy Barcroft, Virginia Christine, Bing Russell; *D:* William Beaudine. **VHS, Beta** *NOS, VYY*

The Black Room

Unique and satisfying story of a contemporary vampire (Stephen Knight) and his sister (Cassandra Gaviota) who lure couples to their mansion home, which they operate as a bed-and-breakfast. They gain a regular supply of victims from an adulterous husband and wife who secretly meet their various lovers at the mansion. Only when it is too late does the couple discover that the vampires have been kidnapping and killing their lovers. In a twist on the standard vampire theme, the vampire portrayed by Knight suffers from a hereditary form of anemia that amplifies his need for a regular infusion of fresh blood. At the same time, he has an aversion to touching his victims, and thus siphons off their blood with transfusion equipment. While not as powerful an exploration of the psychological side of vampirism as the film *Dance of the Damned*, it is nevertheless a moving exploration of social decadence in a world drifting from its moral moorings. A far cry from standard gory vampire fare, this film demonstrates the potential of the vampire genre. Of lesser concern, future scream queen Linnea Quigley makes one of her first screen appearances as one of the vampire's victims. ✐✐✐

1982 (R) 90m/C [Butler/Cronin Productions] Linnea Quigley, Stephen Knight, Cassandra Gaviola, Jim Stathis; **D:** Norman Thaddeus Vane. **VHS, Beta, LV** *VES, LIV*

Black Sabbath

Black Sabbath is comprised of three separate horror stories, including one that features the only motion picture portrayal of a vampire by horror film legend Boris Karloff. The story, "The Wurdalak," is a most effective screen adaptation of a vampire story by nineteenth-century Russian writer Alexei Tolstoy. The story, which was based upon Slavic folk tales, tells of a vampire who returns from the grave to feed, in standard Eastern European fashion, on his family. In the film version, Karloff plays the elderly Gorca, who leaves to kill a local bandit but returns as a vampire. He attacks his grandson first, then uses the cries of the grandson to lure the rest of the family into his clutches. He is opposed by a nobleman who is in love with his daughter. Originally issued as *I Tre Volti della Paura* and for English-speaking audiences as *The Three Faces of Fear*. American International chose the present name of the film to build on the success of director Mario Bava's earlier horror film, *Black Sunday*. **AKA:** I Tre Volti della Paura. ✒✒✒✒

1964 99m/C *IT* [American International Pictures (A.I.P.)] **Boris Karloff**, Jacqueline Pierreux, Michele Mercier, Lidia Alfonsi, Susy Anderson, Mark Damon, Rika Dialina; **D:** Mario Bava; **M:** Les Baxter. **VHS, Beta** *SNC*

Black Sunday

Barbara Steele became an international horror star by successfully taking on two roles in this film, which is now acknowledged as one of the finest horror movies ever produced. Her first role is Princess Ada, who is executed in the seventeenth century for being a witch. Her brother, who was in charge of finding and destroying witches, led the call for her death. Cut to two centuries in the fu-

ture. As two men explore the castle where Ada's body was buried, they are attacked by a bat. The men kill the bat, but some of its blood trickles onto Ada's skeleton, reviving her. Ada, now a vampire, attempts to kill her ancestor Princess Katia, who is also played by Steele. To stay alive for the next century, Ada must vampirize Katia. Though based on an older story (Nicol Gogol's *The Vij*), director Mario Bava's first vampire film brought something new to the film world because it represented a distinct break from the Dracula movies and their clones. The film contains intense and explicit portrayals of death and torture, which caused it to be banned in many countries and heavily edited in the United States. Originally released in Italy as *La Maschera del Demonio* (*The Mask of the Demon*) and later as *House of Fright, Revenge of the Vampire, Die Stinde Wenn Drakula Kommt*, and *La Masque du Démon*. Although Bava's son recently made a new version of the film, it is the original that remains one of the most important horror/vampire movies ever made. ✒✒✒✒

1960 83m/B *IT* [American International Pictures (A.I.P.)] Barbara Steele, John Richardson, Ivo Garrani, Andrea Checchi, Arturo Dominici; **D:** Mario Bava; **M:** Les Baxter. **VHS** *SNC, MRV, MOV*

Black Vampire

African-American vampire story that attempts to reach beyond its blaxploitation roots. Dr. Hess Green, an anthropologist, is also a vampire. As the movie begins, Green is at home, where he kills his first victim. The man's widow (named Ganja) hunts down the professor and eventually becomes his lover, wife, and vampire companion. **AKA:** Blood Couple; *Black Evil, Black Out: The Moment of Terror*, Ganja and Hess; Double Possession. ✒✒

1973 (R) 83m/C [Kelly-Jordan] Duane Jones, Marlene Clark, Bill Gunn, Sam Waymon, Leonard Jackson, Candece Tarpley, Mabel King; **D:** Bill Gunn; **W:** Bill Gunn. **VHS, Beta** *GEM*

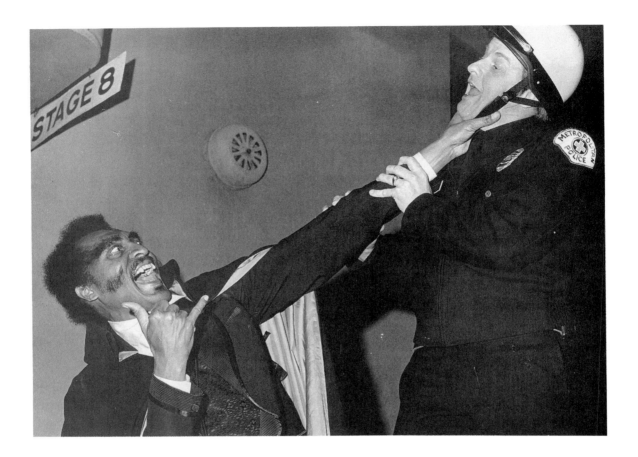

Blacula: "Yeah. Mr. B., that joke was funny, ha ha." Blacula (William Marshall) gets a wee bit defensive over his punchline.

Blacula

What happens when a classically trained Shakespearean actor (William Marshall) encounters a low-budget genre movie? In this case, a better than average B-movie and a classic "blaxploitation" film. Popular in the 1970s, blaxploitation movies adapted popular genres, in this case horror, for an African American audience. *Blacula* opens in 1780, when African Prince Mamuwalde (Marhsall) searches for Dracula to obtain the vampire's assistance in stopping the Atlantic slave trade. In response, Dracula attacks the prince and seals him in a tomb, condemning him to become Dracula's African counterpart, Blacula. Almost two centuries later, the tomb is shipped to California, where Blacula awak-

ens and begins to wreak havoc. The movie proved a great success and led to one sequel (*Scream, Blacula Scream*), several other African American vampire movies, and even a series of other monster movies (Franken-stein, Dr. Jekyll and Mr. Hyde, etc.) for the African American community. 🎵🎵🎵

1972 (PG) 92m/C [American International Pictures (A.I.P.)] **William Marshall**, Thalmus Rasulala, Denise Nicholas, Vonetta McGee; **D:** William Crain. **VHS, Beta, LV** *ORI*

Blonde Heaven

Blonde Heaven is a combination modeling agency and escort service with a nasty twist—the employees are vampires. The

head vampire Illyana (Julie Strain) hires young, naive aspiring actress Angie (Raelyn Saalman) to work for the agency while looking for roles. Before long, Angie is overwhelmed by the vampires and is about to become one herself. Fortunately for her, her hometown boyfriend Kyle (Alton Butler) shows up just in time and, realizing how desperate the situation is, he teams up with a vampire hunter in an attempt to stop the bloodsuckers' plans for his girlfriend. ♫♫

1995 (R) ?m/C [Full Moon Entertainment] **Julie Strain,** Raelyn Saalman, Alton Butler.

Blood

This ultra-low-budget movie was filmed in less than two weeks on Staten Island, New York, by director Andy Milligan, who also wrote the screenplay and did most of the camera work. The low production values are countered by the interesting storyline featuring Regina and Dr. Lawrence Orlovski, a happily married couple. What's unusual about the couple is that Regina is Dracula's daughter and Orlovski is the Wolfman's son. They settle in modern New York and raise carnivorous plants. Unfortunately, the intriguing possibilities of the story are never realized by the film. ♫

1973 74m/C [Bryanston Pictures] **Hope Stansbury,** Allen Berendt, Eve Crosby, Patti Gaul, Pamela Adams; **D:** Andy Milligan; **W:** Andy Milligan; **C:** Andy Milligan.

Blood and Black Lace

Bava invites his audience on a psychological journey into the terrifying world of a vampiric psychotic killer. The killer has targeted the models at a beauty salon run by the Countess Christina. Their bodies are discovered with their clothes ripped off, their throats opened, and their blood drained. As the death toll rises, viewers are forced to confront the horror of the killer's mind. ♫♫♫

1964 90m/C *IT FR GE* [Allied Artists] Cameron Mitchell, Eva Bartok, Mary Arden; **D:** Mario Bava. **VHS, Beta** *MED*

Blood & Donuts

Hungry vampire Boya (Currie) is looking for a rat snack when he stumbles across an all-night donut shop where the pretty cashier (Clarkson) and a friendly cabbie (Louis) seek his help with a local crime boss. Mild horror mixed with comedy and limited gore. ♫♫

1996 (R) 89m/C *CA* [Malofilm Communications] Gordon Currie, Justin Louis, Helene Clarkson, Fiona Reid, Frank Moore; **Cameos:** David Cronenberg; **D:** Holly Dale; **C:** Paul Sarossy. **VHS, LV** *LIV*

Blood and Roses

The earliest attempt to bring to the screen Sheridan Le Fanu's classic vampire tale "Carmilla," which tells the story of a young female vampire. The move to film leaves the story considerably altered. In the film, which is set in the present, Carmilla is the descendent and seeming reincarnation of the nineteenth century vampiress Mircalla. As she begins to identify with her ancestor more strongly, she grows to resemble her as well. The plot centers around Carmilla's unrequited love for her cousin, Leopoldo Karnstein, and her rivalry with Karnstein's fiance, Georgia. In the original story, there is a strong lesbian undercurrent that was approached gingerly by director Roger Vadim (especially when compared to the manner in which sexual themes were handled in soon-to-be-released films from Hammer, such as *Lust for a Vampire*). Still, the American version of the movie was so heavily censored that the plot was all but destroyed. **AKA:** Et Mourir de Plaisir. ♫♫♫

1961 74m/C Mel Ferrer, Elsa Martinelli, Annette Vadim, Marc Allegret; **D:** Roger Vadim; **W:** Roger Vadim. **VHS** *PAR*

Blood Beast Terror

Peter Cushing once called this the worst

in her eyes ...DESIRE! in her veins ...the blood of a MONSTER!

BLOOD OF DRACULA
WILL GIVE YOU NIGHTMARES FOREVER

starring SANDRA HARRISON · LOUISE LEWIS · GAIL GANLEY · JERRY BLAINE · Produced by HERMAN COHEN Directed by HERBERT L. STROCK Screenplay by RALPH THORNTON A JAMES NICHOLSON–SAMUEL ARKOFF Production AN AMERICAN INTERNATIONAL PICTURE

57-368

Blood of Dracula ✝

movie he ever made, and he got no argument from the critics. The bizarre plot features a mad scientist who has a bit of a problem—it seems his daughter periodically turns into a mothlike, blood-sucking monster. His solution? He creates a giant moth as a playmate for his daughter, but his ploy backfires when the two giant moths team up to kill innocent townspeople. Cushing plays the local police inspector who has to figure out who or what is leaving dead bodies laying all over his town. *AKA:* The Vampire-Beast Craves Blood; Deathshead Vampire. ⚔

1967 81m/C *GB* [Arnold L. Miller] Peter Cushing, Robert Flemyng, Wanda Ventham, Vanessa Howard; *D:* Vernon Sewell. **VHS, Beta** *MON*

Blood Freak

An absolutely insane anti-drug, Christian splatter film. A Floridian biker is introduced to drugs by a young woman and eventually turns into a poultry-monster who drinks the blood of junkies. Narrated by a chain smoker who has a coughing fit. Don't miss it. **Woof!**

1972 86m/C Steve Hawkes, Dana Culliver, Randy Grinter Jr., Tina Anderson, Heather Hughes; *D:* Steve Hawkes, Brad Grinter. **VHS, Beta** *NO*

Blood of Dracula

An early attempt to merge the teen movie and vampire genres plays on the perennial

tensions between teenagers and their teachers. An instructor at a girl's school hypnotizes one of the pupils using an amulet from Transylvania and turns her into a vampire. Needless to say, the girl is a little upset by her transformation when she wakes up, leading to a nasty confrontation with the teacher. Adults found it juvenile, but kids loved it. *AKA:* Blood is My Heritage; *Blood of the Demon.* 𝄞𝄞

1957 71m/B [Herman Cohen, American International Pictures (A.I.P.)] Sandra Harrison, Louise Lewis, Gail Ganley, Jerry Blaine, Heather Ames, Malcolm Atterbury; *D:* Herbert L. Strock. **VHS** *COL, MLB*

Blood of Dracula's Castle

Set in modern America, Dracula and his wife live a quiet, aristocratic existence in a desert castle. There they are attended by two servants (a butler played by John Carradine, who goes for a change of pace by *not* playing the vampire; and a hunchback) who keep the couple satisfied by bringing them blood from a group of young maidens who are kept as a living food supply in a twisted version of a wine cellar. Occasionally, the plot is enlivened with a sacrifice of one of the girls to the goddess Luna. *AKA:* Dracula's Castle. 𝄞𝄞

1969 84m/C [Al Adamson, Paragon] John Carradine, Alexander D'Arcy, Paula Raymond, Ray Young, Vicki Volante, Robert Dix, John Cardos; *D:* Jean Hewitt, Al Adamson. **VHS, Beta** *NO*

Blood of Nostradamus

In 1959, Frederico Curiel directed a twelve-part Spanish-language serial (each segment lasting 25 minutes) for release in Mexico. The next year, the twelve parts were edited into four feature-length movies, dubbed into English, and released by American International for American television. The series concerns the nefarious plans of a vampire named Nostradamus, who was portrayed by

German Robles (this Nostradamus was not related in any way to the famous sixteenth-century French prophet). Professor Duran (Domingo Soler) provided the vampire's opposition. In this last of the four features, Nostradamus is on the run, with Duran and the police (who have silver bullets in their guns) not far behind. One of the highlights of the film comes when Nostradamus somehow causes a complete eclipse of the moon, to the obvious consternation of local astronomers. Mexican studios frequently shot serials and later put them together as feature-length films in order to get around a variety of government regulations. *Blood of Nostradamus* included the following episodes from the original serial: "El Aparecido en el Convento," "El Ave Negra," and "La Ultima Victima." Sequel to *Curse of Nostradamus.* *AKA:* La Sangre de Nostradamus. 𝄞𝄞

1960 98m/C [Bosas Priego] **German Robles**, Julio Aleman, Domingo Soler; *D:* Frederick Curiel; *W:* Carlos Enrique Taboada, Alfredo Ruanova; *C:* Fernando Colin.

Blood of the Vampire

Immediately before Jimmy Sangster became well-known for helping Hammer Films revolutionize the horror film business, he scripted this vampire movie that is now remembered as an important transitional movie to his later classics. It tells the tale of Dr. Callistratus, a physician afflicted with vampirism who dies and is revived by Carl, his one-eyed hunchback assistant. He then assumes control of a mental hospital, where the inmates serve as unwilling blood donors. The vampiric doctor is opposed by young Dr. Pierre (Vincent Ball) and his former assistant, who receive help from unexpected sources in their struggle against the doctor. *AKA:* The Demon with Bloody Hands. 𝄞𝄞

1958 84m/C GB [Universal] Donald Wolfit, Vincent Ball, Barbara Shelley, Victor Maddern; *D:* Henry Cass; *W:* Jimmy Sangster. **VHS, Beta** *MPI, MLB*

Blood of the Virgins

Obscure Mexican flick sets vampires after their favorite target, virgin blood. Some movies are obscure for a reason. *AKA:* Sangre de Virgenes. 🦴🦴

1968 ?m/C Ricardo Bauleo, Gloria Prat, Rolo Puente; *D:* Emilio Vieyra.

Blood Pie

An anthology of four pretty much unrelated stories, one of which, "Terror Entre Cristianos," has the ancient Romans fighting Celtic vampires. *AKA:* Pastel de Sangre; Cake of Blood. 🦴🦴

1971 89m/C Marta May, Marisa Paredes, Julian Ugarte, Jaime Chavarri, Carlos Otero, Luis Ciges; *D:* Jose Maria Valles; *W:* Jose Maria Valles.

Blood Relations

In this delightful comedy from the Netherlands, a young nurse discovers that an older doctor is stealing blood from the local hospital. It turns out that he and his son, a policeman, are both vampires. In her attempt to destroy them, the nurse attempts a rather unique method—injecting herself with holy water. *AKA:* Bloedverwanten; Les Vampires en Ont Ras le Bol. 🦴🦴

1977 97m/C [Jaap van Rij Filmproductie, CTIS]

Maxim Hamel, Ralph Arliss, Gregoire Aslan, Sophie Deschamps, Robert Dalban, Eddie Constantine; **D:** Wim Linder; **W:** John Brasom; **C:** Walter Bal; **M:** J.M. de Scarano.

The Blood Spattered Bride

The success of the 1970 Hammer Films movie, *The Vampire Lovers*, which was based on Sheridan Le Fanu's novella "Carmilla," provided the inspiration for continental directors to try their hand at vampire films. In this Spanish effort, a frigid bride falls prey to an attractive vampiress who just happens to have a coffin that easily accommodates two. The two begin an affair, and the bride (Maibel Martin) willingly submits to Carmilla's blood needs. Finally the husband arrives to confront the lesbian vampire lovers, but his macho attitudes are rejected by his bride, who remains loyal to her lover. *AKA:* Blood Castle; La Novia Esangentada; *Til Death Us Do Part.* 𝄢𝄢𝄢

1972 82m/C *SP* [Europix Consolidated] Simon Andrew, Maribel Martin, Alexandra Bastedo, Dean Selmier, Rosa Ma Rodriguez, Montserrat Julio; **D:** Vicente Aranda. **VHS, Beta** *MPI*

Blood Thirst

An American detective in the Philippines uncovers a cult of blood-drinking sun worshippers led by an apparently young vampire priestess and her servant. Largely filmed in 1965, it was completed in 1970 and released in the United States in 1971. Later released as *The Horror from Beyond* and as *Blood Seekers.* 𝄢𝄢

1965 ?m/C Robert Winston, Yvonne Nielson. **VHS** *SNC*

Blood Ties

One of the better attempts to portray vampirism in a modern, urban setting and make it seem to be a believable phenomenon. The vampires, known as the Carpathians, have found a place for themselves in Long Beach, California, and are engaged in a heated debate over how much further they can go public. Their debate is interrupted, however, by the appearance of a young Carpathian whose family has been killed by a group of fanatics from the Southern Coalition Against Vampires, who follow the boy to the Long Beach haven. An exploration of the life of the group is seen through the eyes of Carpathian newspaper reporter Harry Martin, who has fully assimilated into society. Roger Corman continues his 40 years of support for the vampire genre and up-and-coming young actors. 𝄢𝄢𝄢

1992 90m/C Harley Venton, Patrick Bauchau, Kim Johnston-Ulrich, Michelle Johnson, Jason London, Bo Hopkins, Grace Zabriskie; **D:** Jim McBride; **W:** Richard Shapiro. **VHS** *NHO*

Bloodlust

The story of a man whose own victimization has led to his developing a blood fetish. He now breaks into funeral homes to mutilate bodies, and possessed of his fetish, he drinks the blood of the corpses through a pipette. His increasing derangement finally leads him to steal the corpse of a girl he had secretly loved and bring her to his apartment. *AKA:* Mosquito deer Scheander. 𝄢𝄢

1970 ?m/C Werner Pochat, Ellen Umlauf, Peter Hamm; **D:** Marijan Vajda.

Bloodlust

Three modern vampires—Lear (Jane Stuart Wallace), Frank (Kelly Chapman), and Tad (Robert James O'Neill)—are shaken out of their complacency after the murder/mutilation of their friend Dee (Ian Rilen) by a group of religious zealots led by a Brother Ben. Fearing for their own safety, the trio decides to rob a casino to get some quick cash and then leave town. Using their vampiric skills (plus some automatic weapons) the vampires knock off the casino and make their escape, only to be pursued by the casino owner's henchmen. Fleeing the casino

Videos about Vampire Films

In addition to the documentary films that have been made about real vampires, a number of movies about vampire movies have also been made. Several feature collections of trailers from various versions of *Dracula* and other vampire movies; *Dracula: A Cinematic Scrapbook* is one of the best examples from that genre. Others, such as the *Bela Lugosi Scrapbook* and *Mondo Lugosi: A Vampire's Scrapbook*, include rare and interesting footage and biographical material about the man who is still the best-known actor to portray Dracula.

Bela Lugosi Scrapbook (1977)

Dracula: A Cinematic Scrapbook (1991)

Fangs! (1992)

Grandpa's Monster Movies (1990)

Lugosi the Forgotten King (1985)

Mondo Lugosi: A Vampire's Scrapbook (1987)

Witches, Vampires, and Zombies (1988)

goons drives them back towards their religious enemies, so the trio splits up and agrees to meet at a prearranged rendezvous. Each of the vampires is followed by a different threat when they split, with all the elements coming together in a climactic confrontation. 🐾🐾

1992 ?m/C Kelly Chapman, Robert J. O'Neill, Jane Wallace, Paul Moder, Phil Motherwell, James Young; **D:** Richard Wolstencroft, Jon Hewitt.

Bloodlust: Subspecies 3

The third film in the *Subspecies* series. In this installment, the hideous vampire Radu (Anders Hove) is revived by his loving mother, who feeds him the blood of the innocent Michelle (Denise Duff), whom she had captured as *Subspecies II* ended. Radu then takes the attractive and desirable Michelle to his castle and tries to win her love. Michelle wants no part of this, and finally her sister Rebecca (Melanie Shatner) arrives with some help from the American embassy (Kevin Blair). The three battle Radu to the end, which comes when he falls from the castle wall and is impaled as the morning sun rises. Could Radu finally be dead? Maybe, maybe not. At the very end of the film, the demonic creatures who brought Radu back to life in part II reappear. **AKA:** Subspecies 3. 🐾🐾

1993 (R) 83m/C [Vlad Paunescu, Oana Paunescu, Full Moon Entertainment] **Anders Hove, Pamela Gordon**, Kevin Blair, Denice Duff, Ion Haiduc, Michael DellaFemina; **D:** Ted Nicolaou; **W:** Ted Nicolaou. **VHS, Beta, LV** *PAR*

Bloodscent

Julie, a young woman, unearths a golden skull with vampire fangs. While looking at the skull, she has a vision of a woman being attacked by a vampire. Later, she is dismayed to see a television news report about the discovery of a woman's body that has signs of bite marks on her neck. Upset, Julie has her best friend Jill spend the night, but the plan backfires when Jill is overcome and turned into a vampire. Plenty of attacks on scantily clad women follow in this adult erotic movie. 🐾🐾

1994 ?m/C Julie Wallace, Mandy Leigh, Jennifer Fine, Nicole Mentz.

Bloodstone: Subspecies 2

In this sequel to *Subspecies*, the body of the evil and repulsive vampire Radu, killed at

the end of the first film, is resurrected by a group of demons who pull the knife from his heart and replace his severed head. As his first act in his new life, he kills his brother Stefan and steals the precious bloodstone, the powerful stone that holds the life-giving blood of the saints. He is about to kill Michelle (Denise Duff), Stefan's human girlfriend, but is stopped by the rising sun. That day, while Radu sleeps, Michelle steals back the bloodstone and leaves the castle where she had lived with Stefan and heads to Bucharest. Radu, of course, follows. In the city, Radu meets up with his mother (Pamela Gordon), an equally hideous creature with whom he joins forces to regain the bloodstone. By this time, Michelle has gained her own allies—her sister Rebecca (Melanie Shatner) and an old vampire hunter named Popescu (Michael Bemish). Followed by *Bloodlust: Subspecies III*. **AKA:** Subspecies 2. ♪♪

1992 (R) 107m/C [Vlad Paunescu, Oana Paunescu, Full Moon Entertainment] **Anders Hove**, **Pamela Gordon**, Denice Duff, Kevin Blair, Michael Denish, Ion Haiduc; *D:* Ted Nicolaou; *W:* Ted Nicolaou. VHS, LV *PAR*

The Bloodsuckers

Cameron Mitchell portrays Baron von Weser, whose mansion is located on an island off the Italian coast. At the mansion, the baron cultivates a garden of carnivorous plants, including a large, bloodthirsty tree. All similarities to *The Little Shop of Horrors* end there, however, as the plot of this film focuses on how the baron turns his guests into food for the tree. He is finally foiled by a woman named Beth and her boyfriend, who fight off the evil tree and defeat the baron in a rather ironic manner. ♪♪

1967 ?m/C [Orbita/TEFI] Cameron Mitchell, Elisa Montes, George Martin, Kay Fisher; *D:* Ernst R. von Theumer.

The Bloodsuckers

In 1960, Simon Raven published an intriguing novel called *Doctors Wear Scarlet*, which explored the idea of vampirism as a real, but psychological, condition that was simply a form of addiction. In the novel, Richard Fountain runs away to Greece to escape a loveless engagement and an oppressive life. There, he encounters a group of blood-drinking cultists and their seductive female leader. He is eventually rescued and returned to England, where the reader is left to imagine how his experiences in Greece have affected him. Ten years after it was released, Raven's book was finally brought to the silver screen, althought the plot was altered quite a bit in this adaptation. The focus in the film is on a retired Greek general (Patrick MacNee), who is hired by Fountain's fiance (Madeline Hinde) to rescue the somewhat reluctant vampire's victim. In the film, most of Raven's exploration of an alternative form of vampiric existence is lost. Bottom line—read the novel instead of watching this movie. Even Peter Cushing's cameo doesn't help. *AKA:* Incense For the Damned; Doctors Wear Scarlet. ♪♪♪

1970 90m/C *GB* [Graham Harris, Chevron] Patrick Macnee, Peter Cushing, Patrick Mower, Edward Woodward; *D:* Robert Hartford-Davis. VHS, Beta *SNC*

Bloodsuckers from Outer Space

A low-budget comedy that also happens to be low in production values, script-writing skill, humor, and viewer interest. Aliens release a wind that turns Texas farmers into bloodsucking vampire zombies. The farmers were bland and boring before the transformation, and unfortunately, they are just as bland and boring after they pick up their new drinking habits. Equally uninteresting are the forces brought in to stop the fiends—silly scientists, a slightly mad gen-

Videohound salutes: Theda Bara

In her private life she seemed absolutely boring. She was the child of immigrant parents, never suffered a major scandal, never abused drugs, stayed happily married to her first husband, and lived happily ever after with the substantial earnings from her film career. On screen, however, Theda Bara was anything but boring. She had always harbored a secret fantasy to be a tall, dark, and mysterious lady, so the increasingly powerful Fox studio created just such a persona for her, complete with a shadowy French-Arabian past. They issued a photo of her, scantily-clad, with an accompanying skeleton. She was a cinema superstar even before Fox released her first movie, a version of the stage play *A Fool There Was* (1914). The play had been inspired by Rudyard Kipling's poem, "The Vampire" and described the fall of a prominent career diplomat at the hands of an

immoral, uncaring woman. When originally screened, an actor appeared to recite Kipling's poem before the movie began. One reviewer suggested that Bara's character was "quite the most revolting and fascinating character that has appeared on the screen for some time." No one had made the jump to stardom so quickly before.

With no time to rest on her laurels, Bara moved quickly into her next project, *The Kreutzer Sonata* (1915), which appeared only two months after her first film. Again she played the "vampire." And before the year was out she had made her third, *The Clemenceau Case*, where she again vamped her way across the screen. Audiences flocked to see her, Fox made millions, and the defenders of public morals called for censorship against exhibitions of "female depravity." While Bara lived a somewhat normal private life, Fox rented space in a New York hotel,

complete with exotic and occult trappings, where she would don her vampish costumes for her public appearances

It would be during the filming of her next "vampire" film, *The Devil's Daughter* (1915), that she began to be jokingly referred to as the "vamp." By the end of the year, the word vamp had been redefined for moviegoers, and Bara played the part in all of her public appearances as well as on the screen. Her flame burned bright for the next few years, and through 1919 she would star in 35 additional movies, including such classics as *Carmen, Cleopatra*, and *Salome*. But like many who would follow her, she had been typecast by her vampish image. By the end of the decade, though she would continue to look for work through the mid-1920s, her career was over. She lived the rest of her long life as part of New York City's social elite.

In her short career, however, she had expanded the vampire's role and created the vamp, who was later so successfully portrayed by the likes of Greta Garbo. In 1994 she was honored with a picture on a U. S. Postage stamp.

---

eral, and the president of the United States (the otherwise very funny Pat Paulsen). This movie challenges *Plan 9 from Outer Space* as the worst vampire movie ever made. **Woof!**

1983 80m/C [Gary Boyd Latham] Thom Meyer, Laura Ellis, Billie Keller, Kim Braden; **D:** Glenn Coburn. **VHS, Beta** *ORI, WAR*

Bloodthirsty

Low-budget quickie built upon the idea of vampirism as a disease. An accident in a virologist's laboratory turns infected people into blood drinkers. 🐾🐾

1992 ?m/C Ascello Charles, Winston McDonald,

Lia Marino, Stefanie Roumeliotes; **D:** Robert Guy Barrows.

The Bloody Vampire

Lame sequel to *The Invasion of the Vampires* (1961), which introduced the vampire Count Frankenhausen and his equally vampiric daughter Brunilda. Having faced a major setback at the end of the first movie, the Count moves to another village and begins experiments to raise the dead. His is opposed by vampire hunter Count Cagliostro. Originally released as *El Vampiro Sangriento*, it enjoyed great success in Mexico, but bombed in the English version released by American International. ♪♥

1962 ?m/C *MX* Carlos Agosti. **VHS** *SNC*

The Body Beneath

In this 16-mm low-budget production by quickie director Andy Milligan, the Rev. Alger-non Ford is the leader of a family of vampires living in Carfax Abbey (Dracula's London headquarters in the 1931 Bela Lugosi movie) in London. The family is in danger of extinction, which the Reverend attempts to prevent by kidnapping a relative who happens to be pregnant. This is really nothing more than a sexploitation film with heavy doses of violence aimed at an S&M audience. Some of the scenes were filmed at Highgate Cemetery, where rumors abounded that a genuine vampire lived. **AKA:** The Demon Lover. ♪

1970 85m/C [Cinemedia Films, Nova International Film Inc.] **Gavin Reed**, Jackie Skarvellis, Susan Clark, Colin Gordon, Berwick Kaler; **W:** Andy Milligan.

Body Double

Vampires make only a cameo appearance in this 1984 flick, but they do play a small part. Jake is a marginal actor with a job on a vampire B-movie (that's the whole vampire con-nection), but he doesn't have a place to live. He winds up house-sitting for a fellow actor in a trailer court and discovers a neighbor who performs a striptease in front of her window each night, which of course interests Jake. However, when he witnesses a murder, he becomes a suspect because of his "peeping tom" habits. ♪♪♥

1984 (R) 114m/C [Columbia Pictures] Craig Wasson, Melanie Griffith, Greg Henry, Deborah Shelton, Guy Boyd, Dennis Franz, David Haskell, Rebecca Stanley, Barbara Crampton; **D:** Brian DePalma; **W:** Brian DePalma, Robert J. Avrech; **C:** Stephen Burum; **M:** Pino Donaggio. National Society of Film Critics Awards '84: Best Supporting Actress (Griffith). **VHS, Beta, LV** *COL*

Body Snatcher from Hell

Alien vampires attack the survivors of an airplane crash and take possession of their bodies by opening their skulls and climbing inside. Two of the crew members, prepared to tell the world and mobilize a force to fight the aliens, discover to their dismay that other aliens have spread across the earth and the invasion of the vampire aliens had progressed far beyond the isolated site of the downed airplane. **AKA:** Goke, Body Snatcher from Hell; Goke the Vampire; Kyuketsuki Gokemidoro. ♪♥

1969 84m/C *JP* [Shochiku Company] Hideo Ko, Teruo Yoshida, Tomomi Sato, Eizo Kitamura, Masay Takahashi, Cathy Horlan, Kazuo Kato, Yuko Kusunoki; **D:** Hajime Sato. **VHS** *SNC*

Bongo Wolf's Revenge

Bongo Wolf (stage name of William Donald Grollman) is a real person who lives in Los Angeles. This short feature includes a scene in which Bongo Wolf visits the Count Dracula Society, an actual organization that in 1970 was very active in the vampire scene. ♪

1970 ?m/C William Donald Grollman; **D:** Tom Baker.

older audience that horror movies had been made for were turning away from the movie houses to watch television. By the time vampire films became popular again, they were being made especially for teenage audiences. ♫♫

1954 65m/C [Allied Artists] Paul Wexler, Leo Gorcey, Huntz Hall, Bernard Gorcey, Bennie Bartlett, Lloyd Corrigan, Ellen Corby; *D:* Edward L. Bernds. **VHS** *GPV*

Bram Stoker's Dracula

This seventeenth and most recent screen adaptation of Bram Stoker's novel featured a cast of hot Hollywood stars, notable special effects, an expensive advertising budget, and the capable directing skill of Francis Ford Coppola. During its first week of release, it broke attendance records for Columbia, the studio that bankrolled the project. Advertised as the adaptation most faithful to the novel (hence the title variation), it was the first movie to include all of the major characters from the book. Like most screen versions of *Dracula* made since 1972, it also connected Dracula to the real-life Prince Vlad the Impaler (both played by Gary Oldman). Opens with a scene from the end of Vlad's rule, when the Turkish army is overrunning his land. Because accurate historical facts on Vlad are hard to come by, Coppola chose to draw on the legend that suggested Vlad's wife committed suicide. Angered that her suicide would prevent her from joining him in heaven (according to Orthodox thought), Vlad curses God and becomes the vampire known as Dracula. It is important to note that those who know Vlad's story, not to mention the geography of Romania, must constantly remind themselves that *Bram Stoker's Dracula* is entertainment and not a history or geography lesson. From that fifteenth century introduction, the film jumps ahead to the 1800s, where the viewer finds Jonathan Harker (Keaunu Reeves) traveling to Castle Dracula to finalize the paperwork on Count Dracula's purchase of English property. Harker is a replacement for a coworker named Renfield

"No, my neck is a little higher, but that'll do just fine." Gary Oldman and Winona Ryder enjoy a vampire embrace in *Bram Stoker's Dracula*.

Bowery Boys Meet the Monsters

In the decade after World War II, the only vampire (and other monster) movies produced by Universal Studios were comedies. Its final effort before abandoning the horror genre altogether featured the Bowery Boys (a cast of characters that had evolved over two decades and several film studios), who encounter a spectrum of monsters, including a vampire. The boys approach the Gravesend family (their name should have been a hint) to inquire about using their old house as a playground for the local children. The effort turns sour when one of the Boys is turned into a werewolf. They also encounter a gorilla, a robot, a carnivorous plant, and a vampire. By the time this film was made, the

(Tom Waits), who went mad after he returned from an earlier visit to the castle. During Harker's visit, Coppola offers up some of the more memorable scenes of the films, one involving the rather independent movement of the Count's shadow, and another featuring Dracula licking blood off Harker's straight razor. Meanwhile, back in England, the remaining characters in Stoker's tale have assembled. They are led by the two young women at the center of the story—Lucy (Sadie Frost) and Mina (Winona Ryder)—and Lucy's three suitors—Arthur Holmwood (Cary Elwes), Dr. John Seward (Richard E. Grant), and Quincey Morris (William Campbell). Dracula arrives in England on the winds of a storm, and initially focuses his attention on Lucy, who mysteriously takes ill. Baffled, Seward calls in his old friend Dr. Abraham Van Helsing (Anthony Hopkins) for advice. While Lucy is Dracula's first victim, his true interest lies with Mina, who looks exactly like Vlad's long-lost wife from the fifteenth century. In the interactions between Mina and Dracula, Coppola most obviously plays upon the erotic themes so highlighted in contemporary literary criticisms of Dracula. Those themes were touched on earlier in the film—at the castle, three vampire women seduce Harker as they prepare to drain his blood (or are both acts synonymous?), and Dracula graphically rapes Lucy—but never before had the crucial scene of Mina drinking Dracula's blood been portrayed so erotically. After Dracula's attack on Mina, which leaves her drained but not dead, the men plot their revenge against the vampire and chase him back to his castle. There, they encounter fierce resistance from the gypsies who serve Dracula before forcing a final confrontation with the vampire. The release of this movie was celebrated with an appropriately broad range of souvenirs from neckties to postcards. Not only was the screenplay by Coppola and James V. Hart published, but science-fiction novelist Fred Saberhagen (who has written his own series of Dracula novels) joined Hart in writing a novelization of the film. *AKA:* Dracula. 🗡🗡🗡🗡

1992 (R) 128m/C [Francis Ford Coppola, Charles Mulvehill, Fred Fuchs] **Gary Oldman, Sadie Frost,** Winona Ryder, Anthony Hopkins, Keanu Reeves, Richard E. Grant, Cary Elwes, Bill Campbell, Tom Waits; *D:* Francis Ford Coppola; *W:* Jim V. Hart; *C:* Michael Ballhaus. Academy Awards '92: Best Costume Design, Best Makeup, Best Sound Effects Editing; Nominations: Academy Awards '92: Best Art Direction/Set Decoration. **VHS, Beta, LV, 8mm** *COL*

Bram Stoker's Whitby

A brief (10 minutes) documentary featuring the town in the north of England where, in Bram Stoker's novel, "Dracula" originally landed in England. While writing the novel, Stoker vacationed at Whitby, a delightful sea shore community on the mouth of the Esk River. All of the places mentioned in the novel (except for a few which have disappeared with time) are shown, and Stoker's accuracy in describing them noted. 🗡🗡

1994 ?m/C [Coberg Productions]

The Bride's Initiation

In this adult erotic feature, Dracula kidnaps a pair of newlyweds and proceeds to initiate the bride to married life in his own peculiar way. Things don't end there, however, as it turns out that this Dracula wants to initiate the groom as well. Dracula decides he is gay and runs off with the policeman assigned to investigate the couple's disappearance. 🗡🗡

1976 ?m/C [VCX] Carol Connors, Candida Robbins, Mark Brock, Tony Manhall; *D:* Duncan Stewart.

The Brides of Dracula

Second film in Hammer Films' *Dracula* series followed as a result of the notable success of *Horror of Dracula*. Lee was reluctant to again play the role of Dracula just two years after the 1958 film, but most of the other important players returned to *Brides*, including director Terence Fisher, screenwriter Jimmy Sangster, and actor Peter Cushing as vampire hunter Van Helsing. With no Dracula available, the movie features an Eastern European

"Welcome to my home. Enter freely of your own will and leave some of the happiness you bring."

—Dracula (Gary Oldman) to Jonathan Harker (Keanu Reeves) in *Bram Stoker's Dracula* (1992).

27

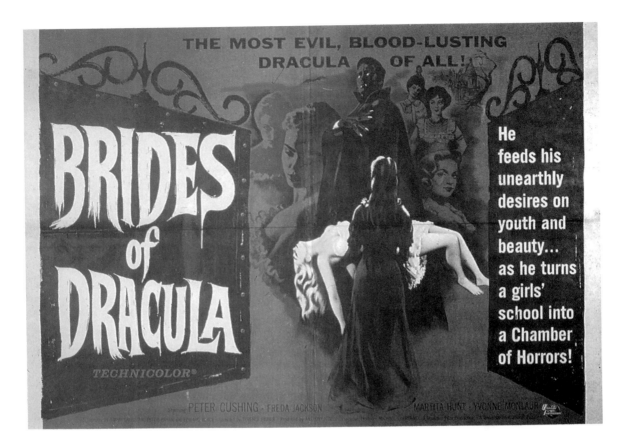

He feeds his unearthly desires on youth and beauty... as he turns a girls' school into a Chamber of Horrors!

BRIDES of DRACULA

TECHNICOLOR®

PETER CUSHING · FREDA JACKSON   MARTITA HUNT · YVONNE MONLAUR

***The Brides
of Dracula***

nobleman clone of Dracula, Baron Meinster. Meinster's mother, unable to gather the willpower to kill her son, keeps him locked up at their home. To keep him alive, she procurs young women for him to meet his minimal need for blood. When his mother is killed, however, Meinster convinces Marianne, a young school teacher, to set him free. The local priest recognizes that a vampire is on the loose and summons Van Helsing to destroy the creature. He tracks Meinster to an old windmill. An epic battle ensues, in which one of the most memorable scenes in any Hammer film occurs when Van Helsing is bitten by the vampire and must cauterize the wound with a red-hot branding iron. Van Helsing, who is not a religious man but instead believes in righteousness, even resorts to calling to the powers of the dark side for assistance in his battle with the creature. Even without Lee, *The Brides of Dracula* carried on the Hammer tradition of high production values that made that generation of vampire films so recognizable. Also released as *Les Maitresses de Dracula* (French). Followed by *Dracula, Prince of Darkness*, in which Lee finally returned to play the title role. ♪♪♪

1960 86m/C *GB* [Hotspur] Peter Cushing, Martita Hunt, Yvonne Monlaur, Freda Jackson, David Peel, Mona Washbourne; *D:* Terence Fisher. **VHS, LV** MCA, FCT

David Peel seems to have spotted a Red Cross van in *The Brides of Dracula*.

The Brides Wore Blood

Low-budget thriller in which four prospective brides are mysteriously murdered, but one is brought back to life and becomes a vampire's mate. **Woof!**

1984 86m/C [Regal Video] **VHS, Beta** *NO*

Bring Me the Vampire

A comedy originally filmed as three shorts for release in Mexico. A group of people have to stay in a castle for a month in order to receive a fortune. While there, they encounter a vampire, or so they think. Turns out the "vampire" is really just the the disinherited brother of the lord of the castle who thinks he can get the fortune for himself by running the people out of the castle. The vampire plot occurred in the third part of the original shorts. Initially released as *Enchenme al Vampiro*, and later as *Throw Me to the Vampire*. 🐾🐾

1961 100m/B *MX* Maria Eugenia San Martin, Hector Godoy, Joaquin Vargas. **VHS** *SNC, MOV*

Buck Rogers in the 25th Century: Space Vampire

From the popular TV series. Episode: "Space Vampire." Buck and Wilma are stranded aboard a quarantined ship that has been in-

vaded by a hideous centuries-old space creature. 𝄢𝄢

1980 47m/C [Universal Television] Gil Gerard, Erin Gray, Tim O'Connor, Christopher Stone, Nicholas Hormann, Patty Maloney; **D:** Larry Stewart; **V:** Mel Blanc. **VHS, Beta** *MCA*

Buenas Noches, Senor Monstruo

This rather disjointed effort is part monster mash for children and part lighthearted musical comedy starring a number of former horror genre stars. Made in Spain at the end of what was known as the horror movie era, it starred Paul Naschy, who earlier had made a name for himself portraying the werewolf Waldermar Danisky in a series of movies. He is joined by several other monsters, including, you guessed it, a singing Count Dracula. 𝄢𝄢

1982 ?m/C [Frade] Paul Naschy, Fernando Bilbao, Regaliz, Luis Escobar; **D:** Antonio Mercero.

Buffy the Vampire Slayer

Critical flop that nonetheless has its share of fans. Buffy (Kristy Swanson) is a stereotypical cheerleader at an even more stereotypical California high school—her only concerns are to finish high school, travel to Europe, and marry a Hollywood idol (or a reasonable equivalent). Her mundane existence is rather rudely interrupted when she receives a visit from a vampire hunter named Merrick (Don-

ald Sutherland). Much to Buffy's disbelief, Merrick informs the Valley Girl teen queen that she is in fact the Chosen One, the descendent of a long line of vampire hunters. It is her job to track down and kill Lothos (Rutger Hauer) the King of the Undead and his cohorts, who have moved into her neighborhood and are planning to feast off of Los Angeles. Several fun moments (including a memorable cameo from Paul Reubens, aka Pee Wee Herman, as one of less fearsome members of the vampire pack) can't mask a movie that can't decide if it's a comedy or drama and in the end succeeds in being neither. A juvenile novelization of Joss Whedon's screenplay was written by Ritchie Tankersley Cusick and released at the same time as the movie. 𝄢𝄢𝄢

1992 (PG-13) 98m/C [20th Century-Fox] **Paul (Pee Wee Herman) Reubens**, **Rutger Hauer**, Kristy Swanson, Donald Sutherland, Luke Perry, Michele Abrams, Randall Batinkoff, Hilary Swank, Paris Vaughan, David Arquette, Candy Clark, Natasha Gregson Wagner; **D:** Fran Rubel Kazui; **W:** Joss Whedon; **M:** Carter Burwell. **VHS, LV** *FXV, PMS*

Bunnicula: Vampire Rabbit

A rather anemic animated version of the children's vampire classic *Bunnicula* by Deborah and James Howe. After a family adopts a vegetable juice-sucking bunny, the family dog and cat team up to prove that it is a vampire. 𝄢𝄢

1982 23m/C [Ruby-Spears Productions] **VHS, Beta** *WOV, GKK*

"The old woman forced me. She's a 1,000-year old tree monster. That old woman controlled my body and used me to lure men to absorb their yang element."

—Nieh Hsalo-Tsing (Joey Wong), the young female ghost in *A Chinese Ghost Story* (1987).

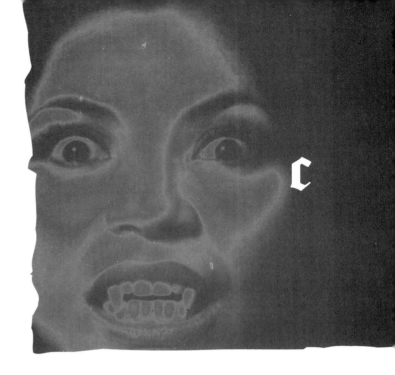

Cafe Flesh

Sci-fi goes adult erotic. After an atomic war, the whole world is divided into sex negatives and sex positives. The former group, which comprises the overwhelming majority of the surviving population, get sick if they attempt to engage in sex. So they force the small group of sex positives to perform sex acts on stage for their entertainment. For some reason, Max Melodramatic (Andrew Nichols), the emcee for the sex programs, is a vampire. The story involves the plight of Lana (scream queen Michelle Bauer), a young positive girl living as a negative. Her growing alienation from her boyfriend and the arrival of Positive Johnny Rico leads her to reconsider her secret life. Released in both hardcore and soft-core versions. *&&&*

1982 ?m/C [Caribbean] **Andrew Nichols**, Michelle (McClellan) Bauer, Paul Gibboneyy, Marie Sharp, Darcy Nichols; **D:** Stephen Sayadian.

Captain Kronos: Vampire Hunter

Tells the tale of Captain Kronos, a former Prussian army officer who once returned from war to discover that his mother and sister had been turned into vampires. That horrible experience causes him to dedicate his life to searching out and destroying the evil bloodsucking creatures. As the movie opens, he arrives in a small town with his partner Professor Grost and discovers that a vampire is attacking and killing the lovely young girls of the village. If these deaths continue, there would soon be no elegible females left. With the help of Dr. Marcus, a local, they follow the trail of blood back to a local aristocrat, Lady Durward, who needs the blood of the maidens to remain young. *Kronos* was actually a pilot for a proposed series featuring a team of vampire hunters, but it was not well received by the youthful audience toward which it was directed. One of the few Hammer vampire movie failures. *&&&*

1974 (R) 91m/C *GB* [Albert Fennell, Hammer Films] Horst Janson, John Carson, Caroline Munro,

"Let me see, it's either right cross left flame or left cross, right flame. Captain Kronos (Horst Janson) and Dr. Marcus (John Carson) plan their strategy in *Captain Kronos Vampire Hunter.*

Ian Hendry, Shane Briant, Wanda Ventham; **D:** Brian Clemens; **W:** Brian Clemens. **VHS, Beta** *PAR*

Capulina contra Los Monstros

In 1972, Mexican comedian Capulina teamed with director Rene Cardona in two similar films, with the comedian squaring off against some monsters. In this one, he encounters Frankenstein's monster, a werewolf, and a vampire. 🦴🦴

1972 ?m/C *MX* [Panorama International Productions, Azteca, Estudios America] Gaspar Henaine, Capulina, Hector Andremar, Gloriella; **D:** Rene Cardona Jr.

Capulina contra Los Vampiros

In the second of his two movies with director

René Cordova, Mexican comedy star Capulina fends off an attack by a group of vampires. 🦴🦴

1972 ?m/C *MX* Gaspar Henaine, Capulina, Hector Andremar, Gloriella; **D:** Rene Cardona Jr.

Carmilla

This fine made-for-television adaptation of Sheridan Le Fanu's novella first ran as an episode of the series "Nightmare Classics" in 1989 and was subsequently released on video. The story is switched to the pre-Civil War American South and begins with the plight of a reclusive widower and his daughter. It seems that Laura is lonely and looking for some companionship, since many of her friends have died from a disease that swept through the community. Her father, unable to help, is suddenly relieved of his burden by the appearance of the Countess Mircalla Karnstein, a woman of noble birth brought to the family home following an accident. She provides some distraction for the father's grief

and needed companionship for Laura. That companionship is not what it seems, however, as Mircalla reveals her evil intentions and has her way with Laura. Roddy McDowell (as a local witch hunter) teams up with Laura's father to battle the evil Mircalla. One of the finer treatments of the "Carmilla" story. *ℐℐℐ*

1989 60m/C [Showtime, Think Ent.] **Meg Tilly**, Ione Skye, Roddy McDowall, Roy Dotrice; **D:** Gabrielle Beaumont. **VHS, Beta** *NO*

Carry On Screaming

This twelfth entry in the British "Carry On" comedy series sends the detective team of Sargent Bung and his assistant Constable Slobotham off to locate a young girl who has been abducted. They are led to a rather spooky mansion overseen by the strange mad scientist, Dr. Watt and his pretty sister, Valeria, who is a vampire. The couple, as it turns out, are kidnapping sweet young things, vampirizing them, petrifying them, and turning them into department store mannequins (which is apparently rather profitable). *AKA: Screaming; Carry on Vampire.* *ℐℐ*

1966 97m/C *GB* [Peter Rogers, Warner Brothers, Pathe] Harry H. Corbett, Kenneth Williams, Fenella Fielding, Joan Sims, Charles Hawtrey, Jim Dale, Angela Douglas, Jon Pertwee; **D:** Gerald Thomas. **VHS** *MOV*

The Case of the Full Moon Murders

An adult erotic comedy film concerning a female vampire who bites her male victims in a rather sensitive place. It was released in both hardcore and softcore versions and under several titles including *Sex on the Groove Tube* and the *Case of the Smiling Stiffs*. One of the vampire's victims was Harry Reems, who had become notorious for his role as the male star of the infamous X-rated film, *Deep Throat* (1972). *AKA:* The Case of the Smiling Stiffs; Sex on the Groove Tube. *ℐℐ*

1974 74m/C [Lobster Enterprises, Dana Films] **Cathy Walker**, Jean Jennings, Satish Kaul, Tulsi Ramay, Harry Reems, Fred J. Lincoln, Sean S. Cunningham; **W:** Jerry Hayling; **C:** Gus Graham; **M:** Bud Fanton, Jacques Urbont.

Castle of Blood

A young poet encounters writer Edgar Allen Poe and a character named Lord Blackwood near a castle where, many years ago, on All Soul's Eve, all the residents died. The poet must spend the night alone in the castle to win a bet with the pair. Just as he is ready to settle in for the evening, all of those who died at the castle return to life for a reenactment of their death. They are led by Lady Blackwood, who is portrayed by Barbara Steele in a role that rivals her classic turn in *Black Sunday*. Inspired by Poe's short story "Dance Macabre," it was originally issued in Italy as *La Danza Macabra* and later reissued as *Castle of Terror* and *Coffin of Terror*. Margheriti remade the movie in color in 1970 as *Web of the Spider. AKA:* Castle of Terror; Coffin of Terror; Danza Macabra. *ℐℐℐ*

1964 85m/B *IT FR* [Woolner Bros. Pictures] Barbara Steele, George Riviere, Margrete Robsahm, Henry Kruger, Montgomery Glenn, Sylvia Sorente; **D:** Anthony (Antonio Margheriti) Dawson. **VHS** *SNC*

Castle of the Living Dead

Christopher Lee again plays an aristocratic vampire, this time named Count Drago. It seems the Count has developed an odd little hobby. He captures animals and mummifies them with a secret drug. In an effort to expand his horizons, he switches from animals to beautiful young women, keeping their beauty preserved forever in a secret lair beneath a castle. A troupe of circus performers stumbles across his evil plot and attempts to stop his unnatural taxidermy service. Donald Sutherland, in his screen debut, plays a dual

VIDEOHOUND SALUTES: MICHELLE BAUER, THE EMPRESS OF THE SCREAM QUEENS

Barbara Steele first created the image of the scream queen, but in the new wave of independent horror movies featuring bad and beautiful stars, no female star has been more popular than Michelle Bauer. She burst upon the scene in 1985 in *The Tomb*, a vampire movie that was based on one of Bram Stoker's more obscure stories and directed by infamous splatter artist Fred Olen Ray. Star and director enjoyed the experience enough to work together again on the delightfully funny *Hollywood Chainsaw Hookers* (1988). In 1987, Bauer joined with two other prominent scream queen stars-on-the-rise, Linnea Quigley and Brinke Stevens, in *Nightmare Sisters*, a fun little vampire flick about three scantily clad sorority sisters who select an unsuspecting nearby fraternity as the object of their demonic bloodlust.

Unlike most movie starlets, Bauer is a California product. After high school, she skipped college and acting school to perfect her thespian skills as a barely legal performer in X-rated features. When she made the jump into horror films, audience members quickly noticed how believable the uninhibited Bauer appeared on the screen. From the beginning of her film career, that ability to communicate her seeming enjoyment of her work quickly earned her a host of fans.

No shrinking violet, Bauer went on to portray a number of sexy alluring females who also just happened to be monsters. As a zombie she attacked yuppies in *Night of the Living Babes* (1987); she enslaved her men in *Phantom Empire* (1987), and she emerged as the instrument of vengeance in *Lady Avenger* (1989). Of course, when the occasion demanded it, she could assume the role of victim, as she did in the not to be missed *Sorority Babes in the Slimeball Bowl-a-Rama* (1987).

Any scream queen worth her salt makes vampire movies, and Bauer actually got her start with a part in the infamous X-rated sci-fi/horror classic, *Café Flesh* (1982), in which she portrayed Lana, a young woman who leads a double life in the warped world of sex positives and sex negatives. She returned to a familiar role as a hooker who attacked her clients in *Beverly Hills Vamp* (1988) and more recently appeared in the story of the vampiric escort agency, *Blonde Heaven* (1995). As an extraterrestrial in *Vampire Vixens from Venus* (1994), she harvested the life essence of her victims as an ingredient in a super mind-blowing drug. In *Red Lips* (1994), you could think of her as a victim, but her seeming enjoyment of the attack of her vampire roommate was not missed by her fans.

Through the 1990s, rumors of retirement have continually swirled around the happily married mother. However, much to the glee of her appreciative fans, she seems merely to have slowed the pace of her work.

role (one of which is a real drag). *AKA:* Il Castello de Morti Vivi. 𝄞𝄞

1964 90m/B *IT FR* [Paul Maslansky] **Christopher Lee,** Gaia Germani, Phillippe LeRoy, Jacques Stanislawsky, Donald Sutherland; *D:* Herbert Wise. **VHS** *SNC, MRV*

Castle of the Monsters

Somewhat inspired by *Abbott and Costello Meet Frankenstein,* Mexican comedians Clavillazo and Elizondo play newlyweds who are trapped in a castle with a set of monsters, including a mummy, a werewolf, and a vampire. In this farce, German Robles plays a parody of the character Count Lavud, whom he had previously portrayed in several horror films. *AKA:* El Castillo se los Monstruos. 𝄞𝄞

1958 85m/C *MX* **German Robles,** Carlos Orellana, Evangelina Elizondo; *D:* Julian Soler; *W:* Carlos Orellana, Fernando Galiana; *C:* Victor Herrera. **VHS** *SMW*

Casual Relations

Despite the fact that this movie opens and closes with scenes from F. W. Murnau's *Nosferatu,* and also includes a spoof called "A Vampire's Love" as one of its short episodes, it barely makes it as a vampire film. 𝄞

1973 80m/C [Mark Rappaport] **Mel Austin,** Sis Smith, Paula Barr, Adrienne Claiborne, Alan Dahl; *D:* Mark Rappaport; *W:* Mark Rappaport; *C:* Mark Rappaport, Alan Raymond; *M:* Jim Burton.

Cave of the Living Dead

In this exploitation cheapie, Inspector Doren (Adrian Hoven) of Interpol squares off against the local vampire, Professor Adels-

berg (Wolfgang Preiss). Doren is investigating the nasty deaths of some local young women. The issue becomes personal when Doren's girlfriend, who also serves as the professor's secretary, is turned into a vampire. Not much to recommend here. *AKA: The Curse of Green Eyes; Night of the Vampire;* Der Fluch Der Gruenen Augen. **Woof!**

1965 87m/B *GE YU* [Film Development Corporation, Richard Gordon] Adrian Hoven, Erika Remberg, Carl Mohner, Wolfgang Preiss, Karin Field, John Kitzmiller, Akos Von Rathony; *D:* Akos Von Rathony. **VHS, Beta** *MSP*

Chanoc contra el Tigre y el Vampiro

In the 1960s, moviegoers in Mexico flocked to films starring masked wrestlers. One of the wrestlers, Santo, became a popular movie star by battling various monstrous characters that he certainly never encountered in a wrestling ring. This installment featured the masked wrestler battling a vampire. 𝄞

1971 ?m/C *MX* German Valdes, Raul Martinez Solares; *D:* Gilberto Martinez Solares.

Chappaqua

Autobiographical study of and by filmmaker Conrad Rooks, who goes to France to kick drugs. While there, he has flashbacks to the beginning of the psychedelic era in 1960s San Francisco. In a comic dream sequence, a doctor sends for blood, and Rooks, as a parody of Lugosi's Dracula, appears. Dracula also bites a woman's neck and hangs around in a coffin. Includes appearances by some of the famous personalities of the era, such as William S. Burroughs and Allen Ginsberg, with music by Ravi Shankar. 𝄞𝄞

1965 92m/C [Rooks Productions] **Conrad Rooks,** Jean-Louis Barrault, William S. Burroughs, Allen Ginsberg; *D:* Conrad Rooks; *W:* Conrad Rooks; *C:* Robert Frank; *M:* Ravi Shankar.

VAMPIRES TO SINK YOUR TEETH INTO: THE ABSOLUTE VERY BEST VAMPIRE MOVIES OF ALL TIME

No doubt about it, some vampire movies continually rise to the top of the heap of the nearly 600 bloodsucker flicks. Possibly the least known of these is *Dance of the Damned*, Roger Corman's quickie which so beautifully explores the essential nature of the vampire trapped in his eternal darkness. There is no way to rate these movies from one to twenty-five; they have each found their way on this list for various reasons. Some are historically important, others have an outstanding story or good special effects, while some are most representative of a particular type of vampire movie. But you won't be sticking your neck out by spending an evening with any of the following:

Black Sunday (1960)

Blacula (1972)

Bram Stoker's Dracula (1992)

The Brides of Dracula (1960)

Cronos (1992)

Dracula (Bela Lugosi, 1931)

Dracula (Spanish, 1931)

Dracula (Frank Langella, 1979)

Dracula's Daughter (1936)

Fright Night (1985)

The Hunger (1983)

Horror of Dracula (1957)

Innocent Blood (1992)

Interview with the Vampire (1994)

Lost Boys (1987)

Love at First Bite (1979)

Nosferatu (1922)

Martin (1976)

Near Dark (1987)

Once Bitten (1985)

The Vampire (1957)

Vampire Hunter D (1985)

Vampyr (1931)

Children of the Night

An evil vampire named Czakyr attempts to take over a small Midwestern town. First he establishes his crypt directly underneath the town's church in a cave that is accessible only by several underground caverns. He first turns to the children of the town for his food supply, abducting the children and placing them in suspended animation underwater so he can dine at his leisure. He then turns to the town's adults, where he finally meets some resistance in the form of teacher Peter DeLuise. Never distributed to theaters, the film is available on video. 🦴

1992 (R) 92m/C Peter DeLuise, Karen Black, Ami Dolenz; **D:** Tony Randel; **C:** Gil Hubbs. **VHS** *COL*

Chillers

A horror anthology made by independent film maker and West Virginia college professor Daniel Boyd. Five people who have missed their ride console themselves by

telling each other scary stories as they wait for the next bus. In one of the stories, a woman encounters a vampire disguised as a TV newsman. 🦇🦇

1988 90m/C [Manson International Pictures] Jesse Emery, Marjorie Fitzsimmons, Laurie Pennington, Jim Wolfe, David Wohl; **D:** Daniel Boyd; **W:** Daniel Boyd. **VHS, Beta** *PSM*

A Chinese Ghost Story

Ning Tsai-Shen (Leslie Cheung), a naive tax-collector, is sent to a small town only to discover that no one will give him shelter for the night. The only protection from the elements is the (haunted) Lan Ro temple. Here he meets and falls in love with the lovely young Nieh Hsaio-Tsing (Joey Wong). He slowly discovers that his new love, a ghost, is bound eternally to a vampiric tree spirit with a very long tongue. Interesting love triangle they've got going. Ning enlists the aid of a swordsman (Ng Ma) in a descent into the netherworld to fight for his true love. Worth searching the independent, mom-and-pop video stores for. The vampiric tree spirit does not appear in the sequel, *A Chinese Ghost Story II*, but does prove central to *A Chinese Ghost Story III*. 🦇🦇🦇

1987 93m/C *CH* Leslie Cheung, Wong Tsu Hsien, Wu Ma; **D:** Ching Siu Tung. **VHS** *FCT*

A Chinese Ghost Story III

The vampiric tree spirit with the long tongue is back. Joey Wong returns as Lotus, a beautiful ghost attached to, and controlled by, the tree. A Buddhist abbott and one of his disciples happen upon the abandoned monastery near the tree. Lotus and fellow ghost Butterfly (Nina Li) attempt to seduce the younger monk and bring him to the tree spirit. The abbott and monk, assisted by a money-grabbing swordsman, must fight the tree spirit after their protective Buddha statue is damaged. Lotus, betrothed by the evil tree spirit to the Mountain Devil, also helps them, hop-

ing to be freed from her imprisonment. Almost as good as the original. 🦇🦇🦇

1991 ?m/C Jacky Cheung, Tony Leung, Joey Wong, Nina Li; **D:** Siu-Tung Ching.

Chosen Survivors

An intriguing premise is the highlight of this 1974 film. An eccentric wants to see what would happen to a group of people thrown together under the worst possible circumstances, so he gathers 11 people together in an underground shelter and convinces them that they are the only survivors of a nuclear holocaust. Things go wrong in the middle of the experiment, however, when hundreds of vampire bats enter the shelter through a vent that was accidentally left open. Faced with the very real threat of the bats, the group must fight for survival. 🦇🦇

1974 ?m/C *MX* [Metromedia Producers Corporation, Alpine Productions, Chrubusco] Jackie Cooper, Alex Cord, Richard Jaeckel, Bradford Dillman; **D:** Sutton Roley.

Chronique de Voyage

A short feature in which a woman is menaced by a vampire. 🦇

1970 ?m/C *FR* Marc Olivier Cayce, Claude Moro, Francine Roussel; **D:** Robert de Laroche.

City of Vampires

The city of Braddock has come under attack by vampires who are killing off a large percentage of the citizens. Sam Helling and his girlfriend find themselves in Braddock after taking a wrong turn. He escapes, but his girlfriend gets left behind. Oops. Being a movie good guy, he goes back to rescue her and confront the evil vampires. 🦇🦇

1995 ?m/C Matthew Jason Walsh; *D:* Ron Bank.

"As your life begins to fill mine you will know peace while I begin to hunger again forever and ever."

—The vampire (Cyril O'Reilly) in *Dance of the Damned* (1988).

The Close Encounter of the Vampire

With an English title inspired by Spielberg's UFO blockbuster, this Chinese horror/comedy is set in medieval China. It has two storylines: the primary one concerns three cowardly exorcists dealing with one of the "hopping" vampires made famous by Chinese supernatural movies. The secondary story concerns a group of orphans who are attacked by a child ghost. ♫♫

1986 ?m/C D: Tuen Ping.

Close Encounters of the Spooky Kind

During the 1980s, Chinese horror/martial arts movies became known for the introduction of a new character, the "hopping" vampire. *Close Encounters* is the original hopping vampire movie, and it borrowed a well-worn plot. An arrogant martial arts expert (Samo Hung Kam-Bo) accepts a dare to spend a night in the proverbial haunted house. The whole situation has been set up by the wealthy lover of Hung's unfaithful wife. Entertaining, if somewhat dated, mixture of action and comedy. ♫♫

1980 ?m/C [Golden Harvest] Hung Kam-Bo, Lam Ching Ying, Wu Ma, Chung Fat, Chan Lung.

Close Encounters of the Spooky Kind 2

Most of the cast of the original *Close Encounters* returns for this comedic kung fu monster mash. Martial artist Hung (Samo Hung Kam-Bo) aligns with the fighting Taoist priest (Lam Ching-Ying) and his apprentice students to battle snake people, zombies, and the hopping vampires. ♫♫♫

1989 ?m/C Hung Kam-Bo, Lam Ching-ying, Wu Ma; **D:** Hung Kam-Bo.

Coming Soon

Attempt to create a new movie by stringing together trailers from old movies. Jamie Lee Curtis narrates, in documentary style, a look at some of Universal's classic horror movies, including *House of Frankenstein* and *House of Dracula*, the two movies that most vividly identified John Carradine with the role of Dracula.. ♫♫

1983 55m/C [Universal] **D:** John Landis; **W:** John Landis, Mick Garris. **VHS, Beta** *MCA, MOV*

Condemned to Live

An early and almost forgotten vampire movie set in the seventeenth century in Africa and New England. Prior to leaving for Africa, a pregnant woman named Marguerite Mane (Maxine Doyle) is bitten by a vampire bat. From Africa, she and her husband make their way to New England, where they settle. The movie jumps to some point in the future and focuses on Prof. Paul Kristan, who is supposedly Mane's son and who had inherited a vampiric condition from the bat bite. Kristan terrorizes the women in the Puritan town where he was raised, causing his wife no small amount of consternation. ♫♫

1935 68m/B [Maury M. Cohen, Invincible Pictures] Ralph Morgan, Maxine Doyle, Russell Gleason, Pedro de Cordoba, Mischa Auer, Lucy Beaumont, Carl Stockdale; **D:** Frank Strayer. **VHS** *SNC, LSV*

"Look into my eyes and give me all your money." Louis Jourdan stares down his inferiors in PBS's Count Dracula.

The Corpse Vanishes

Mad scientist and vampire combined into one in this horror thriller. Dr. Lorenz (Bela Lugosi) entices young brides with his orchids in order to kidnap them and drain their blood. He then gives the blood to his wife (Elizabeth Russell), who sleeps in a coffin, to keep her from aging. Two henchmen, an old woman (Minerva Urecal) and her demented son (Frank Moran), assist Lorenz with his fanatical scheme. Lugosi at his chilling best. Storyline was later used in the nuclear era in *Atom Age Vampire.* ♫♫♫

1942 64m/B [Sam Katzman] Bela Lugosi, Luana Walters, Tristram Coffin, Elizabeth Russell, Vince Barnett, Joan Barclay, Angelo Rossitto; **D:** Wallace Fox. **VHS, Beta** *NOS, MRV, SNC*

Count Dracula

After making six movies with Hammer Films, Christopher Lee returned to the Dracula role in this Jesus Franco film. By making the move, Lee hoped to break away from the direction taken by the British productions and to portray the Count in a manner more closely adhering to Bram Stoker's original novel. Franco turned to the novel for guidance and adhered much more closely to its storyline than had any Hammer film, including the studio's first effort, *Horror of Dracula.* Lee also consulted the text to develop his on-screen appearance, and the look he chose matched the Count's description more closely than any previous attempt—only the hairy palms and the pointed ears and fingers from the book were missing on screen. Also, as in the novel, Lee initially appears as an older man and gradually becomes more youthful in appearance as he consumes the blood of the lead female characters. The early scenes, which take place in Dracula's castle, have been praised as the best presentation of Stoker's book ever put to film. Unfortunately, the remainder of the film degenerated as Franco began to deviate from the book's plot and ran short of money. Still worth watching and

by far the best vampire movie of the several Franco directed. It was the tenth time the novel was brought to the screen. **AKA:** El Conde Dracula; Bram Stoker's Count Dracula; Dracula 71; The Nights of Dracula; Nacht Wenn Dracula Erwacht. 🩸🩸🩸

1971 (R) 90m/C *SP GE IT* [Independent] **Christopher Lee,** Herbert Lom, Klaus Kinski, Frederick Williams, Maria Rohm, Soledad Miranda; **D:** Jess (Jesus) Franco. **VHS** *REP, FCT*

Count Dracula

One of the more faithful retellings of *Dracula*, this version was originally shown on British television and later cut into three segments for viewing in the United States. The story follows Jonathan Harker's trip to Transylvania and his encounter with the thoroughly continental Dracula (Louis Jourdan). When Dracula comes to London and tries to take Lucy, he is opposed by Drs. Seward and Van Helsing, who are unable to prevent Lucy's death. However, her death convinces the men (including Texan Quincey P. Morris) that Dracula is a vampire. Their counterattack leads to Castle Dracula, where Van Helsing has the honor of finally killing Dracula with a stake. In the American showing, the scene of the three vampire women attacking the baby (a most realistic version of the horror in the novel) was cut. Prior to *Bram Stoker's Dracula* (1992), this film, the twelfth attempt to bring *Dracula* to the screen, was the version of *Dracula* that most closely followed Bram Stoker's storyline and included all but one of the major characters. It also included very powerful scenes of Mina drinking Dracula's blood (a necessary scene for understanding how vampires are created) and of her being branded with the eucharistic wafer. 🩸🩸🩸🩸

1978 151m/C [Morris Barry, BBC (British Broadcasting Corporation)] **Louis Jourdan,** Frank Finlay, Jack Shepard, Bosco Hogan, Susan Penhaligon, Judi Bowker, Mark Burns; **D:** Philip Saville; **W:** Gerald Savory; **C:** Peter Hall; **M:** Kenyon Emrys Roberts.

Count It Higher

The famous counting Count of the award-winning children's series *Sesame Street* hosts his own top hits special, "The Count's Count Down," featuring favorite songs from the *Sesame Street* repertoire. For completists or parents of preschoolers. 🩸🩸

1988 ?m/C [Children's Television Workshop] **D:** John Stone.

Count Yorga, Vampire

While several movies prior to this one had tried to fit vampires into comtemporary society, none did so as effectively as *Count Yorga*, a Dracula clone transported to modern Los Angeles. Arriving in his coffin, Yorga establishes his headquarters in a mansion. To attract his female victims, he holds seances and uses his hypnotic powers to put the sexy young females under his control as he turns them into vampires. The plot centers on his attempts to vampirize two women in particular—Donna (Donna Anders) and Erica (Judith Lang). Donna's boyfriend Michael tries to save his girlfriend (with the help of Dr. Hayes) and faces off against Yorga in the climactic battle. One of the movie's memorable scenes features a female vampire draining a cat of its blood. There was one sequel, *Return of Count Yorga* (1971) 🩸🩸🩸

1970 (PG) 90m/C [American International Pictures (A.I.P.)] **Robert Quarry,** Roger Perry, Michael Murphy, Michael Macready, Donna Anders, Judith Lang; **D:** Bob Kelljan. **VHS, Beta** *NO*

Counter Destroyer

A woman retreats to a secluded island to write a film script. But then she is attacked by an army of disgruntled Vampire-zombies. Who can work with all that commotion? Fortunately for her, ninja warriors arrive in the nick of time. 🩸

198? 90m/C VHS, Beta *TWE*

"You'll know that I am no intangible fiend from your imagination when you feel the weight of my hatred. Your life will be a torment. I'll strip you of everything you hold dear."

—A revengeful Dr. Clayton (George Zucco) in *Dead Men Walk* (1943).

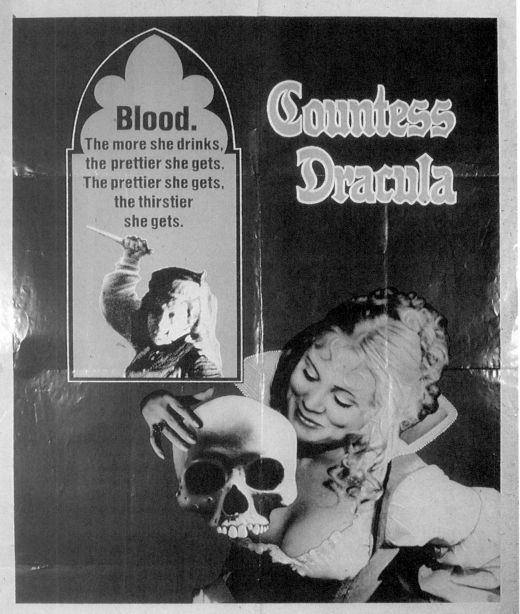

Countess Dracula

Along with *The Vampire Lovers*, this is one of the first films in which Hammer introduced Ingrid Pitt to horror film fans. She plays Countess Bathory, the legendary serial killer linked to vampirism due to her belief that bathing in the blood of young girls would keep her young and allow her to retain her beauty. In Hammer's version, the aged countess actually does undergo a radical transformation after her baths, which must occur with greater and greater frequency to maintain her beautiful appearance. At one point, just as she is saying her wedding vows to a young military officer, she even reverts back to her real age as the effects of her ritual wears off. Typical Hammer fare with lavish sets, plenty of flowing blood, and a Jimmy Sangster script, only slightly marred by an irregular pace that sometimes slows to a crawl. Loosely based upon Valentine Penrose's *The Bloody Countess*, a fictionalized biography of Elizabeth Bathory. A novelization of the movie was released as *Countess Dracula* by Michel Parry. 🦴🦴🦴

1970 ?m/C *GB* [Hammer House of Horror] **Ingrid Pitt**, Nigel Green, Sandor Eles, Maurice Denham; **D:** Peter Sasdy.

The Craving

In this ninth film featuring the famous Italian werewolf Waldemar Danisky (Paul Naschy), the creature is resurrected by graverobbers who discover his body and steal the silver cross that had been plunged into his heart. Danisky soon seeks revenge against Countess Elizabeth Bathory and her group of female vampires. Originally released in Italian as *El Retorno del Hombre Lobo*. 🦴🦴

1980 (R) 93m/C *MX* [Film Concept] Paul Naschy, Julie Saly; **D:** Jack Molina. **VHS, Beta** *VES, LIV*

Crazy Safari

Loosely inspired by the outstanding comedic study of the clash of traditional and modern culture in Africa, *The Gods Must Be Crazy* (1980). A Chinese priest (Lam Chin Ying) is on his way home from an auction in England, where he had purchased a mummified vampire. During the trip, the plane carrying the priest and his assistant runs out of fuel over the African jungle. The vampire falls to Earth and is recovered by a group of natives, setting the stage for laughs when the vampire comes back to life (hopping around, as all good Chinese vampire should). The locals, of course, regard the vampire as a god. The priest and his assistant survive their rough flight and an encounter with some wild animals, arriving in the natives' village just in time to witness the final confrontation between the vampire and a zombie. Not as good as its inspiration, but not a bad product from Hong Kong. 🦴🦴🦴

1990 ?m/C Lam Ching-ying, Sam Christopher Chan, NiXan; **D:** Lo Weng-Tung.

Creature of the Walking Dead

This interesting, but still bad, variation on the vampire motif begins in 1890 with a Dr. Malthus (Fernando Casanova), who has discovered a formula for eternal youth. Unfortunately, the formula requires the blood of several young women, which doesn't slow the murdering doctor down at all. The local constabulary, however, has little appreciation for his accomplishment and hangs him for murder. Several generations later, Dr. Malthus's grandson discovers the doctor's notes and, impressed with the man's discovery, decides to revive him. The resurrected physician requires more blood if he is to stay alive and begins to attack local residents again, causing the grandson to recognize the horror he has unwittingly unleashed. **AKA:** La Marca del Muerto. 🦴🦴

Countess Dracula

the significant absence of blood in the corpses. His investigation leads him to a Spanish dance team (Lupita Tovar, who played Mina in the 1931 Spanish-language version of *Dracula*, and Anthony Caruso) who are suspected of being vampires. The crime doctor's fans may have enjoyed this one, but horror fans were bored by the predictable script in this foray into the vampire genre. 🦇🦇

1945 ?m/B [Columbia Pictures] **Anthony Caruso**, **Lupita Tovar**, Warner Baxter, Hillary Brooke, Jerome Cowan, Robert Scott, Lloyd Corrigan; **D:** George Sherman; **W:** Eric Taylor; **C:** L.W. O'Connell.

Cronos

During the 1970s, Mexico turned out a series of forgettable vampire movies and then more or less abandoned the genre for the entire decade of the 1980s. With that track record, it was quite surprising when this innovative and horrific gem was introduced in Mexico in 1992. The vampire in this tale is actually the small, egg-shaped cronos device originally discovered by a sixteenth-century alchemist. As the movie opens, it is delivered, inside a statue, to a modern-day antiques store dealer. The device quickly gets its hooks into store-owner Jesus Gris and passes along its appetite for blood. Gris is them kidnapped by a wealthy but dying industrialist searching for the secret to eternal life. The story grew out of director del Torre's own love/hate affair with Roman Catholicism (it is no accident that the vampire is named Jesus); his study of alchemy, the occult, and vampires; and his very positive relationship with his grandmother (relived in *Cronos* through the shop owner and his granddaughter). A must-see film for vampire enthusiasts. 🦇🦇🦇🦇

1994 (R) 92m/C MX [Bertha Navarro, Arthur Gorson] Federico Luppi, Ron Perlman, Claudio Brook, Tamara Shanath; **D:** Guillermo del Toro; **W:** Guillermo del Toro; **M:** Ian Deardon. **VHS, LV** *VMK*

1960 74m/B MX [Mexican] Rock Madison, Ann Wells, George Todd, Willard Gross, Bruno Ve Sota; **D:** Frederic Corte, Jerry Warren. **VHS** *NOS, MRV, SNC*

Crime Doctor's Courage

In this third of the ten films featuring Dr. Ordway (Warner Baxter), the criminal psychologist investigates a series of deaths tied together by

Cry of the Vampire

An early Italian film inspired by Hammer's *Horror of Dracula*. The vampire baron at the center of this film even resembles Christopher Lee's Dracula from the Hammer films. Any resemblance to the Hammer quality is purely hypothetical. 🦴🦴

1960 ?m/C [Pao International] **D:** Theodora Fec.

Crypt of the Living Dead

Interesting story has archeologist Professor Bolton searching out the tomb of Queen Hannah (Theresa Gimpera), the thirteenth century spouse of Louis VII. It seems that Louis, upon returning from the Crusades, had discovered that Hannah was a vampire. He had her buried alive on what was known as Vampire Island. Bolton discovers her tomb and she awakens shortly after being uncovered. Her centuries old thirst is momentarily assuaged by the archeologist's blood, but she quickly starts on a bloodsucking rampage, making up for lost time. Bolton's son (Andrew Prine) comes searching for his father, only to find and promptly fall in love with Hannah. *AKA: Hannah, Queen of the Vampires, La Tumba de la Isla Maldita,* and *Vampire Women.* 🦴

1973 (PG) 75m/C Andrew Prine, Mark Damon, Teresa Gimpera, Patty Shepard, Francisco (Frank) Brana; **D:** Ray Danton. **VHS, Beta** *NO*

Curse of Dracula

The anthology series *Cliffhangers,* patterned after the movie serials of the fifties, included this segment, in which Dracula (Michael Nouri) teaches Eastern European history at a San Francisco college (a perfect place to recruit fresh blood). His nemesis is Abraham Van Helsing's grandson Kurt (Stephen Johnson), who is involved with his intended next victim, Mary Gibbons (Carol Baxter). The first four episodes of the show make up this movie. All ten episodes were combined for a longer movie, *World of Dracula.* 🦴🦴

1979 ?m/C [NBC, et al.] **Michael Nouri**, Stephen Johnson, Carol Baxter, Antoinette Stella, Bever-Leigh Banfield, Louise Sorel.

Curse of Nostradamus

In 1959, Frederico Curiel directed a twelve-part Spanish-language serial (each segment lasting twenty-five minutes) for release in Mexico. The next year, the twelve parts were edited into four feature-length movies, dubbed into English, and released by American International for use on American television. In the series Nostradamus (German Robles) was opposed by Professor Duran (Domingo Soler). In this first movie in the series, Duran at first believes that vampires are a thing of the past and nothing more than superstition. Nostradamus challenges that assumption and entices the professor into a contest of wills. Nostradamus builds a vampire cult by vampirizing thirteen local residents and then attacks one of Duran's colleagues and kidnaps his daughter. Duran is able to trace the vampires to their hideout in the mountains, setting up a final confrontation between good and evil. Also released as *La Maldición de Nostradamus* and followed by a sequel, *The Blood of Nostradamus* (1961). 🦴🦴

1960 ?m/B *MX* [American International Pictures (A.I.P.), Mexico] German Robles; **D:** Frederick Curiel. **VHS** *SNC, LOO*

The Curse of the Crying Woman

In Aztec lore, the ancient goddess Culhuacan was a terrifying figure who could transform into a beautiful young woman to seduce men and suck the life out of them. She survived in popular folklore in the post-Roman Catholic era as La Llorona, the Weeping Woman. In this film, a female vampire and her husband find the mummified corpse of La Llorona and attempt to revive her. *AKA: La Maldicion de a Llorona; La Casa Embrujada.* 🦴🦴

1961 74m/B *MX* [American International Pictures (A.I.P.)] Rosita Arenas, Abel Salazar, Rita Macedo. **VHS, Beta** *SNC, HHT*

"Kill me. Please kill me before the night is over, before dawn. Otherwise I'll have to drink your blood and turn you into horrible undead monsters."

—Karl Ulrich (George Hilton) talking to his guests from a *Dinner with a Vampire* (1988).

AFRICAN-AMERICANS AND THE VAMPIRE GENRE— BLAXPLOITATION AND BEYOND

In 1980 when Harry and Michael Medved published *The Golden Turkey Awards*, they gave their award as the worst film of all time to *Plan 9 from Outer Space* and named its director Ed Wood, Jr., the worst director, facts which have followed that movie ever since. Less known are the movies in the other categories (in which surprisingly few vampire movies appear). However, in one category, a vampire movie made the grade. The brothers Medved named *Scream, Blacula Scream* the worst blaxploitation film ever made. They didn't like the title, the editing, or the incoherent plot. They resented the use of a fine actor in such a silly part. In the end, exhausting their vocabulary, they labeled the film simply ridiculous.

It took a long time, but at least some of the powers that be in Hollywood finally discovered in the 1970s that there was a large African American market that was just waiting to watch films made by other African Americans. These "blaxploitation" films, as they are known, didn't necessarily portray African American culture in any accurate way, but at least they created jobs for African American actors and allowed audiences the opportunity to see their own community reflected on the screen rather than the dominant white culture. It was a significant part of the integration of African American into white America.

Several of the blaxploitation movies used vampires as their subject, but at no time in the past nor in the present have African American actors had a prominent place in vampire movies. The vampire is largely based on European mythology, especially the literary and cinematic vampire. There is an important history of African and Caribbean vampire mythology, but it has yet to become the subject of a movie. Blaxploitation vampire movies presented essentially European-style vampires who differ from white vampires only in skin color.

The first African American vampire was Blacula, a character portrayed by William Marshall. A trained Shakespearean actor, Marshall found employment in a number of 1970's motion pictures, most of which he seemed out of place in because of his classical training. In the movie *Blacula*, Marshall's title character began life as an African prince who called upon Count Dracula to help stop the slave trade. For his trouble, Dracula turned him into a vampire and gave him his silly name. Blacula was awakened in contemporary Los Angeles and tried to survive in the modern world. *Blacula* was not a bad movie. While no one at the Academy Awards even considered it, it was given the Ann Radcliffe Award by the Count Dracula Society and found an appreciative audience of vampire fans.

Blacula inspired several other African American vampire movies, including the aforementioned sequel, *Scream, Blacula, Scream*. Possibly the best one was 1973's *Ganja and Hess* (released in video as *Black Vampire)*, which tracked the exploits of Dr. Hess Green, an anthropology professor who was also a vampire, and his seduction of the wife of a young man whom he had previously killed. Another candidate for "best African American vampire movie" of the '70s wasn't even recognized as such at the time. *Old Dracula* (1975) told the story of Dracula (David Nivens), who awakened his wife only to discover that she had turned into an African American after drinking the blood of a young African American woman. Billed for white audiences as a Mel Brooks-type comedy, the film failed when viewed under that context. However, seen as a blaxploitation movie, it is an effective commentary on the racial situation of the era. Dracula has to deal with the fact that Mrs. Dracula (Teresa Graves) is what she is—her skin color is not going to change, so he should learn to accept her.

All of the blaxploitation movies were released within a three-year period. While African Americans have gone on to bigger and better things in Hollywood and the entertainment industry in general, they have still been noticeably absent from vampire films. In the twenty years after *Old Dracula,* only one movie featured an African American person—*Vamp* (1986), in which Grace Jones starred as a vampire/nightclub owner. Finally, in 1995, Eddie Murphy made the first significant attempt in 20 years at making an African American vampire movie.

Murphy's *Vampire in Brooklyn* appeared amidst a spate of movies made in the wake of the very successful *Interview with the Vampire,* a high standard by which each was judged. While the movie had a few humorous moments (as when Murphy morphs into a preacher and delivers a sermon on the goodness of evil), it was not the side-splitting comedy many expected. In fact, *Vampire in Brooklyn* was really just another remake of Dracula, complete with vampire Maximillian's arrival via ship wreck, his recruitment of an insect-eating Renfield, and his attempt to seduce a Mina-like figure from her Jonathan Harker. Like Frank Langella's Dracula, Murphy's was a seductive romancer. *Interview with the Vampire* it is not, but as people have put aside their preconceived notions of what an Eddie Murphy movie should be, the number of appreciative reactions to *Vampire in Brooklyn* have steadily grown.

Given the recent popularity of the vampire, does *Vampire in Brooklyn* signal a new appreciation of the vampire as a subject for African American movies? Probably not. However, movies that draw upon the African vampire mythology and/or the appropriation of European mythology by African Americans would be a welcome addition to the world of vampire films.

✝ E N D ✝

Curse of the Devil

Werewolf Waldemar Danisky (Paul Naschy, also known as Jacinto Molina) meets Elizabeth Bathory in this seventh of Naschy's werewolf movies. The story begins as the vampiric Countess faces off against the local inquisitor (also Naschy), upon whose family she puts a curse. Centuries later, Waldemar Danisky, a descendent of the inquisitor activates the curse by shooting a werewolf—a beautiful woman appears and seduces him to infect him with the "werewolf virus." Afterward, Waldemar goes on a rampage every month when the moon is full. Eventually, his lover is forced to confront him and take drastic action to end his curse. **AKA:** *The Black Harvest of Countess Dracula*; El Retorno de la Walpurgis. ♫♫

1973 (R) 73m/C *MX SP* Paul Naschy, Maria Silva, Patty Shepard, Fay Falcon; **D:** Carlos Aured; **W:** Paul Naschy. **VHS** *SNC*

Curse of the Undead

This, the first vampire western, turned out to be one of the better arguments against attempting to merge the two genres; for that reason, it is largely forgotten by today's vampire film fans. Eric Fleming plays Preacher Dan, who must rise to the occasion when a gun-toting vampire named Drake Robey appears in town to participate in a range war between cattlemen and farmers. He kills several of the town's residents and then goes after his female ranch-owner boss before facing a final showdown with Preacher Dan. **AKA:** *Affairs of a Vampire*; *Mark of the West*; *Mark of the Beast*; *Le Teur Invisible*; *The Invisible Killer*; *Les Griffes du Vampire*; and *The Grip of the Vampire*. ♫

1959 89m/B [Joe Gershenson, Universal Pictures] Eric Fleming, Michael Pate, Kathleen Crowley, John Hoyt, Bruce Gordon, Edward Binns, Jimmy Murphy, Jay Adler; **D:** Edward Dein; **W:** Edward Dein, Mildred Dein; **C:** Ellis W. Carter; **M:** Irving Gertz. **VHS** *MCA*

Curse of the Vampires

Dedicated to the principle that "the family that sucks blood together stays together." A mother passes her vampiric condition on to her son, who in turn then infects the rest of the family. Upon the discovery that his wife is a vampire, Dad banishes her to a basement crypt. This doesn't slow down her son Garcia, however, who wreaks havoc on both his family and that of his sister's fiance. Garcia is opposed by his sister Leonora, who he earlier turned into a vampire; her fiance Fuentes; and, of course, the traditional mob of angry villagers, who use a statue of the Madonna to help them battle the vampires. Also released as *Creatures of Evil*, *Blood of the Vampires*, and *Dugong Vampira*. Director de Leons second attempt at a vampire film far surpassed his initial endeavor. **AKA:** *Creatures of Evil*; *Blood of the Vampires*; *Dugong Vampira*. ♫♫♫

1970 ?m/C Amalia Fuentes, Eddie Garcia, Romeo Vasquez; **D:** Gerardo (Gerry) De Leon.

The Curse of the Vampyr

Carl von Rysselbert, the loving son of a dying baron, invites Dr. Greta Metterlich and her lovely assistant Erika to stay at his creepy mansion. Both Erika and the doctor suffer the consequences when it is revealed that von Rysselbert is really a vampire. Angry villagers realize the danger of the situation and take steps to ensure the vampires are vanquished, putting a merciful end to this amateurish production. **AKA:** *La Llamada del Vampiro*; *Aquellarre de Vampiros*. ♫

1971 ?m/C *SP* **Nicholas Ney**, Diana Sorel, Beatriz Lacy, Ines Skorpio; **D:** Jose Elorieta.

Curse of the Wicked Wife

Two twins separated at birth lead quite different lives, one in poverty and one in wealth. As they meet again in adulthood, they must deal with a vampire, among other horrors. There's also a man who kills people with "deathbugs." Feel free to bug out on this one. *AKA:* Wicked Wife. ♫

1984 ?m/C D: Wong King-Fang.

Cyber City Oedo 808: Data 3

Genetic researchers are turning up dead with fang wounds in their necks. One has left a very unusual retro-virus in his computer and leads pointing to a cryogenic suspension facility. Japanese with subtitles or dubbed. ♫♫♫

1991 49m/C *JP* **VHS** *CPM*

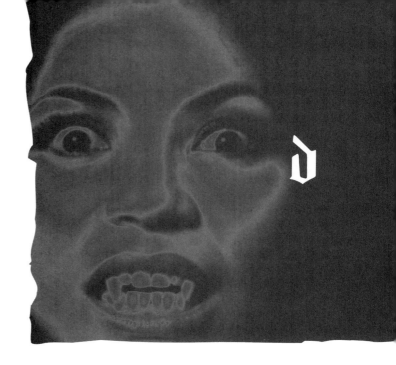

Dance of the Damned

Panned by reviewers (most of whom totally misunderstood it), vampire fans know *Dance of the Damned*—the story of a troubled go-go dancer and the night she spends with a vampire—as one of the truly great vampire movies of the century. Jodi, the dancer (Starr Andreeff), performs in a seedy nightclub, where the hours are keeping her from her son's birthday party. This gives her ex-husband an additional excuse to take the boy away from her. In her despair, she unsuccessfully attempts suicide. The vampire has become privy to her situation due to his very sensitive hearing and confronts Jodi as she is locking up the club. He offers her a way out: spend the night talking with him and he will end her pain. The vampire also has some issues—he misses the daylight and wants the girl to describe the sun and the colorful world he has been denied. At a loss for words, she takes him to the beach and has him lie on a blanket under a spotlight. He takes her to visit her son and a relationship seems to be building. The crucial element remains, however: the vampire needs blood and Jodi actually has a will to live. He waits until the last minutes before dawn to feed, and she must find a way to escape his rather mundane powers. Remade in color as *To Sleep with a Vampire* (1992). ♫♫♫♫

1988 (R) 83m/C [Concorde, New Horizons Pictures] Cyril O'Reilly, Starr Andreeff; **D:** Katt Shea Ruben; **W:** Katt Shea Ruben, Andy Ruben. **VHS, Beta, LV** *NO*

Dark Shadows 1840 Flashback

The original *Dark Shadows* series featured a storyline in which vampire Barnabas Collins and Dr. Julia Hoffman (Grayson Hall) traveled back in time to 1840. This video includes the highlights of their adventures. ♫♫

1967 40m/C [Dan Curtis Productions] **Jonathan Frid**, Lara Parker. **VHS, Beta** *MPI, TPV*

IT CAME FROM CANADA:
THE IMPOSSIBLE NIGHTMARES
OF DAVID CRONENBERG

In the nineteenth century, the writers and dramatists of the Romantic Era wrote of their explorations of their own inner worlds and personal demons. During their darker visions, which were often drug-induced, it was not unusual for horrific creatures such as vampires to be prominently featured. Edgar Allan Poe is a prominent example of a writer from that era who was able to turn his own grotesque visions into a body of ground breaking horror literature.

Decades later, Canadian-born filmmaker David Cronenberg followed the same path as Poe and others of that era by taking his nightmares and transforming them into art. His films have become known for injecting rationally impossible situations into real-life and for the use of effective and vivid presentations that make the impossible both acceptable and horrifying. He burst on the scene in 1977 with *They Came from Within*, a film that caused the Canadian Parliament to debate the appropriateness of its

support for the Canadian Film Development Corporation. Built around a theme that was later popularized in other horror/science fiction movies, the movie told the tale of a parasite that invaded the human body. The parasite, after its incubation period, of course had to eventually leave the host body, and Cronenberg earned his place in the horror hall of fame for a scene in which the parasite bursts out of the stomach of actor Alan Migicovsky.

Cronenberg followed *They Came from Within* with his vampire movie, *Rabid* (1977), which again incorporated his peculiar vision of horror. Borrowing Marilyn Chambers from her lucrative career in adult movies, Cronenberg told the story of a woman (Chambers) who developed strange side effects after an operation. A strange protuberance appeared under her arm, from which protruded a phallic-like growth that was capped by a sharp, pointed object that could easily cut into another person's flesh. Chambers and her

odd growth developed a blood thirst that could only be satisfied by attacking other people, which only served to increase the growth's need for blood.

Cronenberg went from that creative variation on the vampire theme to the likes of *The Brood* (1979), in which a mother gave birth to killer children; *Scanners* (1981), in which psychics willed people to explode; and *Videodrone* (1985), which featured a television of torture and sex. Along with these films, which made him a darling of horror fans, he showed that he had arrived as a big time filmmaker when he was selected to do the film version of Stephen King's novel *The Dead Zone* (1985).

Still very active as a director, Cronenberg will in all likelihood move on to bigger, better, and more controversial movies. One can only hope that he will return to the vampire theme again.

✝ END ✝

Dark Shadows: Behind the Scenes

A history of *Dark Shadows*, told through rare footage, clips from episodes, and interviews with the major actors, such as Jonathan Frid, Alexandra Moltke, David Selby, and Joan Bennett. Dan Curtis, who created the series, provides commentary on the show. 🦷🦷

19?? 60m/C VHS *MOV, TPV*

Dark Shadows Bloopers

Hilarious collection of numerous on-the-air mishaps from the days of almost-live television. *Dark Shadows* was videotaped live (as were most television shows of the period), and the cameras continued to role no matter what happened. The result was shown over-the-air without editing, which was not yet commonly available in the early 1970s. Even if crew members walked on stage, actors forgot their lines, or the set fell apart, the show had to go on, which led to some very funny scenes. 🦷🦷

1993 45m/C VHS *MPI*

Dark Shadows Music Videos

An anthology of scenes from the original *Dark Shadows* television series in which the music associated with the show was highlighted, including the very popular "Quentin's Theme." 🦷🦷

1991 40m/C [MPI Home Video] VHS, LV *MPI, TPV*

Dark Shadows Resurrected The Video

An anthology featuring the cast of the 1991 revival of *Dark Shadows* that includes interviews

with the cast, behind-the-scenes footage, outtakes, and highlights from the series. 🦷🦷

1995 ?m/C Ben Cross, Barbara Steele, Jean Simmons, Roy Thinnes, Lysette Anthony; *D:* Dan Curtis.

Dark Shadows' Scariest Moments

A half-hour anthology of some of the most frightening moments from the original *Dark Shadows* series, which during its run explored a wide variety of frightening situations, especially attacks by Barnabas Collins (Jonathan Frid) and other vampires. 🦷🦷

199? ?m/C *MPI*

Dark Shadows: Vampires & Ghosts

A collection of clips from the *Dark Shadows* series that features Barnabas Collins and the several other characters who were turned into vampires at some point during the series. 🦷🦷

1995 60m/C VHS *MPI*

Dark Shadows 25th Anniversary

In 1991, the actors from the original *Dark Shadows* TV series celebrated the show's 25th anniversary. This hour-long video includes clips of the various stars on stage answering questions from fans, along with scenes from the show. 🦷🦷

199? ?m/C *MPI*

Dark Universe

In a less than original plot, borrowed directly from *The First Man into Space* (1957), a

"There's not room enough in this town for two doctors... or two vampires."

—Max Adrian to Donald Sutherland in *Dr. Terror's House of Horrors* (1965).

spaceship crashes in the Florida swamp. The pilot (Steve Barkett), had been transformed into a large bloodsucking monster by an alien entity. Like most sci-fi vampire creatures, this one wants to take over the Earth and feed on humans. It's been done, better, elsewhere. 🗡🗡

1993 (R) 83m/C [Patrick Moran, Curb Entertainment, American Independent/Sharan] Blake Pickett, Cherie Scott, Bently Tittle, John Maynard, Paul Austin Saunders, Tom Ferguson, Steve Barkett, Joe Estevez, Patrick Moran; *D:* Steve Latshaw; *W:* Patrick Moran. **VHS, Beta** *PSM*

Darkness

This low-budget splatter quickie features a group of vampires who attack a small community, starting with the customers at a convenience store who happen to be in the wrong place at the wrong time. A sole survivor becomes a modern knight who seeks to slay the army of the undead. His weapons include a shotgun, a chainsaw (standard splatter prop), and holy water (a nod to traditionional vampire lore). Along the way, he finds a few survivors who assist him in his final confrontation with Liven (Randall Aviks), the vampire king. 🗡🗡

1992 ?m/C Randall Aviks, Jake Euker, Timo Gilbert, Veronica Page Denne, Steve Brown; *D:* Leif Jonker.

Daughter of Darkness

In this made-for-TV movie, a young Ameri-

can woman (Mia Sara) goes to prerevolutionary Romania in search of her family roots. She discovers that her father is Anton Crainic (Anthony Perkins), a 200-year-old vampire, and that by coming to Romania she has placed herself in great jeopardy from the rest of the family. Crainic must help her escape their clutches. 🗡🗡🗡

1989 (R) 93m/C Mia Sara, Anthony Perkins, Robert Reynolds, Jack Coleman; **D:** Stuart Gordon. **VHS** *VMK*

The Daughter of Dr. Jekyll

Janet Smith, a proper young British girl, is told by her guardian, the kindly Dr. Lomas, that she is really the daugher of the notorious Dr. Jekyll. At the same time, her village is rocked by a series of murders that appear to have been committed by a vampire. Angry villagers believe that Smith must be the perpetrator, but she and her fiance George Hasting take steps to reveal the true villian. Even B-movie veteran John Agar must have had second thoughts about this flick, which was originally released on the same bill with *Dr. Cyclops.* 🗡

1957 71m/B [Allied Artists] John Agar, Arthur Shields, John Dierkes, Gloria Talbott; **D:** Edgar G. Ulmer. **VHS, Beta** *FOX*

Daughter of Dracula

One of Jesus Franco's quickie vampire films, *Daughter of Dracula* combines elements of the Dracula legend with Sheridan Le Fanu's story "Carmilla." Just months after Dracula is killed, a dying mother tells her daughter Maria Karnstein (Britt Nichols) that she is a descendent of Dracula. This revelation causes Maria great mental distress, and she flees to the apparent tranquility of a nearby estate. There, she meets and befriends a young woman who eventually becomes her lover. Unfortunately, the happiness comes to an end when Maria's true vampiric nature rises to the surface. As is typical of Franco's '70s

films, he attempts to disguise poor narrative content with a surplus of naked bodies and violence. A weak story line is often further destroyed by the cuts of various national censors. **AKA:** A Filha de Dracula; La Hija de Dracula; La Fille de Dracula. 🗡🗡

1972 87m/C *SP* [Interfilme, Comptoir Francais de Film] **Howard Vernon, Britt Nichols**, Anne Libert, Alberto Dalbes, Soledad Miranda; **D:** Jess (Jesus) Franco; **C:** Jose Climent; **M:** Rene Silvano.

Daughters of Darkness

By far the best of the movies that use a contemporary setting to retell the legend of Elizabeth Bathory, *Daughters of Darkness* takes place at a largely empty hotel during the off-season. Guests include two couples—honeymooners Valerie and Stefan and a lesbian couple, Ilona and her aristocratic companion. One of the hotel employees recognizes Ilona's companion as the same person who had stayed at the hotel decades before but who appears not to have aged in the intervening years. It turns out that she is the Countess Elizabeth Bathory, a famous vampire/serial killer who, legend has it, survives by bathing in the blood of young women. Plot twist after plot twist follows when Ilona and Valerie become tired of their relationships and Valerie finds herself attracted to the Countess. **AKA:** *Blut on den Lippen, The Promise of Red Lips. Le Rouge aux Levres.* 🗡🗡🗡

1971 (R) 87m/C *BE GE IT FR* [Gemini Film Productions] Delphine Seyrig, John Karlen, Daniele Ouimet, Andrea Rau, Paul Esser, Georges Jamin, Joris Collet, Fons Rademakers; **D:** Harry Kumel. **VHS, Beta** *NO*

Dawn

Low-budget British offering from producer/director Johnson. Louis (Geoff Sloan) is 200 years old, but he's aged well, so he can still get the girls. One of his conquests, whom he has impregnated, sets out to show her dis-

Def by Temptation: "First I'll tease him, then I'll kill him. Oops, was that out loud?" Temptress Cynthia Bond puts the moves on one of her victims.

pleasure with him. Weak plot, performances, and direction. ⚔

1990 ?m/C [Shooting Gallery] **Geoff Sloan**, Elizabeth Rees, Craig Johnson, Kate Jones Davies; **D:** Niall Johnson.

Dead Men Walk

George Zucco portrays the Clayton brothers, twins who both happen to be doctors. One of the twins has an evil streak and is fascinated by the occult, a fascination that causes his death. His trusted assistant (Dwight Frye, who is best known for playing Renfield in the famous 1931 version of *Dracula*) comes to his aid by bringing him back to life as a vampire. When he begins to kill some of the local residents, his good twin, who is mistakenly accused of the killings, is forced to uncover the truth and save his own life. **AKA:** *Creatures of the Devil.* ⚔⚔

1943 65m/B [Sigmund Newfeld] George Zucco, Mary Carlisle, Dwight Frye, Nedrick Young, Al "Fuzzy" St. John; **D:** Sam Newfield. **VHS, Beta** *NOS, MRV, SNC*

Deadly Love

Career woman Dey is looking for love—not so unusual except she happens to also be a vampire. She finds a potential soulmate in homicide detective McHattie, but his latest case involves a serial killer whose victims die from puncture wounds to the neck. Nasty coincidence? Somewhat silly cable thriller. ⚔⚔

1995 ?m/C Susan Dey, Stephen McHattie, Eric Petersen, Julie Khaner, Robert S. Woods.

Deafula

Director Wechsburg stars in this low-budget but noble attempt to film a vampire movie entirely in sign-language for the hearing impaired (there is a voice over for hearing audience members). Steve Adams, a theology

student, is bitten by Count Dracula, causing him to periodically grow fangs and transform into Deafula. Wechsburg went on to produce America's first sign-language newscast. ♪♪

1975 90m/C [Signscope] **Peter Wechsberg, Gary R. Holmstrum**, Lee Darrel, James Randall, Dudley Hemstreet, Katherine Wilson; **D:** Peter Wechsberg; **W:** Peter Wechsberg.

Deathdream

A mother learns the hard way the truth of the old adage "Watch out what you wish for or you just might get it." After her son (Richard Backus) is killed in Vietnam, she wishes him back from the grave. He comes back, but is now a bloodthirsty revenant. He attains his nourishment by way of a syringe. **AKA:** Dead of Night; Night Walk; The Veteran. ♪♪♪

1972 98m/C *CA* [Bob Clark, Europix Consolidated] John Marley, Richard Backus, Lynn Carlin; **D:** Bob (Benjamin) Clark; **W:** Alan Ormsby. **VHS, Beta** *MPI*

The Deathmaster

Long-haired vampire Korda is washed ashore in his coffin in 1970s Los Angeles and subsequently becomes a guru to a group of hippie beach people. The beach crowd provides him with a steady diet of young blood. **AKA:** Khorda. ♪♪

1971 ?m/C [American International Pictures (A.I.P.)] **Robert Quarry**, Brenda Dickson, John Fiedler; **D:** Ray Danton.

Def by Temptation

Joel, a young African American ministerial student (James Bond III) experiences troubling dreams that call into question his desire to join the ministry. He goes to New York to share his doubts with a friend, unaware that he has been lured to the big city by a succubus (Cynthia Bond) who wants to suck the life and soul out of him and his friend. In a chilling and gory confrontation with the su-

pernatural, Joel is offered a chance to reestablish his faith. The atmosphere is bolstered by brief appearances by pop singers Freddie Jackson, Melba Moore, and Najee. ♪♪

1990 (R) 95m/C [Troma Team] **Cynthia Bond**, James Bond III, Kadeem Hardison, Bill Nunn, Samuel L. Jackson, Minnie Gentry, Rony Clanton; **D:** James Bond III; **W:** James Bond III. **VHS, Beta, LV** *SGE, IME*

Demon Queen

A demonic vampiress seeks out men to seduce and murder. ♪♪

198? 70m/C [Donald Farmer, David Reed] Mary Fanaro, Dennis Stewart, Cliff Dance; **D:** Donald Farmer. **VHS, Beta** *NO*

Demonsoul

The thriller features Erika (Kerry Norton), who suffers from horrible nightmares featuring ritual sacrifices, black magic, and a mysterious red-headed female. Eventually the nightmares become waking visions. This sends her to Dr. Charles Bucher (Daniel Jordan), a hypnotherapist who regresses her to a past life in which she was a vampire. The red-head, Selena (Eileen Daly), was her servant. Bucher become infatuated with Dana, the vampire entity who comes forth when Erica is hypnotized, and conspires with her to take over Erica's waking consciousness. Erica is forced to fight for her sanity as the nighttime—Dana's time—approaches. ♪♪

1994 ?m/C [Vista Street Ent.] **Kerry Norton**, Daniel Jordan, Eileen Daly; **D:** Elisar C. Kennedy.

A Deusa de Marmore Escrava do Diabo

A 2,000-year-old vampire (Rosangela Maldonado) survives by sucking the life out of her endless string of lovers. ♪♪

> "I am Dracula. . .
> I bid you
> welcome."
>
> —Dracula (Bela Lugosi) in *Dracula* (1931).

The female Dracula?

She was just a sweet young girl, but in the world of vampires, looks can and often are deceiving. Carmilla, a young female vampire, was the creation of Irish novelist and short story writer Sheridan Le Fanu. She made her first appearance a quarter of a century before Dracula in a novella that bore her name. Or at least one of her names. It seems that Le Fanu tried to create a new part of the vampire myth in his story, saying that vampires had to choose a name that was an anagram of their real name. Carmilla's real name was Mircalla, and she was also known as Millarca. By what ever name, Carmilla, who was part of the noble

Karnstein family, enjoyed the company of young adult females who were near her own age (or at least the age she appeared to be).

Carmilla did not make it to the screen as early as her aristocratic male counterpart. She was somewhat of an inspiration for Theodor Dreyer's *Vampyr* (1932), but it was not until 1961, when censorship laws were loosened, that French director Roger Vadim decided to cast his wife Annette Stroyberg in the role of Carmilla. Vadim moved the story into the present, but centered the action on the relationship between Carmilla and her cousin's fiancé. The

next year, director Camillo Mastrocinque, who was building his career churning out sexploitation quickies, convinced Christopher Lee to star in his Carmilla production, *La Maldicion de los Karnsteins* (released in English as *Terror in the Crypt*). Lee's presence easily overshadowed that of Carmilla, who in the film version was a mere servant girl who summoned Carmilla's spirit and then attacked the members of the family for whom she worked.

The 1970s were the heyday for Carmilla films. Hammer, searching for material to exploit the goldmine they had found in bloodsucking movies, found Le Fanu's anti-heroine the perfect character to test the boundaries of British censorship laws. At the beginning of the decade they made three Carmilla movies, *Lust for a Vampire* (1970), *The Vampire Lovers* (1970), and *Twins of Evil* (1971), each of which made good use of the aspiring, young starlets in the Hammer stable.

1978 ?m/C [Panorama do Brazil] **Rosangela Maldonado**, Jose Mojica Marins, Joao Paulo, Luandy Maldonado; *D:* Rosangela Maldonado.

The Devil Bat

Mad scientist Dr. Paul Carruthers (Bela Lugosi) develops a unique way to get even with his enemies. He devises a shaving cream with a unique scent, gives a sample of his mixture to people he doesn't like, and then releases a giant "vampire" bat that is trained to attack anyone smelling of the cream. This movie, also released as *Killer Bats* and as *Devil Bats*, represents one of several low

points in Lugosi's career. Someone liked it enough, however, to cause the Producers Releasing Company to redo the film after World War II with a slightly different creature and a new name—*The Flying Serpent*. A sequel, *The Devil Bat's Daughter*, was also produced. **AKA:** *Killer Bats.* 🦇

1941 67m/B [Producers Releasing Corporation] Bela Lugosi, Dave O'Brien, Suzanne Kaaren, Yolande Donlan; *D:* Jean Yarbrough. **VHS, Beta** NOS, SNC, PSM

The Devil Bat's Daughter

In this sequel to *The Devil Bat*, Nina, the daughter of the angry scientist who had sent

out the murderous bats, begins to have night-mares about her late father, whom she was told was a vampire. She goes to a psychiatrist for help, but instead he uses her in a plot to kill his wife, convincing Nina that she is the one who killed her. Rosemary La Plache, who played Nina, was Miss America in 1941. 🦇🦇

1946 66m/B [PRC] Rosemary La Planche, Michael Hale, John James, Molly Lamont; *D:* Frank Wisbar. **VHS, Beta** *COL, MRV*

The Devil's Commandment

Appearing the year before Hammer's *Horror of Dracula,* this fountainhead of the Italian cinematic vampire launched the modern era of vampire movies in Europe. Set in post-war Paris, it concerned a mad doctor (Antoine Belpetre) who takes blood from young women in order to perpetuate the youth of the Duchess Marguerite (Gianna Maria Canale), his aristocratic patient somewhat loosely modeled on Elizabeth Bathory. A somewhat mediocre production, notable for the camera work of future star director Mario Bava. *AKA:* I, Vampiri; Lust of the Vampires. *The Devil's Commandment; Lust of the Vampire; and The Vampire of Notre Dame.* 🦇🦇

1956 90m/B *FR* [RCIP, Ermanno Donati, Luigi Carpentieri] Gianna Maria Canale, Dario Michaelis, Carlo D'Angelo, Wandisa Guida, Paul Muller, Renato Tontini; *D:* Riccardo (Robert Hampton) Freda. **VHS, Beta, LV** *OUP, SNC*

The Devil's Mistress

A low-budget independent movie in which a female psychic vampire (portrayed by Joan Stapleton) attacks the four men who killed her husband in the old West. 🦇🦇

1968 66m/C [Emerson Film Enterprises] **Joan Stapleton,** Robert Gregory, Forrest Westmoreland, Douglas Warren, Oren Williams, Arthur Resley; *D:* Orville Wanzer; *W:* Orville Wanzer. **VHS** *SNC*

Devils of Darkness

Pioneering effort in British filmmaking is the first film to attempt to place the vampire in a contemporary setting. Because of that and because of its extremely low budget, it's easier to understand and forgive some of the film's shortcomings. Sylvester and Reed play two friends who investigate the death of a young man killed on vacation in Breton. They discover Count Sinistre, the local vampire, who threatens to turn Reed into his next victim. 🦇🦇

1965 90m/C *GB* [20th Century-Fox] **Hubert Noel,** Diana Decker, Rona Anderson, Victor Brooks, William Sylvester, Tracy Reed, Carole Gray; *D:* Lance Comfort; *W:* Lyn Fairhust; *C:* Reg Wyer; *M:* Bernie Fenton.

The Devil's Plaything

Adult erotic film has a group of nuns awaiting the return of a vampire burned at the stake during the Middle Ages. *AKA:* Veil of Blood. 🦇

1973 88m/C [Leisure Time Products/3M, Monarex Hollywood Corporation] **Nadia Senkowa,** Untel Syring, Maria Forssa, Ulrike Butz; *D:* Joe Sarno; *W:* Joe Sarno.

Devil's Vindeta

Among the more unique vampire productions from Hong Kong (though the title was misprinted and should be *Devil's Vendetta*). The devil feasts on a Buddhist priest's heart, resulting in the priest both changing sex and turning into a demon. She then comes back to life as a vampiress. 🦇🦇

1986 ?m/C *D:* L. Chang-Xu.

Devil's Wedding Night

1970s sexploitation flick in which twin brothers, both archeologists (and both

Videohound salutes: the Chaneys.

Lon (short for Alonzo) Chaney, Sr., was called the man with a thousand faces. The legendary actor was willing to go to outrageous extremes to create the most grotesque of characters through novel makeup and facial distortions. He became best known for his roles in *The Hunchback of Notre Dame* and *The Phantom of the Opera* (1925), but he appeared in more than 150 films (an average of nine a year). It is a clear statement on how difficult it is to preserve old movies that, even as big a star as he was, only forty of his pictures have survived.

Included in the more than one hundred lost Chaney films was *London After Midnight*, a pet project of director Tod Browning. Chaney portrayed a police inspector who assumed the role of a vampire in order to force the guilty person to reveal himself. This would be the last of several collaborations between Chaney and Browning, though the director had signaled his intent to sign his favorite actor to play the lead role in the 1931 production of *Dracula*. Chaney developed cancer and died, opening the door for a young Hungarian actor named Bela Lugosi who was to take the part and make it his own.

Deciding to do what so many children do and pursue his father's profession, Lon Chaney, Jr., tried his hand in acting. Only two years after his father's death, the young man appeared in *Bird of Paradise* with Joel McCrea. He came into his own in 1941 as Larry Talbot, the title character in *The Wolf Man*, a part that made him a horror star at Universal. In that movie, Bela Lugosi portrayed the man whose bite transformed him into a werewolf.

In an odd turn of fate, Chaney was in the right place at the right time when Universal decided to bring Dracula back for another celluloid treatment in 1943. In *Son of Dracula*, Chaney won the part of Dracula that many expected would go to Lugosi, much like Lugosi had won the role after the elder Chaney passed away in 1931. Not the suave, continental type, Chaney's Dr. Alucard (Dracula backwards) in *Son of Dracula* (1943) was an adequate vampire, but he had nowhere near the impact of his predecessor. He would go on to play the Wolf Man in several of the Universal monster movies—opposite John Carradine's Dracula in *House of Frankenstein* and *House of Dracula* and opposite Lugosi's Dracula in *Abbott and Costello Meet Frankenstein*.

Chaney carried on the family tradition for many decades longer than his father. He closed out his career in 1969, over 55 years after his father's first part in *Poor Jake's Demise* (1913). Unfortunately that last appearance was in one of director Al Adamson's cinematic disaster's, *Dracula vs. Frankenstein*, in which Dracula and an alien attempt to reanimate the world's monsters. That mistake aside, the Chaneys provided the world with more than a half-century of monstrous thrills.

✝ END ✝

played by Mark Damon), are searching for the ring of the Nibelungs, which they believe has magical powers. One brother learns that it's in the possession of the Countess del Vries (a thinly disguised Elizabeth Bathory clone) who keeps herself young by bathing in the blood of virgins. The brothers go after the ring and one is victimized by the Countess. The other one must battle the Countess and his brother to obtain it. *AKA: El Returno de la Drequessa Dracula; The Return of the Duchess Dracula; Full Moon of the Virgins.* ♪

1973 (R) 85m/C [Dimension Pictures] Mark Damon, Rosalba (Sara Bay) Neri, Frances Davis; **D:** Paul Solvay. **VHS, Beta** *NO*

Dinner with the Vampire

Director Lamberto Bava, son of the legendary Mario Bava, continues his father's tradition in this story of Karl Urich, a world famous horror director who has taken up residence in a castle. Unbeknownst to the rest of world, Urich is also a centuries-old vampire who has grown tired of his existence. At an audition, two actors and two actresses win a weekend with Urich, during which the depressed vampire hopes one of the lucky winners will kill him, as he has been unable to face the idea of suicide. Killing Urich proves no easy task, however—his power is immense, and he is unaffected by most traditional vampire weapons such as garlic, crosses, or even the stake in the heart. Urich is so powerful, in fact, he can even cause a person's heart to jump out of his or her body and into his (Urich's) hands. In fact, the only sure method of dispatching him is to destroy a piece of film made in the 1920s, when a film crew accidentally released him from his tomb and captured part of his soul on celluloid. ♪♪♪

1988 ?m/C [Dania Film, Reteitalia] **George Hilton**, Patrizia Pellegrino, Riccardo Rossi, Valeria Milillo, Yvonne Scio; **D:** Lamberto Bava.

Disciple of Death

A very different vampire movie, drawing on Satanism themes. An eighteenth-century vampire (Mike Raven) is resurrected by a drop of blood falling on his tomb. The unwitting donor (Virginia Weatherall) becomes his first victim and joins him in his vampiric life. The vampire then establishes himself as a priest, of sorts, and plans to sacrifice virgins. ♪

1972 (R) 82m/C *GB* [Avco Embassy] **Mike Raven**, Ronald Lacey, Stephen Bradley, Virginia Wetherell; **D:** Tom Parkinson. **VHS, Beta** *UNI*

Doctor Dracula

In 1977 Paul Arator did a film called *Lucifer's Woman*. Nobody noticed. So three years later Al Adamson took the film, added some footage with the aging John Carradine and came up with *Doctor Dracula*. Still, nobody but a few vampire completists cared. For the few who care, the revised story concerns a devil-cult, led by Carradine, attempting a ritual that will result in their attaining everlasting life. A vampire among them has other plans for the participants. Adamson, cutting the budget from low to practically non-existent, got what he paid for. Don't even bother. **Woof!**

1980 ?m/C [Independent International] **Geoffrey Land**, John Carradine, Larry Hankin, Susan McIver; **D:** Al Adamson, Paul Aratow.

Dr. Terror's House of Horrors

Peter Cushing and Christopher Lee are among the several stars of this collection of horror shorts, although, neither are in the vampire story. Cushing plays a tarot card reader who introduces each episode as an account of how each of his fellow train passengers will die. One of the passengers, an American doctor played by Donald Suther-

Dracula: Van Helsing looks alarmed at Dracula's (Bela Lugosi) strange method of high five.

land, suspects his wife is a vampire. This rather fine horror anthology is the first of several produced by Amicus. *The Blood Suckers.* As mentioned above, not related to *Dr. Terror's Gallery of Horrors.* **AKA:** The Blood Suckers. ♫♫

1965 92m/C *GB* [Hammer] Christopher Lee, Peter Cushing, Donald Sutherland; *D:* Freddie Francis. **VHS** *REP, MLB*

Doctor Vampire

A Hong Kong physician traveling in England visits a house of vampire prostitutes after his car breaks down. He takes advantage of his situation, and ends up giving good blood to his partner of the evening (Ellen Chan), in one of the more sensual bloodsucking episodes ever. As the couple exchanges bodily fluids, they fall in love. When the pimp gets a taste of the doctor's blood, he becomes obsessed with acquiring more. The doctor returns to Hong Kong, where he begins to manifest vampiric tendencies, including taking blood from the patients in the hospital while his love tries to cure him. The pimp, who still can't get enough of the stuff, goes to Hong Kong to find the missing pair. One of the better Chinese vampire flicks.. ♫♫

1991 ?m/C *HK* **Ellen Chan**, Bowie Lam Bo-Yi; *D:* Q. Xen Lee.

Dracula

Tod Browning's classic is the most important vampire movie ever made. Bela Lugosi, an immigrant from Hungary who spoke little English, was perfect for the part that made him famous and forever typecast him. Dracula, as scripted by playwright Hamilton Deane in the 1920s was a suave, cultured, continental nobleman who covered his evil intentions well. He was at home everywhere, especially in a proper English drawing room, even in the most tense situations. Lugosi brought an unexpected sensuality to the part, which was only recognized later, when thousands of letters poured in from female fans. Lugosi's

Dracula, with his penetrating eyes and debonair manner, presented a very seductive anti-hero to the audiences who filled the theater. Even without the fangs (they weren't added until the 1950s), Lugosi set most of the popular images of Dracula and the vampire. Possessed of a widow's peak, vampires dress in evening clothes, complete with the all-important opera cape. Only in recent years have male cinematic vampires tended to deviate from that standard dress. The script for the 1931 movie version (and its Spanish counterpart, shot simultaneously) was the John Balderston revision of the original Hamilton Deane play, written for the New York stage. That play was further edited by screenwriter Louis Bloomfield, who seems to be responsible for changing the Carfax estate, Dracula's London home base, to Carfax Abbey. He also began to provide answers for some of the questions not dealt with in the novel, such as the reason for Renfield's madness. The movie opens with Renfield, not Jonathan Harker, traveling to Transylvania in search of Count Dracula, an exciting part of the book dropped from the earlier stage presentations. Renfield (Dwight Frye) completes the sale of property in England to the Count, but in the process is victimized by Dracula's three vampire brides. He returns to England completely insane. In England, Dracula begins to target, and then quickly disposes of, Lucy Weston (Francis Dale) before turning his attention to Mina Seward (Helen Chandler). In the novel, Lucy was a young girl with three suitors. As in the play, the movie collapsed the three men into one, Dr. John Seward (Herbert Bunston), who was transformed into Mina's middle-aged father. Emerging to counter Dracula, of course, is Dr. Abraham Van Helsing (Edward van Sloan), the knowledgeable and grandfatherly vampire hunter. He confirms Dracula's true nature with a mirror and then leads the charge to destroy him. At the close of the movie, he interrupts the credits to deliver a famous speech on the possible reality of vampires. Tod Browning had previously collaborated with Lon Chaney on another feature-length vampire movie, *London After Midnight*. A look at the Spanish version, shot on the same stage at Universal each evening after the English-speaking cast was finished, reveals Browning's limited use of the camera, especially in the scenes in the castle. The Spanish version was the cinematographic superior. The body of the film also comes off as exactly what it was, a stage play brought to the screen. Still, the limitations of the directing and camera work fade beside the enormous (and lasting) impact of the film on popular culture. Lugosi's Count attained a mythical status in modern society worldwide and fathered one of the most intriguing movie genres to grace the screen. *Dracula* was to open on Friday the 13th, in February of 1931. Manhattan was plastered with blood-red notices and the movie had a relatively successful eight-day run. With a silent version prepared for those theaters not yet equipped for sound, it opened nationally with little fanfare; Universal was in a financial crunch at the time, and its future was very uncertain. In spite of the lack of publicity and the panning by critics (who as a rule tend to dislike horror movies), *Dracula* caught on and became the largest grossing movie of the year for Universal. The studio did not close and is still with us today. The one who suffered was Lugosi. While he had played Dracula on the New York stage, he was by no means the first choice for the movie role. Lon Chaney was chosen, but he died of cancer. Several other actors turned it down. Little appreciated, Lugosi was paid a small salary commensurate with the (lack of) respect accorded him by industry types. The movie made him a star, but also typecast him, and he was unable to break out of horror movies and into the kind of roles that promised mainstream stardom. In later years, when horror movies went through periods of decline, he was often without work and living in poverty, occasionally having to resort to playing a parody of himself. In more recent years, other actors such as Christopher Lee and Frank Langella would learn from his mistake. ♫♫♫♫

1931 75m/B [Universal] Bela Lugosi, David Manners, Dwight Frye, Helen Chandler, Edward Van Sloan; *D:* Tod Browning; *C:* Karl Freund. **VHS, Beta, LV** MCA, TLF, HMV

"Look ma. 3-D."
Yes. Frank Langella
tests his spooky
charm in *Dracula*.

Dracula

This 11th remake of Dracula, a made-for-television production, was at the time of its release the most faithful of the several feature film versions of the novel. Scriptwriter Richard Matheson bypassed the play by Hamilton Deane and John L. Balderston (used in the several versions of *Dracula* produced by Universal Studios) and instead went straight to Bram Stoker's novel for his outline. In addition to using Stoker's novel, Matheson also became the first to integrate parts of the legend of Vlad the Impaler into the plot of *Dracula*. The connection solved several problems not resolved in the novel—for example, why did Dracula choose Lucy Westenra as his first victim? Viewers learn the answer during the initial action in the movie, which occurs at Castle Dracula. The main hall of the castle is dominated by a painting of Vlad on horseback. In one corner of that painting is the picture of Vlad's lover—a woman who could have been Lucy's twin. Vlad/Dracula (Jack Palance) be-

comes obsessed with finding his lost love and spends eternity searching for her. When he sees Lucy, he abandons his castle (leaving Jonathan Harker in the clutches of a trio of vampire women) and travels to England. That combination of the two legends sets the stage for Dracula's attempts to make Lucy his own and for his final battles with vampire hunter Van Helsing and his band of allies. Palance has received mixed reviews for his performance. Some critics have charged that he failed to capture the range of emotions appropriate to the part, while others have found in Palance the quintessential villain perfectly suited for the part. 𝄞𝄞𝄞𝄞

1973 105m/C [Dan Curtis Productions] Jack Palance, Simon Ward, Fiona Lewis, Nigel Davenport; *D:* Dan Curtis. **VHS, Beta, LV** *LIV*

Dracula

For this 15th remake of Dracula, screenwriter W. D. Richter rewrote the play by Hamilton Deane and John Balderston to pre-

sent Dracula as a magnetically attractive seducer, a part ideally written for actor Frank Langella (who had been starring in the revived play on Broadway). Skipping the scenes in Castle Dracula that appeared at the beginning of the earlier Universal Studios' version with Bela Lugosi, this lavish new version opened with the wreck of the ship bringing Dracula to England. Dracula leaves the ship as a wolf and in one of the more sensual moments in any Dracula remake, slowly transforms back into a human-like being (the sensuality of this scene is rivalled by another scene later in the film when Dracula shares his blood with his beloved Lucy). In human guise, this Dracula woos and charms his female victims (although he is not above a few supernatural parlor tricks if it serves his purpose) and views the males who oppose him with complete disdain. Legendary stage and screen actor Laurence Olivier provides an interesting counterpart to Langella's Dracula in his portrayal of vampire hunter Abraham Van Helsing. When Universal released its version of *Dracula* in 1931, it was surprised when female viewers were captivated by, and fell in love with Bela Lugosi as the Count. This 1979 version seemed to acknowledge Dracula's inherent sex appeal, and self-consciously played upon females' romantic attachment to the handsome yet evil Count. 🦇🦇🦇🦇

1979 (R) 109m/C [Universal] Frank Langella, Laurence Olivier, Kate Nelligan, Donald Pleasence; **D:** John Badham; **W:** W.D. Richter; **M:** John Williams. **VHS, Beta, LV** *MCA*

Dracula

During the 1970s, Marvel Comics published "The Tomb of Dracula," one of the most successful vampire comic book series ever. In the series, Dracula was alive and well and living in London and America. Shortly after the series ended, Japanese cartoonists turned the last issues into this animated feature. The plot centers around Dracula's battles with his daughter Lilith, the product of his union with a mortal, who is unaffected by the sunlight.

An entertaining adaptation of writer Marv Wolfman and artist Gene Colan's classic comic. 🦇🦇🦇

1980 ?m/C *JP* [Toei Animation] **D:** Minori Okazaki.

Dracula: A Cinematic Scrapbook

An anthology of movie trailers from *Dracula* and other vampire movies. Also includes brief interviews with Bela Lugosi and Christopher Lee. 🦇🦇🦇

1991 60m/C [Rhino Video] **D:** Ted Newsom; **W:** Ted Newsom. **VHS, Beta** *RHI, FCT*

Dracula A.D. 1972

Christopher Lee returned to England for his sixth (and by most accounts, worst) go-round as Dracula for Hammer Films, where the creative juices seemed to be drying up. The decision was made to turn Dracula loose in the modern world. The movie actually opens in 1872 with a scene that is one of the highlights of the entire production—an action scene that features Dracula battling his nemesis Van Helsing (Peter Cushing) atop a speeding stagecoach. When the coach is wrecked, Dracula is impaled on a wheel spoke and dies. From that point, the scene immediately jumps ahead one century. A Satanist named Johnny Alucard and a group of naive hippie teenagers revive the long-dead vampire in an abandoned church building in England. The teens and Dracula are opposed by Van Helsing's grandson (Cushing) and his granddaughter Jessica (Stephanie Beacham). Hammer's unwillingness to pay Lee to speak more than a few lines, together with a sterile plot that had Dracula essentially paralyzed by the modern world, forced the teenagers to carry the story. It appears that the idea for *Dracula A.D. 1972* came from the Count

Yorga movies, which had some success in placing an Old World vampire in modern Los Angeles. However, the Yorga movies were only moderately successful and this Hammer copy did not even do that well. *Dracula A.D. 1972* was the sequel to *The Scars of Dracula* (1971) and was followed by *The Satanic Rites of Dracula* (1973). 🦴🦴

1972 95m/C *GB* [Hammer Films, Warner Brothers] **Christopher Lee**, Peter Cushing, Christopher Neame, Stephanie Beacham, Michael Coles, Caroline Munro, Marsha Hunt, Philip Miller; *D:* Alan Gibson; *W:* Don Houghton; *C:* Richard Bush; *M:* Michael Vickers.

Dracula & Son

A horror comedy that begins with much the same premise as George Hamilton's better-known 1979 film, *Love at First Bite*. The ruling Communist government in Transylvania has decided that Dracula presents the wrong image to the modern word and thus exiles him and his son to England. From that point

the two films completely diverge. In *Dracula and Son*, Dracula (Christopher Lee) is welcomed as a celebrity and immediately hired to play a vampire in a movie. This is Lee's last appearance as Dracula, and unfortunately it is not very funny, especially in its dubbed American video version. Based on the novel "Paris V." Released in the U.S. in 1979. **AKA:** *Dracula, Father and Son; Dracula Pere et Fils.* 🦴

1976 (PG) 88m/C *FR* [Quartet Films] Christopher Lee, Bernard Menez, Marie Breillat; *D:* Edouard Molinaro; *M:* Vladimir Cosma. **VHS, Beta** *GKK*

Dracula Bites the Big Apple

A low-budget and unauthorized variation on *Love at First Bite* (1979) that features Dracula having difficulty adjusting to his new life in New York City. 🦴🦴

1979 ?m/C [Independent Films] **Peter Lowey**, Barry Concula; *D:* Richard Wenk.

Dracula Blows His Cool

Stan, a fashion photographer, returns to his family's castle in Bavaria, where several generations earlier an ancestor had been a vampire. Stans soon learns that the ancestor—his great grandfather Count Stanislaus—is still alive and well and living with the striking Countess Olivia in the castle's lower recesses. The couple initiates a willing Stan and some of his models into the vampiric life in a series of soft-core shots of naked women and lustful men. In the end, they restore the ancient castle and open it to the public as a disco, Hotel Dracula. This lighthearted comedy was originally released in Germany as *Graf Dracula Beisst Jetzt* 🦇🦇

1982 (R) 91m/C [Luna Video] John Garco, Betty Verges; **D:** Carlo Ombra; **W:** Carlo Ombra. **VHS, Beta, LV** *MED*

The Dracula Business

In the early 1970s, in the wake of the publication of "In Search of Dracula" by Raymond T. McNally and Radu Florescu, the Romanian government began to develop its tourist industry in Transylvania around genuine (Dracula's birthplace at Sighisoara) and not so genuine (Castle Bran) historical Dracula sites. *The Dracula Business* is a BBC documentary on that effort. 🦇🦇

1974 ?m/C [BBC (British Broadcasting Corporation)] **D:** Anthony de Latbiniere.

Dracula: Dead and Loving It

In the mid 1970s, Mel Brooks produced a hilarious spoof of *Frankenstein* called *Young Frankenstein*. Unfortunately, George Hamilton's *Love at First Bite* (1979) stole much of the thunder that Brooks might have put into a follow-up movie spoofing *Dracula*. Not until 20 years later would Brooks make fun of the toothy Count in this 1996 production, which did not receive the critical acclaim that his earlier effort had. The film definitely has its moments, however, with Leslie Nielsen continuing his latter-day success as the bungling hero in the *Airplane* and *Police Squad* films. Imagine Dracula slipping on vampire bat droppings as he ambles through his home, or the timeless and epic struggle between vampire hunter Van Helsing (Brooks) and Dracula reduced to a petty spat. Peter MacNicol steals the show with his take-off on Dwight Frye's portrayal of Renfield in the 1931 version of *Dracula*, and Anne Bancroft is equally funny in her brief cameo appearance as a gypsy. The script follows the outline of the 1931 *Dracula*, with Renfield rather than Harker going to Dracula's Castle in the opening scenes. Along the way, it manages to poke fun at several of the Hammer Dracula movies and even at *Nosferatu* (1922). 🦇🦇🦇

1995 (PG-13) 90m/C [Mel Brooks] Leslie Nielsen, Mel Brooks, Peter MacNicol, Lysette Anthony, Amy Yasbeck, Steven Weber, Harvey Korman, Anne Bancroft; **D:** Mel Brooks; **W:** Mel Brooks, Rudy DeLuca, Steve Haberman; **C:** Michael D. O'Shea; **M:** Hummie Mann. **VHS, LV** *COL*

Dracula Exotica

In this adult erotic film released in both hardcore and softcore versions, Jamie Gillis revives his portrayal of Dracula from *Dracula Sucks* (1979) to pursue a female CIA agent who is the reincarnation of a virgin he had raped five centuries earlier. **AKA:** Love at First Gulp. 🦇🦇

1981 ?m/C [Entertainment Ventures Inc., VCA] **Jamie Gillis**, Vanessa del Rio, Samantha Fox; **D:** Warren Evans; **W:** K. Schwartz.

Dracula: Fact or Fiction

A documentary look at vampirism. Includes a biography of Vlad Tepes, the 15th century prince who is thought to be the basis for the character of Dracula; background on Bram Stoker's novel; a woman who interviews

modern-day vampires; and a brief overview of vampire films and their appeal. A somewhat campy production with lurid music and black and white re-enactments of historical events but interesting nonetheless. 𝄞𝄞

1992 40m/C VHS *WOV*

Dracula/Garden of Eden

The abridged version of the chilling vampire film "Nosferatu" is coupled with "The Garden of Eden," in which Tini Le Brun meets her Prince Charming while vacationing with her Baroness friend. Silent. 𝄞𝄞

1928 52m/B [Janus Films, Lewis Milestone] Max Schreck, Alexander Granach, Corine Griffith, Charles Ray, Louise Dresser. **VHS, Beta** *CCB*

Dracula Has Risen from the Grave

Christopher Lee's third appearance in a

Dracula movie from Hammer Films. At the end of the previous film, Dracula was destroyed when he was trapped in the layers of ice surrounding Castle Dracula. As expected, he is reborn in this film when he gets a taste of blood from a Catholic Monsignor, who falls to his death in the ice while attempting to exorcise the castle. For the second film in a row, the revived Dracula doesn't speak much thanks to budget-saving measures by Hammer (fewer lines for Lee meant a smaller paycheck from Hammer). Dracula, kept out of his castle by a large cross nailed to the door by the monsignor before he died, subjects a local priest to his control and attempts to take revenge against the monsignor's family. Noticeably absent is Peter Cushing in the role of Van Helsing. Film is also notable for the infamous scene in which Dracula pulls a stake out of his own chest. Sequel to *Dracula: Prince of Darkness* (1965), it was followed by *Taste the Blood of Dracula*. 𝄞𝄞𝄞

1968 (G) 92m/C *GB* [Hammer House of Horror, Warner Brothers] Christopher Lee, Rupert Davies, Veronica Carlson, Barbara Ewing, Barry Andrews,

Michael Ripper; **D:** Freddie Francis; **M:** James Bernard. **VHS** *WAR*

Dracula in the Movies

A collection of trailers from old vampire and Dracula movies. A nostalgic trip down memory lane. 𝄞𝄞

1992 ?m/C

Dracula: Prince of Darkness

Christopher Lee skipped Hammer Films second vampire movie, *Brides of Dracula* (1960), but he returned to the Hammer fold in 1965 to make this sequel to the 1958 film, *Horror of Dracula.* Lee, who had become an international star since the first film was made, was reunited with screenwriter Jimmy Sangster and director Terence Fisher. Missing from the original film was Peter Cushing, who had other plans and was unable to reprise his role as Abraham Van Helsing. Sangster had a prepared a fine screenplay, but Hammer was experiencing money woes and was unable to pay Lee's full fee. Instead, Dracula was left with little more than a few grunts and hisses as he attacked his victims. Artistically offended, Sangster withdrew his name from the credits and had it replaced with a pseudonym John Samsom. It would have been interesting to see what Sangster could have done to liven up the movie's standard story line, which dealt with a group of travelers who are forced to spend a night in Dracula's castle. **AKA:** *Disciple of Dracula; Revenge of Dracula; The Bloody Scream of Dracula.* 𝄞𝄞𝄞

1965 90m/C *GB* [Hammer Films, Warner Brothers] **Christopher Lee**, Barbara Shelley, Andrew Keir, Francis Matthews, Suzan Farmer, Charles Tingwell, Thorley Walters, Philip Latham, Walter Brown; **D:** Terence Fisher; **W:** John Sansom; **C:** Michael Reed; **M:** James Bernard.

Dracula Rises from the Coffin

Though it sounds like a Hammer feature, *Dracula Rises from the Coffin* is actually a Korean production made the same year that Hammer was attempting to keep its vampire series alive by mixing in some Asian martial arts. The better of the two efforts turns out to be the Korean production, in part because it uses Dracula as a metaphor representing the contamination of Asian culture by Western influences. Dracula becomes obsessed with a young Korean exchange student and follows her to her homeland. With the help of a foreign businesswoman (who also represents the evil Western influence), Dracula attempts to make the girl his own. He is opposed by the girl's fiancé and a Buddhist monk team. The final confrontation pits Dracula against the kung-fu fighting monk in a Korean forest. 𝄞𝄞𝄞

1982 ?m/C [Tai Chang, ROK] Kang Yong Suk, Park Yang Rae, Lee Hyoung Pyo.

Dracula Rising

The young and lovely Teresa (Stacy Travis) has been hired by a man named Alec (Doug Wert) to restore a painting of Vlad Tepes, the infamous Vlad the Impaler and father of the Dracula legend. What Teresa does not know is that Alec is a vampire who intends to make her his. That's when Vlad enters the picture, and the plot thickens. Vlad also lusts after Teresa, his desire having originated when the trio were together in a past life. Vlad, it turns out, is also a vampire, and the son of Vlad Tepes. He and Alec lived in the same monestary hundreds of years ago, but Vlad turned away from his vows when he fell in love with Teresa. Alec, apparently unable to stand the fact that Teresa would not be his, accused her of being a witch and had her burned at the stake. A grieving Vlad was then turned into a vampire by his father, who promised his son that one day he would be reunited with his love. 𝄞𝄞𝄞

"He is already dead. He is undead. He can be destroyed but not killed."

—Father Sandor in *Dracula Prince of Darkness* (1965).

Dracula (Spanish Version): "Hey, someone's been sleeping in my bed, and she's still there!"

1993 **(R) ?m/C** [Roger Corman] Christopher Atkins, Stacy Travis; **D:** Fred Gallo. **VHS** *NHO*

Dracula (Spanish Version)

At the same time that Tod Browning and Bela Lugosi version were creating the first talking Dracula movie, the powers that be at Universal Studios decided to film a second version in Spanish for distribution in Mexico and South America. The move to sound had cut deeply into Universal's revenues, as it had widely distributed its silent movies to foreign markets. Thus, every evening as the English-speaking cast and crew left the set of Browning's *Dracula*, a Spanish-speaking cast and crew would work on a Spanish-language ver-sion of the same film, which essentially fol-lowed the same script. Cast in the role of Mina was Lupita Tovar, whom Universal had just made into a star south of the border, while Carlos Villarias played Dracula. The Spanish version was a hit and continued to play in Latin America throughout World War II. For some reason, however, Universal lost interest in the film, failing even to renew its copyright and also failing to make extra copies of the film to preserve it for future gen-erations. During a recent period of height-ened interest in vampire films, it was discov-ered that the only surviving copy of the film at the Library of Congress had a decomposed third reel. However, in 1989, vampire writer David Skal discovered a complete copy in Cuba and facilitated the production of a clean copy of the film. The new copy was ini-

tially shown in the United States in 1992, the first time since the 1930s that the film had been seen by American filmgoers. It was subsequently released on video with English subtitles. While most film critics agree that it is far superior to the Tod Browning/Bela Lugosi version, its contemporary audience has been limited to a relatively small number of vampire enthusiasts and film history buffs. 🦴🦴🦴🦴

1931 104m/B [Universal Pictures, Paul Kohner] Carlos Villarias, Lupita Tovar, Eduardo Arozamena, Pablo Alvarez Rubio, Barry Norton, Carmen Guerrero; **D:** George Melford; **W:** Garrett Fort. **VHS** *MCA*

Dracula Sucks

The most renowned of the many adult-oriented, erotic vampire movies. It relied heavily on the storyline of Lugosi's 1931 classic, but featured X-rated movie star Jamie Gillis as Dracula (who preferred his victim's breasts to their jugular veins) and the attractive Annette Haven as Mina. It was released in both hardcore and softcore versions and released under various titles including *Lust at First Bite* and *Dracula's Bride*. Thirteenth adaptation of Bram Stoker's novel. 🦴🦴

1979 (R) 90m/C James Gillis, Reggie Nalder, Annette Haven, Kay Parker, Serena, Seka, John Leslie; **D:** Philip Marshak. **VHS, Beta** *UNI, OM*

Dracula Tan Exarchia

Most noteworthy as one of the very rare examples of a Greek horror movie. Dracula slips down to Athens from his Transylvanian homeland. Once there, the Count and said servants attempt to create a Frankenstein-like monster, who they hope to turn into a rock music superstar. Their monster is built from parts taken from the bodies of famous musicians, including none other than Jimi Hendrix. 🦴🦴

1983 ?m/C *GR* [Allagi Films] Kostas Soumas, Yannis Panousis, Vangelis Contronis; **D:** Nikos Zervos.

Dracula: The Ballet

Features a full-length ballet about the legend of Count Dracula. 🦴🦴

1983 90m/C [KTXT Lubbock] **VHS, Beta** *NO*

Dracula, The Dirty Old Man

In this low-budget quickie, Vince Kelly plays a descendent of Dracula who comes to America to feed on naked virgins. He makes his home in an abandoned mine, where his assistant brings him young women to feast on. The end to this pitiful excuse for entertainment comes when the assistant falls in love with one of the women slated to be the vampire's next meal. 🦴

1969 55m/C William Whitton, Vince Kelly, Ann Hollis, Libby Caculus; **D:** William Edwards. **VHS** *SMW, TPV*

Dracula: The Great Undead

An evocative documentary about vampires—in history and movies. Narrated by Vincent Price. 🦴

1985 60m/C [Active] **VHS, Beta** *AHV, FCT*

Dracula: Up in Harlem

If you think the Watts Riot was something, you haven't seen the effects of the problem when Dracula aligns himself with the street people in New York's Harlem. It takes the military to counter the disturbance. 🦴🦴

1983 90m/C [Mike Rodgers] **VHS, Beta** *NO*

Dracula vs. Frankenstein

Scientists from another planet travel to Earth to pave the way for an invasion force. To

speed their plan along, they reanimate the world's monsters and inhabit their bodies. The aliens are in for a surprise, however—the monsters' willpower is stronger than their own, causing the monsters to fight each other instead of doing the aliens' bidding. This puts a serious crimp in the invasion plan. Curiously, the battle between Dracula and Frankenstein implied in the title never occurred. Michael Rennie, as the leader of the invasion force, seems as if he's forgotten how to act in this film, and the indifferent performances by other veteran European actors (such as Paul Naschy) lower the quality of the film even further. With good reason, this flick regularly appears on lists of the worst vampire movies ever made. *AKA: El Hombre que Vino del Ummo; Blood of Frankenstein; Assignment Terror; The Man*

Who Came from Ummo; Dracula Jagt Frankenstein. **Woof!**

1969 91m/C *IT GE SP* Michael Rennie, Paul Naschy, Karin Dor, Patty Shepard; *D:* Hugo Fregonese, Tulio Demicheli; *W:* Paul Naschy. **VHS** *UAV*

Dracula vs. Frankenstein

J. Carroll Naish and Lon Chaney, Jr. closed out their Hollywood careers in this disjointed story of a crippled Dr. Frankenstein (Naish), who is trying to discover a cure for his dysfunctional legs. He is surrounded by a community of monsters, including Dracula and Groton the Mad Zombie (Chaney). The monsters are opposed by a young couple. Forest J. Ackerman, editor of *Famous Monsters of Filmland* makes a cameo appearance. *AKA:*

Blood of Frankenstein; Satan's Bloody Freaks; They're Coming to Get You; Dracula Contra Frankenstein; The Revenge of Dracula. **Woof!**

1971 (R) 90m/C *SP* [Al Adamson, Independent International] J. Carrol Naish, Lon Chaney Jr., Regina Carrol, Russ Tamblyn, Jim Davis, Anthony Eisley, Zandor Vorkov, John Bloom, Angelo Rossitto; *Cameos:* Forrest J. Ackerman; *D:* Al Adamson. **VHS** *NO*

Dracula's Daughter

One of those rare sequels that is actually the equal of, if not better than, the original film (in this case the 1931 version of *Dracula*). It operates under the same premise as the original and continues its storyline, taking it in refreshing directions. An example of this creativity is the film's willingness to explore vampirism as an affliction from which the vampire earnestly sought release, a theme that was hardly touched on in the first movie. It is also significant to note that this is the first movie to feature a female vampire. The story begins with the final scene from *Dracula*, after which Van Helsing is arrested for killing Dracula. Dracula's daughter, Countess Marya Zalesky (Gloria Holden), steals the Count's body and burns it, hoping that this will free her from vampirism and allow her to lead a normal life. Alas, her wish goes unfulfilled. Her servant, Sandor, places Dracula's ring on her finger, and soon afterward the Countess begins claiming female victims (a fact not lost on lesbian vampire fans). Marya then has a chance encounter with psychiatrist Dr. Geoffrey Garth (Otto Kruger), who offers to help her overcome her vampirism. Her struggle to overcome her affliction takes her back to Transylvania, with Garth not far behind. Marya hopes to force Garth to stay with her, but a jealous Sandor has other plans and causes her undoing. *Dracula's Daughter* found some of its inspiration in "Dracula's Guest," a story published by Bram Stoker that had originally been written to be an opening chapter in the *Dracula* novel. In 1977, Carl Dreadstone wrote a novel, *Dracula's Daughter*, inspired by the movie. 🩸🩸🩸🩸

1936 71m/B [Universal Studios] Gloria Holden, Otto Kruger, Marguerite Churchill, Irving Pichel, Edward Van Sloan, Nan Grey, Hedda Hopper; *D:* Lambert Hillyer. **VHS** *MCA*

Dracula's Daughter

Another boring, low-budget quickie churned out by Jesus Franco in the early 1970s. Continues the storyline developed earlier in *Dracula, Prisoner of Frankenstein* and again features Howard Vernon as the Count. This time out, Franco mixes together the legends of Dracula and Carmilla, doing justice to neither. **AKA:** *La Hija de Dracula; A Filha de Dracula*. **Woof!**

1971 ?m/C *FR PT* [Interfilme, Comptoir Francais de Film] **Howard Vernon**, Britt Nichols, Anne Libert, Alberto Dalbes; *D:* Jess (Jesus) Franco.

Dracula's Great Love

Low-budget, Spanish imitation of the Hammer horror flicks that failed outside Spain because strict Spanish censorship rules kept the gore factor low. While living in an abandoned nursing home, Dracula is presented with a veritable feast when a carriage transporting four virginal young women breaks down nearby. The Count makes the mistake of falling in love with one of the women, but true love and a happy ending just aren't in the cards for the bloodthirsty vampire. *AKA:* Cemetery Girls; Gran Amore del Conde Dracula; Count Dracula's Great Love; Dracula's Virgin Lovers. 🩸

1972 (R) 96m/C *SP* [Cinema Shares International] Paul Naschy, Charo Soriano; *D:* Javier Aguirre. **VHS, Beta** *SNC, MPI*

Dracula's Last Rites

Low-budget film set in a small town in mod-

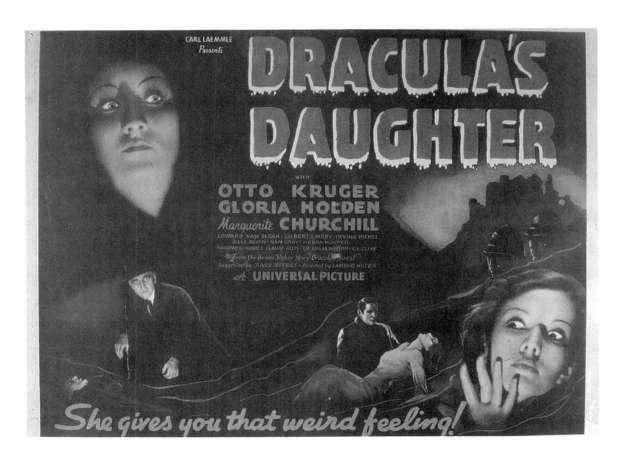

Dracula's Daughter ✝ ern upstate New York. The town's sheriff, doctor, and mortician are all vampires who use the victims of automobile accidents as a steady source of food. After taking their fill, the mortician (called "Lucard") stakes the victims prior to burial to prevent them from becoming vampires. If you've missed this poorly made film, you haven't missed much. **AKA:** Last Rites. **Woof!**

1979 (R) 86m/C [Kelly Van Horn, Cannon Films] Patricia Lee Hammond, Gerald Fielding, Victor Jorge; **D:** Domonic Paris. **VHS, Beta** *MGM, CAN, FCT*

Dracula's Widow

Countess Dracula (Sylvia Kristel) is mistakenly shipped to Hollywood from Romania's Castle Bran (the small castle which for many

years was passed off as Dracula's Castle by the Romanian Tourist Board). Awakened in the Hollywood House of Wax Museum, she quickly takes control of its owner Raymond Everett and initiates plans to return to Romania to find her long lost husband. Informed that he is dead, she goes on a killing spree and is pursued by police, Raymond's girlfriend, and Van Helsing's grandson. Completed just as De Laurentis Entertainment failed financially, causing it to be sent direct-to-video instead of being released on the big screen. Directed by the nephew of Francis Ford Coppola, it falls short of his uncle's high standards and is nothing more than run-of-the-mill vampire fare. 🎬🎬

1988 (R) 85m/C [De Laurentiss Ent. Group] **Sylvia Kristel**, Josef Sommer, Lenny Von Dohlen; **D:** Christopher Coppola. **VHS, Beta** *HBO*

Dragon Against Vampire

Disjointed story of a Chinese vampire who kills two of three grave robbers it meets in the cemetery. The survivor seeks help from the local vampire hunter, a Shaolin magician who lives in a nearby cave. The best element of the movie may be the background music by Tangerine Dream. *AKA:* Dragon vs. Vampire. 🦇🦇

1984 ?m/C *D:* Lionel Leung.

Dragstrip Dracula

Last of a series of ultra low-budget amateurish productions by Donald Glut. Aimed at the teen audience and receiving only limited exposure on a horror double or triple feature. No copy of this film is known to have survived. Dracula, having been revived and killed in the earlier movies, is revived once again to hang around a dragstrip. Don't even bother looking. It's not available and you wouldn't want to see it if it was. 🦇

1962 ?m/C [Independent Productions Corporation] *D:* Don Glut.

Drakula in Istanbul

Legendary Turkish movie talked about but never seen, even by hard-core vampire fans in the West. This first non-Western adaptation of "Dracula" appeared in Turkish theaters but was never shown in America or Great Britain. It tells the story of Amzi, an accountant who becomes Drakula's personal secretary. Amzi discovers Drakula in his coffin and flees back to Istanbul, where he is pursued by the vampire. Amzi then teams with a Turkish version of vampire hunter Abraham Van Helsing in an effort to stop Drakula's attacks on Amzi's family. According to the standard lore about this film (possibly nothing more than rumors), it was unique in linking Drakula to the fifteenth-century Vlad the Impaler and in using much of the dialogue from Bram Stoker's novel in an attempt to be faithful to his vision. Originally released as *Drakula Istanbulda*. This was the sixth film based upon Stoker's novel; it also utilized Ali Riga Seifi's *Kastgli Voyvoda* (The Impaling Voivode) as a source for information on Vlad. It is included here for its significance in the cinematic *Dracula* progression, and may be extremely difficult (if not impossible) to find. *AKA:* Drakula Istanbulda. 🦇🦇🦇

1953 ?m/C *TU* [Demirag] **Atif Kaptan**, Consuelo Osorio, Lito Legaspi, Gina Laforteza, Joseph Gallego; *D:* Mehmet Muhtar; *W:* Umit Deniz.

Drakulita

This low-budget comedy that was never released in the United States features a vampiress names Drakulita (Rossana Ortiz) who harasses a a group of people trapped in an old dark house. 🦇

1969 ?m/C Rossana Ortiz, Gina Laforteza, Joseph Gallego; *D:* Consuelo Osorio.

Dry Kisses Only

This independent production presents a look at cultural icons of femininity and feminism through a montage of lesbian films. Along the way, commentators Dykenna and Dykella discuss lesbian vampire stereotypes. 🦇🦇

D: Jane Cottis, Kaucyila Brooke. **1990 75m/C VHS** *VDB*

Dungeon Master

Independent production in which the vampire tortures his female victims, several of whom are turned into vampires like himself. 🦇

1968 ?m/C

Ed Wood

A delightful celebration of the life and times of the man who won the Golden Turkey Award as the worst movie director of all time, best known for his cult classic *Plan 9 from Outer Space*, which also won the Golden Turkey Award as the worst movie of all time. Having seen a host of vampire flicks, I must dissent at least as regards *Plan 9*. Though unintended by Wood, at least it's entertaining in its wretchedness and good for an evening of laughs. Some vampire movies are just plain boring and/or ludicrous in the extreme. *Ed Wood*, however, is neither bad nor boring. Quite the opposite, it is a delightful retelling of the life of a genuine real life character (portrayed by Johnny Depp) haunted by the social disapproval of his transvestitism and possessed of a kind heart which he opened to an ill and dying Bela Lugosi, portrayed movingly by Martin Landau, who earned an Academy Award for his effort. Appropriately, director Tim Burton filmed in black and white returning viewers to the B-movie era of the 1950s. *Ed Wood* earns its pres-

ence in this volume from its treatment of *Plan 9 from Outer Space*, and for Woods' recruitment of horror hostess Vampira and relationship with Bela Lugosi. *Plan 9* also happens to be a vampire movie which includes Vampira playing Vampira, some old film clips of Bela Lugosi, and an actor imitating Lugosi as Dracula. The segment dealing with the filming of *Plan 9*, the filming of which was underwritten by a Baptist church, is one of the highlights of Burton's masterpiece. 🎵🎵🎵🎵

1994 (R) 127m/B [Denise DiNovi, Tim Burton, Casual Pictures Inc.] Johnny Depp, Sarah Jessica Parker, Martin Landau, Bill Murray, Jim Myers, Patricia Arquette, Jeffrey Jones, Lisa Marie, Vincent D'Onofrio; ***D:*** Tim Burton; ***W:*** Scott Alexander, Larry Karaszewski; ***C:*** Stefan Czapsky. Academy Awards '94: Best Makeup, Best Supporting Actor (Landau); Golden Globe Awards '95: Best Supporting Actor (Landau); Los Angeles Film Critics Association Awards '94: Best Cinematography, Best Supporting Actor (Landau), Best Original Score; New York Film Critics Awards '94: Best Cinematography, Best Supporting Actor (Landau); Screen Actors Guild Award '94: Best Supporting Actor (Landau); Nominations: British Academy Awards '95: Best Supporting Actor (Landau); Golden Globe Awards '95: Best Actor—Musical/Comedy (Depp), Best Film—Musical/Comedy. **VHS, LV** *TOU*

DON'T LET FANGS GET IN THE WAY OF A GOOD LAUGH: VAMPIRE COMEDIES

For those who want a more humorous bite of vampiric life, vampire stereotypes in popular culture have provided seemingly endless possibilities for bad (and not-so-bad) jokes, beginning with the "original" Dracula, Bela Lugosi. So pervasive was the image of Dracula created by Lugosi that he spent his last years portraying a parody of himself, a career direction he was forced into by typecasting. Thanks to his co-starring turn in the first vampire comedy, *Abbott and Costello Meet Frankenstein* (1949), that film remains one of the best. Thirty years later, another contender for funniest vampire film was released—George Hamilton's *Love at First Bite* (1979). And not to be missed are Lauren Hutton's search for virgin blood in *Once Bitten* (1985), the dancing vampires in The Fearless Vampire Killers, *or* Pardon Me, but Your Teeth Are in My Neck *(1967), and Mel Brooks' recent madness,* Dracula: Dead and Loving It *(1995).*

Any sampling of vampires who tickle the funny bone instead of the neck would have to include The Munsters' *Grandpa Dracula (Al Lewis) and mother Lily (Yvonne De-Carlo). In addition to the TV series, the pair also made several made-for-television movies, including* Munster, Go Home *(1966),* The Munster's Revenge *(1981), and* Here Come the Munsters *(1995). Additional vampire comedies include:*

Blood & Donuts *(1995)*

Blood for Dracula (Andy Warhol's Dracula)

Bordello of Blood *(1996)*

El Castillo del los Monstruos *(1958)*

Dracula and Son *(1975)*

El Jovemcito Dracula *(1975)*

My Best Friend is a Vampire *(1987)*

Rockula *(1990)*

Transylvania 6-5000 *(1985)*

Transylvania Twist *(1989)*

Who Is Afraid of Dracula? *(1985)*

El Vampiro Negro

This is the third cinematic attempt to tell the story of serial killer Peter Kürten, who killed a number of people in Germany in 1929-30 and then drank their blood. His story was first told in the silent movie *M*, which was made in Germany in the immediate aftermath of the killings and Kürten's capture. *M* was later remade in the United States as a sound movie in 1951. A French version of the story, *Le Vampire of Düsseldorf*, would appear in 1963. *El Vampire Negro* was released in English-speaking countries as *The Black Vampire*. **AKA:** The Black Vampire. 🗡🗡

1953 ?m/B [Argentinian Sono] Olga Zubarry, Roberto Escalada, Nathan Pinzon, Nelly Panizza; **D:** Ramon Barreto.

Elusive Song of the Vampire

More fun with the hopping vampires. In ancient China, a man has to put up with a vam-

pire infestation in his home. Who you gonna call? In this case, the local kung fu sorcerer gets the nod over the Ghostbusters. At the same time, the local ruler, who just happens to be a transvestite, steals the soul of a princess and demands the soul of a virgin male as ransom. ♪♪♪

1987 ?m/C TW D: Takako Shira.

Elvira, Mistress of the Dark

Elvira, Cassandra Peterson's famous B-movie horror hostess character, is really a witch, but she certainly draws much of her image from that of the classic vamp. In this campy romp, the rather well-endowed terror queen inherits a house in a conservative Massachusetts town and moves there to take possession. While all of the teenage boys in town might be excited by her presence, most of the conservative townsfolk want her out. What passes for a plot centers around an ancient book of spells that is hidden in the house and Elvira's efforts to keep the book out of the hands of her wicked uncle. ♪♪

1988 (PG-13) 96m/C [New World Pictures] Cassandra Peterson, Jeff Conaway, Susan Kellerman, Edie McClurg, Daniel Greene, W. Morgan Shepherd; D: James Signorelli; C: Hanania Baer. VHS, Beta, LV VTR, NWV

Embrace of the Vampire

Charlotte (Alyssa Milano) is a virgin college student who has a steady boyfriend but is still hot and bothered over some very sexually explicit dreams she has been having that feature a vampire (Martin Kemp). As often happens in vampire movies, Charlotte bears a strong resemblance to the vampire's long lost love of centuries past. If she can keep her boyfriend at bay for just three days, then she and the vampire can find their eternal life together. ♪♪

1995 (R) 92m/C [Marilyn Vance, Alan Mruvka] Alyssa Milano, Martin Kemp, Harrison Pruett, Charlotte Lewis; Cameos: Jennifer Tilly; D: Anne Goursaud; W: Halle Eaton, Nicole Coady, Rick Bitzelberger; M: Joseph Williams. VHS, LV TTC, IME

The Empire of Dracula

As she is dying, a mother sends her son Luis (Cesar del Campo) to Castle Draculstein, where he is to seek revenge against the Count for killing his father many years earlier. Heavily based on Hammer's Horror of Dracula (1958), it was originally released as El Imperio de Dracula and later as Las Mujeres de Dracula and Sinfonia del Mas Alla. Possibly the first Mexican horror film shot in color. AKA: El Imperio de Dracula; Las Mujeres de Dracula; Sinfonia del Mas Alla. ♪♪

1967 90m/C MX [Filmica Vergara] Eric del Castillo, Ethel Carrillo, Cesar del Campo, Lucha Villa; D: Frederick Curiel.

The Evil of Dracula

The last of three vampire films directed by Yamamoto. A young psychology teacher at a girl's school discovers that the principal is a vampire (Hunie Tanaka). He must enter into a demonic pact to finally defeat the vampire and her lover (Mia Oto). One of the many films that is loosely based on Sheridan Le Fanu's classic story "Carmilla." AKA: Chi O Suu Bara. ♪♪♪

1975 87m/C JP [Fumio Tanaka, Toho] Kunie Tanaka, Mia Oto, Toshio Kurosawa, Mariko Mochizuki, Shin Kishida, Katsuhiko Sasakai, Yunosuke Ito; D: Michio Yamamoto; W: Ei Ogawa, Masaru Takasue; C: Kazutami Hara; M: Richiro Manabe.

The Evil Within

An amoeba-like vampiric entity that can take the shape of a phallus attacks and enters into the body of a circus girl. Once inside her, the creature both demands to be born and to be fed male blood. This black comedy gets some points for plot originality, but little else. *AKA:* Baby Blood. ⚔️

1994 (R) 88m/C [Dimension Films] Emmanuelle Escourrou, Jean-Francois Guillotte; *D:* Alain Robak; *W:* Alain Robak, Serge Cukier. **VHS** *APX*

Evil's Commandment

Original vampire film which started the classic Italian horror cycle. A gorgeous Countess needs blood to stay young, otherwise she reverts to a 200-year-old vampire. ⚔️⚔️

1956 ?m/B *IT* Gianna Maria Canale; *D:* Riccardo (Robert Hampton) Freda. **VHS** *SMW*

Evils of the Night

In one of his last movies, the aging John Carradine is paired with Julie Newmar as alien vampires who force two young men to capture young girls to meet their needs for a regular diet of blood. It was the last of Carradine's many appearances as a vampire and lacks the unique vigor of his previous portrayals. *AKA:* Space Monsters. ⚔️

1985 85m/C [Mars Film Productions] John Carradine, Julie Newmar, Tina Louise, Neville Brand, Aldo Ray, Karrie Emerson, Bridget Hollman; *D:* Marti Rustam; *W:* Phillip D. Connors. **VHS, Beta** *LIV*

Face of Marble

Another entry in the underrated, and under-used vampire dog category. Mad professor. Randolf (John Carradine), conducting experiments on corpses, succeeds in resurrecting them, but only briefly. Surprisingly enough, when he switches from people to a Great Dane, his experiment succeeds in a very odd way. The deceased doggie doesn't come back to life, but it does become a sort of vampire dog, attacking people and drinking their blood. As an unexpected bonus, the pooch is able to become invisible and walk through walls. A dog's life indeed.

1946 70m/B [Monogram] John Carradine, Claudia Drake, Robert Shayne, Maris Wrixon, Thomas E. Jackson, Rosa Ray; ***D:*** William Beaudine; ***W:*** Michael Jacoby; ***C:*** Harry Neumann; ***M:*** Edward Kay.

Fade to Black

Eric Binford has a bit of a problem—it seems he isn't very schooled in the social graces

and has trouble relating to people. He finds his escape in the imaginary world of the movies, which slowly take over his life and becomes the only reality he knows. Eventually, he begins to assume the roles of some of his favorite characters, including Bela Lugosi's Dracula. As he crawls deeper into his fantasy world, he begins to kill real people who have offended him. His modus operandi is acting out cinematic scenes of death and mayhem. An effective exploration of what happens when the effects of everyday pressures become overwhelming. A novelization of the movie was written by Ron Renauld.

1980 (R) 100m/C [Irwin Yablans Company, Sylvio Tabet] **Dennis Christopher**, Tim Thomerson, Linda Kerridge, Mickey Rourke, Melinda Fee; ***D:*** Vernon Zimmerman. **VHS, Beta** *MED, MLB*

Fangs!

Veronica Carlson, best-known for being turned into a vampire by Christopher Lee in *Dracula Has Risen from the Grave* (1968),

hosts this nostalgic documentary romp through seventy years of vampire flicks, starting with 1922's *Nosferatu*. 🎞🎞

1992 ?m/C [Pagan Video] **D:** Bruce G. Hallenbeck.

Fangs of the Living Dead

Count Wolduck (Julian Ugarte), a vampire, tries to convince his niece Silvia (Anita Ekberg) that she is a reincarnation of Malenka, an ancestor who was burned for practicing witchcraft. In reality, she does not resemble Malenka, but Wolduck tells her this as part of a plot to drive her insane. In the end, his plot fails, and he is killed by the light of the rising sun. **AKA:** Malenka, the Vampire; La Nipote del Vampiro; The Niece of the Vampire; The Vampire's Niece. 🎞🎞

1968 80m/C *SP IT* [Europix Consolidated] Anita Ekberg, Rossana Yanni, Diana Lorys, Fernando Bilbao, Paul Muller, Julian Ugarte, Andriana Ambesi; **D:** Armando de Ossorio; **W:** Armando de Ossorio. **VHS** *SNC*

Fascination

Made near the midpoint of his 30-year career in the vampire filmmaking business, director Jean Rollin's *Fascination* tells of a group of blood-drinking women who gather in a remote castle for ritual murders and subsequent blood drinking. All of the victims are male, so it comes as no surprise when one of the women falls in love with one of the prospective victims. As is usual with Rollin films, plot and action are sacrificed in an attempt to project image and atmosphere. 🎞🎞🎞

1979 80m/C *FR* [Les Films ABC, Comex] **Franca Mai**, Jean-Marie Lemaire, Brigitte Lahie, Fanny

Magier; **D:** Jean Rollin; **C:** Georges Fromentin, Daniel Lacambre; **M:** Philippe D'Aram.

Father, Santa Claus Has Died

A post-Berlin Wall Russian effort loosely based upon nineteenth-century author Alexei Tolstoy's classic tale, "The Wurdalak" (originally adapted by Mario Bava in *Black Sabbath*). The story concerns a man who becomes a vampire and turns on his own family. 🎞🎞🎞

1992 ?m/C *RU* Anatoly Egorov, Evan Ganzha, Ljudmila Kozlovskava; **D:** Ugeny Ganzha.

The Fear Chamber

This Mexican quickie was actually shot after Boris Karloff's death, but included footage filmed shortly before he died. A mutant stone that feeds on human fear is fed' by Doc Karloff and his myriad assistants. Women are taken to the lab and scared just before their blood is taken. As more and more women are sacrificed to the stone, it begins to grow tentacles. Karloff was quickly written out of the script, the slack being taken up by an unusually high number of assistants, including a hunchback and a dwarf. The film has been heavily criticized not only for its ineptitude, but for its emphasis on sadism and the underlying racism of the script. **AKA:** Torture Zone; Chamber of Fear; La Camara Del Terror. **Woof!**

1967 88m/C *MX* [Azteca] Boris Karloff, Yerye Beirut, Julissa, Carlos East; **D:** Juan Ibanez, Jack Hill. **VHS** *SNC, MPI*

> "We shall drink to the heir, the future Count Dracula and to his mother without whom he could not exist."
>
> —Dracula speaking to his granddaughter in *Dracula, the Bloodline Continues* (1972).

Shhh. I just want to borrow your Head and Shoulders. Count Von Krolock (Ferdinand "Ferdy" Mayne) disturbs Sarah's (Sharon Tate) bath in *The Fearless Vampire Killers*.

85
VAMPIRES on VIDEO

Videohound salutes: Roger Corman

In a career spanning four decades, Roger Corman has been responsible for the production of more than a hundred movies—many were unmitigated trash, a few were high quality *avant garde*, and most fell somewhere in between. Almost without exception, however, they were all rather interesting. Along the way Corman helped launch the careers of many hungry young actors and directors who would later go on to stardom with major studios (Jack Nicholson and Francis Ford Coppola head that list). With so many B-movies under his belt, it comes as no surprise that Corman managed to produce more vampire films than any other person.

Soon after he began his producing/directing career in the mid-1950s, he produced the first science-fiction vampire movie, *Not of This Earth* (1957), about an alien who comes to earth in search of a viable blood supply. It was such a good movie that Corman made it two more times during his career (1987 and again in 1995). A couple of years later Corman produced the delightful dark comedy *Little Shop of Horrors*. A unique vampire movie, the bloodsucker was a large carnivorous plan. Again the movie was so good, it was shot a second time as *Please Don't My Mother* before being transformed into a musical play on Broadway. Finally the Broadway production was brought to the screen in 1986 as *Little Shop of Horrors* (starring Rick Moranis and Steve Martin). The list of other vampire movies Corman produced over the years includes *Queen of Blood* (1966), *The Velvet Vampire* (1971) *Transylvania 6-5000* (1985) *Vamp* (1986), and *Transylvania Twist* (1989)

In 1988, his new company (Concorde/New Horizons) found a perfect script for a low-budget movie called *Dance of the Damned*. It had only two characters—a vampire lamenting the fact that he could no longer remember what daylight looks like, and a young woman who had reached the end of her rope and was contemplating suicide. He wanted a victim who could tell him about sunlight before he killed her and thought the woman was the perfect choice since she wanted to die anyway. In her confrontation with the vampire, the woman changes her mind and reaffirms her will to live. It was an unpretentious movie quickly put together (and later remade as *To Sleep with a Vampire*), but vampire fans now consider it to be one of the best vampire movies ever made.

Corman told the tale of his rise to king of the B-movies in the autobiography *How I made a Hundred Movies in Hollywood and Never Lost a Dime*.

✝ END ✝

The Fearless Vampire Killers

Unusual and distinctive comedy unfortunately moves too slowly some of the time. Renowned professor of vampirology Dr. Ambrosius and his bungling assistant Alfred (director Polanski) are busy searching for vampires in a small village in Transylvania. There, local vampire Count Von Krolock is hard at work trying to get the lovely Sarah (Sharon Tate) into his clutches. Ambrosius and Alfred must hurry to save Sarah, but will they get there in time? Added significance since this is Sharon Tate's last movie. Just a few months after the film was completed, she was brutally murdered by Charles Manson and his followers in one of the most infamous crimes of this century. Other than the pacing, there's plenty to recommend this one. *AKA:* Pardon Me, Your Teeth are in My Neck; Dance of the Vampires. 𝄐𝄐𝄐

1967 98m/C *GB* [MGM] Jack MacGowran, Roman Polanski, Alfie Bass, Jessie Robbins, Sharon Tate, Ferdinand "Ferdy" Mayne, Iain Quarrier; **D:** Roman Polanski; **W:** Roman Polanski, Gerard Brach. **VHS, Beta, LV** *MGM*

Ferat Vampire

Featuring perhaps the first vampire car, this bit of Marxist escapism makes fun of horror movies. A vampiric automobile finds a diet of blood (drawn from drivers) far superior to gasoline. *AKA:* Upir z Feratu. 𝄐𝄐

1982 ?m/C *CZ* [Barrandov Film Studios] Jiri Menzel, Jiri Menzel, Dagmar Veskrnova, Jana Brezkova; **D:** Juraj Herz.

First Man into Space

Fortunately, when astronauts really did venture into space in the 1960s, it proved less hazardous than in this early guess at how space travel might turn out. Set in 1958, it tells the tale of Commander Prescott, the first man into space. He safely guides his space-ship through a radioactive cloud, but unfortunately the cloud has some nasty side effects, turning Prescott into a rather ugly monster that craves human blood. *AKA:* Satellite of Blood. 𝄐𝄐

1959 78m/B [Producers Associates] Marshall Thompson, Marla Landi, Bill Edwards; **D:** Robert Day. **VHS, Beta** *DVT, RHI, HEG*

First Vampire in China

Standard Hong Kong vampire fare which moves at a rather slow pace after an exciting opening. Features an attack by a horde of vampire bats and a particularly nasty vampire creature. 𝄐𝄐

1990 ?m/C **D:** Yam Chun-Lu.

Flesh of Your Flesh

The producers dedicated this political satire of upper class life in Columbia to Roger Corman and Roman Polanski. No word yet on whether they were flattered. Wealthy family's life revolves around incest and vampirism. *AKA:* Carne de Tu Carne. 𝄐𝄐

1984 85m/C [Producciones Visuales] Adriana Herran, David Guerrero; **D:** Carlos Mayolo; **W:** Elsa Vasquez, Jose Nieto; **C:** Luis Beristain.

Fools

Two lonely people—he an aging horror film actor and she a young woman estranged from her husband—start a warm romance when they meet in San Francisco. The husband reacts violently. Good cast seems lost. 𝄐

1970 (PG) 93m/C [Cinerama, Translor Productions] Jason Robards Jr., Katharine Ross, Scott Hylands; **D:** Tom Gries. **VHS, Beta** *PSM*

Frankenstein Meets Dracula

Independent project, all of 3 minutes long, has Dracula (Victor Fabian) reviving Franken-

> "And I returned to living again. A long life lay ahead of me. I would continue to feed myself with blood and remain eternally lonely. But the line of the Draculas lives on."
>
> —The deceased Count Dracula reborn in his great grandson at the end of *Dracula, the Bloodline Continues* (1972).

stein's monster (producer/director Don Glut). Dracula plans to hypnotize the monster and use him as a killing instrument. 🗡

1957 ?m/C [Don Glut] **Victor Fabian**, Don Glut; **D:** Don Glut.

Frankenstein, the Vampire and Co.

Mexican remake of *Abbott and Costello Meet Frankenstein* starring the comedy team of Manuel Loco Valdes and Jose Jasso. They deliver two crates to a castle unaware that they contain the bodies of a vampire and Frankenstein's monster. The castle's resident mad scientist and the vampire conspire to have Valdes' brain transplanted into the Frankenstein monster. Vastly inferior to the original. **AKA:** Frankenstein, El Vampiro, y Cia; Frankenstein, El Vampiro y Compania. 🗡🗡

1961 80m/C MX [Cinematografica Calderon] Manuel Valdez, Jose Jasso, Nora Vetran, Arturo Castro; **D:** Benito Alazraki; **W:** Alfredo Salazar; **C:** Enrique Wallace.

Frankenstein's Bloody Terror

This is the first film starring Paul Naschy in the role of a wolfman named Count Waldemar Daninsky. Naschy went on to make a series of films as Daninsky and became a monster movie superstar throughout the Spanish-speaking world. In this initial effort, the Count turns to some occult specialists in hopes of finding a cure for his lycanthropic condition. Unfortunately, the specialists turn out to be vampires, which leads to a bit of a brouhaha. Filmed in 3-D at the height of the 3-D craze. **AKA:** La Marca del Hombre Lobo; The Vampire of Dr. Dracula; The Wolfman of Count Dracula; Hell's Creatures; The Mark of the

Wolfman. 🗡🗡

1968 ?m/C SP **Julian Ugarte**, **Rossana Yanni**, Paul Naschy, Dianik Zurakowska; **D:** Enrique L. Eguiluz.

Fright Night

Charley Brewster (William Ragsdale) has a big problem: his neighbor Jerry Dandridge is a rather nasty vampire, a fact that no one but Charley believes. Desperate for help in stopping Dandridge, he's forced to turn to Peter Vincent (Roddy McDowell), the host of a local, late-night, horrorfest called "Fright Night." Vincent claims to be a "great vampire hunter," but it turns out at first that he is practically scared of his own shadow. When Dandridge kidnaps Brewster's girlfriend and the chips are down, however, Vincent must show his mettle. The rather predictable plot is aided greatly by some excellent special effects, especially the transformations of various characters into animals and back again. Novelized in "Fright Night" by John Skipp and Craig Spector, which was based on Tom Holland's screenplay. Followed in 1989 by *Fright Night II*. 🗡🗡🗡

1985 (R) 106m/C [Herb Jaffe, Columbia Pictures] **Chris Sarandon**, **Amanda Bearse**, **Stephen Geoffreys**, William Ragsdale, Roddy McDowall, Jonathan Stark, Dorothy Fielding; **D:** Tom Holland; **W:** Tom Holland; **M:** Brad Fiedel. **VHS, Beta, LV** COL

Fright Night 2

Charley Brewster, the young hero from *Fright Night*, discovers that Regine, the sister of the vampire he killed in the first movie, has come to reside near his college. While therapy has helped him overcome his previous trauma, his psychiatrist has failed to fully convince him that his earlier experiences were an illusion. He is trying to convince himself that he lives in a world without vampires, but Regine is very real. He has to re-

Hey, I had onions for lunch, can you smell 'em? Amanda Bearse isn't quite herself in *Fright Night*

cruit Peter Vincent for another fight and convince his new girlfriend Alex (Traci Lind) that he isn't crazy. Slow to get started, the tension builds gradually and reaches an exciting if predictable climax. 🗡🗡

1988 (R) 108m/C [Vista Organization, New Century] **Julie Carmen**, Roddy McDowall, William Ragsdale, Traci Lind; **D:** Tommy Lee Wallace; **W:** Tommy Lee Wallace, Tim Metcalfe; **M:** Brad Fiedel. **VHS, Beta, LV** *LIV*

Frightmare

A great horror star dies but refuses to give up his need for adoration and revenge. 🗡

1981 (R) 84m/C [Patrick Wright, Tallie Wright] **Fer-**

dinand **"Ferdy" Mayne**, Luca Bercovici, Nita Talbot, Peter Kastner; **D:** Norman Thaddeus Vane. *VES*

From Dusk Till Dawn

A pair of desperate amoral bank robbers, Richard (Quentin Tarantino) and Seth Gecko (George Clooney), are heading for safety in Mexico. Along the way, they murder a convenience store clerk and kidnap ex-preacher Jacob Fuller (Harvey Keitel). Along with his two teenage children, Kate (Juliette Lewis) and Scott (Ernest Liu), they head for the border in Fuller's motor home. The unlikely group ends up at a sleazy bar just across the border where the two killers must spend the hours from dusk to dawn waiting for their

connection to arrive and guide them to their new life. Simple right? Well, that's only half the movie—the real fun has yet to begin. At the bar, the five Americans settle down to enjoy some refreshments and entertainment while they wait. Before long, however, they realize that the bar is, well, a little different when, one by one, the bar employees reveal themselves to be vampires. It's a perfect situation for the two killers, but it's complicated by the fact that any close encounter with one of the bloodsuckers leads to a relatively rapid transformation into a vampire. In the ensuing battle, the vampire fighters discover every conceivable method for killing vam-pires, and then some. Cheech Marin has three separate (and very distinct) roles. Plays like two separate movies: one a gritty gang-sters-on-the-run story, and the other an all-stops-out vampire gore fest. Both provide plenty of action. ♫♫♫

1995 (R) 108m/C [Gianni Nunnari, Meir Teper, Dimension Films, A Band Apart, Los Hooligans] **Salma Hayek**, George Clooney, Quentin Tarantino, Harvey Keitel, Juliette Lewis, Fred Williamson, Richard "Cheech" Marin, Michael Parks, Tom Savini, Ernest Liu, Kelly Preston, John Saxon, Danny Trejo; **D:** Robert Rodriguez; **W:** Quentin Tarantino; **C:** Guillermo Navarro; **M:** Graeme Revell. MTV Movie Awards '96: Breakthrough Performance (Clooney). **VHS, LV** *TOU*

"Sandor, look at me. What do you see in my eyes?"

"Death."

—Countess Marya Zaleska (Gloria Holden) conversing with her man servant Sandor (Irving Pinchel) in *Dracula's Daughter* (1936).

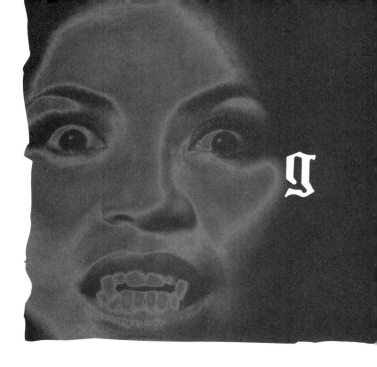

Gandy Goose in Ghosttown

A short animated film in which Gandy Goose has a nightmare and meets up with a few ghosts as well as the monsters Franken-stein and Dracula. 🦴🦴

1944 ?m/C [Twentieth Century-Fox] **D:** Manny Davis.

Geek Maggot Bingo

Underground low-budget monsterfest satire with a guest appearance from TV horror show host Zacherle. Featured monsters in-clude Scumbalina the vampire queen (Donna Death), a mad scientist (Robert Andrews), a hunchback (Bruno Zeus) and a Formaldehyde Man. Features amateurish acting, cheesy cardboard sets, and a warning halfway through that "it isn't going to get any better." That piece of information should've come a

lot sooner, like the opening credits. **AKA:** The Freak From Suckweasel Mountain. 🦴

1983 70m/C Richard Hell, Donna Death, John Zacherle; **D:** Nick Zedd. **VHS** *MWF, MOV*

Genie of Darkness

The ashes of Nostradamus himself are re-trieved in a bid to destroy his vampiric de-scendent. Edited from a Mexican serial; if you were able to sit through this one, look for "Curse of Nostradamus" and "The Mon-ster Demolisher." 🦴

1960 ?m/B *MX* [American International Pictures (A.I.P.), Mexico] German Robles; **D:** Frederick Curiel. **VHS** *SNC, NOS, LOO*

The Ghost Brigade

In the midst of the Civil War, Union and Confederate soldiers find a more dangerous foe when some mysterious force begins slaughtering troops on both sides of the bat-

Hey! We'll turn this bar around and go home if you kids don't settle down! Harvey Keitel along with George Clooney and Juliet Lewis fight off barflies that happen to be vampires in *From Dusk Till Dawn.*

tlefield. The Union general (Martin Sheen) sends out a search team consisting of a captain (Adrian Pasdar), a Confederate prisoner (Corbin Bernsen), and a slave (Cynda Williams) who soon find the source of the trouble— a brigade of vampires. *AKA:* The Killing Box. 🗡🗡🗡

1993 (R) 80m/C [Brad Krevoy, Steve Stabler, Motion Picture Corporation of America] Adrian Pasdar, Corbin Bernsen, Martin Sheen, Cynda Williams, Ray Wise, Roger Wilson; *D:* George Hickenlooper; *W:* Matt Greenberg. **VHS** *TTC*

Ghost Punting

Accomplished martial artist Samo Hung and his buddies can't get a date, so they decide to explore a local haunted house. What they find is a sadistic spirit vampiress. They report the haunting to the local police sergeant who, along with her four specially-trained assistants, investigates. Played more for laughs than scares. 🗡🗡🗡

1991 ?m/C Hung Kam-Bo.

Ghost Stories: Graveyard Thriller

An anthology of supernatural horror stories with ghosts and vampire. 🗡🗡

1986 56m/C [Alamance] *D:* Lynn Silver. **VHS, Beta** *LIV, VES*

Ghostly Mouth-to-Mouth Resusitation

The irreconcilability of the ghostly world with that of the living is featured in this Taiwanese movie about a woman who, through mouth-to-mouth breathing, revives a man and falls in love with him. A consulting exorcist informs her that he is now a vampire, though he seems to act like a ghost. The ghost/vampire tries to explain to the woman that he is of another realm and to forget him.

Just goes to illustrate the extent to which some people will go for a good time. 🗡🗡

1985 ?m/C

The Girl with the Hungry Eyes

Driven to commit suicide in 1937 after she discovers her husband is cheating on her, a beautiful young woman is reborn in 1995 as a vampire. Once reborn, she sets out to restore the luxury hotel she once owned, turning to modeling to raise the cash after she realizes that her pallid complexion is in demand in the fashion world. Still holding a grudge against her long-ago lover, she takes her revenge on the men she meets in her new occupation. 🗡🗡

1994 (R) 84m/C [Michael Kastenbaum, Seth Kastenbaum, Smoking Gun Pictures] Christina Fulton, Isaac Turner, Leon Herbert, Bret Carr, Susan Rhodes; **D:** Jon Jacobs; **W:** Jon Jacobs; **M:** Paul Inder. **VHS** COL

Go for a Take

Unfunny comedy in which two gangsters on the run hide out in a movie studio. While there, they run into actor Dennis Price (playing himself), who is dressed up for a part as Dracula. Nothing to see here. Just go about your business. 🗡

1972 ?m/C [Century Film Studios] **Dennis Price**, Reg Varney, Norman Rossington, Sue Lloyd; **D:** Harry Booth.

Goliath and the Vampires

Goliath (Gordon Scott), who has sworn to protect the weak from supervillains, is called upon to rescue his girlfriend (Leonora Ruffo) and a group of slave women from the vampire Kobrak and his evil zombies. Once he has overcome the zombies and released the women, a whole new challenge arises. The vampire assumes Goliath's identity, and in the climactic scenes he must engage himself

in a fight to the finish. **AKA:** *Maciste Contro il Vampiro; The Vampires.* 🗡🗡🗡

1964 ?m/C *IT*

The Gong Show Movie

Tasteless self-serving movie about a tasteless TV amateur talent show. Amateur being the key word. Among the entries was one Count Banjola, who hung upside-down while playing the banjo. Avoid at all costs. **Woof!**

1980 ?m/C [Chuck Barris] **Count Banjola**, Chuck Barris, Jaye P. Morgan, Robin Altman, Buddy Didio.

Gore-Met Zombie Chef From Hell

You haven't seen how bad a greasy-spoon restaurant can be until you visit this gourmet seafood place where "serving the customers" is taken quite literally. In this gore fest, the owner-chef, who just happens to be a demon vampire, slaughters his customers for food. Its a graphic gore-fest over acted and played for the fun of it. Not for the squeamish. **Woof!**

1987 90m/C [Camp Pictures] Theo Depuay, Kelley Kunicki, C.W. Casey, Alan Marx, Michael O'Neill; **D:** Don Swan. **VHS, Beta** NO

Gothic

Not a vampire picture itself, *Gothic* is a fictionalized account of the famous summer in 1816 on Lake Geneva when Lord Byron, Percy Shelley, Mary Shelly, and John Polidori gathered for a meeting of the minds. At the gathering, Mary Shelley wrote the first chapter of what became *Frankenstein* and Byron produced a story fragment later developed by Polidori into "The Vampyre," the first modern vampire novella. Though it moves slowly in places, director Russell imagines the mental processes of several of the literary elite of the day, who were taking opium and dabbling in occultism. 🗡🗡🗡

"She must desire me before I empty her life into my throat and take back the love I lost so long ago."

—Martin Kemp in *Embrace of the Vampire* (1994).

1987 (R) 87m/C [Vestron Pictures] Julian Sands, Gabriel Byrne, Timothy Spall, Natasha Richardson, Miriam Cyr; **D:** Ken Russell; **W:** Stephen Volk; **M:** Thomas Dolby. **VHS, Beta, LV** *LIV, VES*

Grampa's Monster Movies

Al Lewis as Grandpa Dracula (from "The Munsters" television series) plays host to a nostalgic look at some classic horror films. Retrospective pays tribute to Dracula, Frankenstein, Wolfman, and the Mummy. Includes segments on Bela Lugosi, Lon Chaney, and Boris Karloff. Worth a look for the enthusiast. Followed by a sequel on science fiction movies. 🎝🎝🎝

1990 65m/C VHS, Beta *NO*

Grampa's Sci-Fi Hits

Nostalgic look at some of the famous science fiction movies, hosted by Al Lewis in his "Munsters" regalia. 🎝🎝🎝

1990 65m/C VHS, Beta *NO*

Grave of the Vampire

Vampire Caleb Croft (Michael Pataki) assaults a young woman, who subsequently becomes pregnant and bears a son. The child craves blood, not milk, and eventually the woman dies of anemia. The lineage is passed on, and twenty years later, the lad (William Smith) has grown to manhood. He has learned to control his craving for blood, but when he finds his father teaching at a local university, it brings out the worst in him and causes big problems for his father. Based on the novel "The Still Life" by David Chase. ***AKA:*** Seed of Terror.

1972 (R) 95m/C [Daniel Cady] William Smith, Michael Pataki, Lyn Peters, Diane Holden, Jay Adler, Kitty Vallacher, Jay Scott, Lieux Dressler; **D:** John Hayes. **VHS, Beta** *UNI*

Graveyard Disturbance

Made-for-television movie in which a group of teenagers visit hell. They begin their jour-

ney in a graveyard inn and encounter a variety of creatures, including some vampires. At the close of their trip they confront Death. **AKA:** Dentro il Cimitrio. 🦇🦇

1987 ?m/C [Reteitalia, Dania Film] Gregory Lech Thaddeus, Lea Martino, Beatrice Ring; **D:** Lamberto Bava.

Graveyard Shift

Not great drama, but a pretty good story nonetheless. Stephen Tsepes, a New York cabby working the night shift, is actually a powerful 300-year-old vampire who feeds off his fares. He is especially attracted to women close to death or ready to die. His bite saves them and preserves him. His life is changed when he encounters Michelle, a young woman (Helen Papas) who has just found out that she's dying. This film is not to be confused with the Stephen King movie of the same name. Followed by the sequel *Understudy: Graveyard Shift II.* 🦇🦇

1987 (R) 89m/C *IT* [Cinema Ventures] Silvio Oliviero, Helen Papas, Cliff Stoker; **D:** Gerard Ciccoritti. **VHS, Beta** *VTR*

Guess What Happened to Count Dracula?

Guy (John Landon) offers the lonely Count Adrian/Dracula a deal. The vampire can have his girlfriend Angelica (Claudia Barron)

in return for Guy becoming a star. The Count agrees to the deal, which leaves Guy killing time in Hollywood in a boring round of orgies, drugs, and disco. Meaningless movie with no depth. **AKA:** *The Master of the Dungeon.* 🦇🦇

1970 80m/C [Merrick International] **Des Roberts,** Claudia Barron, John Landon; **D:** Lawrence Merrick; **W:** Lawrence Merrick; **C:** Robert Caramico; **M:** Des Roberts.

Guru, the Mad Monk

Another low-budget dreck-a-thon from writer/director/producer Milligan. Father Garu (Neil Flanagan) of the Lost Souls Church in medieval Mortavia (subtle) is also the chaplain at the local prison, where he enjoys torturing the prisoners. He is assisted by his hunchback sidekick Igor and his lesbian vampire mistress Olga (Jacqueline Webb). Wow! This movie has everything. Except a reason to watch. **Woof!**

1970 57m/C Neil Flanagan, **Jacqueline Webb,** Judith Isral, Julia Willis; **D:** Andy Milligan; **W:** Andy Milligan; **C:** Andy Milligan.

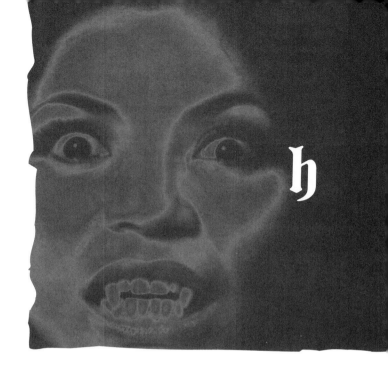

h

Halloween with the Addams Family

Over a decade after the demise of the television series, several members of the original Addams Family cast revived their parts for a new story in which they encounter the Countess Dracula (Suzanne Krazna). The film was a rough transition from TV to the theater for the popular horror family. *Halloween with the New Addams Family.* 🦴🦴

1979 87m/C John Astin, Carolyn Jones, Jackie Coogan, Ted Cassidy. **VHS, Beta** *GKK*

Haunted Cop Shop I

Special Hong Kong Monster Police Squad swings into action when vampires invade the local meat-packing plant. The cops lose round one, and the police commissioner demotes them until the vampires reappear at the local hospital. Noteworthy for the special effects. Popular enough to spawn the aptly-named *Haunted Cop Shop II.* 🦴🦴🦴

1984 ?m/C

Haunted Cop Shop II

Action is the focus of this sequel as the Monster Police Squad goes after the most recent vampires to invade its territory. Contains one of the more creative, if somewhat gross, methods of killing a vampire. Let's just say it involves bodily functions and electricity. 🦴🦴

1986 ?m/C D: Jeff Lau.

Haunted Summer

During the summer of 1816, Lord Byron (Philip Anglin), Percy Shelley (Eric Stoltz), Mary Shelley (Alice Krige), and John Polidori (Alex Winter) spent a week on Lake Geneva. Retreating inside when a storm blew across the lake, they told supernatural stories to

THE BLOODY COUNTESS

Prince Vlad Tepes (the real Dracula) is not the only historical personage to inspire modern vampire tales. Almost his equal, in her own small way, was Elizabeth Bathory, a Slovakian Countess who lived in the late sixteenth century. Obsessed with keeping her youthful appearance, she discovered that blood seemed to do the trick. However, she didn't drink it like a vampire, she bathed in it. Unfortunately, it took a lot more blood for a bath than it did for a cocktail—over a period of years until she was discovered and stopped, Bathory had more than 600 young women tortured, killed, and drained of their blood.

Interestingly enough, while a number of movies have been based on the Bathory legend, all have originated in Europe. This is rather surprising in light of Hollywood's constant and extensive search for new vampire material. The first attempt to tell the Countess' story was produced by Hammer Films to showcase their new voluptuous star, Ingrid Pitt. In *Countess Dracula* (1970), Pitt portrayed a woman driven by her lust for youth and her desire to keep her young lovers. Taking full cinematic liberty, the movie showed the aging, wrinkled countess being spectacularly rejuvenated and reverting to young adulthood after each bath.

Like *Dracula,* Bathory rarely appears in her contemporary setting but instead is continually shown in the present, having survived the ordeal that ended her historical existence. For example, the very first Bathory movie, *The Devil's Commandment* (1956), told the story of an evil modern doctor draining the blood of patients to keep the Countess alive. A far more effective use of the Bathory persona is found in *Daughters of Darkness* (1971). Her castle is now an empty off-season hotel. Along with her female servant/lover, she invades the bedroom of a honeymooning couple, thus destroying their lives and her own in the process.

Several movies have been built around the Bathory legacy. In *The Female Butcher* (1972), beauty queen Lucia Bosé as a descendent of the Countess takes up her illustrious ancestor's ways to preserve her own beauty. Her husband Karl fakes his own death and then secretly begins acquiring young women for his wife's use. The various scenes in which the Countess's bath is filled in the uncut version of the film ensure the movie's place in spatter flick history, but it is usually seen in its edited version under the title *The Legend of Blood Castle.*

Some people can make light of anything, and *Mama Dracula* (1980) is a comedic version of Elizabeth Bathory's life. In homage to *Andy Warhol's Dracula*, the Countess is finding it ever more difficult to find virgin (also pronounced "wirgin") blood. Needing a constant supply, she hires a mad scientist to make synthetic blood. In the meantime, her fanged offspring are competing for the dwindling supply of the needed life-giving substance.

After a spate of movies in the 1970s, movie makers seem to have concluded that Bathory's story has been largely exhausted, and she has had only a few additional appearances. Among the rare cinematic references from around the world to her habit of bathing in blood are the movies *Krvava Pani* (1981); an animated version of her story, the *Legend of the Eight Samurai* (1984); and the *Mysterious Death of Nina Chereau* (1987).

✝ END ✝

each other. Out of that storytelling session, Mary Shelley produced the first chapter of what became "Frankenstein" and Byron offered a story fragment that he left unused. It was later taken by Polidori and turned into "The Vampyre," the first modern vampire novella. This fictionalized account of that week suggests the time was also spent in various bacchanalian pursuits. Inspired by Anne Edwards' novel. Ken Russell's *Gothic* also explores this subject. 🗡🗡

1988 (R) 106m/C [Cannon Films] Alice Krige, Eric Stoltz, Philip Anglim, Laura Dern, Alex Winter; **D:** Ivan Passer; **W:** Lewis John Carlino. **VHS, Beta, LV** *MED*

Heartstopper

Benjamin Latham, an innocent physician in Pittsburgh, was accused of being a vampire in colonial times and hung. 200 years later, he emerges from the grave, unscathed. While trying to figure out what has happened, he falls in love with a photojournalist, who helps him find his own descendent, Matthew Latham. Unfortunately, his deep freeze has left him with the compulsion to kill, but only evil members of society. 🗡

1992 96m/B Moon Zappa, Tom Savini, Kevin Kindlan. **VHS** *TEM, MOV*

Hello Dracula

Dracula comes to China when his dead body is transformed after its reanimation by a child-vampire. Local officials attempt to counter the Count by bringing in three European vampire hunters, who are joined in their efforts by a local magician and his gang of bug children. This bizarre vampire feature includes a vampire baseball game and musical dance number. 🗡🗡

1985 ?m/C D: Henry Wu-Leung.

Hercules in the Haunted World

Director Mario Bava and actor Christopher Lee combine talents to redeem a less than stellar script. Building on Greek mythology, the story finds Hercules (Reg Park) and Theseus (Giorgio Ardisson) coming to the aid of Daianara (Leonora Ruffo), who has gone insane under the influence of the evil Lico (Christopher Lee), the vampiric agent of Hell. In order to cure her, they seek to retrieve a golden apple from Hesperides and a magic stone from Hades. The muscular pair must fight off Procrustes, the stone giant, an army of flying ghouls, and a lake of boiling lava. A demigod's work is never done. *AKA:* Ercole al Centro Della Terra; *Hercules contra les Vampires*; and *Hercules at the Center of the Earth.* 🗡🗡🗡

1964 91m/C *IT* [SPA Milan, Woolner Bros. Pictures] Reg Park, Leonora Ruffo, Christopher Lee, George Ardisson; **D:** Mario Bava. **VHS, Beta** *CCB, RHI, MRV*

Here Come the Munsters

A second generation cast takes over as the popular and friendly Munster family in this third movie spin-off. The family is forced out of their Transylvania home by the locals and heads for the United States, finally settling on Mockingbird Lane in Los Angeles. The following encounters with modern Western suburban life are supposed to induce amusement. Al Lewis (the original Grampa), as well as fellow original cast members Pat Priest (Marilyn) and Butch Patrick, (Eddie) make cameo appearances. 🗡🗡

1995 ?m/C [Fox] **Robert Morse, Veronica Hamel,** Edward Herrmann.

Hollywood on Parade

Ten-minute short (one of a series produced by Paramount), features various characters in a wax museum that come to life. Bela Lu-

"That's why I've come to you, to seek release from a curse of misery and horror."

—Count Dracula (John Carradine) to Dr. Edelmann in *House of Dracula* (1945).

gosi, playing Dracula for fun, approaches Mae Questel (playing Betty Boop) and is heard to say, "Boop! You have booped your last boop!" 🗡🗡

1934 59m/B [Paramount Pictures] Fredric March, Ginger Rogers, Jean Harlow, Jeanette MacDonald, Maurice Chevalier, Mary Pickford, Jackie Cooper. **VHS, Beta** NOS, DVT, RXM

Horrible Orgies of Count Dracula

A group of Satanists gather in an underground room of an old castle to resurrect a witch dead for four centuries. The sadistic ceremony is to include the sacrifice of seven naked young women, presumably all virgins. The evening's festivities are interrupted by a victim's boyfriend and the Satanists transform into vampires. Eventually the residents of the nearby village join in. What could have become a shock classic was all but destroyed by inept acting and writing. *AKA:* Reincarnation of Isabel; Riti Magie Nere e Segret Ogre del Trecento; The Ghastly Orgies of Count Dracula. 🗡🗡

1973 100m/C Mickey Hargitay, Rita Calderon, Max Dorian, Consolata Moschera; *D:* Renato Polselli; *C:* Ugo Brunelli; *M:* Gianfranco Reverberi, Romolo Forlai.

The Horror of Dracula

Second in importance only to Universal's *Dracula* (1931), *The Horror of Dracula* transformed actor Christopher Lee into an international star, second only to Bela Lugosi in terms of identification with the part of Dracula. The seventh film adaptation of *Dracula* also initiated a new cycle of vampire and horror movies characterized by their gothic setting, beautiful women in various stages of disrobe, and the use of color. By the end of World War II, Universal was, for all practical purposes, out of the horror film business. Hammer Films picked up Universal's licenses for a song and made their new versions of the classic horror flicks. The tall and imposing Christopher Lee was chosen to be the new Dracula. He had played Frankenstein's monster beneath a wall of makeup, but was now able to take center stage. Peter Cushing, who had played the scientist Victor Frankenstein, returned to play Van Helsing. He would go on to assume numerous roles in which he was the knowledgeable professor/scientist, either creating the horror or helping to end it. The new film was helped immensely by Terence Fisher's directing skills and the scripting of Jimmy Sangster. Color added a new dimension to horror movies and seems to be the major factor in their revival through the 1960s. New freedoms in what could be portrayed also helped. Lee donned fangs for the first time, and the extended toothy look became a popular toy with which vampire movie makers could play. The sensual nature of the vampire's bite, never shown in the 1931 *Dracula*, was evident to all. Beginning with *Horror of Dracula*, Hammer would continually explore, in ever more literal presentations, the relationship between vampirism and sexuality. Hammer's *Dracula* opens with the arrival of Jonathan Harker (John Van Eyssen) at Castle Dracula to assume the role of castle librarian. The first person he meets is a beautiful female (Valerie Grant) dressed in negligee. She bites Harker who becomes a vampire. (Thus spreading the idea that a single bite by the vampire turns the victim into a vampire. In the novel, one had to receive blood from the vampire to be transformed and it took more than one such incident.) As is later revealed, Harker has come to Castle Dracula as part of a covert operation planned by Van Helsing to kill the vampire.

The Horror of Dracula: "Uh, hon, do you know where I left the car keys. I'm late for work." Arthur Holmwood (Michael Gough) looks on, concerned, at wife Mina (Melissa Stribling). But Van (the Man) Helsing (Peter Cushing) knows this ain't no ordinary morning sickness.

starring PETER CUSHING

also starring MICHAEL GOUGH

and MELISSA STRIBLING

with CHRISTOPHER LEE

as DRACULA

Screenplay by JIMMY SANGSTER
From the novel by BRAM STOKER
Directed by TERENCE FISHER
Executive producer: MICHAEL CARRERAS
Associate producer: ANTHONY NELSON-KEYS
Produced by ANTHONY HINDS

PRODUCED BY HAMMER FILMS · RELEASED BY SEVEN ARTS PICTURES

The Horror of Dracula

However, Dracula flees, and when Van Helsing arrives, he discovers that his agent has been turned. Van Helsing kills Harker with the traditional stake. The scene now shifts to England, where still another rearrangement of the characters from the novel was to be found. Lucy (Carol Marsh) and Mina (Melissa Stribling) are sisters. Mina is married to Arthur Holmwood (Michael Gough) and Lucy was the fiancee of the late Jonathan Harker. John Seward, Renfield, and Quincey Morris do not appear. Dracula turns his attention first to Lucy, whose picture he had taken from Harker before leaving the castle. Van Helsing arrives on the scene to thwart his plans. Angered, Dracula goes after the vulnerable Mina. He kidnaps her and heads for his castle. The men eventually overtake him and rescue Mina. While Holmwood

stays with his traumatized wife, Van Helsing moves on to confront the count in his lair. In one of the most famous scenes in vampire movies, Dracula defeats Van Helsing and is about to kill him, but pauses just a moment to enjoy his success to the fullest. That pause is his undoing. Van Helsing recovers, brushes Dracula aside, and rushes across the room. He has one last weapon, the morning sun. When he rips the drapes from the window, the sunlight catches Dracula by surprise, Using a cross, Van Helsing pushes Dracula into the deadly stream of light. Dracula burns to ashes which blow away in a breeze. Only his ring is left on the floor. At the time, there was no particular thought of a sequel, but several years later, the manner of death would necessitate some creative thinking to resurrect a character so thoroughly destroyed. Sangster and others proved equal to the task. **AKA:** Dracula. 🎜🎜🎜🎜

1958 82m/C *GB* [Hammer, Universal] Peter Cushing, Christopher Lee, Michael Gough, Melissa Stribling, Carol Marsh, John Van Eyssen, Valerie Gaunt; **D:** Terence Fisher; **W:** Jimmy Sangster; **M:** James Bernard. **VHS, Beta, LV** *WAR, FCT, MLB*

Horror of it All

Young American pop singer Pat Boone worked with horror director Terence Fisher (fresh from his landmark work with Hammer) on this light story of a traveling salesman who falls in love. The problem begins when his new love (Erica Rogers) takes him home to meet the family. They include a madman locked in the basement, a patriarch who appears ready for the grave, and a sister who happens to be a vampire (Andree Melly). Music fans will be disappointed to hear that Boone survived, but Fisher's reputation was not helped by association with this loser. 🎜🎜

1963 ?m/C [20th Century-Fox, Lippert Productions] **Andree Melly**, Pat Boone, Dennis Price, Valentine Dyall, Erica Rogers; **D:** Terence Fisher.

The Horror of It All

An inside look at how horror movies are created and a celebration of some of the great stars including Boris Karloff, John Carradine, Lionel Atwell, Vincent Price, and, of course, Bela Lugosi. Includes insightful commentary on the dark side of human experience, which leads the imagination to create horror in the first place. 🎜🎜

1991 58m/C [MPI Home Video] Boris Karloff, Lon Chaney Sr., Bela Lugosi, John Barrymore, Lionel Atwill, John Carradine, Vincent Price. **VHS** *MPI, FCT*

Horror of the Blood Monsters

One of an unfortunate series of bad cheapie movies made by John Carradine at the end of his career, *Horror of the Blood Monsters* spliced action scenes from a primitively colorized Philippine movie into new scenes shot by B-movie legend Adamson. Without benefit of computers or Ted Turner, the ineffective coloring process (pretentiously named "Spectrum X") didn't quite cut it. The plot doesn't provide much help. Carradine portrays a scientist who, along with his assistant Valerie (Vicki Volante) and a military representative, discover an alien plot to invade earth. They plan to counter the attack with a preemptive strike at the aliens, all of whom are vampires. On a hastily constructed rocket, they fly to the bloodsucker planet where they encounter the "Philippine" monsters. Earth is saved, but by this time no one cares. As word of mouth spread on how bad this movie was, the names under which it was released were quickly changed. **AKA:** Vampire Men of the Lost Planet; Horror Creatures of the Prehistoric Planet; Creatures of the Prehistoric Planet; Creatures of the Red Planet; Flesh Creatures of the Red Planet; The Flesh Creatures; Space Mission of the Lost Planet. **Woof!**

1970 (PG) 85m/C *PH* [Independent International] John Carradine, Robert Dix, Vicki Volante, Jennifer Bishop; **D:** Al Adamson, George Joseph. **VHS, Beta** *REP*

Horroritual

A three-minute comic short originally shown in the United States along with *Dracula A. D. 1972.* Barry Atwater revived the vampire he played on television the previous year in *The Night Stalker.* 🎜🎜

1972 3m/C [Warner Brothers]

"I am Count Dracula. You see before you a man who has lived for centuries, kept alive by the blood of innocent people."

—Dracula (John Carradine). *House of Dracula* (1945).

House of Dark Shadows

Not bound by the television censors, *House* could retell the story of popular daytime television vampire Barnabas Collins, without cutting out the violence and sexuality inherent in the vampire's attack. The familiar story opens with the discovery of the 375-year-old vampire's coffin and his reawakening in the contemporary world. His family still owns the land, so Barnabas presents himself to matriarch Elizabeth Collins (Joan Bennett) as a long-lost cousin from England. He falls in love with Carolyn (Kathryn Leigh Scott), Elizabeth's daughter, and turns Carolyn into a vampire. Meanwhile, a female physician, Dr. Hoffman (Grayson Hall) has emerged on the scene. She falls in love with Barnabas and offers to cure him. The cure works for a while and Barnabas, sensitive neither to the sun nor the good doctor's feelings, courts Victoria Winters (Lara Parker), the family governess. The spiteful doctor, her love unreturned, alters the medicine upon which Barnabas' recovery is based. He quickly ages, but stops what appears to be a quick slide into death by killing Dr. Hoffman and refreshing himself on her blood. He then attempts to leave with Victoria. Barnabas does not appear in the 1971 sequel, *Night of Dark Shadows*, which drops the vampire theme altogether. Also released in France as *La Fiancée du Vampire*. 🗡🗡🗡

1970 (PG) 97m/C [MGM] Jonathan Frid, Joan Bennett, Grayson Hall, Kathryn Leigh Scott, Roger Davis, Nancy Barrett, John Karlen, Thayer David; **D:** Dan Curtis. VHS, Beta *MGM, FUS*

House of Dracula

This less than spectacular sequel to *House of Frankenstein* (1944), finds scientist Dr. Edelman (Onslow Stevens) attempting to turn the Universal monsters (Dracula, Frankenstein's monster, and the Wolfman) into normal people. He is looking for a serum which will kill the parasites that cause vampirism and lycanthropy. Lawrence Talbot (Lon Chaney, Jr.), ever searching for a cure to his werewolf curse, readily becomes a patient. Dracula, again named Baron Latos, however, not only rejects the offer of a cure but turns Edelman into a vampire. The doctor then goes truly mad and, in the frenzied disturbance that follows, releases Frankenstein's monster. Inspector Holtz (Lionel Atwill) and the local villagers don't take too kindly to the monstrous goings-on. Talbot escapes only to discover that he is no longer a werewolf, though that situation could and would change were he needed again. Carradine's Dracula character saves the production from total disaster. Together, the two movies established Carradine's partial ownership of the part and he would return to it periodically over the next forty years. Released in Italy as *La Casa Degli Orrori* ("The House of Horror"). 🦇🦇🦇

1945 67m/B [Universal] Lon Chaney Jr., Martha O'Driscoll, John Carradine, Lionel Atwill, Onslow Stevens, Glenn Strange, Jane Adams, Ludwig Stossel; **D:** Erle C. Kenton; **W:** Edward T. Lowe. **VHS, LV** MCA, FCT

House of Frankenstein

The original monster mash brought together Dracula, Frankenstein's monster, and the Wolfman, with Boris Karloff as a mad scientist, Dr. Niemann. It also marked the first of what would be many appearances by John Carradine as Count Dracula (actually named Count Latos in the movie). Niemann and his hunchbacked assistant Daniel (J. Carrol Naish) escape from a prison for the criminally insane and take over a traveling freak show, which conveniently features the exhibition of such horrors as the late vampire Dracula. Released briefly from his deathlike state, he faces final death in the sunlight. But not before having possibly the best scene in the movie as he attempts to vampirize the character played by Anne Gwyne. Niemann then goes after Frankenstein's diary. Instead he finds the monster and the wolfman. He revives them with hopes of controlling both. Although it hasn't worn well over the decades, *House of Frankenstein* was a crowd pleaser in the 1940s and prompted a sequel, *House of Dracula*, and a condensed version released as *Doom of Dracula*. 🦇🦇🦇

1944 71m/B [Universal Studios] Boris Karloff, J. Carrol Naish, Lon Chaney Jr., John Carradine, Elena Verdugo, Anne Gwynne, Lionel Atwill, Peter Coe, George Zucco, Glenn Strange, Sig Rumann; **D:** Erle C. Kenton. **VHS, LV** MCA

The House that Dripped Blood

Four short features originally written by master horror writer Robert Bloch are tied together by the history of an old house, as told by the real estate agent. In the last tale, the present renter of the house, a horror movie actor (Jon Pertwee) has disappeared. As the story unfolds, he is seen buying a cloak. When the co-star of his current production (Hammer veteran Ingrid Pitt) puts it on, she becomes a real vampire and turns Pertwee into her next victim. 🦇🦇🦇

1971 (PG) 101m/C GB [Max Rosenberg, Milton Subotsky, Amicus Productions] Christopher Lee, Peter Cushing, Jon Pertwee, Denholm Elliott, Ingrid Pitt, John Bennett, Tom Adams, Joss Ackland, Chloe Franks; **D:** Peter Duffell; **W:** Robert Bloch. **VHS, Beta** PSM

Howl of the Devil

Horror veteran Paul Naschy stars in his first film shot in English. Playing a slightly insane actor, he takes the viewer on a nostalgic, if gory, tour by assuming the roles of classic

monsters such as a werewolf (for which Naschy is most famous), Fu Manchu, Mr. Hyde, and, of course, a vampire. Viewed in passing, a portrait features Mexican horror star German Robles, who played the vampire Count Lavud in the 1950s. Another horror veteran, Howard Vernon, plays Naschy's eerie manservant. *AKA:* El Allido del Diablo. 🗡🗡

1972 ?m/C [Lorion] **Paul Naschy**, Caroline Munro, Howard Vernon; **D:** Paul Naschy.

Howling 6: The Freaks

"The Howling" was an outstanding horror novel which led to two sequels and then a very fine atmospheric movie. The movie generated its own series of inferior sequels, most shot for the video and television market rather than the theaters. This sixth of the Howling "epics" pits the werewolf lead against a vampire. Harker (Bruce Martyn Payne) captures the werewolf (Brendan Hughes) and turns him into a side show exhibit at his traveling carnival freak show. In the ultimate and inevitable confrontation, the vampire changes into a huge bat in which form he battles the werewolf. One of the more entertaining episodes in the mediocre series. 🗡🗡

1990 (R) 102m/C Brendan Hughes, Michelle Matheson, Sean Gregory Sullivan, Antonio Fargas, Carol Lynley, Jered Barclay, Bruce Martyn Payne; **D:** Hope Perello. **VHS, LV** *LIV, IME*

The Hunger

Rational speculation encounters the vampire legend in what is by consensus (among vampire-horror fans) one of the best vampire movies of the century. *The Hunger* brings to the screen the innovative vision of author Whitley Streiber. Miriam Blaylock (Catherine Deneuve), a beautiful 2000-year-old vampire (or lonely extraterrestrial, depending on your take) has been creating human companions, one after the other, over the centuries. The latest is John (David Bowie), who seems to be enjoying himself as the movie opens.

Modern science provides a new possibility of Miriam as she is now able to initiate a search for the underlying chemical distinctiveness of her blood which yields immortality as well as an appetite for more. Her search for understanding is given immediacy by John's deterioration. It seems that she cannot fully pass on her immortal condition to humans. After a century or so they begin to age rapidly. The signs of Bowie's changing spurs Blaylock to contact a specialist in the aging process, Dr. Sarah Roberts (Susan Sarandon). Soon entranced by the strange Miriam, the doctor (along with the vampire) provides the most lively (and torrid) scenes. But the movie is not about life, it speaks to death and damnation, and in the end no cure is forthcoming. John continues to age. He is soon left old and helpless, but conscious, unable to die completely. His only solace is Miriam's promise to visit him regularly in his attic depository. His two hundred years of life has been rewarded with a new hell of consciousness void of life or meaning. ♫♫♫

1983 (R) 100m/C [MGM/UA] Catherine Deneuve, David Bowie, Susan Sarandon, Cliff DeYoung, Ann Magnuson, Dan Hedaya, Willem Dafoe; **D:** Tony Scott; **W:** Michael Thomas, Ian Davis. **VHS, Beta, LV** *MGM*

Hysterical

To overcome his writer's block, a burned-out writer moves into a lighthouse in the town of Hellview. He discovers that his new home is also the residence of a spirit (Julie Newmar) who wants the writer to replace her lost love. However, that lost love is also brought back to life, a good indication that there's more going on than one lonely ghost could pull off. At times, the movie actually lives up to its title. ♫♫

1983 (PG) 86m/C [Gene Levy] Brett Hudson, William Hudson, Mark Hudson, Cindy Pickett, Richard Kiel, Julie Newmar, Bud Cort; **D:** Chris Bearde; **M:** Robert Alcivar. **VHS, Beta, LV**

"I went to unholy Cross University where I majored in dead. . . languages. But the atmosphere there was so grave that I Transylvanianed to Nosferatu Dame where I got my Draculaerate."

—Viola (Rachel Golden) in *I Married a Vampire* (1984).

I Bought a Vampire Motorcycle

A surprisingly good gimmick B-flick comedy starring a motorcycle with a life of its own. In a confrontation between Satanists and bikers, the cycle is turned into a vampire. Gasoline no longer suffices, it must have blood. It develops appropriate fangs, does not go out until the evening, and recoils from a crucifix. There is even a running joke about the halitosis of a garlic-eating cop. Though reviewed at Cannes in 1990, it never circulated widely in the United States and is relatively hard to find. Catch it on your London vacation. 🦴🦴

1990 ?m/C [Majestic Films International] Nick Morrisey, Amanda Noar, Michael Elphick; **D:** Dirk Campbell.

I, Desire

Made-for-television movie has David Naughton as a law student who becomes aware that a vampire is living in town, in this case, contemporary Los Angeles. As might be expected, no one wants to believe him. He sets out on his own to search out and destroy the bloodsucker, who turns out to be a prostitute. The somewhat predictable storyline climaxes with the inevitable confrontation between vampire and hunter. **AKA:** Desire the Vampire. 🦴🦴🦴

1982 97m/C [Green/Epstein Productions, Audrey Balsdel-Goddard, ABC, Columbia Pictures Television] David Naughton, Dorian Harewood, Marilyn Jones, Barbara Stock; **D:** John Llewellyn Moxey; **C:** Robert L. Morrison; **M:** Don Peake.

I Like Bats

As contact with the outside world has increased in post-Communist Poland, the horror genre has begun to make a comeback there. In this unique story, into which a variety of levels of meaning can be read, Katarzyna Walter portrays a vampire who sustains herself by dining on the bats that live in her attic. She withdraws from society

VIDEOHOUND SALUTES: TOM CRUISE

When it was announced that Tom Cruise had been selected to play the sensitive androgynous vampire Lestat—the hero of Anne Rice's "Vampire Chronicles"—angry cries went up from Rice and all of Lestat's fans. How could this young, All-American boy, who had made a career out of playing masculine, heterosexual men, bring the needed depth to the character. Many of the protesters had seen only a few of Cruise's movies and concluded that he was nothing more than a one-dimensional actor. Very few people gave Cruise the benefit of the doubt, refusing to believe that maybe he was mature enough to play such a complex role.

In all honestly, there was little in Cruise's background to suggest he was ready for the part. He went into acting right out of high school appeared in his first movie, *Endless Love*, when he was just 19-years-old. He reached stardom two years later in the comedy *Risky Business* playing a teenager left at home by wealthy parents. He followed that up with roles that again cast him as a well-to-do, in-control, white male in *All the Right Moves* (1983) and *Top Gun* (1986). Later efforts included *A Few Good Men* (1992) and *The Firm* (1993). Even as

his characters grew a little older in each film, critics couldn't help but notice a sameness in the roles he was portraying. Maybe all he could do was play himself, they commented.

Those who defended Cruise offer several counterarguments. First, Cruise had shown a great deal of depth (hidden up to that point) in his portrayal of a Vietnam veteran in *Born on the Fourth of July*. He had clearly extended the boundaries of his ability, and his peers acknowledged his performance with an Academy Award nomination. Second, those who had worked with Cruise had come to know him as a serious actor who had a strong perfectionist streak. Finally, it was reported that Cruise, already a superstar, had agreed to less than his normal salary to play Lestat. He wanted the part. He had something to prove to himself and to the public—that he was a talented actor who could demonstrate a range of emotions and identify with different realities, two talents that are apparent in all accomplished actors.

The movie was made under tight security. Information on the filming was sought by the media and a picture of Cruise in his makeup as Lestat was considered the ultimate prize

(eventually obtained by the tabloids, of course). Leaks were held to a minimum, however, and few could anticipate what the final product would look like when the movie was finally released in the fall of 1994.

All the worries proved to be unfounded. *Interview with a Vampire* turned out to be just another notch on Cruise's gun. He overwhelmed Anne Rice, he surprised his critics, and won over many skeptical fans. Cruise was able to project the power of a Rice vampire and manifest the strength of Lestat's will. He magnetically drew the audience to him, irresistible and horrific at the same time. He offered the possibility of eternal life while showing just how meaningless and full of despair such a life was. Little wonder that the film went on to become an immense financial success.

Amid rumors (and hopes) that he would soon make the sequel, Cruise moved on to other projects, the most notable being the revival of the old television series, *Mission Impossible* (1996). *Vampire* Co-stars Brad Pitt and Antonio Banderas have likewise seen their career flower elsewhere. Will the sequel ever be made? At this point, all fans can do is hope.

✝ END ✝

and has trouble associating with humans, a concern leading her to consult a psychiatrist. He first commits her, and then falls in love and marries her. Becoming a good housewife seemingly cures her of her vampirism. Gee Mrs. Cleaver, that's a lovely death shroud you're wearing today. Originally released in Polish as *Lubie Nietoperze*. 🩸🩸

1985 90m/C **D:** Grzegorz Warchol. **VHS** *FCT*

I Married a Vampire

In this low-budget comedy production, Brendan Hickey portrays Robespierre, a promiscuous vampire who indulges in a new sexual/drinking encounter each evening. The comedic element derives from Robespierre being married, and the upset and anger experienced by his wife after she becomes aware of his round of affairs. 🩸🩸

1987 85m/C [Troma Team] Rachel Gordon, Brendan Hickey; **D:** Jay Raskin. **VHS, Beta** *PSM*

I Was a Teenage Vampire

First there was the reasonably successful *I Was a Teenage Werewolf* in 1957, then *I Was a Teenage Frankenstein* in 1959. So why not *I Was a Teenage Vampire*? Because there's such a thing as taking a decent concept too far. Written, directed, produced, and (surprise!) starring Donald Glut (with a host of unnamed not-exactly-professional thespian friends). The title says it all in this extremely low-budget independent production so forgettable that neither the writer, producer, director, nor star remembered to save a copy. 🩸

1959 81m/B [Independent Productions Corporation] **Don Glut**; **D:** Don Glut; **W:** Don Glut.

Il Cavaliere Costante Nicosia Demoniaco Ovvero

A titillating sexual comedy in which Sicilian comic Buzzanca plays a businessman who travels to Romania, where he is bitten by Dragulescu. His main fear after this attack? Not that he will become a vampire, but rather that he will become a homosexual (horrors!) However, the story has a happy ending when he discovers that in reality, his sexual prowess has been greatly increased by his new habit of consuming blood. A factory owner, he makes sure that he always has a fresh supply of blood from his pool of employees (the metaphor of factory owner as bloodsucker is not lost on the audience). **AKA:** Dracula in Brianza; Dracula in the Provinces. 🩸🩸

1975 100m/C *IT* [R. Marini, Titanus, Coralta Cinematografica] **John Steiner**, Lando Buzzanca, Sylva Koscina, Christa Linder, Valentina Cortese, Ciccio Ingrassia; **D:** Lucio Fulci; **W:** Lucio Fulci, Pupi Avati, Bruno Corbucci, Mario Amendola; **C:** Sergio Salvati; **M:** Franco Bixio.

Immoral Tales

Four adult erotic stories, the third of which is an account of Elizabeth Bathory (Paloma Picasso) which focuses upon her lesbianism and her habit of bathing in the blood of virgins in order to stay youthful. **AKA:** Contes Immoraux; Three Immoral Women. 🩸🩸

1974 103m/C [Argos Films] **Paloma Picasso**, Lise Danvers, Charlotta Alexandra, Pascale Christophe, Fabrice Luchini; **D:** Walerian Borowczyk; **W:** Walerian Borowczyk; **C:** Bernard Daillencourt, Michel Zolat, Noel Very; **M:** Walerian Borowczyk, Maurice Le Roux.

In Search of Dracula

In 1972, the landmark historical text *In Search of Dracula*, by Raymond T. McNally and Radu Florescu, hit the shelves. It served to tie together Count Dracula, Eastern European vampire mythology, and the historical Dracula, Prince Vlad Tepes. The 1976 documentary, based on the McNally/Florescu volume, featured Christopher Lee as both narrator and actor in dramatic scenes recreating episodes in the life of Vlad Tepes. First of a

Urgh! I bit you where? Marie (Anne Parillaud) gets a little upset over her "food" in *Innocent Blood.*

Incubus

Experimental film using Esparanto (the artificial universal language) with English subtitles. A succubus, a female sex demon seduces the future Captain Kirk (William Shatner) while an incubus, a male sex demon, goes after his sister. The incubus/succubus was an evil entity from Central European folklore, a cross between the vampire and the *mara* (for which the nightmare is named). Inspiration from folklore was not enough to save this cinematic atrocity. **Woof!**

1965 ?m/C [Daystar-Villa Di Stefano U.A.]

Incubus

A doctor and his teenage daughter move to a small town in New England. It seemed like a good idea, but wouldn t you know it, it's inhabited by an energy sucking demon who's into sex murders and is attracted to the beautiful young girl. Unfortunately, what could have been a good psychic vampire thriller never gets the blood pressure up. 🦴🦴

1982 (R) 90m/C *CA* [Artists Releasing Corporation, Mark Boyman] John Cassavetes, Kerrie Keane, Helen Hughes, Erin Flannery, John Ireland; **D:** John Hough; **C:** Conrad Hall. **VHS, Beta, LV** *VES*

number of similar documentaries, several of which were made for television and then later released on video. 🦴🦴

1976 24m/C [Alan Landsburg Productions] **VHS, Beta** *PYR*

Incredible Melting Man

Remake of an early sci-fi flick, *First Man into Space* (1958), stars Alex Rebar as an astronaut who returns from his mission orbiting Saturn with peculiar side effects—he has become a vampire. The most outstanding element of the film is its special effects, which are disgusting enough to satisfy hard-core horror fans, if not science fiction aficionados. 🦴🦴

1977 (R) 85m/C [Orion, American International Pictures (A.I.P.)] Alex Rebar, Burr de Benning, Cheryl "Rainbeaux" Smith; **D:** William Sachs. **VHS,**

The Inn of the Flying Dragon

"Carmilla" is the Sheridan Le Fanu short story most associated with vampires, but this movie is based on another of his stories, "The Room in the Dragon Volant." A youthful aristocrat (Patrick Magee) finds himself drawn to a beautiful and equally youthful countess (Marilu Tolo). Her vampiric nature is suggested by the series of strange deaths which occur prior to Magee's spotting an old woman dressed in the Countess' clothes. Originally released in Swedish as *Ondskans Vardshus*. *AKA:* The Sleep of the Dead. 🦇🦇

1981 ?m/C [Aspekt Film, Dragon Co., National Film School of Ireland] **Marilu Tolo**, Per Oscarsson, Patrick Magee, Curt Jurgens; *D:* Calvin Floyd.

Innocent Blood

As a vampire, Marie (Anne Parillaud) follows a tight set of rules—she feeds only on bad guys, she doesn't play with her food, and she always cleans up after a meal. Things go wrong, however on the night she decides to "dine Italian." While sucking up to crime boss Sal "The Shark" Macelli (Robert Loggia), she is interrupted before she can finish off Macelli, turning him into a vampire. Since he doesn't know about the rules that Marie lives by, he begins to quench his thirst on innocent people, which of course turns them into vampires. Marie's guilty conscience forces her to seek out the assistance of a handsome young policeman (Anthony LaPaglia), who slowly recognizes that he also needs Marie's help to stop "The Shark." Oh, the problems of being a modern vampire. A good vampire tale with a romantic subplot and just the right mixture of dark humor. Forrest Ackerman makes a cameo, as does Alfred Hitchcock via a brief clip from one of his movies. 🦇🦇🦇

1992 (R) 112m/C [Warner Brothers, Lee Rich, Leslie Belzberg] **Anne Parillaud**, **Robert Loggia**, Anthony LaPaglia, David Proval, Don Rickles, Rocco Sisto, Kim Coates; *D:* John Landis; *C:* Mac Ahlberg; *M:* Ira Newborn. **VHS, Beta, LV** *WAR, PMS*

Insomnia

Not much story development in this short film in which a woman, whose husband is reading a book on vampires, turns out to be one herself. *AKA:* Insomnie. 🦇

1963 ?m/B Pierre Etaix; *D:* Pierre Etaix.

Interview with the Vampire

After almost two decades of waiting, ardent fans of Anne Rice's blockbuster novel were rewarded for their patience when it was announced that the book was finally going to make it to the big screen. Then following Tom Cruise's selection to play the role of Lestat, the months leading to the release of the film were marked with controversy. Many fans of the book—especially Rice herself—simply could not picture Cruise filling Lestat's large fangs. Rice went so far as to call for a boycott of the film before finally backing down after seeing a preview screening of the movie. The controversy only added to the attention being paid the long-awaited film, which was Hollywood's second major treatment of the vampire theme in the decade (*Bram Stoker's Dracula* being the first). While the novel *Interview with the Vampire* is really more Louis's story than Lestat's, in the years since the novel first appeared Lestat has emerged as the more important character in Rice's vampire writings (he has been the subject of the several additional novels in the series), and thus his role in *Interview* was elevated and made more central. The movie largely follows the novel. Reluctant vampire Louis (Brad Pitt) narrates the tale as he grants an interview to an eager young writer (Christian Slater). He recounts his life-changing encounter with Lestat in eighteenth century Louisiana and his slow adaptation to a vampire's existence. After the pair settles in New Orleans, Lestat turns a lovely young girl into a vampire to join him and Louis. Louis quickly develops a fatherly concern for the petite Claudia (Kirsten Dunst), and the trio proceeds to live a life of debauchery and blood drinking until a conflict within their artificial family causes Louis and Claudia to make an attempt on Lestat's life. The pair escapes to France, where they make contact with Armand (Antonio Banderas) and the Theatre of the Vampires, the first vampires they have found in the world

besides themselves. Here some of the more exciting scenes in the movie occur—posing as a daringly risque theatre troupe, the Theatre of Vampires ravage an unsuspecting woman on stage in front of an adoring audience whose members think they are simply witnessing magnificent acting and a grand morality play. Louis and Claudia are not safe among their own kind, however. For killing one of their own (Lestat), Claudia is condemned to die in the sun and Louis is entombed. With Armand's help, Louis escapes and exacts his revenge on the group of vampires before returning to America, where he discovers that Lestat, while near death, is not dead at all. In fact, Lestat proves to be very much alive at the film's end. *Interview* is as faithful to the novel as a film could be. It is strengthened by magnificent photography,

which effectively conveys a world without sunlight, where color exists but is always muted. Most importantly, the film captures the dark and amoral nature of the vampire's life dominated by the blood thirst. To that life Louis must eventually accomodate while in it Lestat revels, savoring the eternal nature of his existence. It is interesting to note that after all the prerelease controversy, Rice admitted she was wrong about Cruise. He was widely praised for his performance as Lestat, and it helped him to escape his pretty boy image and prove that he was a better actor than previously thought. 🗡🗡🗡🗡

1994 **(R)** 123m/C [Stephen Woolley, David Geffen, Geffen Pictures] **Tom Cruise, Brad Pitt, Kirsten Dunst, Antonio Banderas,** Christian Slater, Stephen Rea, Domiziana Giordano; **D:** Neil Jordan; **W:** Anne Rice; **C:** Philippe Rousselot; **M:** Elliot Goldenthal.

Chicago Film Critics Awards '94: Most Promising Actress (Dunst); MTV Movie Awards '95: Best Male Performance (Pitt), Breakthrough Performance (Dunst), Most Desirable Male (Pitt); Nominations: Academy Awards '94: Best Art Direction/Set Decoration, Best Original Score; Golden Globe Awards '95: Best Supporting Actress (Dunst), Best Original Score; MTV Movie Awards '95: Best Film, Most Desirable Male (Slater, Cruise), Best On-Screen Duo (Tom Cruise/Brad Pitt), Best Villain (Cruise). **VHS, LV** *WAR*

Invasion of the Blood Farmers

Cheap, sleazy bit of schlock cinema in which a Druid blood cult slices and dices neighborhood women looking for a rare blood type needed for a special ritual. They plan to resurrect their queen in time to celebrate a blood feast. Plot takes a back seat to graphic, gratuitous gore. **Woof!**

1972 **(PG)** 86m/C [Ed Adlum] Norman Kelley, Tanna Hunter, Bruce Detrick, Jack Neubeck, Cythia Fleming, Paul Craig Jennings; **D:** Ed Adlum. **VHS, Beta** *NO*

Invasion of the Dead

Blue Demon is the wrestler who comes out of the ring to fight the forces of evil, represented by no less than Dracula himself (Cesar Silva). The Count brings along a tag team of the Frankenstein monster and a zombie. **AKA:** La Invasion de los Muertos. ♪♫

1972 78m/C [Azteca]

Invasion of the Vampires

First of two low-budget Mexican offerings featuring the vampiric Dracula-clone, Count Frankenhausen. In this initial outing, the Count's victims attack a small medieval town. They are countered by a knowledge-able vampire hunter who seeks the aid of the

Count's unsuspecting daughter. No surprises await the viewer in this very predictable battle between aristocratic vampire and beleaguered villagers. The Count eventually returns for a sequel, *The Bloody Vampire*. **AKA:** La Invasion de Los Vampiros. ♪

1961 78m/B *MX* [K. Gordon Murray] Carlos Agosti, Rafael Etienne, Bertha Moss, Tito Junco, Erna Martha Bauman, Fernando Soto, Enrique Garcia Alvarez, David Reynoso; **D:** Miguel Morayta; **W:** Miguel Morayta. **VHS** *SNC*

Isle of the Dead

In spite of his long history in the horror genre, Boris Karloff rarely played in vampire movies, and only once portrayed a vampire. In this early offering from RKO, he is a Greek military commander serving on an isolated island during the Balkan War in 1912. He is in the extreme minority in believing that a vampire (*vrykolakas*) is killing off the island's residents. Flick was effective enough to earn the wrath of British censors, protective of post-war sensitivities, for over a decade. ♪♪♪

1945 72m/B [Val Lewton] Boris Karloff, Ellen Drew, Marc Cramer; **D:** Mark Robson. **VHS, Beta, LV** *TTC, MED, FCT*

It! The Terror from Beyond Space

In one of the earliest science fiction vampire movies, a blood-drinking Martian (Ray "Crash" Corrigan) stows away on a space ship and begins attacking the crew one by one. The captain and few remaining crew are able to isolate the creature in a section of the ship, but it escapes and the crew becomes the pursued. The special effects of this low budget film are quite unconvincing, but *It!* broke new ground and led to more notable features such as *Planet of the Vampires* (1965), and *Queen of Blood* (1966). Its remake, sans the vampiric element, became the blockbuster scifi thriller *Alien* (1979).

"My first rule —Never play with the food. . . . My second rule — always finish the food."

—The vampire Marie (Anne Parillaud) in *Innocent Blood* (1992).

DAUGHTERS OF DARKNESS: YOUR FAVORITE FEMALE VAMPIRES

The first female vampires on screen were beautiful, inviting, and the very epitome of temptation. However, those "brides" of *Dracula* from the 1931 movie were strictly the creation of a male vampire (Dracula) and were there just to do his bidding. They were not independent creatures who acted of their own free will. Additionally, they were not considered central to the story and had limited screen time.

The first vampiress to act on her own was the old woman who controlled the village in Carl Theodor Dreyer's *Vampyr* (1932). She was followed a few years later by *Dracula's Daughter* (1936), the Countess Marya Zaleska. The countess, who was played very effectively by Gloria Holt, drew both men and women to her fateful kiss. In spite of these initial roles for female vampires, the early decades of horror were male dominated. Dracula and his compatriots ruled the screen—they occasionally lured a woman into becoming a vampiress, but it seemed as if the female always met a disastrous end.

It really was not until the 1960s that female vampires got their chance to get even with the boys. From Italy came the unforgettable

Barbara Steele as the vampire Princess in *Black Sunday* (1960), and from France came Annette Stroyberg, the cinema's first Carmilla in *Blood and Roses* (1961). Carmilla, a young and sexy female vampire, was the title character in a short story created by Irish writer Sheridan Le Fanu. During a brief period in the 1970s, the number of appearances Carmilla made on the silver screen was equaled only by Dracula. Like the Countess Marya Zaleska, she drew fawning audiences of both sexes. Her starring turns in the three Hammer movies in the early 1970s (*The Vampire Loves*, *Lust for a Vampire*, and *Twins of Evil*), did more to establish the presence and staying power of female vampires than any vamp who had come before her.

At the same time that Carmilla became so popular, another female vampire also rose to prominence. Countess Elizabeth Bathory was a real person, who, according to legend, killed more than 600 young women, drained their blood, and then bathed in it to retain her youthful appearance. No sooner had Hammer brought Carmilla to the screen than production began on the Bathory legend. Rather than return-

ing Ingrid Pitt to the second Carmilla movie, the studio cast her as the *Countess Dracula* (1970), which was based on the Bathory legend. Today, Pitt is still remembered for her infamous bath scene from that film in which she hurriedly exits her bath and is left standing, dripping blood from her voluptuous body. After Hammer, other filmmakers repeatedly found Bathory a source of inspiration, from Jorge Grau's quickie production, *The Legend of Blood Castle* (1972) to the haunting classic, *Daughters of Darkness* (1971).

Once female vampires showed how powerful they could be on-screen, they earned a permanent place in vampire cinema. Today, while any vampire fan knows Count Yorga, Blacula, Barnabas Collins, or Lestat, they are sure to recognize the bloodthirsty tactics of such female vampires as Venessa (*Dracula's Widow*), Miriam (*The Hunger*), the Countess (*Once Bitten*) and Marie (*Innocent Blood*). In the meantime, women have also joined the ranks of the vampire hunters, as demonstrated in *Buffy the Vampire Slayer* (1992).

✝ END ✝

Based on A. E. van Vogt's story "The Black Destroyer." **AKA:** It! The Vampire From Beyond Space. 🗡🗡🗡

1958 68m/B [United Artists] Marshall Thompson, Shawn Smith, Kim Spalding, Ann Doran, Dabbs Greer, Paul Langton, Ray Corrigan; **D:** Edward L. Cahn. **VHS, Beta** *MGM, MLB*

It's Alive

As Mr. Davis (John P. Ryan) awaits the birth of his second child, he hears screaming just before a nurse, covered with blood, comes out of the delivery room and collapses. The doctor and other attendants lie dead on the delivery room floor; only Mrs. Davis is alive. The newborn is nowhere to be seen. The child, complete with fangs, has come out of the womb and gone on a murderous blood-drinking rampage. The Los Angeles Police are called in to track it down, and the family members must one-by-one decide what their relationship with the newest family member will be. A cheaply-made horror movie that rises above its origins to focus questions about human interference in the birth process, as well as posing a challenge to the family values crowd. Not to be confused with the 1968 monster movie of the same name. The Davis family adventure spawned two sequels: *It's Alive 2: It Lives Again* and *It's Alive 3: Island of the Alive.* 🗡🗡🗡

1974 (PG) 91m/C [Larry Cohen] John P. Ryan, Sharon Farrell, Andrew Duggan, Guy Stockwell, James Dixon, Michael Ansara; **D:** Larry Cohen; **W:** Larry Cohen. **VHS, Beta** *WAR, FCT*

It's Alive 2: It Lives Again

The Davis's fanged baby from *It's Alive* turned out to be just the first in a crop of killer kids that were about to be born around the country. When the government establishes a hit squad to eliminate the mutant newborns, Mr. Davis (John P. Ryan) runs around to expectant parents both to warn them of what is to come and to gain their support for saving and loving their vicious little bundles of joy. Another couple, the Scotts, agree with Davis and join him when he shows up soon after the birth of their child and leads the whole family to momentary safety at a rural hideaway. Davis and others try to study the babies and teach them that humans are not food. However, the hit squad eventually finds the safe house, and the babies, quickly grasping the situation, simply see the officers as their next meal. Kids these days. The story is continued in *It's Alive 3.* 🗡🗡

1978 (R) 91m/C [Larry Cohen] Frederic Forrest, Kathleen Lloyd, John P. Ryan, Andrew Duggan, John Marley, Eddie Constantine; **D:** Larry Cohen. **VHS, Beta** *WAR, FCT*

It's Alive 3: Island of the Alive

Surprise! The killer mutant infants that were supposedly wiped out at the end of *It's Alive 2* weren't killed after all. Instead, they were taken to a remote island and left to fend for themselves. One of the children's parents launches a crusade to save the children who, he hypothesizes, may be the next level of human evolution. This third film in the series hints at but does not answer some basic questions: How do you love, much less potty train, an ugly, fanged offspring who might devour you at any moment? 🗡🗡

1987 (R) 94m/C [Larry Cohen] Michael Moriarty, Karen Black, Laurene Landon, Gerrit Graham, James Dixon, Neal Israel, MacDonald Carey; **D:** Larry Cohen; **W:** Larry Cohen. **VHS, Beta** *WAR*

The Jail Break

In this Mighty Mouse cartoon, Dracula and Frankenstein's monster are inmates at Alcatraz (still an active prison in the 1940s). the monster breaks down the door to his cell and Mighty Mouse is called in. 🦴🦴

1946 ?m/C D: Eddie Donnelly.

Jaws of the Jungle

An obscure film from an obscure corner of the filmmaking world. In this independent production, a host of giant vampire bats (which aren't indigenous to the area) attacks a Sri Lankan village. 🦴

1936 ?m/B Teeto, Minta, Gukar; **D:** J.D. Kendis.

The Jitters

What would happen if the unique Chinese hopping vampires came to North America? This important question dogging the consciousness of every true vampire fan is answered here as the murdered dead turn on their killers and seek revenge. A vampire (James Hong) and his son hop around Toronto and Los Angeles, transforming recently deceased murder victims and organizing them into a cadre to direct vengeance against a street gang. One can rest assured that the LAPD has never tried this alternative solution to the gang problem. 🦴

1988 (R) 80m/C [Gaga Communications] Sal Viviano, Marilyn Tokuda, James Hong, Frank Dietz; **D:** John Fasano. **VHS, Beta** *PSM*

Jonathan

Count Dracula (Paul Albert Krumm) needs a descendent to carry on the family name, so he decides to adopt the young Jonathan Harker (Jurgen Jung) and introduce him to the vampire's life. In an important bit of political commentary, Harker turns out to be a member of a resistance movement sent to

121

VAMPIRES on VIDEO

VIDEOHOUND SALUTES: PETER CUSHING

Veteran of more than a hundred movies, Peter Cushing humbly noted that of the many movies in which he had appeared, *The Blood Beast Terror* (1968) was the worst he had ever made. But that leaves the opposite question unanswered: What was the best? One certainly has a large variety from which to choose. The British-born Cushing (1913-1994) made his first movie, *The Man in the Iron Mask*, in 1940 just as World War II was beginning. His career really took off in 1957 when he starred in Hammer's initial horror production, *The Curse of Frankenstein*, in which he played the slightly mad scientist who created the monster. The film not only brought him together with director Terence Fisher and acting colleague Christopher Lee for the first time, but established a persona he was to play over and over again in the movies, that of the highly educated expert who could use his great knowledge either for good or evil. The epitome of that persona emerged the next year when he played Dr. Abraham Van Helsing opposite Lee's Dracula.

The Horror of Dracula must certainly be in the running for Cushing's best. He portrayed a man who had known evil and dedicated his heart and mind to defeating it. His final scene in which he suddenly turns the tables on Dracula just as death seems inevitable is one of the most unforgettable (and copied) in vampire films. He revived the part, but without Lee, the next year in *The Brides of Dracula*, another film many consider to be his best. The scene in which he cauterizes the bite of the vampire Baron Meinster with a branding iron is another memorable one.

Cushing would return to his roles as Van Helsing (or a descendent) and Baron Frankenstein on several occasions, and fans soon began to expect him to always play a variation of one of the parts. His most extreme variation came in *Twins of Evil* (1971), in which he portrayed a fanatical witch-hunter. On occasion, however, he drifted out of the horror field. For example, he portrayed the evil villain opposite Richard Green in the *Sword of Sherwood Forest* (1960), and 25 years later he joined Sean Connery in a second Robin Hood film, *Sword of the Valiant*. His most notable nonhorror role, however, had to be his 1977 appearance in *Star Wars*.

So, what was his best film? For this one the Hound must choose between his portrayals of Van Helsings in *Horror of Dracula* and *The Brides of Dracula*, and the scales seem to tilt slightly towards the latter.

✝ END ✝

Peter Cushing, the consummate Dr. Van Helsing.

destroy Dracula, a rather Hitleresque persona. **AKA:** Jonathan, Vampire Sterben Nicht; Jonathan, le Dernier Combat contre les Vampires. 🗡🗡

1970 ?m/C [New Yorker Films] **Jurgen Jung, Paul Albert Krumm,** Thomas Astan, Oskar von Schaab; **D:** Hans W. Geisendorfer.

Jonathan of the Night

Obscure ten-minute short designed more as an advertisement for possible backers of a full-length vampire movie than for commercial release. Focuses on a vampire at a party in contemporary New York. Its lackluster performances and low-budget production guaranteed that a feature film would not be forthcoming. 🗡

1987 ?m/C Don Striano, Mitch Maglio, Melissa Tait, Eric Collica; **D:** Buddy Giovinazzo.

Jugular Wine: A Vampire Odyssey

Anthropologist James Grace (Shaun Irons) has a problem—he fell in love with Alexandra, a vampiress who bit him but was killed before she could give him some of her blood and thus complete his transformation into a vampire. Now, strongly affected by the bite but still living, he tries to find an explanation for his condition. His only lead is the mysterious Dr. Donna Park, a scholar who vanished some years earlier while supposedly searching for the secret of the vampires. Grace begins his search for Park, but is quickly opposed by Legion, the head of the vampire world (and Alexandra's killer) who sends his minions to harass Grace every step of the way. Eventually, Grace must confront and overcome Legion to reach the end of his quest. This better than average low-budget film features a cameo by Stan Lee of Marvel Comics fame. 🗡🗡🗡

1994 95m/C Bill Moynihan, Jacqueline Sieger, Shaun Irons, Lisa Malkiewicz, Vladimir Kehkaial, Frank Miller, Henry Rollins, Michael Colyar; **Cameos:** Stan Lee; **D:** Jacqueline Sieger; **W:** Jacqueline Sieger; **C:** Baird Bryant; **M:** John Butler. **VHS** *TPV*

Kathavai Thatteeya Mohni Paye

In this Indian film made in the Tamil language, a private detective is called upon to end the arbitrary rule of a prince (the character partially inspired by Dracula) cursed to be a vampire. 🂠🂠

1975 ?m/C [Anuradha International] C. R. Patiban, Sanjivirajan, Desikan; **D:** M. A. Rajaraman.

The Keep

Much of the vampiric element in the original novel by F. Paul Wilson is lost in this unique war tale. Nazi soldiers in Romania camp outside a mysterious fortress-like building. The Keep is notable for the numerous crosses embedded in the wall, which any vampire fan recognizes as a clue that there's an evil vampiric entity stored somewhere on the premises. Two soldiers searching for treasures succeed in breaking the Keep's seal and allowing Molasar (now transformed into a more Lovecraftian demon) to come forth. The havoc he causes the first night is blamed on anti-Nazi partisans, and the local commander orders villagers shot. Help is on the way in the form of Glacken, an ancient watcher who was awakened by Molesar's appearance. He is assisted by the historian Dr. Cuza. Evil opposes evil as Nazis and creature square off. The equally unlovable Gracken (who tries to romance Cuza's daughter) has the talisman, which can thwart the monster. The film unfortunately loses much of its logic due to the elimination of the monster's vampiric nature and never constructs a rationale for Molasar's destructiveness. It does, however, offer an enjoyable evening of horror viewing. 🂠🂠

1983 (R) 96m/C [Gene Kirkwood, Howard W. Koch] Scott Glenn, Alberta Watson, Juergen Prochnow, Robert Prosky, Gabriel Byrne; **D:** Michael Mann; **W:** Michael Mann, Dennis Lynton Clark. **VHS, Beta, LV** *PAR*

The Ketchup Vampires

Elvira narrates this animated movie which

DRIVE-IN VAMPIRES FROM INDEPENDENT INTERNATIONAL

Drive-in movies were still the vogue in the mid 1960s, not yet the victim of air conditioning, and companies like Hemisphere and American-International (and their stellar director Roger Corman) had filled a niche by turning out inexpensive movies shown for the open-air crowd. In 1968, young independent film makers Sam Sherman and Al Adamson felt that there was a huge market just waiting for escapist films that offered nothing more than a hearty belly laugh or a good scare. The films weren't works of art, but they offered a little diversion from the work-a-day world.

Sam Sherman got started at the City College of New York, where he learned the basics of filmmaking. His interest in horror movies was fueled by the numerous horror films made in the thirties and forties that were being shown on television, and by pioneering double-feature horror movies released by American-International. While getting his career off the ground, he found work restoring and preserving old movies and moved Los Angeles in 1962. Sherman went to work for Hemisphere and was employed there when it turned out its last vampire movie,

The Blood Drinkers (1966). While in Los Angeles, he met Al Adamson, the son of a movie professional who had migrated from Australia.

With Adamson (who came to specialize in completing a film in a week) directing, Sherman began to turn out a series of cheapie sexploitation films, such as *Swinging Stewardesses*, and horror spectaculars, such as the infamous *Dracula vs. Frankenstein* (1969). The latter, an almost unwatchable film, featured a cast of horror stars that included Michael Rennie, Paul Naschy, and J. Carroll Naish and Lon Chaney, Jr., both of whom were making their last screen appearance.

One of I-I's secrets was advertising. They shifted funds from production and salaries into promoting their films in major markets; it was not unusual for a film's marketing budget to far exceed what it cost to make it. As Sherman put it, "It's a hard job making a picture with nothing and making it look like something." I-I also had no problem releasing films two or even three times, often under very different titles. The re-released films were often used to complete a double- or triple-feature that was headlined by a new

film. *Dracula vs. Frankenstein*, for example, was also released as *Blood of Frankenstein*, Satan's Bloody Freaks, and *Assignment Terror* (a fact which has confused vampire film fans ever since).

While I-I could never be described as specializing in vampire flicks, it did return to the genre from time to time. For instance, *Dracula vs. Frankenstein* was followed a year later by *Horror of the Blood Monsters*. At one point Adamson even took footage from one movie—*Lucifer's Woman*, a 1975 film directed by Paul Aratow—and used it to create an entirely different movie—*Doctor Dracula*—five years later.

One might think that I-I would fade into the past amid the wave of new independent companies in the 1990s, but that has not been the case. The home video market gave company new life. While I-I has ceased to produce new films, Sherman has formed his own company called Super Video and released his older movies for a new generation. Al Adamson passed away in 1995.

✝ END ✝

features a group of kids, and a kooky castle located in Transylvania. ♫♫

1995 90m/C [Just for Kids] **VHS** *JFK*

Killer Klowns from Outer Space

Aliens land on earth, dress up as clowns, put up a circus tent, and drink the blood of anyone foolish to wander by through a crazy straw. Their landing was seen by a couple parked in their car for a little bit of R&R. Seeing what appeared to be a meteor, they discovered a tent and decided to take a look inside. It seemed to be an ordinary tent but soon they find a body of one of the local residents in none too good a shape. They try to warn people, but its hard to make anyone believe them. Suspense, coupled with some dark comedy make this possibly unbelievable storyline tolerable. ♫♫

1988 (PG-13) 90m/C [Trans World Ent.] Grant Cramer, Suzanne Snyder, John Allen Nelson, Royal Dano, John Vernon, Peter Licassi, Michael Siegel; **D:** Stephen Chiodo; **W:** Charles Chiodo, Stephen Chiodo; **M:** John Massari. **VHS, Beta, LV** *MED, CDV*

Kingdom of the Vampire

In this low budget quickie, bad acting only emphasizes the blandness of the story. A 90-year-old vampire poses as Jeff, a young man (Matthew Jason Walsh) who works the late shift at the local liquor store. He lives at home with his mother Elizabeth (Cherie Patrey), a very hostile, possessive, and controlling person. She preys on local children and expects him to clean up her mess. Jeff is befriended by a young girl, Nina (Shannon Doyle). She eases his loneliness but incurs his mother's jealousy in the process. Meanwhile, the local sheriff (Tom Stephan) is investigating the disappearances of the children. Vampire family, cops, and girl in distress end up in the woods, but by that time the audience is sawing logs. ♫

1991 ?m/C Matthew Jason Walsh, Cherie Patry, Shannon Doyle, Tom Stephan; **D:** J.R. Bookwalter.

The Kiss

A mysterious aunt visits her teenage niece in New York and tries to apprentice her to the family business of sorcery, demon possession and murder. Aunt Felicity's kiss might lead you to some appreciation of all that harmless but annoying affection from your own aunts. Pretty ordinary entry in the "possession-by-disgusting-creature" genre ♫♫

1988 (R) 98m/C [Tri-Star Pictures] **Joanna Pacula**, Pamela Collyer, Peter Dvorsky, Meredith Salenger, Mimi Kuzyk, Nicholas Kilbertus, Jan Rubes; **D:** Pen Densham; **W:** Tom Ropelewski. **VHS, Beta, LV** *COL, IME*

Kiss Me Quick!

A spoof, in part on Peter Sellers' *Dr. Strangelove, or How I Learned to Stop Worrying and Love the Bomb*, it was even released at one point under the title *Dr. Breedlove, or How I Learned to Stop Worrying and Love*. Sterilox, an alien from an all-male planet visits earth in hopes of finding a mate. He encounters a mad earth scientist who has been cloning monsters, including Dracula, and has been experimenting on the creation of females. This very forgettable, low-budget flick is often mistakenly listed as having been directed by famed soft-porn producer Russ Meyer. **AKA:** Dr. Breedlove, or How I Learned to Stop Worrying and Love. ♫

1964 ?m/C [Fantasy Films, G & S Films] Jackie De-Witt, Althea Currier, Frank Coe; **D:** Peter Perry, Max Gardens.

Kiss of the Vampire

With Christopher Lee still on his hiatus from playing Dracula, Hammer for a second time turned to a reputed disciple of the Count, Dr. Ravna (Noel Williams) to be the villain. The

VIDEOHOUND SALUTES: ELVIRA

While she's really a witch and not a vampire, Elvira is every bit a vamp. In 1981, after all of the other horror movie hosts had come and gone and were remembered only in the pages of horror movie magazines, Elvira was just getting started. At that time, she began hosting Movie Macabre on KHJ-TV in Los Angeles. Her rise to near-instant stardom was confirmed when she made her first appearance on *The Tonight Show* with Johnny Carson the next year.

Elvira is the stage name assumed by comic actress Cassandra Peterson, who is a one-woman marketing blitz. During her early days at KHJ, the station was unable to afford to give her her pay raises on schedule, so she accepted the rights to the Elvira character instead. That proved to be a very smart move. There has been no shortage of demand for Hollywood's reigning Mistress of the Night ever since that time. Today Elvira's image is everywhere. She has her own successful comic book, *Elvira Mistress of the Night,* from Claypool Comics; appears at the annual Halloween show at Knots Berry Farm; and heads up her own company, Queen B Productions. In the stores, you can purchase Elvira cosmetics, calendars, t-shirts, and games, and her slinky black dress is perennially among the best selling Halloween costumes. She has a very active fan club that can be reached at 14755 Ventura Blvd., 10710, Sherman Oaks, CA 91403.

Elvira is the latest in the long line of classic vamps on film, carrying on the tradition started by the legendary Theda Bara and carried on by any number of femme fatales, including Morticia Addams from *The Addams Family.* It doesn't matter if the vamp is a witch, a spider lady, or a vampire, as long as she is breathtakingly beautiful. Elvira's incarnation of the vamp includes a heaping dose of irreverence—she exaggerates her obvious physical assets while spewing forth all the bad puns and trashy little remarks we wished we had thought of.

Elvira assisted the comeback of low-grade horror movies on video by adding her pithy (and earthy) comments on the world's worst horror flicks in her successful video series "Thriller Theater." Her comments are merciless: from the hopeless plots, to the attempts at acting, to the highly predictable monster attacks, Elvira skewers them all.

In 1988, Elvira even made her own feature-length movie entitled *Elvira, Mistress of the Dark* (1988). The movie, which portrayed her almost as a comic book superhero, finally supplied her with a family history and gave her fans a full 90-minutes of her one-liners. Attention Elvira fans: There actually is a vampire in the movie, but can you be quick and observant enough to see it? The movie was completed on schedule and ready to be released to the world when New World Pictures, the distributor, went bankrupt. The movie was eventually released to a national audience on television. Peterson has authored the script for her next movie (possibly to be called *The Return of Elvira, Mistress of the Night*), but there's no telling when, or if, it will go into production. In the meantime, fans can pick up Elvira's first vampire novel, *Transylvania 90210.*

✝ END ✝

script drew on a very tried and true story line. A young couple (in this case honeymooning in Bavaria in 1910) run out of gas, and eventually find themselves guests in Ravna's castle. After enjoying an evening meal, they are invited to a masked ball the next evening. The ball is a cover for the gathering of the local vampire "cult," with the evening's entertainment scheduled to be the initiation of the young bride, Marianne (Jennifer Daniel), into the group. Marianne is drugged and her husband (Edward de Souza) tossed out of the castle. He eventually finds an ally in Dr. Zimmer (Clifford Evans), the local vampire expert. A horde of bats makes an appearance—in this case against the vampires. In spite of the worn-out plot, one of Hammer's finest. *AKA:* Kiss of Evil. 🦇🦇🦇

1962 88m/C *GB* [Anthony Hinds, Hammer Films, Universal Pictures] Clifford Evans, Noel Willman, Edward De Souza, Jennifer Daniel, Barry Warren, Jacqueline Wallis; *D:* Don Sharp; *W:* Anthony John Elder Hinds; *C:* Alan Hume; *M:* James Bernard. **VHS** *MCA*

Krvava Pani

Hey kids, what time is it? It's Countess Bathory time! Just what the kiddies need, a full-length animated version of the story of aristocratic blood bather Countess Elizabeth Bathory, who murdered hundreds of her servant girls and drained their blood in order to keep her youth and beauty. All it needs are some songs and a happy ending... 🦇🦇

1981 ?m/C [CFP/Koliba] *D:* Viktor Kubal.

Kung Fu Vampire Buster

The soul of our hero (Ricky Hui) is fused with the specter of a woman who committed suicide. Originally released as *New Mr. Vam-* *pire* to cash in on the popularity of the *Mr. Vampire* series in which Hui had starred. A sequel was released as *New Mr. Vampire II* and *One Eye-Brow Priest.* 🦇🦇🦇

19?? 90m/C Lu Fang, Wang Hsiao Feng, Chien Hsiao Hou. **VHS, Beta** *MGI*

Kuroneko

One of the unique elements of Japanese mythology is the frequency with which vampires appear as cats. In the twelfth century, two women, a soldier's mother (Nobuko Otowa) and her daughter-in-law (Kieako Taichi), await his return from the war. Instead, they encounter a group of Samurai warriors who have their way with the pair and then kill them. They arise, however, as vampires who regularly transform into cats and attack any Samurai warriors they meet. The effectiveness of their revenge eventually leads to the emergence of a noble champion (Kichiemon Nakamura) assigned to kill the vampires. That champion turns out to be the son-husband who had not made it home in time to prevent the original tragedy. When he discovers his situation, a complicated set of social rules comes into play. He cannot bring himself to kill his loved ones and thus, unable to fulfill the command of the feudal lord, should commit suicide. He works out an alternative arrangement with his wife, who agrees to return to her grave. The mother, however, doesn't like the arrangement, and destroys the couple. While not the first Japanese vampire film, *Kuroneko* was the first to have a measurable impact on Japanese audiences and became an inspiration for those which followed. 🦇🦇🦇

1968 ?m/C [Kindai Eiga Kyokai, Nihon Eiga Shinsha, Cinecenta] **Nobuko Otowa, Kwako Taichi,** Kichiemon Nakamura, Kei Sato; *D:* Kaneto Shindo.

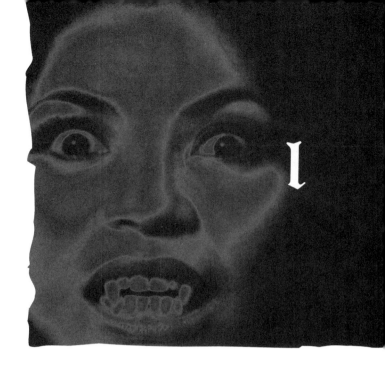

La Bonne Dame

A short fantasy feature starring French film star Valeska Gert as a fairy who, like Elizabeth Bathory, bathes in the blood of her victims. ⚟⚟

1966 ?m/B *FR* [SOFCA] **Valeska Gert**, Constantin Nepo, Germain Kerjean; **D:** Pierre Philippe.

La Maschera del Demonio

Inferior remake of the classic horror film *Black Sunday* (1960) which had made Barbara Steele the queen of horror pictures for a generation and launched Mario Bava's directing. In this remake, a group of vacationing skiers discovers the frozen body of the vampire/witch Anibas (Debora Kinski). Brought back to life, she begins to seek revenge and must deal with her contemporary descendent (also played by Kinski). Director

Lamberto Bava is the son, but not yet the filmmaking equal of, Mario Bava. ⚟⚟⚟

1990 ?m/C Debora Kinski, Michele (Michael) Soavi, Eva Grimaldi, Piero Nomi; **D:** Lamberto Bava.

La Reine des Vampires

After making his very successful short, *La Viol du Vampire*, director Jean Rollin was asked to expand it into a full-length feature by producer Sam Selsky. The resulting film has a disjointed plot tying together a set of rich photographic images and a large dose of nude females. The plot, such as it is, concerns two crazy blood-drinking sisters who believe that they have been cursed by a sword-welding vampire. ***AKA:*** Les Femmes Vampires; Queen of the Vampires; The Rape of the Vampire; Sex and the Vampire. ⚟⚟

1968 100m/C [Sam Selsky] Bernard Letrou, Solange Pradel, Ursule Pauly, Nicole Romain; **D:** Jacqueline Sieger, Jean Rollin.

Just the Facts, Bloodsucker: Vampire Documentaries

Beginning in the 1970s, some filmmakers began using the documentary format to try to tell the real story of vampires on film. Each of these efforts has value, in large part because each features interviews with different vampire experts and fans. Two recent videos readily available through you local outlet—*Vampire Interviews (1995)* and *Vampires* (1994)—do a tolerable job of entertaining while separating fact from fiction. Both include interesting interviews with people who claim to be vampires. The complete list:

Bram Stoker's Whitby (1994)

Count Dracula, the True Story (1979)

In Search of Dracula (1976)

Vampire Interviews (1995)

Vampires (1994)

Vincent Price's Dracula (1982)

Vlad Tepes (1978)

Winter with Dracula (1971)

La Vampire Nue

Erotic vampire artist Jean Rollin jumped to color for this second of his horror fantasies. In the sketchy plot, the son of a scientist (Oliver Martin), falls in love with a vampire upon whom a slightly mad father has been conducting experiments. The pair escape into the underground world of a vampire cult who conduct strange pagan, even Satanic, rituals. Eventually the young man grows weary of the scene and goes back home. The film is not known for its storyline as much as its bevy of nude women and its rich imagery and atmosphere. ***AKA:*** Nude Vampire; Naked Vampire. 🦇🦇

1969 ?m/C Caroline Cartier, Maurice Lemaitre, Olivier Martin, Ly Letrong; *D:* Jean Rollin.

Lady Dracula

An entertaining horror comedy if you can believe the basic premise. In 1876 Dracula bites a little girl who is subsequently staked and buried. A century later, the body is exhumed and the little girl has grown into a lovely young woman (Evelyn Kraft). She now must find five liters of blood per day (or night, as the case might be), and takes a job in a hospital where there is both a blood bank and plenty of patients. Unfortunately, her needs cause the death of a number of people, which leads to an investigation. The investigating officer (Brad Harris) discovers her secret, but then falls completely in love with her. 🦇🦇

1977 86m/C [Guenther Sturm, Kurt Kodal, TV 13, IFV Production] **Evelyn Kraft**, Christine Buchegger, Brad Harris, Theo Lingen, Eddi Arent, Walter Giller; *D:* Franz-Joseph Gottlieb; *W:* Redis Read; *C:* Ernst W. Kalinke.

The Lair of the White Worm

Scottish archaeologist uncovers a strange skull, and then a bizarre religion to go with it, and then a very big worm. An unusual look at the effects of Christianity and paganism on each other, colored with sexual innuendo and, of course, giant worms. A cross between a morality play and a horror film. Adapted from Bram Stoker's last writings, done while he was going mad from Bright's disease. Everything you'd expect from Russell. 🦇🦇🦇

1988 (R) 93m/C *GB* [Vestron Pictures] **Amanda Donohoe**, Sammi Davis, Catherine Oxenberg, Hugh Grant, Peter Capaldi, Stratford Johns, Paul Brooke, Christopher Gable; *D:* Ken Russell; *W:* Ken Russell; *M:* Stanislas Syrewicz. **VHS, Beta, LV** *VES, LIV, TPV*

Lake of Dracula

One of three loosely connected vampire films by director Yamamoto. Akiko (Midori Fujita) is a young artist who, along with her sister Natsuko, has moved near a lake (thus explaining the movie's title) where she relives some nightmares of her childhood. She eventually discovers that a nearby mansion is inhabited by a vampire (Mori Kishida), who proceeds to attack the young women. The film owes much to *Horror of Dracula* and the other Hammer vampire films, from which scenes are borrowed and reworked. *AKA:* Chi O Suu Me; Bloodthirsty Eyes; Dracula's Lust for Blood. 🩸🩸🩸

1971 ?m/C [Toho Company] **Mori Kishida**, Midori Fujita, Sanae Emi, Choei Takahashi; **D:** Michio Yamamoto.

The Last Man on Earth

In 1954 Richard Matheson wrote *I Am Legend,* one of the most important modern vampire novellas. The Italians were the first to bring it to the screen, with Vincent Price starring as the beleaguered, eponymous Robert Morgan. He is opposed by Ben Courtland, the chief vampire in a world where a plague has turned almost all of humankind into vampires. Most of the action revolves around the hordes trying to get through the barricades Morgan has erected to protect himself and a women, Ruth, whom he has saved from vampirism with a transfusion. Read the book, then see the movie. An American remake, stripped of its vampiric content, was released in 1971 as *The Omega Man. AKA:* L'Ultimo Uomo Della Terra. 🩸🩸🩸

1964 86m/B *IT* [Robert L. Lippert Productions, American International Pictures (A.I.P.)] Vincent Price, Franca Bettoya, Giacomo "Jack" Rossi-Stuart, Emma Danieli; **D:** Ubaldo Ragona, Sidney Salkow. **VHS** *SNC, MRV*

Le Frisson des Vampires

Third vampire film by prolific vampire film director Jean Rollin followed quickly on the heels of the unexpectedly successful flicks *Le Voil de Vampire* and *La Vampire Nue.* Vampire leader Isolde has a mission: to expand and perpetuate her species. In this endeavor, she first attacks two brothers who are would-be vampire hunters. She then engages in a rather erotic and violent scene at a medieval castle, into which walks a young couple on their honeymoon. Faster paced than most of Rollin's offerings, but still representative of his attempts to create highly atmospheric cinematic poetry. *AKA: Sex and the Vampire, Terror of the Vampires, Shudder of the Vampire,* and *The Vampire's Thrill.* 🩸🩸🩸

1970 ?m/C *FR* [Production Films Modernes] **Dominique**, Jean Durand, Sandra Julien, Nicole Nancel; **D:** Jean Rollin.

Le Nosferat ou les Eaux Glacees du Calcul Egoiste

Directors have occasionally attempted to use the vampire film as a vehicle for social comment and political satire. In this 1970s diatribe against fascism, a vampire terrorizes prostitutes in a misguided crusade to purify society. Quenching his own lust while interacting with the women of the street, he spouts Nazi speeches and the confessions of crimes, thus uniting vampirism and murder with Nazism. The film, originally shot on 16mm film, was based on the director's play. It raised questions of the appropriateness of using the vampire myth for political ends and the sophistication of director Rabinowicz's politics. 🩸🩸

1974 100m/C [Les Films du Groupe de Chambre] Veronique Peynet, Maite Nahyr, Martine Bertrand, Guy Pion, Quentin Milo; **D:** Maurice Rabinowicz; **W:** Maurice Rabinowicz; **C:** Jean-Jacques Mathy.

> "Don't be afraid. I'm going to give you the choice I never had. I've drained you to the point of death. If I leave you here you die. Or you can be young always, friend, as we are now. But you must tell me, will you come or not?"
>
> —Lestat (Tom Cruise) in *Interview with a Vampire* (1994).

Le Vampire du Dusseldorf

The fourth cinematic version of the story of Peter Kürten, the serial killer with vampiric habits. In early screen versions, the setting of the story had been changed, usually to Berlin, to protect sensitivities in Dusseldorf (where Kurten had committed most of his crimes). As time passed, and the immediate horror faded from memory, it became acceptable to set the account in the city of its origin. Abused as a child, Kurten first killed during his juvenile years. It was in 1929-30 that he went on his famous killing spree, which included men, women, and children. He fooled police for many months by continually changing his methods. 🎬

1964 86m/C [Rome-Paris Film] **Robert Hossein**, Marie-France Risier, Roger Dutoit, Annie Andersson, Paloma Valdes; *D:* Robert Hossein; *W:* Claude Desailly, George Tabet, Andre Tabet; *C:* Alain Levent.

Le Viol du Vampire

La Viol du Vampire launched Jean Rollin's career as the most acclaimed director of nudie vampire films. He was asked to create on almost no budget a short film released to accompany an American vampire film being shown in France. It proved far more popular than the American film and led to *La Viol du Vampire* being turned into a full-length film, *La Reine des Vampires*. He created *La Viol du Vampire* using a set of amateur actors, some of whom he has continued to work with repeatedly over his lifetime. As with his

later films, this first offering emphasized imagery over plot and atmosphere over character development. 🎬🎬

1967 100m/C [ABC Films] Bernard Letrou, Solange Pradel, Ursula Pauly, Nicole Romain; **D:** Jean Rollin; **C:** Guy Leblond, Antoine Harispe; **M:** Yvon Geraud, Francois Tusques.

The Leech Woman

While in Africa, an older woman (Coleen Gray) is able to restore her youth through a mysterious tribal ritual. The catch is that the ritual requires her to become a serial killer to obtain the pineal gland of young males. Like Elizabeth Bathory, she is quite willing (and for a while quite able). Not a vampire film in the strict sense, but close enough to the Bathory story to qualify. 🎬🎬

1959 77m/B [Joe Gershenson, Universal] Coleen Gray, Grant Williams, Gloria Talbot, Phillip Terry; **D:** Edward Dein; **W:** David Duncan. **VHS** *MCA*

Legacy of Satan

Independent horror film centered on a group of satanic vampires led by Dr. Muldavo (John Francis). A young woman, Maya (Lisa Christian), is drawn into the group's strange rites, which culminate in her being transformed into a monstrous corpse. It appears that this rather dull film was originally enlivened with several sex scenes that have been cut from the only surviving copies. Producer/director Damiano is best known for his porn classic, *The Devil in Miss Jones.* 🎬

1973 68m/C [Damiano Films] **Lisa Christian, John Francis,** Paul Berry, Christ Helm, Deborah Horlen; **D:** Gerard Damiano.

The Legend of Blood Castle

A movie based upon the Elizabeth Bathory legend. In this tale, a descendent of Countess Bathory continues her ancestor's habit of bathing in blood in order to retain her youth. Her vampire husband assists her by capturing the needed victims, all young, virginal females. **AKA:** The Female Butcher; Blood Ceremony; Ceremonia Sangrienta. 🎬🎬

1972 (R) 87m/C *IT SP* [Film Ventures International] Lucia Bose, Ewa Aulin; **D:** Jorge Grau. **VHS, Beta** *NO*

Legend of Eight Samurai

An ancient Japanese princess hires eight samurai, all accomplished in the martial arts, to destroy the vampire-witch who rules over her clan. The vampire stays young by bathing in blood in this fantasy adventure loosely based on the Elizabeth Bathory legend. 🎬🎬

1984 130m/C [Toei] **VHS, Beta** *PSM*

Lemora, Lady Dracula

Released under a variety of names since it first debuted in 1973, *Lemora* follows the adventures of the youthful Lila Lee (Cheryl Smith), the daughter of a gangster who has been taken in by a minister. While under the minister's care, Lila takes center stage at his church because of her singing talent. One of the people who's eye she catches is Lemora, the leader of a vampire coven who sends Lila a message that her father is dying and that she should come quickly because he wants to have a last moment with his daughter to beg her forgiveness. She leaves her new home to journey to Astroth; along the way, a bus driver warns her about the town, telling her stories of the strange people who live there who have been changed by an "epidemic." It seems that some of them are pallid and have fangs, while others are covered in decaying flesh. Overcoming the problems of the trip, she finally reaches Lemora's home only to be locked in a stone shed, where she is taunted by a group of vampire children. Eventually she joins into

VIDEOHOUND SALUTES: TERENCE FISHER

As Dracula and Van Helsing in the Hammer Films' Dracula productions, Christopher Lee and Peter Cushing are immediately recognizable to fans. What those fans need to remember, however, is that Lee and Cushing were turned into international stars in large part due to the work of their director, Terence Fisher. Fisher placed a distinctive stamp on horror films that would forever influence the genre.

Fisher was born in 1904 in London. He spent time at sea as a young man in the late 1920s before getting a job at Shepherd's Film Studios, where he learned how to edit films. He finally got his first opportunity to direct in 1948 for the Rank Organization and then joined the upstart Hammer Films in 1952. By 1957, when he received the assignment to direct the first of the Hammer remakes of classic Universal horror films of the 1930s, he had directed more than twenty features, none of which were particularly notable. Starting with *The Curse of Frankenstein*, however, he directed a series of films that brought him international renown, at least among vampire fans.

Fisher's unique touch with the relatively new medium of Technicolor brought a level of excitement to horror films that immediately caught the audience's attention. Most notable was the fact that Fisher actually showed, in full color, the horrid acts committed by the villains and the flow of blood that followed. His use of blood, which was prominent, can be directly tied to more recent splatter films. His colleagues immediately noticed the balanced editing patterns of his films, which translated to the audience level as coherent story lines and loose ends in the plot. Censors appreciated the clear moral vision evident in his films—good and evil were clearly marked, and the final victory always went to the former. As Fisher's work matured, however, a certain ambiguity began to appear. In later films, he began to communicate the message that, good does not always triumph. This was a powerful message for moviegoers, who had been comforted by his earlier resolution of conflict.

While Fisher directed more than a dozen films for Hammer, the epitome of his work can be seen in the vampire trilogy, *The Horror of Dracula* (1957), *The Brides of Dracula* (1960), and *Dracula Prince of Darkness* (1965). *The Horror of Dracula*, a remake of Stoker's novel (with appropriate liberties), put Hammer on the map. In between these career peaks,

he worked on other important horror films such as *The Mummy* (1959), *The Curse of the Werewolf* (1961), and the *Phantom of the Opera* (1962).

Fisher seemed to thrive in the atmosphere of creative teamwork that flourished at Hammer, and in return, his films earned the studio an excellent reputation. It should be noted that once Fisher and his associates (such as screenwriter Jimmy Sangster) created the Hammer style, succeeding directors at the studio followed it, though not always as successfully. In addition, when Fisher worked outside of Hammer, his work suffered. In fact, his last vampire film, *The Horror of It All*, which he made for 20th Century Fox in America, is little more than a cinematic disaster.

Fisher slowed his pace in the late 1960s, and after one last film at the beginning of '70s, retired and deservedly rested on his laurels. He had created a body of work that set the standard for horror directors around the world. He had lifted the horror genre, so despised by many in mainline cinematic productions, to new heights and set the direction of its development for a decade.

† END †

the blood drinking cult. Some have dismissed Lemora as a slow-paced irrelevant movie, others have seen the attempt to use the vampire theme to open up issues of child abuse and the sexual awakening of Lila the young girl after whom all the adults, from the preacher to Lemora, lust. **AKA:** The Lady Dracula; The Legendary Curse of Lemora *Lemora, Lemora, A Child's Tale of the Supernatural, The Lady Dracula, Blood Kiss.* 𝄽

1973 (PG) 80m/C [Robert Fern, Media Cinema] Leslie Gilb, Cheryl "Rainbeaux" Smith, William Whitton, Steve Johnson, Monty Pyke, Maxine Ballantyne, Parker West, Richard Blackburn; **D:** Richard Blackburn. **VHS** *FRG*

Leonor

Retelling of a medieval fairy tale as told by Ludwig Tieck (and popularized in the nineteenth century) of a knight obsessed with his prematurely deceased wife. In this version the knight (Michel Piccoli) makes a deal with the Devil. His wife (Liv Ullman) comes back as agreed, but she is a vampire who brings a plague with her. You have to read the fine print in these deals. 𝄽𝄽

1975 90m/C *FR SP IT* [France] Liv Ullmann, Michel Piccoli, Ornella Muti; **D:** Juan Bunuel; **M:** Ennio Morricone. **VHS, Beta** *FOX*

Les Charlots contre Dracula

In this French farce, Dracula's son, Dracounet, lays plans to become a vampire like his famous father. Crucial to achieving his goal is locating a woman similar to his mother who can give him a secret potion to make the transformation. 𝄽𝄽

1980 ?m/C *FR* [Planfilm/Belfast Productions, Stephan Films, Films de la Tour] Amelle Prevost, Andreas Voutsinas, Gerard Jugnot, Vincent Martin; **D:** Jean-Pierre Desagnat.

Lesbian Vampires
The Heiress of Dracula

Spanish horror director Jesus Franco drew on multiple sources (including Sheridan Le Fanu's "Carmilla," Bram Stoker's "Dracula's Guest," and the story of Countess Elizabeth Bathory) for this adventure into his world of pornographic fantasy. Nadina (played by Soledad Miranda) is a descendent of Count Dracula. She lives isolated from society on an island, but is able to lure young women to her home where she kills them and bathes in their blood. However, she makes the mistake of falling in love with one of her victims who turns on Nadina and kills her. The superficial plot seems to have been concocted as simply a rationale for the series of scenes of sex and violence. Two versions were created, The more explicit version in which credit for direction was given under a pseudonym and which intended for initial release in Germany included very explicit scenes of lesbian sex and sadomasochism. The more tame version designed for Spanish audiences tended to imply more than was shown. **AKA:** Vampyros Lesbos Die Erbin des Dracula; Lesbian Vampires; El Signo del Vampiro; The Heritage of Dracula; The Sign of the Vampire; The Strange Adventures of Jonathan Harker. 𝄽𝄽

1971 92m/C [Fenix] **Soledad Miranda**, Dennis Price, Ewa Stroemberg, Paul Mueller; **D:** Jess (Jesus) Franco; **W:** Jess (Jesus) Franco, Jaime Chavarri; **C:** Manuel Merino; **M:** Mannfred Hubler.

Let's Scare
Jessica to Death

Better-than-its-parts debut by director John Hancock, who later directed *Bang the Drum Slowly* and *Weeds*. Jessica (Zohra Lambert) comes home to a Connecticut farmhouse after her stay in a mental hospital. But she, her husband, and a family friend discover a strange woman living in the new homestead.

"Do you know how few vampires have the stamina for immortality? How quickly they perish of their own will. The world changes, we do not: there in lies the irony that finally kills us."

—Armand (Antonio Bandaras) in *Interview with a Vampire* (1994).

The unexpected tenant is later revealed to be a vampire, and Jessica notices more of the undead strolling around town. Problem: no one believes the crazy lady. Maybe she's having another breakdown. Hancock shows how to get the most out of a low budget, inadequate script, and less than stellar cast. 🎵🎵

1971 (PG) 89m/C [Charles B. Moss, Jr., Paramount Pictures] Zohra Lampert, Barton Heyman, Kevin J. O'Connor, Gretchen Corbett, Alan Manson; **D:** John Hancock. **VHS, Beta** *PAR*

Lifeforce

A group of astronauts from England and the United States examining Halley's Comet find what appears to be an old abandoned space craft sitting in the corona. The crew investigates the craft, which turns out to be inhabited by giant bat-like creatures They also discover three humanoid bodies, one woman and two men. Brought on board, the three decimate the crew, except for the captain. The life-energy vampires make their way to earth, where they are initially confined to a London scientific facility before they escape to wreak havoc on the city. Exciting, fast-paced scifi effort is notable for its outstanding special effects and the strong direction by Tobe Hooper (who also directed *Salem's Lot*). Based on Colin Wilson's "The Space Vampires." 🎵🎵🎵

1985 (R) 100m/C [Cannon Group] Steve Railsback, Peter Firth, Frank Finlay, Patrick Stewart, Michael Gothard, Nicholas Ball, Aubrey Morris, Nancy Paul, Mathilda May, John Hallam; **D:** Tobe Hooper; **W:** Dan O'Bannon, Don Jakoby; **M:** Henry Mancini, Michael Kamen. **VHS, Beta, LV** *MGM, LIV, VES*

Little Shop of Horrors

A typical Roger Corman low-budget quickie now seen as an innovative black comedy classic. Corman and associates outlined the movie in a week and shot it in two days. Who cares, it was good entertainment. Loser Seymour works in a small flower shop where he discovers a carnivorous plant that survives on human blood. He names it after his girlfriend Audrey (some relationship issues there?), then discovers that Audrey can talk; after awakening each day at sunset, it demands its sustenance by shouting "Feed me!" At first the powerless Seymour identifies with the plant, and even commits several murders to supply it with food. But the plant grows to monstrous proportions, and Seymour must show his moral fiber. Jack Nicholson, a Corman discovery, makes a cameo appearance as Wilbur Force, a masochist who visits a sadistic dentist. Remade as *Please Don't Eat My Mother* (1972) and then turned into a very successful off-broadway musical which was released on film in 1986. 🎵🎵🎵

1960 70m/B [Roger Corman, Filmgroup] Jackie Joseph, Jonathan Haze, Mel Welles, Jack Nicholson, Dick Miller; **D:** Roger Corman. **VHS, Beta, LV** *CNG, MRV, NOS*

Little Shop of Horrors

A quarter of a century after the original 1960 movie, Roger Corman's film was transformed into a successful off-Broadway musical. During a solar eclipse, the nerdish Seymour (Rick Moranis) purchases a plant for the flower shop where he is employed. As the plant, which he named Audrey after his girlfriend, grows far beyond what he had planned, he learns that the plant is intelligent, can talk, and demands blood to sustain it. The plant also becomes somewhat of a public attraction, bringing people into the shop. Seymour begins to search out "deserving" victims. As the number of victims mount, the dark comedy, along with such songs as "Mean Green Mother from Outer Space," keeps the mood light and campy. 🎵🎵🎵

1986 (PG-13) 94m/C [Warner Brothers] Rick Moranis, Ellen Greene, Vincent Gardenia, Steve Martin,

Director Terence Fisher helmed many of Hammer Films' classic vampire movies.

The Lost Boys:
The Beavis
and Butthead
of vampires.

James Belushi, Christopher Guest, Bill Murray, John Candy; **D:** Frank Oz; **M:** Miles Goodman, Howard Ashman. Nominations: Academy Awards '86: Best Song ("Mean Green Mother from Outer Space"). **VHS, Beta, LV** *WAR, HMV, MVD*

The Living Dead Girl

After several years away from vampire films, director Rollin returned to the genre with a story of a dead woman (Francoise Blanchard) resurrected by a chemical waste spillage. She encounters a friend who assists her in locating victims for her growing thirst for blood. As the need rapidly increases, the vampire soon turns and attacks her friend. As with all of Rollin's films, atmosphere and aesthetic cinematic values take priority over storyline and character development. Personal tastes will determine if that's good or bad. **AKA:** La Morte Vivante. 🎜🎜🎜

1982 98m/C [Les Films ABC, Films Aleria, Films Du Yaka, Sam Seisky] **Francois Blanchard**, Marina Pierro, Mike Marshall, Carina Barone; **D:** Jean Marie Rollin; **C:** Max Monteillet; **M:** Philippe D'Aram.

Living Skeleton

Interesting tale of two men (Masumi Okada and Nobuo Kaneko) who murder the crew of a ship to steal its cargo of gold. Unbeknownst to them, the ship's doctor (Akira Nishamura), survives their attack and lives off of the bodies of the crew as the ship drifts. Later, the sister of one of the victims (Kikko Matsuoka) lures the two thieves back on board. They encounter the doctor, who has been transformed into a vampire creature. Together, the vampire and girl exact their revenge. Retribution comes in many forms. **AKA:** Kyuketsu Dukorosen. 🎜🎜

1968 ?m/C [Shochiku Company] **Akira Nishimura**, **Akira Nishimura**, Masumi Okada, Nobuo Kaneko, Kikko Matsuoka, Masumi Okada, Nobuo Kaneko, Kikko Matsuoka; **M:** N. Nishiyama.

Los Vampiros de Coyoacan

After several years away from vampire films, German Robles returns as a vampire battling

those stalwart merchants of justice, the masked wrestlers. 🗡️🗡️

1973 87m/C MX [Azteca, Madera] **German Robles**, Sasha Montenegro, Mil Maschras; **D:** Arturo Martinez. *MAD*

The Lost Boys

One of the most successful of the several attempts to break away from both the aristocratic European vampire and the Hammer gothic tradition, *The Lost Boys* is set in the teen culture of the fictional modern-day community of Santa Clara, California. Oscar-winner Dianne Wiest plays a recently divorced mother attempting to make a new life for herself and her two sons Michael (Jason Patric) and Sam (Corey Haim). Mom finds a new love in the boss of the video store where she is employed. Michael takes up with a sweet young thing who, unbeknownst to him, is a vampire-in-training. Sam makes friends with two knowledgeable locals, the Frog brothers, who warn him of the vampires in town. David (Kiefer Sutherland) heads the group of teenage toughs for whom the film is named, all vampires. As Michael is slowly sucked into the vampire world, Sam and the Frogs unite to fight the bloodsuckers. They come to believe that Mom's beau is the real secret leader of the Lost Boys and set out to prove it. Critics panned it (for, among other things, copying scenes from *Salem's Lot*), but the younger crowd (who make up the largest segment of horror film audiences) responded to it. It has stood the test of time and is now thought of as one of the outstanding efforts of the decade. 🗡️🗡️🗡️🗡️

1987 (R) 97m/C [Warner Brothers] **Kiefer Sutherland, Edward Herrmann**, Jason Patric, Corey Haim, Jami Gertz, Dianne Wiest, Corey Feldman, Barnard Hughes, Billy Wirth; **D:** Joel Schumacher; **W:** Jeffrey Boam; **M:** Thomas Newman. **VHS, Beta, LV, 8mm** *WAR, FUS*

The Lost Platoon

This low-budget vampire/war movie begins when a war correspondent (William Knight)

uncovers a group of four soldiers who are actually vampires. The group has followed the world's wars through the centuries, always finding a fresh source of blood—one of the group (Hancock, played by David Parry) may even be Dracula. This interesting concept—vampires living off the carnage of war—has been explored in several recent vampire novels 🗡️🗡️

1989 (R) 120m/C [Kimberley Casey] **David Parry**, William Knight, Sean Heyman; **D:** David A. Prior. **VHS, Beta, LV** *AIP*

Love After Death

In this sixties adult movie, a vampire is buried alive, but digs his way out of the grave to seek revenge for the unneighborly actions of those who tried to kill him. *AKA:* De Vampier van New York; Le Vampire de New York; The Vampire of New York. 🗡️🗡️

1969 ?m/C **D:** Glauco del Mar.

Love at First Bite

In what is generally recognized as the best of the vampire comedies, suntanned Hamilton masterfully satirizes the 1931 Lugosi *Dracula* while bringing the obsolete Count into Ceaucescu's Romania at the end of the 1970s (1979 was a blockbuster year for vampire movies). Mixing one liners ("Children of the night shut up!") with a situation comedy, the story begins as the Count is kicked out of his ancestral castle by the unfeeling Communist government. So, along with faithful assistant Renfield (Arte Johnson), he travels to New York to find Cindy Sondheim (Susan Saint James), the woman he decides will end his centuries of loneliness. While wooing her, he must contend with her psychiatrist boyfriend, a descendent of Van Helsing, Dr. Jeffrey Rosenberg (Richard Benjamin). The modern Van Helsing is more nuisance that threat and

> "If I'm alive, what am I doing here? On the other hand, if I'm dead, why do I have to wee-wee?"
>
> —A self-reflective Dracula (John Carradine) in *Las Vampiras* (1967).

1979 (PG) 93m/C [American International Pictures (A.I.P.)] **George Hamilton**, Susan St. James, Richard Benjamin, Dick Shawn, Arte Johnson, Sherman Hemsley, Isabel Sanford; **D:** Stan Dragoti; **M:** Charles Bernstein. **VHS, Beta, LV** *ORI, WAR*

Love Vampire Style

Because of his sexual stamina, a postman (Patrick Jordan) faces the jealousy of a psychiatrist in this early sexploitation movie. Women seem to prefer the postman's ministrations to any counseling provided by the shrink. In his frustration, the psychiatrist grows fangs. Hmm, not too Freudian. *AKA:* Beiss Mich, Leibling; Bite Me, Darling. 🗡🗡

1970 ?m/C Patrick Jordan, Eva Renzi, Amadeus August; **D:** Helmut Foernbacher.

The Loves of Irina

Spanish producer Jesus Franco, with international financing, directed this tale of a mute descendent of Carmilla Karnstein (the female vampire featured in Sheridan Le Fanu's classic story "Carmilla") who kills her lovers by biting them on their genitals. This destructive behavior inevitably leads to a tragic ending. Using a mute lead character meant that the film could easily be dubbed into various languages. The original version of the film, released for the adult erotic market, was edited in different ways and issued under a variety of names in an attempt to appeal to a variety of audiences. However, even the sex can't save this boring, slow-moving film. A softcore version currently circulates in American video stores as *Erotikill. AKA: La Comtesse Noire, Les Avaleuses, Jacula, Sicarius The Midnight Party, The Bare Breasted Countess, La Comtesse aux Siens Nus, Yacula, The Last Thrill.* 🗡

198? 95m/C [Foreign] Lina Romay, Monica Swin, Jack Taylor, Alice Arno; **D:** Jess (Jesus) Franco. **VHS, Beta** *MED*

"Look Renfield. I see my whole career passing before my eyes." Renfield (Arte Johnson) keeps Count Vlad (George Hamilton) company in *Love at First Sight.*

continually bungles his attempt to stop the Count from stealing Cindy. In between the laughs, the movie also makes a contribution to the evolving vampire myth. Sex and vampirism mix as Dracula draws his first blood during his seduction of Cindy in her bedroom. She initially misunderstands his bite as merely kinky sex. He then informs her that three bites will lead to her transformation. A Fotobook was also released. 🗡🗡🗡🗡

Lugosi the Forgotten King

This biographical documentary of the ups and downs of the life of Bela Lugosi includes some rare interviews and clips of the movies that framed his American cinematic career, *Dracula* (1931) and *Plan Nine from Outer Space* (1956). ♫♫♪

1985 ?m/C D: Mark S. Gilman, Dave Stuckey.

The Lurking Vampire

One of the more obscure vampire films. In a dream, a young boy opposes a vampire who attacks small children. German Robles portrays the vampire, but not his popular Nostradamus character. Based on a story by Cornell Woolrich, who wrote it under the name William Irish. *AKA:* El Vampiro Aechecha. ♫♫

1962 ?m/C German Robles, Abel Salazar, Nestor Zavarce, Blanca del Prado.

Lust for a Vampire

The second episode in the Hammer "Carmilla" trilogy features the reincarnation of Carmilla Karnstein (Yutte Stengaard) attending a girl's boarding school. She attacks the other students and then turns on the school master (Ralph Bates), an easy conquest. She finally goes after a traveling writer (Michael Johnson), who is more difficult but finally succumbs. Her real problem is the wrath of the irate townspeople, who object to the many incidents of vampirism. You'd think that the vampires would learn to be more discreet. While many liked the final product (and what's not to like about Stensgaard), even the most devoted Hammer fans rated *Lust for a Vampire,* along with *Legend of the Seven Golden Vampires,* as one of the worst of the Hammer bloodsucker epics. But even the worst from Hammer was better than most of what was being cranked out elsewhere. William Hughes wrote a novelized version, originally released as *To Love a Vampire.* *AKA:* To Love a Vampire. ♫♫♪

1971 (R) 95m/C *GB* [Hammer, EMI, Levitt-Pickman] Ralph Bates, Barbara Jefford, Suzanna Leigh, Michael Johnson, Yutte Stensgaard, Pippa Steele; **D:** Jimmy Sangster. **VHS, Beta, LV** *MLB*

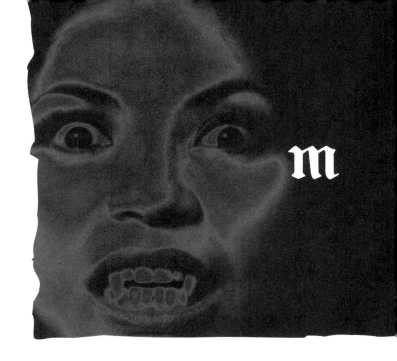

M

Peter Kürten, one of the first of what is now referred to as serial killers, was known as the "Vampire of Düsseldorf." While not a vampire in any traditional sense, he did have an obsession with blood and became sexually aroused when he saw spouting arteries. Peter Lorre made his screen debut as the Düsseldorf vampire in this early sound film by Fritz Lang. As the film opens, a serial killer is threatening Berlin (the setting of the fictionalized account having been shifted because the events that inspired it had occurred only a year before). The police have been frantic in their attempts to find the perpetrator, and their efforts have interfered with and angered the criminal underground. The murderer is introduced just before he kills his next victim, a young girl, after which he is seen humming Tchaikovsky's "Dance of the Sugar Plum Fairies," the tune which signals his deadly acts. The police and the criminal community are both searching for him, and the criminals find him first. The first to locate him marks him with the letter "M." Captured by the criminals, he is put on trial by a kangaroo court, whose proceedings raise important questions about claims of insanity and the legitimacy of capital punishment. This haunting film, one of the classics of the decade, made Lorre a star. Available on video in German with English subtitles, it was remade in 1964 as *Le Vampire de Düsseldorf* and was recently the subject of a four-part graphic novel. 🗡🗡🗡🗡

1931 99m/B *GE* [Nero] **Peter Lorre**, Ellen Widmann, Inge Landgut, Gustav Grundgens; **D:** Fritz Lang; **W:** Fritz Lang. National Board of Review Awards '33: 10 Best Films of the Year. **VHS, Beta, LV, 8mm** *SNC, NOS, HHT*

M

David Wayne portrays Peter Kürten, the so-called Vampire of Dusseldorf, a serial killer who operated in Germany in 1929-30 and drank the blood of many of his victims. The plot follows the storyline of the original thriller from Fritz Lang. 🗡🗡🗡

VIDEOHOUND SALUTES: GERMAN ROBLES, MEXICO'S BELA LUGOSI

German Robles arrived in Mexico from Spain in 1946, and in the 50 years that have followed, he has carved out one of the most memorable careers in Mexican cinema. During that time, Robles managed to create not one, but two, screen vampires of all-time. From his humble beginnings reading poetry in nightclubs, Robles went on to become one of the biggest stars in the vampire film world.

His first great vampire role was that of the suave, debonair, Count Karol Lavud, who arose from his coffin formally dressed in a tuxedo complete with high-collared opera cape. Mexico's film industry, which managed to survive World War II practically intact, began churning out horror films in the 1950s, and Robles was at the center of it all. His Count Lavud character was invented by director Fernando Mendez and screenwriter Ramon Obon, who wanted to create a Lugosi-like vampire that had some important differences from the traditional screen vampire. Like Lugosi's Dracula, Count Lavud had royal roots—he was a Hungarian who had at some point moved to Mexico. However, he was younger and much more handsome. Count Lavud, while building on the image of Dracula perpetuated by Lugosi, Lon Chaney, and John Carradine, was the first major vampire character who used his physical attractiveness to assist in the hypnotic seduction of his female victims.

Released a year prior to Christopher Lee's Horror of Dracula, El Vampiro (The Vampire, 1957) was Robles first lead role and first film as Lavud. It had a successful international distribution in various languages and was more directly the model for the image Lee would develop and immortalize than was Lugosi. El Vampiro was quickly followed by The Vampire's Coffin, also released in 1957.

The second major vampire role that Robles portrayed came a few years later when he played the vampire Nostradamus, who was not to be confused with the medieval French prophet. The story of Nostradamus was originally told in the form of 12, 25-minute episodes of a serial in which the vampire attempted to build a vampire cult. Later the episodes were reassembled into four feature-length movies released during 1959 and 1960—The Curse of Nostradamus, The Blood of Nostradamus, Nostradamus and the Destroyer of Monsters, and Nostradamus and the Genie of Darkness.

The still active Robles has appeared in almost a hundred movies and many plays in Mexico, where he is still a prominent star. However, with all due credit for the many parts he has portrayed in an outstanding career, his immortality still rests upon those few years when he bit young damsels and sucked his way into the hearts of horror fans.

✝ END ✝

1951 ?m/B **David Wayne**, Howard da Silva, Luther Adler, Karen Morley.

The Macabre Mark

Obscure Mexican production about vampire children. **AKA:** La Huella Macabra. 🗡

1962 ?m/B [Azteca] Guillermo Murray, Rosa Carmina, Carmen Molina, Jaime Fernandez.

The Macabre Trunk

Using a storyline that would later be adopted by such movies as *Atom Age Vampire*, *The Macabre Trunk* relates the plight of Dr. del Vialle (Ramon Pereda), who kills young women with a high purpose in mind. He uses the blood he obtains to keep his wife alive. Originally released in Spanish as *El Baul Macabro*. René Cardona, who had a co-starring role in this film, went on to direct a number of vampire films. **AKA:** El Baul Macabro. 🗡🗡

1936 ?m/B [Ezet] Rene Cardona Jr., Ramon Pereda, Manuel Noriega; **D:** Miguel Zacarias.

The Mad Love Life of a Hot Vampire

In this low-budget underground adult film, Dracula (Jim Parker), is surrounded by a family of female vampires who suck their needed blood from the nearest male organ. In the end the Count is killed as the light of the sun shines on his dark life. **Woof!**

1971 ?m/C **Jim Parker**, Jane Bond, Kim Kim.

Mad Monster Party

Frankenstein is feeling his age and had decided to retire as senior monster. He calls a convention of all of the monsters, including Dracula, to make his decision known and to designate a successor. An animated children's puppet film featuring the voices of such stars as Boris Karloff (as the Frankenstein Monster) and Phyllis Diller, as well as impressionists who mimic Bela Lugosi, Peter Lorre, James Stewart, and Charles Laughton. 🗡🗡🗡

1968 94m/C [Avco Embassy] **D:** Jules Bass; **V:** Boris Karloff, Ethel Ennis, Phyllis Diller. **VHS, Beta** COL

Madhouse

Vincent Price shows the range of his entertaining abilities in this story of aging movie star Paul Toomes, famous for his role as Dr. Death. Some years after his career is ended by the unfortunate death of his fiancée, a scriptwriter (Peter Cushing) offers him the opportunity to revive his role in a British television production. Once in England, however, he encounters a series of brutal murders that appear to copy the new script. Price sings the closing song (but no, we do not know where to purchase the soundtrack). 🗡🗡

1974 92m/C GB [Max J. Rosenberg, Milton Subotsky, Amicus Productions, American International Pictures (A.I.P.)] Vincent Price, Peter Cushing, Robert Quarry, Adrienne Corri, Natasha Pyne, Linda Hayden, Michael Parkinson; **D:** Jim Clark. **VHS, Beta** HBO

Magic Cop

The star of the *Mr. Vampire* series (Lam Ching Ying) continues his vampire fighting ways as a policeman who places his faith in traditional magical practices more than modern police techniques. His instincts serve him well in his latest case, which involves a living corpse that is controlled by a vampiress and sorceress (Michiko Nishiwaki). Aided by two young colleagues (who are really just interested in the older policeman's niece), he must fight an assortment of supernatural creatures before the climatic fight with the vampire. A better than average addition to the series, the version released in the

"One thing about living in Santa Clara I never could stomach was all of the damn vampires."

—Grandpa (Bernard Hughes) in *The Lost Boys* (1987).

VIDEOHOUND SALUTES: HAMMER FILMS

From the late 1950s until the mid-1970s, no studio was more associated with horror films in general and vampire films specifically than Hammer Films. Its lavish, full-color productions seemed to literally drip blood from the screen, so vivid were the scenes. The studio's vampire films were the most recognizable ever produced, and they turned Christopher Lee into a superstar.

Founded immediately after World War II, Hammer took the lead in rebuilding the British film industry. In 1957, Hammer ventured into horror for the first time with its version of the Frankenstein legend called *The Curse of Frankenstein*. That movie was successful enough to convince the studio to try another horror film, and in 1958, it released *Dracula* (better known by its American title, *Horror of Dracula*). It proved to be spectacularly successful, and over the next decade, Hammer turned out more than a dozen vampire movies using the Gothic settings that were still available in rural England at that time.

The *Horror of Dracula* was rather tame by contemporary standards, but it featured plenty of attractive young females who swooned at Dracula's deadly kiss. Moviegoers were quick to take notice and demanded more. Hammer continually tested the boundaries of censorship rules by making the vampire attacks ever more bloody and by increasing the amount of skin shown by its seemingly endless supply of beautiful starlets. While many of the films are now considered to be little better than average horror film fare, they were the best of their era. The Hammer films that featured both Lee and Peter Cushing are still considered to be among the best horror movies ever made.

In the early 1970s, Hammer was suffering from financial instability. The vampire had always been a stable money maker, so the studio jumped at the chance to mix its vampires with the martial arts films that had become popular in the Far East. The move proved to be the studio's undoing. With a deal for American distribution in hand, it gave the go

ahead for the first vampire kung-fu movie, *Dracula and the Seven Golden Vampires*. It was a pioneering effort, but like an earlier attempt to merge the vampire and the western genres, it just didn't work. The film was so bad that the American distributor withdrew from the project, leaving Hammer with a film but no audience. The company folded.

Hammer left an important legacy in the vampire film world, having turned on millions of fans to vampire flicks for the first time. Its movies were copied by directors from around the world for years. Even its last product, the ill-fated *Golden Vampires*, was a good idea that was poorly executed. Ten years after the failure of that movie, Hong Kong directors were inspired to develop a series of new vampire/martial arts movies, and this time they worked. Films such as *Mr. Vampire* and *Chinese Ghost Story* are good enough to compete with the best vampire movies from around the world.

✝ END ✝

West unfortunately suffers from hard to read English subtitles. *AKA:* Mr. Vampire. 🦴🦴🦴

1989 ?m/C Lam Ching-ying; *D:* Tang Wei.

The Magic Sword

Witch Sybil raised her foster son George in the forest and as he comes of age gives him a magic sword and the associated armor. In order to rescue a princess from the evil sorcerer Lodac (George Rathbone), he must overcome seven curses. Amid his various trials, George much deal with a vampiress played by Maila Nurmi in her persona as Vampira. A delightful children's adventure. *AKA: St. George and the 7 Curses; St. George and the Dragon.* 🦴🦴

1962 80m/C [United Artists] Basil Rathbone, Estelle Winwood, Gary Lockwood; *D:* Bert I. Gordon. **VHS, Beta** *MGM, MRV, VYY*

The Malibu Beach Vampires

A vampire movie for aficionados of pop political culture, the vampires turn out to be a group of sexy young women kept by three unscrupulous American leaders: Congressman Teri Upstart, Col. Ollie West, and the Rev. Timmy Fakker. Subtlety was obviously not a priority. The three men are unaware that the women, including infamous billboard lady Angelyne, with whom they are having their private affair, are really vampires and that they have injected each of their male benefactors with a truth serum. The rest of the film asks and answers the question, "Will these leaders finally come clean with the American public?" The bigger question, however, is "Will the audience care?" 🦴🦴

1991 (R) 90m/C [Peacock Films] Angelyne, Becky Le Beau, Joan Rudelstein, Marcus A. Frishman, Rod Sweitzer, Francis Creighton, Anet Anatelle, Yvette Buchanan, Cherie Romaors, Kelly Galindo; *D:* Francis Creighton. **VHS** *NO*

The Maltese Bippy

Fresh from their hit television show Rowan and Martin's Laugh-In, the comedy team of Dan Rowan and Dick Martin decided to make this comedy-horror movie. The plot centers around an old house on Long Island, where the pair find themselves in the midst of a monster mash. Dennis Weaver shows up as a vampire named Ravenwood and Martin gets turned into a werewolf. Not nearly as funny as the TV show, this flick was quickly forgotten. 🦴🦴

1969 ?m/C [Metro-Goldwyn-Mayer] **Dennis Weaver**, Dan Rowan, Dick Martin, Carol Lynley; *D:* Norman Panama.

Mama Dracula

A contemporary Elizabeth Bathory (Louise Fletcher) must periodically bathe in the blood of virgins, so she sends her twin vampire sons, Vlad and Lad (Marc-Henri Wajnberg and Alexander Wajnberg) to lure victims to her castle. One twin is a gay dress designer and the other is too shy to bite anyone. Among those unlucky enough to wind up at the castle is a young scientist trying to develop an artificial blood. Such blood could possibly free Bathory from her constant need to kill people. The opportunity to pursue this new possibility is thwarted by the arrival of vampire hunter Nancy Hawaii (Maria Schneider). Her plans to kill Bathory are momentarily detoured by the countess arguing her case. 🦴

1980 90m/C *FR* [UGC] Louise Fletcher, Bonnie Schneider, Maria Schneider, Marc-Henri Wajnberg, Alexander Wajnberg, Jess Hahn; *D:* Boris Szulzinger. **VHS** *TWE*

The Man in Half Moon Street

A 104 year old surgeon/mad doctor/vampire discovers a formula to prolong his life and

youth. The only problem is that he has to kill to obtain the main ingredient. He encounters a former colleague who recognizes him in his new life and confronts him. The surgeon confesses to his activities, which include the murder of someone every six years. The two begin to work on an alternative solution which doesn't require someone to die. However, the prescribed time passes and the surgeon kills a young medical student, creating a rift in the doctors' relationship. Originally taken from the play by Barré Lyndon, it was remade in 1959 by Hammer, with the vampiric elements deleted, as *The Man who Could Cheat Death* ♫♫

1944 ?m/B [Paramount Pictures] **Nils Asther**, Helen Walker, Paul Cavanagh, Reinhold Schuenzel, Edmund Brown; *D:* Ralph Murphy.

The Mark of Lilith

This low-budget half-hour short, shot on 16mm film by a collective of feminist directors, centers on a black lesbian filmmaker who is researching the myths of monstrous women. Her search leads to an encounter with the immortal Lillia (Susan Franklin), a bisexual vampire. They share an interest in horror films, political correctness, and the problems of patriarchal society, which leads Lillia to confide that she wants to dump her male vampire companion. Fun for a change of pace. ♫♫♫

1986 32m/C [Bruna Fionda] **VHS, Beta** *WMM*

Mark of the Vampire

One of Lugosi's best appearances as a vampire came not as Dracula but as the pseudo-vampire Count Mora. Director Tod Browning obviously loved this movie, which had originally been filmed as *London After Midnight,* a silent feature starring Lon Chaney. After the success of *Dracula,* however, both Browning and Lugosi found themselves at MGM where the former was free to complete a remake, with sound, of his original film. Lugosi brought along Carol Borland, with whom he had worked on stage. Sir Karell Borotyn (Holmes Herbert) and his daughter Irena (Elizabeth Allen) have moved into a castle in rural Czechoslovakia. Rumors suggest that Count Mora (Lugosi), the previous resident, had killed his daughter Luna (Borland) and then committed suicide. It is believed that they walk the castle grounds as the undead and would attack any new residents. Meanwhile, Irena is developing a serious relationship with Count Feodor Vincenty (Henry Wadsworth). After Borotyn is murdered and found with two wounds in his neck and his blood drained, Inspector Neumann (Lionel Atwill), Dr. Doskill (Donald Meek), and Baron von Zinden enter the picture, determined to solve the murder. They are joined by Prof. Zelen (Lionel Barrymore), a vampire hunter brought in to rid the castle of the vampire residents. The Inspector and Baron von Zinden sneak up to the castle at night and see Count Mora and his daughter. After the murderer has been caught, Count Mora and Luna are revealed to be actors hired to assist in forcing the real killer out into the open. Interestingly enough, Lugosi never speaks until the end of the film. *Mark of the Vampire* gets high marks as a horror flick until the very end. As a murder mystery, the elaborate plot unravels and loses believability. Browning (who shot the movie without revealing the ending to the actors) would not change the script even in the face of a threatened palace revolt instigated by the cast. All believed that it was a straight horror movie, and only discovered as the last scenes were filmed what Browning really intended. *AKA: Werewolf of Paris* and *The Vampire of Prague.* ♫♫♫

Mark of the Vampire: "Don't hate me because I'm ghoulish." Carol Borland strikes a pose.

"That boy gives me the willies." thinks Uncle Cuda (Lincoln Maazel) of his nephew *Martin*.

1935 61m/B [MGM] Lionel Barrymore, Bela Lugosi, Elizabeth Allan; *D:* Tod Browning; *C:* James Wong Howe. **VHS, Beta** *MGM, MLB*

Martin

Since World War II, vampire movies have explored the possibility that vampires might be living among us in the contemporary world. While most have kept the gothic characters, merely making superficial changes in the costumes and scenery, some have seriously attempted to reflect the rationalistic world and remove the superstition. Of the latter group, *Martin* stands out as the story of a psychopathic teenager (John Amplas) who kills and drinks the blood of his victims. The ambiguity of modern life is represented in his religious (and thoroughly Germanic) uncle Cuda who would rather lead his nephew to salvation than kill him. Meanwhile, Martin has come to believe that he is a descendent of Nosferatu, the character portrayed in Murnau's classic German vampire film. His blood thirst is likened to drug addiction, and he often resorts to the use of a hypodermic needle to acquire the needed venous fluid. In the face of his nephew's activity, Cuda retreats into tradition and fills his home with mirrors, garlic, and crucifixes. These, of course, have no effect on thoroughly modern Martin. However, a stake in the chest is just as effective now as in the seventeenth century. Director Romero showed what could be done on a low-budget film with talented acting and competent

production, and *Martin* has assumed an important position in the history of vampire cinema. A novelization, by George A. Romero and Susan Sparrow, is also available, but may be harder to find. 🗡🗡🗡🗡

1977 (R) 96m/C [Richard Rubinstein] John Amplas, Lincoln Maazel; **D:** George A. Romero; **W:** George A. Romero. **VHS, Beta, LV** *NO*

Mary, Mary, Bloody Mary

One of a series of Mexican vampire movies built around the aging John Carradine. A bisexual female vampire (Christina Ferrare) is caught between a mysterious figure who haunts her and the police who are pursuing her. The haunting figure cloaked in black is her vampire father (Carradine), attempting to destroy his daughter so she will not share his fate as a rotting, aging vampire. Her death would also end the family curse. This largely incoherent tale is far from Carradine's finest hour. 🗡🗡

1976 (R) 85m/C [Translor Productions] **Christina Ferrare**, **John Carradine**, David Young, Helena Rojo; **D:** Juan Lopez Moctezuma; **M:** Tom Bahler. **VHS, Beta** *NO*

Men of Action Meet the Women of Dracula

As the title implies, a group of tumblers/wrestlers are forced to do battle with a group of vampire women headed by no less a personage than Dracula. 🗡

1969 ?m/C Dante Varona, Eddie Torrente; **D:** Artemio Marquez.

Mickey's Gala Premier

In one of his earliest outings, Mickey Mouse dreams of attending the premiere of his new movie. During the festivities, he meets various cartoon caricatures, including Franken-stein's monster, Quasimoto, and Lugosi's Dracula, the original Universal movies being at the time still very much in the public consciousness. Dracula and his companions are viewed sitting in the audiences enjoying Mickey's antics on the screen. A seven-minute short. 🗡🗡🗡

1933 ?m/B [United Artists, Walt Disney Productions] **D:** Bert Gilbert.

The Midnight Hour

Three teenagers break into their town's historical museum and steal a ring, journal and costumes from the witchcraft exhibit. It's Halloween, so it seemed like a good idea at the time to go to the town's cemetery and perform a ritual to resurrect the vampire witch Lucinda (Shari Belefonte-Harper), an ancestor of one of the teens (also played by Belefonte-Harper). Once loose, she brings an assortment of ghouls, zombies, and vampires with her. Townspeople soon learn that the strange Halloween creatures are not their children in disguise. Standard made-for-TV fare with more musical numbers and attempts at humor than horror. For added atmosphere, disc jockey Wolfman Jack is heard spinning the platters in the background. 🗡🗡

1986 97m/C Shari Belafonte, LeVar Burton, Lee Montgomery, Dick Van Patten, Kevin McCarthy, Jonelle Allen, Peter DeLuise, Dedee Pfeiffer, Mark Blankfield; **D:** Jack Bender; **M:** Brad Fiedel. **VHS** *VMK*

Midnight Kiss

When a woman police detective investigates a mysterious series of deaths—women whose blood has been drained—she gets more than she bargains for. She's attacked by a vampire and is herself turned into a reluctant bloodsucker. Quick moving and some gross special effects. Also available in an unrated version. 🗡🗡🗡

The Women of Hammer

Everyone knows Christopher Lee, the world's most famous Dracula, and his nemesis, Peter Cushing as Van Helsing But just where would the pair have been if not for the many beautiful women who swooned into Dracula's arms and who breathlessly waited for Van Helsing to rescue them? The stable of sexy young females that Hammer Films used as both vampire and victim drew fans into the theaters every bit as much as the leading men.

It all began with the seductive Valerie Gaunt, who appeared at the beginning of *Horror of Dracula* (1957) as the "bride" of Dracula who attempted to seduce Jonathan Harker soon after his arrival at Castle Dracula. While each of the Hammer starlets had their fans, the first to rise above the crowd was undoubtedly Barbara Shelley, whom Dracula transformed from a frigid wallflower into the very embodiment of lust. Shelley had had her first encounter with a vampire in *Blood of the Vampire* while still with Universal Studios in 1965. She moved to Hammer later that same year and made *The Camp on Blood Island*. In one of the more memorable scenes from Hammer's *Dracula, Prince of Darkness*

(1965), a screaming Shelley was punished for her new (admittedly kinky) sexuality with a stake in the heart delivered by a group of male churchgoers. Her road to stardom took her through several Hammer horrors before her final and fatal coupling with Lee.

Veronica Carlson's, Lee's next co-star in *Dracula Has Risen from the Grave* (1968), has been touted as possessing the most desirable neck ever punctured by Dracula's fang. She made her mark in this fourth of the Hammer vampire movies as Maria, the primary object of Dracula's bloodlust. In vampirizing her, Lee stretched out the act of biting her neck, thereby transforming it into something resembling a seduction scene. As he seemed to make love to the ravishing blonde, she returned his advances with a willing surrender and waited expectantly for him to penetrate her exposed jugular.

By the end of the 1960s, Hammer had stretched the boundaries of British censorship regulations and was ready to expand its vampire cycle to feature female vampires, most notably Carmilla (from Sheridan Le Fanu's novella) and the very real historical figure Elizabeth Batho-

ry. Enter Ingrid Pitt to the Hammer roster. Having escaped from the Nazis as a child, Pitt grew up to become what one author has termed the very embodiment of pure sexuality. As Carmilla in *Lust of the Vampire* (1970), her drive for blood, especially that which flowed through the veins of young women, carried her to the bedroom of the lovely Laura (Pippa Steele). There she began the seduction of her naive hostess, who was just coming into her womanhood. Some of the forcefulness of Pitt's Carmilla was carried over to her portrayal of the aging Elizabeth Bathory, a woman totally obsessed with retaining her youth. Pitt effectively flipped between the old woman and the artificially rejuvenated young woman, who had an increasingly large need for fresh blood. Her most impressive scenes as the youthful *Countess Dracula* (1970) were too much for American censors, who trimmed them from the final cut. However, anyone who saw those scenes, in which she emerged from her blood bath dripping fresh, red blood, could never forget them.

Just like Lee, Hammer turned Pitt into such a big star that it was unable to afford her services. Thus, for the second Carmilla movie, *Lust of a Vampire* (1970), Hammer choose a young Danish actress named Yutte Stengaard for the lead role. One of Stengaard's admirers referred to her as the "cutest" vampire in Hammer history. She had moved to England during her late teen years and begun her professional career in modeling. By 1970, her total film experience consisted of a handful of bit parts in a string of forgotten movies. Then suddenly she was pulled from the Hammer stable to replace Pitt. Stengaard created a completely different persona for Carmilla in this, her only starring role. Saddled with a weak script, the inexperienced actress lost the assertive vitality of Pitt and remained the focus of attention only as she allowed the action to come to her. In the most memorable scene, Ralph Bates facilitated her resurrec-

tion, after which the camera found her slowly sitting up in the tomb with blood streaked across her unclad body. Lacking the forceful thrust of Pitt, she is remembered most for her aesthetic presence, a quiet sensuality that continually acted as a magnet, drawing the camera, the other actors, and eventually, the audience to her.

In Hammer's last Carmilla epic, *Twins of Evil* (1971), the victims upstage the vampire. The recently resurrected vampire (played by Katya Wyeth) affected every home in the community, even that of vampire hunter Gustav Weil (Peter Cushing). Eventually, her attempts to locate new victims led to Weil's niece Madeleine and her sister Mary, who were the twins for whom the film was named. Hammer didn't miss a trick

and used real-life twins Freida and Maria Geldhorn, who had begun their film career in sexploitation movies, in the roles of Madeleine and Mary. In the films standard nude scenes, the twins supplied the audience with twice as much skin for their money. Additionally, the Gelhorn girls were also seen as symbols of (albeit in an extreme form) trouble with a parental authority figure and the suffering which resulted from their powerlessness.

The number of Hammer women seems endless, and though most are known only to diehard fans, those fans continue to celebrate the ladies' brief cinema careers. The glamour they projected is as eternal as the celluloid fantasy that is the movie world.

✝ E N D ✝

FROM HONG KONG THEY COME

Once the Far East recovered from World War II, a thriving movie industry developed quickly. Vampire films, of course, could not be far behind. As early as 1957, an original (and now obscure) vampire movie appeared named *Vampire Love*. A few additional vampire films were made in the 1960s, but no large wave developed even after the popular full-color productions from Hammer Films were released worldwide.

Throughout the '60s, Hong Kong (the Hollywood of the Far East) was busy kicking its way onto the world market with martial arts movies. It was inevitable that someone would have the idea to put the two genres together, which was a tricky proposition. After all, vampire westerns had proved a disaster, while sci-fi vampires had been most entertaining. The end result turned out to be one of the most unusual films in vampire cinema, *Dracula and the Seven Golden Vampires* (1974). A joint project between the Shaw Brothers of Hong Kong and Hammer Films, the film met with chilly audience reception and bombed. In the wake of this disaster, Hammer soon went out of business.

However, the folks in Hong Kong still thought that vampires and mar-

tial arts had potential. The idea just needed some time to mature—ten years to be exact. In 1984 the first of a new breed of Hong Kong-produced vampire movies was released. *Dragon versus Vampire* brought together most of the elements that would become standard fare in Chinese vampire movies—the vampire, the damsel in distress, the martial arts hero, and the Taoist priest who possessed the knowledge to fight supernatural evil. The combination of kung-fu and supernatural power was needed to defeat the bloodsucking revenants. Only one more thing was needed—some kind of original character to provide an additional uniqueness to Hong Kong horror.

That unique character made its first appearance in 1985's *Mr. Vampire* in the form of the infamous "hopping vampire." *Mr. Vampire* would prove to be a landmark vampire movie. It not only introduced the strange, rigid vampires dressed in Ming Dynasty clothes who hopped up and down as if they were on pogo sticks, but it also started a tradition of building a Chinese perspective on vampires that drew on both Western movies and Chinese folklore. *Mr. Vampire* also introduced Lam Ching-Ying (the Asian Peter

Cushing) as the Taoist priest/vampire fighter with one eyebrow. Robed in yellow garb with a black hat, he used paper charms, magic mirrors, dog's blood, and a wooden sword to fight the vampires and the evil spirits who helped them. Usually accompanying Ching-Ying was a bungling student who had to be rescued from his own incompetence, a standard form of comic relief.

Mr. Vampire spawned three sequels and inspired many more kung-fu vampires features. They range from comedy to action, from romance to horror. Production values have steadily improved, and in the 1990s, the films have found distribution channels in the West. European and American vampire fans have known for some time about the *Mr. Vampire* movies, but they now have the opportunity to view some of the finer Hong Kong vampire films, such as the three entries in the *Chinese Ghost Story* series. Of course, with the good comes the bad, and fans can also check out such terrible films as *Robovampire*, which has been called Hong Kong's *Plan 9 from Outer Space*.

✝ END ✝

1993 **(R)** 85m/C [Manette Rosen, Marion Zola] Michelle Owens, Gregory A. Greer; **D:** Joel Bender; **W:** John Weidner, Ken Lamplugh. **VHS** *ACA*

Mrs. Amworth

Half-hour cinema version of the classic vampire story by E. F. Benson, produced as the pilot for a Canadian television series, *Classics Dark and Dangerous*. A strange sickness is spreading through an English village. Francis Urcombe (John Phillips) is sure that the source is Mrs. Amworth (Glynis Johns), seemingly a kindly, respectable lady and perfect hostess. He sets out to prove that she is really a vampire. ♫♫♫

1973 29m/C [Learning Corporation of America, William Deneen] Glynis Johns; **D:** Alvin Rakoff. **VHS, Beta** *LCA*

Mr. Vampire

In one of the most successful Hong King vampire movies, lead character Mr. Yan (Wong Ha) is going through the reburial ceremony of his deceased father. However, things go amok when the priest notices that the body has not decomposed; before the priest can act, the corpse rises from the dead as a vampire (Yuen Wah) and claims his son as a victim. The priest and his two bungling assistants are left with the task of tracking down and finally destroying the vampire. Fast-paced kung fu action, hopping zombies, and a psychic vampire ghost who attacks one of the priest's assistants add their color to the more memorable scenes—scenes that are often unintentionally funny to Western audiences. One of the must-see vampire videos from the East, it spawned three sequels. ♫♫♫

1986 99m/C *CH* Ricky Hui; **D:** LauÇKoon Wai. **VHS** *FCT*

Mr. Vampire II

In this second installment in the *Mr. Vampire* series, a group of archaeologists finds three well-preserved bodies, each with a piece of paper pasted to its forehead. As they will later learn, the paper is a spell that keeps the three (a man, a woman, and a child) from coming to life as vampires. When the paper on the child is accidentally removed, he goes searching for his parents, who also eventually come to life. The day is saved when a local herbalist comes to the rescue. ♫♫♫

1986 91m/C *CH* Ricky Hui; **D:** LauÇKoon Wai. **VHS** *FCT*

Mr. Vampire III

The third *Mr. Vampire* series moves the action back to the beginning of the twentieth century when a Taoist priest (Lam Ching Ying) must battle a demoness who leads an army of vampires. One subplot features a con man (comedian Richard Ng) who receives help from two nice vampires right in the middle of the battle between the priest and the demoness. ♫♫♫

1987 95m/C *CH* Ricky Hui; **D:** LauÇKoon Wai. **VHS** *FCT*

Mr. Vampire IV

Very inferior fourth entry in the popular series is missing most of the cast from the earlier films (especially Lam Ching Ying), and it shows. Two rival Taoist priests, who supposedly hold the secrets of fighting (and defeating) vampires, play a game of one-upmanship with each other. Soon they must face the real threat, a fierce vampire, and are suddenly forced to call upon their rusty powers to defeat it. ♫♫

1988 90m/C *CH* **D:** LauÇKoon Wai. **VHS** *FCT*

Mixed Up

A group of teens find themselves caught between a vampire and a Frankenstein-like monster. In the climax, the two monsters, for

VIDEOHOUND SALUTES: TOBE HOOPER

How would you feel if your first movie screening caused a riot? Well, if your name was Tobe Hooper and you had just witnessed the first screening of the independent horror film that you had slaved over, you'd be delighted. In 1973, Hooper unveiled his movie *The Texas Chain Saw Massacre* to an unsuspecting audience at a San Francisco theater. The audience, horrified by the tale of a madman who butchered teenagers, turned into a mob and demanded their money back from the theater manager, who refused to issue refunds. The film went on to be one of the top grossing films of the year, in spite of its being banned in Paris. Hooper followed his festival of gore with *Eaten Alive* (1976), in which Leatherface the chainsaw wielding madman was replaced by crocodiles.

In his prolific career, Hooper has directed two important and very different vampire movies: *'Salem's Lot* and *Lifeforce Salem's Lot*, a three-hour made-for-television movie, was a more traditional vampire tale, while *Lifeforce* featured an extraterrestrial psychic vampire.

Hooper made *Salem's Lot*, which was based on Stephen King's World Fantasy Award-winning book, in 1979. Working with scriptwriter Paul Monash, Hooper had 190 minutes of screen time with which to work and was able to stick closely to King's main plot and even introduce several of the subplots. Possibly the most significant change from the novel concerned the main vampire named Barlow. Hooper moved away from the Dracula archetype that King had used in the his mouth, and elongated ears and fingers. Barlow was too hideous to function in normal society and so had to hide behind the facade provided by his human assistant, the urbane James Mason.

In *Lifeforce*, a cinematic version of Colin Wilson's novel, *The Space Vampires*, Hooper told the story of an attractive-but-deadly vampiress who hitched a ride to earth on a returning space craft. Hooper used the sci-fi atmosphere and bang-up special effects to give the film an added dimension of terror. *Salem's Lot* was undoubtedly one of Hooper's finer films, while *Lifeforce* effectively transferred the horror of Wilson's life-draining monsters to the silver screen.

Most recently, Hooper has returned to his first love, the splatter movies with which he began, and wrote the script for *The Mangler* (1994), which was also based on a Stephen King story.

whatever reason, find themselves on a yacht battling it out to the finish. 🦴🦴

1985 ?m/C D: Henry S. Chen.

Mom

Clay Dwyer's (Mark Thomas Miller) life becomes a bit more complicated after a vampire (played by Brion James) bites his mother (Jeanne Bates). She dons sunglasses and begins to act like the undead. The dutiful son tries to keep her locked up, but soon realizes that's only a temporary solution. Attempts to answer the question "How do you tell your own mother that she must be destroyed?" Someone should have asked "Why is this a good idea for a movie?" 🦴🦴

1989 (R) 95m/C [Epic Productions] Mark Thomas Miller, Art Evans, Mary McDonough, Jeanne Bates, Brion James, Stella Stevens, Claudia Christian; **D:** Patrick Rand. **VHS, LV** *COL*

Mondo Keyhole

Adult erotic feature in which a pornographer who also happens to be a rapist is punished by a group of vigilante lesbians while his wife is left to be vampirized by Dracula. Sounds like they did her a favor. You'll do yourself no favors by tuning in to this trash. Also released under the more descriptive title *The Worst Crime of All*, obviously a reference to this movie. **AKA:** The Worst Crime of All. *✸*

1968 ?m/C [Ajasy, Boxoffice International] **D:** John Lamb.

The Monster Club

An all-star cast highlight this musical-horror film aimed at the younger crowd and based on several short stories by Ronald Chetwynd-Hayes. The stories are tied together by the conversation between Eramus (Vincent Price), a vampire, and Chetwynd-Hayes (John Carradine), who is bitten by Eramus and taken to the Monster Club to meet friends and hear some stories. The third story is a vampire tale about a small boy with a grown-up task. He must protect his parents, including his vampire father (Richard Johnson), from the Bleeny (the blood patrol). A delightful set of stories which were later adapted for the comic books by graphic artist John Bolton. *✸✸*

1985 104m/C *GB* [Milton Subotsky, ITC Film Distributors] Vincent Price, Donald Pleasence, John Carradine, Stuart Whitman, Britt Ekland, Simon Ward, Patrick Magee; **D:** Roy Ward Baker. **VHS, Beta, LV** *LIV*

The Monster Demolisher

Nostradamus' descendent shares the family penchant for sanguine cocktails, and threatens a professor who protects himself with an electronic wonder of modern technology. Edited from a sombrero serial; if you make it through this one, look up its Mexican siblings, "Curse of Nostradamus" and "Genie of Darkness." *✸✸*

1960 ?m/B *MX* [American International Pictures (A.I.P.), Mexico] German Robles; **D:** Frederick Curiel. **VHS** *NOS, LOO*

The Monster Squad

Teenagers really are smarter than their parents in this tale of a small band of monster enthusiasts (ages 5-15) who discover that Dracula (Duncan Regehr) has come into their small Southern town in search of a life-sustaining amulet. Van Helsing (played by Jack Gwillian) had stolen the amulet in 1888 and brought it to the United States. Dracula plans to take the amulet and unleash a reign of terror and destruction. To accomplish these ends, he gathers together famous monsters, including a Frankenstein monster, a wolfman, a mummy and the creature from the Black Lagoon. One of the girls turns Frankenstein with her childish charm, and he joins the good guys. Children will like it, but adults will have problems with the indecision of director Dekker over whether to highlight the comedy or the horror. *✸✸*

1987 (PG-13) 82m/C [Tri-Star Pictures] Andre Gower, Stephen Macht, Tom Noonan, Duncan Regehr; **D:** Fred Dekker; **W:** Fred Dekker, Shane Black; **M:** Bruce Broughton. **VHS, Beta, LV** *LIV, VES*

Moon Legend

Chinese supernatural love story has a young knight experience recurring dreams about Moon-Cher, a beautiful vampire with whom he is infatuated. He becomes convinced that she is in danger and needs his assistance. His attempts to rescue her consume most of the film. Moon-Cher is one variety of those unique Chinese vampire creatures; in her case, she drinks her blood through a hollow reed. Another of those very different Chinese vampire tales, which will expand your vision of what vampires are all about. *✸✸✸*

1991 ?m/C D: Joey Wang.

Morning Star

Exotic Russian ballet performed by the ballet corps of the Kirghiztan State Opera brought to the screen with the accompaniment of the Leningrad Philharmonic Orchestra. Young hero prince Nurdin (U. Sarbasgev) encounters 100-year-old vampiress Al-Dal (B. Beishenova) who, with the wave of a magic wand becomes a beautiful young woman. Unable to resist her charms, he is saved by the intervention of the virtuous Cholpon (R. Chokoeva), his girlfriend. As might be expected, the beauty of the dancing take precedence over the story. There is also an unusual, for a Russian film of the Stalinist era, amount of nudity. In one scene, the king attempts to cheer up his son with a group of dancers whose routine seems closer to that of a dance-hall stripper than ballet. ♫♫♫

1962 C [Frunze Film Studio] **B. Beishenova**, R. Chokoeva, U. Sarbasgev, N. Tgelev; **D:** Roman Tikhomirov.

Mr. Vampire 1992

Part of the second series of *Mr. Vampire* movies. The priest with one eyebrow (Lam Ching-Ying) returns to fight the hopping vampire. His battles are occasioned by the activity of a group of people who have decided that the vampire's teeth have the same curative powers often ascribed to the tusks of some large animals in Chinese medicine. ♫♫♫

1992 ?m/C Lam Ching-ying, Sandra Ng Kwun Yu, Ricky Hui Koon-Ying, Chin Siu Ho.

Munster, Go Home!

The TV monster family travel to England to visit Munster Hall. Years earlier, following his creation, Herman had assumed the name Munster from the Munster Family and is now due an inheritance. Problems begin during the trip over when Grandpa, after getting stuck in the form of a wolf, is placed in the ship's kennels. Upon arrival at the family home, they have to contend with Cousin Freddy, who tries to drive them away with inappropriate scary effects. Herman and Grandpa also discover that the mansion is being used by some counterfeiters as their headquarters. Having cemented its relationship with the rest of the British relatives, the American branch of the family finally heads home to America. Based on the popular TV series (1964-66), this movie spin-off was also released as *La Famille Frankenstein* (French), *Frankenstein et les faux monnayeurs* (French), *La Dolce Vita non piace ai Mostri* (Italian), and *La Herencia de los Munsters* (Spanish). Sequels, *The Munsters Revenge* and *Here Come the Munsters*, appeared in 1981 and 1995 respectively. ♫♫♫

1966 96m/C [Universal] **Al Lewis, Yvonne De Carlo,** Fred Gwynne, Butch Patrick, John Carradine, Debbie Watson, Hermione Gingold; **D:** Earl Bellamy; **C:** Benjamin Cline.

Munster's Revenge

In the second reunion of The Munster's television cast, the family has to prove their innocence when the villainous Dr. Dustin Diablo (Sid Caesar) creates robot doubles who are subsequently sent on a crime spree. Marred by uninspired directing and an inept supporting cast. ♫♫

1981 96m/C [Universal] **Yvonne De Carlo, Al Lewis,** Fred Gwynne, Jo McDonnel, Sid Caesar, Ezra Stone, Howard Morris, Bob Hastings, K.C. Martel; **D:** Don Weis. **VHS, Beta** *MCA*

The Musical Vampire

A non-Chinese doctor (mad scientist) steals a corpse and injects it with a mysterious formula that transforms it into a nearly invincible hopping vampire. The renowned one eye-browed Taoist priest vampire fighter (Lam Ching-Ying), and the beautiful Loletta Lee, cannot defeat it even though they exhaust the whole spectrum of incantations.

They subsequently discover, however, that a simple melody ("London Bridge Is Falling Down"), is a good way to control the vampire. 🦇🦇

1990 ?m/C Lam Ching-ying, Loletta Lee Lai-Chun, Lee Ka-Sing, Stanley Fung Shui-Fan; **D:** Tong Wai-Sing.

My Best Friend Is a Vampire

Better than average, if somewhat predictable, teenage vampire story finds innocent and naive delivery boy Jeremy Capello (Robert Sean Leonard) making the rounds, which include an old mansion. For a tip, he gets a roll in the hay and a bite from the resident vampire and slowly begins the transformation. He is assisted in his new life by a suave vampire-mentor (René Auberjonois) who comes in handy when vampire hunter Professor McCarthy (David Warner) and assistant show up to make (after)life miserable for Jeremy and his cohorts. The chase to destroy the vampires has been done before, but usually not with the vampires as the good guys, and usually not with this many car crashes. Treats the vampires as another misunderstood minority and has Jeremy's parents mistake his behavioral changes as signs that he's gay, but overall it's your basic, innocuous, mid-'80s teen comedy. Solid supporting cast helps things along. 🦇🦇🦇

1988 (PG) 90m/C [Kings Road Entertainment, Dennis Murphy] **Robert Sean Leonard, Rene Auberjonois,** Evan Mirand, Cheryl Pollak, Cecilia Peck, Fannie Flagg, Kenneth Kimmins, David Warner, Paul Wilson; **D:** Jimmy Huston; **M:** Stephen Dorff. **VHS** *HBO*

My Grandpa is a Vampire

Al Lewis, who played grandpa Dracula in The Munsters' television series, returns as lovable vampire grandpa Vernon T. Cooger in this film from down under. The story opens with his twelve-year-old son Lonny (Justin Gocke) arriving from Los Angeles for a visit. Lonny makes friends with a peer, Kanziora, and the pair soon learn grandpa's secret, that he is a 300 year-old vampire. He seeks their help in protecting him from Aunt Leah's boyfriend Ernie, who wishes to drive a stake through Gramps' heart. Vampire fun for the entire family. Also released as *Moonrise* and as *Grampire*. 🦇🦇🦇

1992 (PG) 90m/C Al Lewis, Justin Gocke, Milan Borich, Noel Appleby; **D:** David Blyth. **VHS** *REP*

My Lovely Monster

Silvio Francesco is dressed as the vampire in *London After Midnight* (the character played by Lon Chaney) in this film within a film. As Maximillian, he suddenly finds himself thrust out of the old film and into a contemporary German theater. A young woman (Nicole Fischer) helps the speechless vampire (he's from a silent movie) back to his true home. Forrest J. Ackerman, former editor of the classic fan magazine "Famous Monsters of Filmland," appears as the owner of a horror film museum. It's all played for fun in this low-budget satire of low-budget horror flicks. A delightful time for vampire film buffs. 🦇🦇

1991 ?m/C [Xenon Video] **Silvio Francesco,** Forrest J. Ackerman, Nicole Fischer, Matthias Fuchs; **D:** Michael Bergmann.

My Son, the Vampire

Comic vampire encounter between the star of a British movie series and Bela Lugosi. Released in the United States in the 1960s. **AKA:** Old Mother Riley Meets the Vampire; The Vampire and the Robot; Vampire Over London; Mother Riley Meets the Vampire. 🦇🦇

1952 72m/B *GB* [Renown Pictures, Blue Chip Productions] Bela Lugosi, Arthur Lucan, Dora Bryan, Richard Wattis; **D:** John Gilling. **VHS** *NOS, SNC*

"Children of the night... Shut up!"

—Dracula (George Hamilton) in *Love at First Bite* (1979).

GETTING RID OF BLOODSUCKERS...
THE VAMPIRE HUNTER'S GOAL

Every vampire film fan knows the standard ways to kill a vampire—a stake in the heart or fire do the trick every time. However, once the first hundred or so vampire movies had been made, the death scenes were getting a little boring and predictable. How many new ways can someone be staked or set on fire after all? Thus it is no wonder that screenwriters and special effects experts have combined their talents to find additional creative ways to dispatch the nocturnal fiends.

The third most popular method of destroying a vampire is to expose him to sunlight. This method was actually created for the movies and is not a part of traditional vampire lore. In 1922, F. W. Murnau significantly revised the vampire myth in his film *Nosferatu*. Contrary to Stoker's novel, in which Dracula could walk around in the daylight without his powers), Count Orlock was a totally nocturnal creature. He not only wilted under the sun's rays but was actually destroyed by them. Legal problems kept *Nosferatu* out of circulation until the 1950s, but Columbia used its idea of deadly sunlight in the 1943 film *The Return of the Vampire*. Sunlight was thoroughly integrated into the vampire myth by Peter Cushing's destruction of Christopher Lee in *Horror of Dracula* (1958).

Since most vampires don't wear watches and seem to be easily distracted, sunlight has become a standard means to demonstrate the triumph of good over evil —see Frank Langella's *Dracula* or *Near Dark* for examples. If we are to believe the movies, after centuries of existence, even the smartest of the night's creatures seem to slip up.

Other methods have been used to kill off vampires. Christopher Lee's six Dracula adventures from Hammer Films proved especially challenging to screenwriters, as each film began where the previous film had ended. The writers thus had to find creative ways of getting rid of Dracula that would allow him to be revived a year or so later. The old bloodsucker must have felt terribly abused as he and his vampire women were incinerated by the sun, staked, impaled on a wagon spoke, burned, and beheaded. While the cross is generally used to ward off a vampire, in *Taste the Blood of Dracula*, the Transylvanian Count is trapped under the shadow of a cross as he wanders into a church. In possibly the most creative ending in the Hammer series, *The Satanic Rites of Dracula* reached back into eastern European folklore and had Dracula impaled on a hawthorn bush. Finally, in *Scars of Dracula,* Lee found himself stuck on a metal rod and destroyed with a bolt of lightening.

As Asian vampire movies have become popular in the United States, fans have found that Eastern mythology is quite different from Western. Chinese hopping vampires do not fight crosses and wolfbane, but instead battle the local kung fu expert and ward off magical incantations, written on small pieces of rice paper with a blood-ink mixture. And in China, you know a vampire is finally destroyed when it explodes. It should be noted that one Hong Kong movie, *Magic Cop,* wins the all-time award for creativity in dispatching a vampire. The evil monster is fittingly blown up when the hero urinates into a pool, thus completing an electrical circuit. It's hard to imagine a more dramatic ending.

✝ END ✝

My Soul Is Slashed

An employee of a pharmaceutical company is killed by his bosses after he begins to suspect that they are up to no good. He dies on the operating table from wounds received in the attack, but there is one complication—some of Dracula's blood is used as part of a transfusion during the operation. His daughter learns the truth when she is approached by a female scientist who had smuggled the blood out of Transylvania in the first place. The scientist tells the daughter that if she is a virgin, a few drops of her blood will revive her father—she follows the scientist's instructions, and sure enough, her father returns from the dead one year later. The man realizes all that has happened to him, so he uses his vampiric powers to settle the score with the men who killed him. The moral of the story? While most people might consider the vampire to be a monster, the truly evil monsters in this movie are the corporate executives who thought nothing of killing their employee. Also, while in his vampiric state, he discovers feelings he never knew he had, especially a new appreciation for his neglected daughter. Fine acting, excellent camera work, and appropriate background music contribute to making this one of the best Japanese vampire films ever made. ♫♫♫

1992 ?m/C Ken Ogaka, Narumi Yaseda, Hikari Ishida; **D:** Saka Kawamura, Shusuke Kaneko.

The Mystery of Dracula's Castle

Made-for-TV movie aimed at teens tells the story of two brothers, one of whom (Johnny Whitaker) is a Dracula fan who is about to make a movie. They decide to transform a local lighthouse into the stage for a horror movie, only to realize that some jewel thieves are already using it as a hide out. Originally shown in two parts on the *World Of Disney.* ♫♫♫

1973 ?m/C [Walt Disney Productions] Johnny Whitaker, Scott Kolden, Clu Gulager, Mariette Hartley.

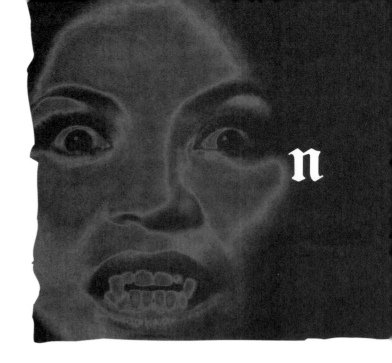

Nadja

Vampire hunter Van Helsing (Peter Fonda) dispatches the king of the bloodsuckers and then goes after the vampire's children Nadja (Elina Lowensohn) and her twin brother Edgar (Jared Harris), who have moved to New York City, where their activities blend into the urban landscape. Van Helsing recruits his nephew Jim (Martin Donovan) to assist in his crusade, only to discover significant complications. Nadja has seduced Jim's wife Lucy (Galaxy Craze), and his half-sister Cassandra (Suzy Amis) is in love with Edgar. Vampirism is simply used as a backdrop to tell the tale of children coming to grips with the violent death of their father, as well as the fragile nature of family life in the modern world. A serious attempt to lift the vampire movie above its usual B-movie level and a noteworthy use of black-and-white film to emphasize the dark world in which vampires operate. ♫♫♫

1995 (R) 92m/B [Mary Sweeney, Amy Hobby, Kino Link Productions] Elina Lowensohn, Suzy Amis, Galaxy Craze, Martin Donovan, Peter Fonda, Karl Geary, Jared Harris; *Cameos:* David Lynch; *D:* Michael Almereyda; *W:* Michael Almereyda; *C:* Jim Denault; *M:* Simon Fisher Turner. Nominations: Independent Spirit Awards '96: Best Actress (Lowensohn), Best Cinematography, Best Director (Almereyda). **VHS** *HMK*

The Naked Witch

The first of a series of low-budget Milligan quickies with a vampire theme. Beth Porter stars as the vampire witch who is revived when a college student researching witchcraft pulls the stake from her body. Just a tip here: If you find a body with a stake in the chest, leave it alone! Since nobody seems to be able to grasp this simple rule, she is free to take her revenge on the village that staked her in the first place. In 1967 an additional twenty minutes was added and the film was re-released. The additional scenes didn't help. *AKA:* The Naked Temptress. **Woof!**

1964 60m/C [Claude Alexander] Beth Porter, Robert Burgos, Bryarly Lee, Lee Forbes; *D:* Andy Milligan. **VHS** *SNC*

possessed of a single-minded, ruthless survival instinct. Farm boy Caleb (Adrian Pasdar) knows about girls but is innocent in the ways of the world. He moves in on Mae (Jenny Wright), the new girl in town, and she introduces him to vampire existence. The problem is, he's in a transitional state on his way to becoming a vampire. To be a full-blooded bloodsucker, he has to kill and feed. The vampire test is the most gruesome scene in the movie as one-by-one they take out the unsuspecting roadhouse patrons and employees. However, Caleb is not up to taking a human life and must be sustained by Mae. The vampires raise the stakes by bringing Caleb's family into the picture. The impossibly pat ending frustrates what up to that point had been an exciting ride. 𝄛𝄛𝄛𝄛

1987 (R) 95m/C [F/M Ent., De Laurentiis Entertainment Group] Adrian Pasdar, Jenny Wright, Bill Paxton, Jenette Goldstein, Lance Henriksen, Tim Thomerson, Joshua Miller; **D:** Kathryn Bigelow; **W:** Kathryn Bigelow, Eric Red; **M:** Tangerine Dream. **VHS, Beta, LV** *HBO, IME*

Nick Knight

Passable made-for-television pilot for what became the *Forever Knight* series. Nick Knight, a 400-year-old vampire currently working as a policeman on the night shift in Los Angeles attempts to atone for past sins while engaging in a quest to become human again. He is assigned to investigate a series of murders in which the victims have been drained of blood. One of the murders occurs in a museum which had housed a goblet used in ancient ceremonies, which turns up missing. In the process of pursuing the murderer, Nick meets Alyce Hunter, an archeologist who becomes his trusted human confidant. She discovers that the goblet was used in a blood-drinking ceremony to cure vampirism. The murders have a rather mundane solution, but the investigation discloses that a second vampire, Nick's old nemesis Lacroix, is in Los Angeles. In the resulting television series the story line (including Nick's biography) was altered at several sig-

Near Dark: "I'll have a Bloody Mary," declares rebel vampire Bill Paxton.

166

VAMPIRES on VIDEO

Near Dark

Among the best of the 1980s vampire flicks, *Near Dark* followed the exploits of a group of modern-day outlaw vampires in a most mundane contemporary rural American setting. The small band is shown as close-knit, vicious with their food (any human), and

nificant points, not the least of which was the movement of the series location to Toronto and the elevation of Lacroix to a continuing dark character. 🗡🗡🗡

198? 92m/C Rick Springfield, Michael Nader, Laura Johnson. **VHS** *VTR*

Night Angel

A nocturnal villainess combines the characteristics of Lilith, the ancient vampiric demon of Hebrew folklore, and the modern vamp. Lilith (Isa Anderson) attempts to persuade the editor (Karen Black) of a fashion magazine to put her picture on the cover, the initiation of a scheme to seduce the world via mass media. Some of the male employees immediate fall for her, only to meet tragic ends, and soon the editor is just as infatuated. The instrument of Lilith's destruction is true love, a quality possessed by Craig (Linden Ashby) the magazine's art director who is loved by the editor's younger sister. He learns the secrets of getting rid of the vampire from a 70-year old voodoo-practicing cabbie (Helen Martin). 🗡

1990 (R) 90m/C [Emerald Pictures/Paragon Arts International] Isa Anderson, Linda Ashby, Debra Feuer, Helen Martin, Karen Black; **D:** Dominique Othenin-Girard; **W:** Joe Augustyn. **VHS, Beta, LV** *FRH*

Night Hunter

Jack Cutter's (Wilson) vampire-hunting parents were killed by a group of bloodsuckers so he teams up with a tabloid reporter (Smith) to eliminate the last nine vampires who have gathered together in Los Angeles and plan to multiply. 🗡🗡

1995 (R) 86m/C Don "The Dragon" Wilson, Melanie Smith, Nicholas Guest, Maria Ford; **D:** Rick Jacobson. **VHS** *NHO*

Night Life

A teenager gets the all-out high-stakes ride of

his life when four cadavers are re-animated in his uncle's mortuary. 🗡🗡

1990 (R) 92m/C [RCA] Scott Grimes, John Astin, Cheryl Pollak, Alan Blumenfeld; **D:** David Acomba; **W:** Keith Critchlow; **M:** Roger Bourland. **VHS, LV** *COL*

Night of Dark Shadows

An abominable film which even fans of the TV show have a hard time liking. The last of the Collins family and his new bride are sent 150 years into the past. Sequel to "House of Dark Shadows." **AKA:** Curse of Dark Shadows. **Woof!**

1971 (PG) 97m/C [MGM] David Selby, Lara Parker, Kate Jackson, Grayson Hall, John Karlen, Nancy Barrett, James Storm; **D:** Dan Curtis. **VHS, Beta** *MGM*

Night of the Devils

Attempts to bring Alexis Tolstoy's short story "The Wurdalak," previously filmed by Mario Bava as part of his Black Sunday trilogy, into a more contemporary setting. Young doctor Nicola (Gianni Garko) encounters a peasant family seemingly involved with vampirism, and falls in love with the young woman of the household, Sdenka (Agostina Belli). The family patriarch has returned from a failed attempt to kill a witch. For his efforts, he has been turned into a vampire and gradually infects the family. Nicola is able to extract himself from the setting and returns to his medical practice in the city. Playing to the immediate tastes of horror film audiences, director Ferroni dropped many of the subtle features of the original story in favor of dead bodies and zombie-like vampires. While seemingly a straightforward vampire movie, it raises the possibility, that the vampirism was all an imagined product of Nicola's own paranoia. **AKA:** La Notte dei Diavoli; La Noche de los Diablos. 🗡🗡🗡

1971 91m/C [Filmes Cinematographica, Due Cinematographica, Copernices] Agostina Belli, Mark Roberts, Cinzia de Carolis, Teresa Gimpera, Umberto Raho; **D:** Giorgio Ferroni; **W:** Romano Migliorini,

"Remember this: without me Transylvania will be as exciting as Bucharest on a Monday night."

—Dracula (George Hamilton) in *Love at First Bite* (1979).

Gianbattista Mussetto, Eduardo Brochero; *C:* Manuel Berenguer; *M:* Girogio Gaslini.

Night of the Sorcerers

On an expedition to the Congo, explorers uncover a bizarre tribe of beautiful women dressed in leopard skins. They turn out to be vampires who lure young girls to their bloody death. Hmm. Beautiful women. Leopard skin outfits. How did it all go wrong? Little things like plot, acting, and any semblance of moviemaking skill got left out. *AKA: La Noche de Los Brujos.* 🦴

1970 85m/C [Avco Embassy] Jack Taylor, Simon Andrew, Kali Hansa; *D:* Armando de Ossorio. **VHS, Beta** *UNI*

Night of the Vampire

An attempt to mix Japanese ghost traditions and the western Vampire myth. Yuko, the young woman who is the focus of the story, was conceived when her mother was raped by Dr. Yamaguchi. Her mother made a pact with the devil to ensure Yuko's survival, but as a result she lives as a vampire, part of the undead whose only goal is to take revenge on the world. For director Yamamoto, this film was a follow-up to his vampire film, a Japanese version of *Dracula* that was released in English as *Lake of Dracula*. *AKA:* Chi O Suu Ningyo; Yureiyashiki no Kyofu-Cho Wo Sun Ningyo. 🦴🦴

1970 ?m/C *JP* [Toho Company] Yukiko Kobayashi, Atsuo Nakamura, Kayo Matsuo, Akira Nakao; *D:* Michio Yamamoto.

Night Owl

Jake (James Raferty), a handsome vampire who is also a serial killer, operates out of a sleazy tavern in New York City, targeting unattached females who patronize the bar. Beginning with some fervent love-making with victim number one, Jake moves on to a series of relatively quick kills before he falls in love with Anne (Ali Thomas), who he meets when his first victim's brother shows up at the bar to search for his missing sister. As moody as Franco's earlier films but without any hint of a fresh thought or growing appreciation for the vampires he has so frequently photographed. Forget it. 🗡🗡

1995 ?m/C [Franco Film]

Night Stalker

The popularity of the vampire in the 1970s was evident in the January 11, 1972, airing of *Night Stalker*, the highest rated made-for-TV movie to that date. It would not only encourage the production of other made-for-television movies, but turn into a popular horror series the next season. The Night Stalker turns out to be luckless reporter Carl Kolchak (Darren McGavin), always pursuing the great story. One finally comes his way when someone starts killing Las Vegas showgirls. He is convinced that the murderer is a vampire of sorts, but no one, least of all the police, wants to believe him. After battling the culprit with no assistance, the final insult comes when the story is discarded by his editor. Jeff Rice's novelization of Richard Matheson's script appeared in 1974. 🗡🗡🗡

1972 75m/C [ABC] **Barry Atwater**, Darren McGavin, Carol Lynley, Simon Oakland, Ralph Meeker, Claude Akins, Charles McGraw, Kent Smith; *D:* John Llewellyn Moxey; *W:* Richard Christian Matheson; *C:* Michael Hugo; *M:* Robert Colbert.

The Night Stalker: Two Tales of Terror

Two episodes from the television series "Kolchak: The Night Stalker" in which McGavin plays a nosy newspaper reporter who constantly stumbles upon occult phenomenon. Episodes are "Jack the Ripper" and "The Vampire." 🗡🗡🗡

1974 98m/C [Dan Curtis Productions, ABC] Darren McGavin, Simon Oakland. **VHS, Beta** *MCA*

Nightlife

In this made-for-cable-television comedy, Count Vlad Dracula (Ben Cross) travels to Mexico City to find his former lover Angelique (Maryam D'Abo). Now freed from her coffin, Angelique wants nothing to do with Vlad. She assumes the life of a modern liberated woman, complete with swanky apartment, and begins to date a doctor who wants to find a cure for her blood disease. The jealous Vlad pursues and woos, but is continually frustrated. Has its funny moments but appears somewhat anemic beside *Love at First Bite* and *Once Bitten*. 🗡🗡

1990 93m/C [Universal] **Ben Cross, Maryam D'Abo**, Keith Szarabajka, Jesse Corti, Oliver Clark, Glenn Shadix, Camille Saviola; *D:* Daniel Taplitz. **VHS, Beta, LV** *MCA*

Nightmare Castle

This low-budget horror tale concerns Dr. Derek Joyce (Lawrence Clift) a mad scientist experimenting on the regeneration of human blood with electricity. While he is concentrating on his work, his wife Jenny (Barbara Steele) has found more attentive company in the arms of David, the gardener (Rik Battaglia). The scientist, finding her activities unacceptable, kills the adulterous couple, uses their blood to revive a dead servant, and courts his wife's sister for her inheritance. Now he has real problems, as the late lovers return as angry ghosts. *AKA:* Amanti d'Oltretomba; Night of the Doomed; The Faceless Monsters; Lovers From Beyond the Tomb. 🗡🗡🗡

1965 90m/B *IT* [Allied Artists] Barbara Steele, Paul Muller, Helga Line; *D:* Allan Grunewald; *M:* Ennio Morricone. **VHS, Beta** *SNC, HHT*

Matthews makes a brief appearance in one of Malekai's movies shown at the convention. No one cares. If you haven't seen it you haven't missed anything of importance. *AKA:* Horror Convention. ♫♫

1975 90m/C [John Stanley] Kerwin Mathews, Jerry Walter, Barrie Youngfellow; *D:* John Stanley. **VHS, Beta** *VCD*

Nightwing

Usually overlooked simply because there aren't any vampires in it. There are, however, vampire bats, and it did come out in 1979, the same year as Frank Langella's *Dracula,* the remake of *Nosferatu,* and *Love at First Bite.* In the great Southwest, a group of bats begin to attack humans and devour them. (Hey, why not? By this time just about every other species had been given its cinematic day in the sun.) They are also carrying a plague which threatens to do even more damage. To the Indians, the bats are on a mission of revenge. To the whites, they're just bad. Boring version of a cliched theme. Based on the novel by Martin Cruz Smith, which was also released as a Fotonovel. ♫♫♫

1979 (PG) 103m/C [Image Associates, RCA Video Productions, Columbia Pictures] Nick Mancuso, David Warner, Kathryn Harrold, Strother Martin; *D:* Arthur Hiller; *M:* Henry Mancini. **VHS, Beta, LV** *COL*

The Nine Demons

Joey's father and best friend have been murdered. In order to get revenge on the bad guys, the Prince of Darkness gives him the use of nine demon vampires that he has control of through a necklace of mini-skulls. When Joey tosses the necklace, the skulls materialize into the demons and head for the nearest neck. Eight of the demons appear as children who briefly entertain their victims before pouncing. In the end, Joey gains his revenge against the killers, but he must take responsibility for the mistake he made in loosing the demons. ♫♫

1983 ?m/C

Nosferatu (1922): "Thank you, come again." Nosferatu (Max Schreck) awaits new guests.

Nightmare in Blood

A low budget, hastily constructed, and boring film. What little action there is occurs during a horror film convention. Malekai (Jerry Walter) is a veteran horror actor who also happens to be a real vampire. Kerwin

Ninja, the Violent Sorcerer

Murderer, with the help of Chinese vampires, does battle with the ghost of a dead gambling lord's wife and the gambling lord's living brother. Often tedious even with above average production and incredible plot. 🗡🗡

1986 90m/C [Foreign] **D:** Bruce Lambert; **W:** Daniel Clough. **VHS, Beta** *TWE*

Ninja Vampire Busters

Vampire fans beware. Ninja fans beware. There are no ninja and not enough vampires to worry about in this misnamed movie. There are lots of martial arts fights and a host of supernatural creatures, but a weak plot merely serves to tie together what the advertising for the film describes as a fight between the undead and the braindead. Hong Kong contributes to the list of "Worse Than *Plan 9 from Outer Space* Movies." **Woof!**

1989 ?m/C Jacky Cheung, Nick Chang; **D:** Norman Law, Stanley Siu.

Nocturna

Disco spoiled everything it touched, and Count Dracula was no exception. In this disco horror comedy, the aging John Carradine winds down his illustrious career with one of his all-time lows. Nocturna rejects the old ways of her grandfather Drac, takes up with a musician, and turns the family castle into a dance club. Can you find the vampire's victims among the fashion victims? This film must join the bottom-ten list of worse vampire movies. **AKA:** Nocturna, Granddaughter of Dracula. **Woof!**

1979 (R) 82m/C [Compass International Pictures] Yvonne De Carlo, John Carradine, Tony Hamilton, Nai Bonet; **D:** Harry Tampa; **C:** Mac Ahlberg. **VHS, Beta, LV** *MED*

Nosferatu

The first film adaptation of Bram Stoker's "Dracula" remains one of the creepiest and most atmospheric versions. Murnau knew how to add just the right touches to make this one of the best vampire films ever made. All it lacks is the name of Dracula, which was changed due to copyright problems with Stoker's widow. Filmed in Bavaria. Silent with music and English titles. Remade by Werner Herzog in 1979. **AKA:** Nosferatu, Eine Symphonie des Grauens; Nosferatu, A Symphony of Terror; Nosferatu, A Symphony of Horror; Nosferatu, The Vampire. 🗡🗡🗡🗡

1922 63m/B GE [Prana] **Max Schreck**, Alexander Granach, Gustav von Wagenheim, Greta Schroeder; **D:** F.W. Murnau. **VHS, Beta, LV** *GPV, MRV, NOS*

Nosferatu the Vampyre

The original *Nosferatu,* the German retelling of Stoker's *Dracula,* became legend among vampire fans. It introduced new elements to the mythology, such as the destructive power of the sun, and left a lasting image in the rat-like vampire Count Orlock. In 1979, a modern technicolor version of the old silent flick was shot simultaneously in English and in German (and the shorter English version lacks material important to the continuity of the story line). Given the passage of time, with *Dracula* in the public domain, there was no need to continue the disguises adopted by F. W. Murnau in his silent version. The character names in Stoker's novel were returned, though both the plot deviations by Murnau, as well as Dracula's appearance (made so memorable by Max Schreck in 1922) were retained. The movie had its moments, such as the scene in which the vampire hungrily eyes Harker as blood oozes from his cut finger, but overall the plot moved much too slowly. *Nosferatu* wasn't as well received as its 1979 rivals *Dracula* with

"I am experiencing a terrible shortage of 'wirgin' blood."

—Countess Dracula (Louise Fletcher) in *Mama Dracula* (1980).

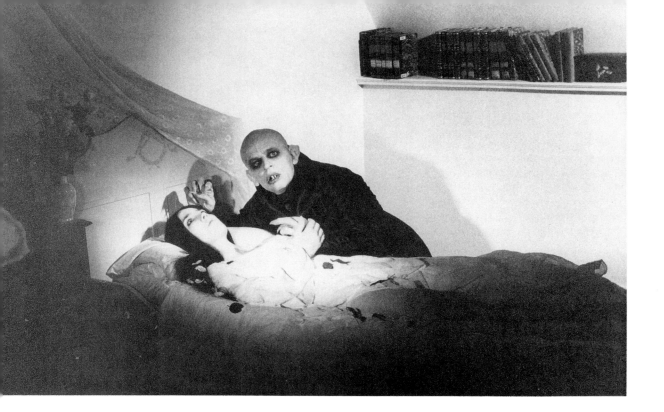

Nosferatu The Vampyre: "See, even I, an ugly creature of the night, can bed Isabelle Adjani." With this Vampyre (Klaus Kinski) love is truly blind.

Frank Langella and *Love at First Bite*. The sixteenth attempt to bring "Dracula" to the screen, a novelization of *Nosferatu the Vampyre* by Paul Monette was based on Werner Herzog's screenplay. *AKA:* Nosferatu: Phantom der Nacht. 🦇🦇🦇🦇

1979 106m/C [20th Century-Fox] **Klaus Kinski**, Isabelle Adjani, Bruno Ganz, Jacques Dufilho, Roland Topor, Walter Laderigast; *D:* Werner Herzog; *W:* Werner Herzog.

Nostradamus and the Destroyer of Monsters

The fourth and final feature of the Nostradamus series has the vampire's nemesis Professor Duran (Domingo Soler) creating a device which destroys bats through sound waves. *AKA:* Nostradamus y el Destructor de Monstruos; The Monsters Demolisher. 🦇🦇

1962 77m/C [Bosas Priego] **German Robles**, Julio Aleman, Domingo Soler, Aurora Alvarado; *D:* Frederick Curiel; *W:* Alfredo Ruanova, Carlos Enrique

Taboada; *C:* Fernando Colin.

Nostradamus and the Genie of Darkness

In this third of the series, Nostradamus (German Robles) the vampire is resurrected by the genie of Tinebra. Instead of being destroyed, frequently the fate of someone reviving a vampire, she becomes Nostradamus' love object. In the meantime, his nemesis Professor Duran (Domingo Soler) attempts to get at Nostradamus by stealing the ashes of his ancestor, the original Nostradamus. The storyline is ultimately brought to a climax in the sequel, *Nostradamus and the Destroyer of Monsters*. *AKA:* Nostradamus y el Genio de las Tinieblas; Genie of Darkness. 🦇🦇🦇

1960 77m/C [Bosas Priego] **German Robles**, Julio Aleman, Aurora Alvarado, Domingo Soler; *D:* Frederick Curiel; *W:* Alfredo Ruanova, Carlos Enrique Taboada; *C:* Fernando Colin.

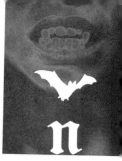

Not of this Earth

Another entertaining classic movie from Roger Corman, a pioneer of the scifi vampire movie. A humanlike alien (Paul Birch) from the planet Davanna, now suffering the effects of a nuclear war, explores Earth as Mr. Johnson, to see if human blood is a viable substitute for that of his own race. In this endeavor, he enlists the assistance of a physician and his nurse (Beverly Garland). Soon afterwards, residents of the small town turn up dead and drained of their blood. Davanna also has the ability to destroy minds with his eyes, which he hides behind sunglasses. One of the more memorable and eerie revelations occurred when he took off his glasses to reveal eyes without pupils. Corman remade the film in 1987. *AKA:* El Vampiro del Planeta Rosso. 🎬🎬

1957 67m/B [Allied Artists, Roger Corman] **Paul Birch**, Beverly Garland, Morgan Jones, William Roerick, Jonathan Haze, Dick Miller; *D:* Roger Corman; *W:* Charles B. Griffith, Mark Hanna; *C:* John Mescall; *M:* Ronald Stein.

Not of This Earth

A close reproduction by Roger Corman of his 1957 scifi vampire classic of the same name. An alien comes to earth in search of blood to replace that of the inhabitants of his home planet, which is drying up. Arthur Roberts took over Paul Birch's role as Mr. Johnson,

the alien, and Traci Lords replaced Beverly Garland as the nurse who discovers the plot to steal earth's bloody resources. The remake did not have the cultural impact of the original (after 30 years we seem to have learned to live with the nuclear threat), and lines which were received with all seriousness in the 1950s appeared humorous in the 1980s. Audiences also demanded greater acting ability even from Corman's up and comers, and subsequently the second *Not of This Earth* did not fair as well at the theaters. 🎬🎬

1988 (R) 92m/C [Concorde, MGM/UA] Traci Lords, Arthur Roberts, Lenny Juliano, Rebecca Perle, Ace Mask, Roger Lodge; *D:* Jim Wynorski; *W:* Jim Wynorski, R.J. Robertson. **VHS, Beta** *MGM*

Not of This Earth

Third incarnation of the classic vampire science fiction movie from Roger Corman. Mr. Johnson, the human-like alien (Parker Stevenson) from a planet devastated by an atomic war, is testing the hypothesis that human blood is a viable substitute for that of his own alien race. Corman had originally made the film in 1957 and made it a second time in 1988. This version was specially made for the emerging cable television movie market. 🎬🎬

1996 (R) 92m/C [Showtime, Roger Corman] Michael York, Elizabeth Barondes, Richard Belzer, Parker Stevenson; *D:* Terence H. Winkless. **VHS** *NHO*

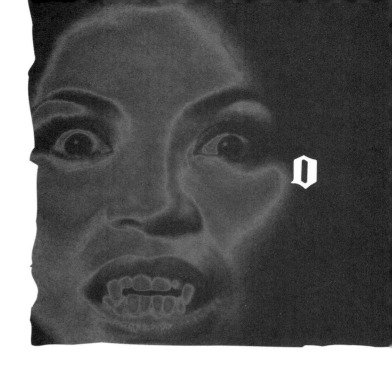

O Macabro Dr. Scivano

One of the rare entries from the Brazilian film industry into the vampire genre. Traces the fall of the title character (Raúl Calhado), beginning with a foray into voodoo. As a part of the ritual, he offers some gold nuggets in exchange for which he is made a vampire by magic. 🎞🎞

1971 72m/C [Natus] **Raul Calhado**, Luiz Lime, Oswaldo de Souza, Lauro Sawaya; *D:* Raul Calhado, Rosalvo Cacador; *W:* Raul Calhado; *C:* Raul Calhado, W. Silva.

Old Dracula

"If you liked *Young Frankenstein,*" the Mel Brooks horror farce of 1974, "you'll love *Old Dracula,*" promised the ads. While this British production did not live up to the memorable comedic masterpiece that had supplied its immediate inspiration, *Old Dracula* has its share of laughs. David Niven was nowhere close to winning any acting awards for *Old Dracula,* but his one attempt at playing the Count did turn into a delight-fully entertaining period (1970s) piece. In the late twentieth century, the noble monster has become a *Playboy*-reading tour host, allow-ing people to visit his castle as a means of luring them into the range of his fangs. He also decides to revive his mate by giving her the blood of one of his victims, who hap-pened to be a young black woman. His wife Vampira (Teresa Graves) revives, but is now also black. While the joke did not go over well with American audiences, Old Dracula did provide one of the few opportunities for an African American to play a vampire in the movies. Dracula, possessed of hundreds of years worth of old-world prejudices and tra-ditions, is appalled at the idea of interracial marriage and sets out for London to find some means of rectifying the situation in a politically correct fashion. *AKA:* Vampira; Old Drac. 🎞🎞🎞

1975 88m/C [World Film Services Ltd., American International Pictures (A.I.P.)] **David Niven, Teresa Graves**, Peter Baylis, Jennie Linden, Nicky Henson, Bernard Bresslaw, Veronica Carlson, Freddie Jones, Linda Hayden; *D:* Clive Donner; *W:* Jeremy Lloyd; *C:* Tony Richmond; *M:* David Whitaker.

Once Bitten

A delightful comedy set in present-day Los Angeles, drawing upon a theme from *Blood for Dracula* (1973) that the vampire needs not just any blood, but the increasingly rare blood of a virgin. Halloween is approaching and the Countess (Lauren Hutton) needs her regular dose of the potent elixir. Also taking inspiration from the Countess Bathory legend, the needed blood primarily keeps the aged Countess in her youthful state. Integrating an idea from *Love at First Bite* (1979), the Countess requires three shots of the blood, the bites having the additional side effect of transforming her victim into a vampire. She finally locates her virgin in the person of young Mark Kendall (Jim Carrey, before super stardom). Meanwhile, Kendall is trying in every way possible to put an end to his amateur status, and wants girlfriend Robin (Karen Kopins) to provide the necessary assistance. Unable to seduce her, he goes bar hopping in search of an alternative and ends up with the Countess. He is soon dressing in black, wearing sunglasses, and quaffing cow's blood as if it were orange juice. Critics attacked *Once Bitten* for not achieving what it could have and Hutton had some harsh words to say about her role, which she seemed to want to play with some greater degree of seriousness. However, the movie has stood the test of time and remains second only to *Love at First Bite* as a vampire comedy of note. ♂♂♂♂

1985 (PG-13) 94m/C [Samuel Goldwyn] **Lauren Hutton, Jim Carrey,** Cleavon Little, Karen Kopins, Thomas Balltore, Skip Lackey; **D:** Howard Storm; **W:** Jonathan Roberts; **M:** John Du Prez. **VHS, Beta, LV** *LIV, VES*

One Dark Night

Two high school girls plan an initiation rite for one of their friends who is determined to shed her "goody-goody" image. The girl (Meg Tilly) must spend the night in a mausoleum, where she's attacked by a psychic vampire. *AKA: Entity Force.* ♂♂

1982 (R) 94m/C [Michael Schroeder] Meg Tilly, Adam West, David Mason Daniels, Robin Evans; **D:** Tom McLoughlin. **VHS, Beta** *NO*

One Eyebrow Priest

It's all fun and games when an old priest, the most effective of the vampire hunters, must square off against a group of Hong Kong hopping vampires. This one has a little of everything, including dance numbers, flatulence as a vampire defense, vampire kids, and breakneck pacing. Worth looking for, especially for the attention span-challenged. *AKA:* New Mr. Vampire II. ♂♂

1987 ?m/C **D:** Mason Ching.

Orgy of the Vampires

Classic Ed Wood production (from his own novel) with a variety of beautiful women in various stages of undress. An otherwise innocent young couple is captured by a group of baddies that includes the "Emperor of the Dead" (Hollywood psychic Criswell), Vampira (the television horror hostess created by Maila Nurmi), and the "Princess of Darkness" (Fawn Silver). The trio forces the travelers to watch as they pass judgment on a group of "topless sinners" in a cardboard graveyard. Silly nonsense, marginally vampiric but hilariously bad. *AKA:* Vampire's Night Orgy. ♂

1973 (R) 86m/C *SP IT* [Jose Frade, International Amusement Corporation] Jack Taylor, Charo Soriano, Dianik Zurakowska, John Richard; **D:** Leon Klimovsky. **VHS** *SNC*

"Did you watch me, I was greater than any real vampire!"

—Count Mora (Bela Lugosi) as the pseudo-vampire in *Mark of the Vampire* (1935).

Director/Producer Roger Corman

Out for Blood

An adult erotic feature shot on video in both hard- and softcore versions. During the day, Tori (Tori Wells) is unaware that she is really the child born of two vampire parents. In the evening, a second personality emerges and she become a sex-craving tuxedo-wearing bloodsucker who knows just which part of the male anatomy from which to assuage her thirst. ♫♫

1990 ?m/C [Vivid Productions] **Tori Wells**, Raquel Darian, Randy Spears, Kelly Royce; *D:* Paul Thomas. **VHS**

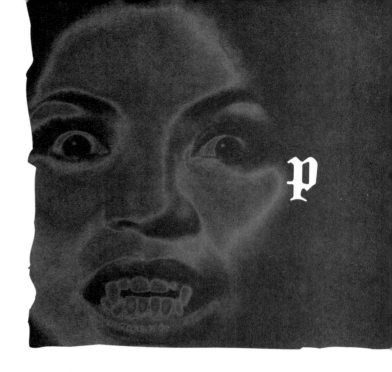

Pale Blood

A serial killer in Los Angeles is leaving his victims drained of blood. Michael Fury (George Chakiris), a real vampire, begins looking for the killer in the hopes of finding another like himself. In the process he teams up with a vampire-obsessed researcher (Pamela Ludwig), and together they track the killer. Slow paced story has its moments. 🎬🎬

1991 (R) 93m/C [Noble Ent.] George Chakiris, Wings Hauser, Pamela Ludwig, Diana Frank, Darcy Demoss; **D:** V.V. Dachin Hsu. **VHS, LV** *NO*

Paris When It Sizzles

Richard Benson (William Holden) is a writer with a drinking problem. Hollywood producer Alexander Meyerheimer gives him a second chance. He hires Benson to write a movie script and sends him to Paris to complete the work. Benson spends the time en-joying the city, and now has 48 hours to complete the script. He hires a secretary, Gabrielle Simpson (Audrey Hepburn) to assist this rush to deadline. Together they act out Benson's fantasies, one of which happens to be a brief vampire episode. 🎬🎬

1964 110m/C [Paramount Pictures] William Holden, Audrey Hepburn, Gregoire Aslan, Raymond Bussieres, Tony Curtis, Fred Astaire, Frank Sinatra, Noel Coward, Marlene Dietrich, Mel Ferrer; **D:** Richard Quine; **W:** George Axelrod. **VHS, Beta** *PAR*

Pepito y Chabelo vs. los Monstruos

The popular and youthful Mexican comedy team confronts a series of monsters including Frankenstein's monster, the Wolf Man, the mummy, Mr. Hyde, the Creature from the Black Lagoon, and, of course, Dracula. *AKA:* Chabelo y Pepito contra los Monstruos. 🎬🎬

1973 ?m/C [Alameda] Martin Ramos, Xavier Lopez, Silvia Pasquel; **D:** Jose Estrada.

Once Bitten: Oh sure, he can strut his stuff now but before he became Mr. Megabucks, Jim Carrey played Lauren Hutton's love slave in this campy vampire comedy.

Plan 9 from Outer Space

Though it earned the Golden Turkey Award as the worst movie ever made, *Plan 9 from Outer Space* is an unintentionally humorous and entertaining movie featuring a trite story, stilted acting, and many well-known on-screen blunders. "Plan 9" is the scheme of a pair of aliens dressed in silk pajamas who believe that all Earthlings are stupid. They land on Earth near a cemetery in California (in a flying saucer that looks suspiciously like a paper plate) and begin the process of animating the dead. Although they move at snail-like speed, these first representatives of a proposed army of vampire-zombies are supposed to conquer the cities of the world.

Included among the living dead is Vampira, the TV horror hostess character who was created and portrayed by Maila Nurmi. In the end, the plan is of course foiled, but not before Bela Lugosi (who died before shooting of the film began) makes a brief appearance via a clip from an old home movie shot by Wood. An actor imitating the deceased Lugosi, also makes several brief appearances in the film, peering out from behind his vampire's cape as he sneaks across the screen. The elevation of this movie to cult status has recently prompted the release of a documentary video *Flying Saucers Over Hollywood, the Plan 9 Companion* (1992) and the inclusion of some additional footage Wood shot of Lugosi in the video biography *Lugosi the Forgotten King* (1985). *AKA:* Grave Robbers from Outer Space.

1956 78m/B [Edward Wood Jr., DCA] Bela Lugosi, Tor Johnson, Lyle Talbot, Vampira, Gregory Walcott; **D:** Edward D. Wood Jr. **VHS, Beta, LV** *NOS, SNC, MED*

Planet of Blood

One of the finest sci-fi vampire movies finds an expedition sent to Mars to investigate an unusual phenomenon. Once there, members of the crew (John Saxon, Judi Meredith, Dennis Hopper) find a crashed spacecraft with a lone survivor, an alien with green skin (Florence Marly). She is allowed to come on board, but soon crew members are turning up dead with, you guessed it, their blood missing. Marly is the sole survivor of her race and aims at breeding a new race. The captain (Basil Rathbone) also discovers the eggs she has laid and takes them back to earth for study. Probably not a good idea. Rathbone's final film also included a cameo appearance by scifi editor/writer Forest J Ackerman. Based on the story, "The Veiled Woman." *AKA:* Queen of Blood. 🎵🎵🎵

1966 81m/C [George Edwards, American International Pictures (A.I.P.)] John Saxon, Basil Rathbone, Judi Meredith, Dennis Hopper, Florence Marly; **D:** Curtis Harrington. **VHS** *SNC, NOS, MRV*

Planet of the Vampires

Planet of the Vampires stands as one of legendary Italian horror director Mario Bava's more interesting films. Working on a shoestring budget with popular American actor Barry Sullivan, he attempts to bring the public interest in space flight together with the horror genre. Sullivan leads an expedition to the planet Aura, where a previous ship and its crew had vanished. They find the corpses of the original crew and bury them. The dead astronauts, now possessed by a vampiric alien life form, arise and begin to vampirize the second crew as part of their attempt to escape the planet. Sullivan is left to decide who is a vampire, who isn't, and

what to do about it. *AKA:* Terror in Space; Terreur dans l'Espace; Space Mutants; The Demon Planet. 🎵🎵🎵

1965 86m/C *IT* [American International Pictures (A.I.P.)] Barry Sullivan, Norman Bengell, Angel Aranda, Evi Marandi; **D:** Mario Bava. **VHS, Beta** *ORI*

Playgirls and the Vampire

In his second vampire movie, director Pierro Regnoli took a little from several earlier productions beginning with the stranded people who take refuge in a castle. In this case, five young attractive showgirls and a pair of male companions come to the home of Count Kernassy (Walter Brandi). The Count, while a good and trustworthy man himself, has a nasty vampire ancestor (also Brandi). The vampire seizes the opportunity to appear and attack the women, who are left in various stages of undress. Maria Giovanni becomes a vampire and begins to prey upon the others. Regnoli tested the loosening guidelines for sex and nudity in post-war Italy and provided inspiration for Jean Rollin's later celebrations of sex and vampirism. *AKA:* L'Ultima Predadel Vampiro The Last Victim of the Vampire, The Last Prey of the Vampire, The Vampire's Last Victim, Desires of the Vampire, Daughters of the Vampire, and Curse of the Vampire. 🎵🎵

1960 85m/C [Tiziano Longo] **Walter Brandi**, Lyla Rocco, Alfredo Rizzo, Maria Giovannini; **D:** Pietro Regnoli; **W:** Pietro Regnoli; **C:** Ugo Brunelli, Aldo Greci; **M:** Aldo Piga.

Please Don't Eat My Mother

Roger Corman's low-budget classic dark comedy, *Little Shop of Horrors*, was remade as a soft core adult movie in which Seymour, the lowly worker at a flower shop, has become a voyeur. Audrey, the blood-thirsty

plant, still stars in this obscure and better-left-forgotten version. *AKA:* Hungry Pets; Glump. **Woof!**

1972 95m/C Buck Kartalian, Renee Bond; *D:* Carl Monson. **VHS** *MOV, VDM, TPV*

A Polish Vampire in Burbank

Low-budget quickie concerns the coming of age of Dupah (Mark Pirio), a young adult vampire who is finally being forced to get his own victims. His aging father kicks him out of the family home to fend for himself amidst the night life of the Los Angeles suburb of Burbank. While the acting is amateurish and the production not much better, the movie was highly successful in video after it appeared on cable television. *AKA: Polish Vampire.* 🗡🗡

1980 84m/C [Vistar International] Mark Pirro, Lori Sutton, Eddie Deezen; *D:* Mark Pirro. **VHS, Beta** *NO*

Project Vampire

Vampire concocts a serum that will change humans into vampires within three days. His first guinea pig fights to stop the evil from succeeding. 🗡🗡

1993 90m/C Brian Knudson, Mary-Louise Gemmill, Christopher Cho, Myron Natwick; *D:* Peter Flynn. **VHS** *AIP*

Pure Blood

A rich Colombian businessman needs a constant supply of blood. His son (and heir) recruits victims and drains them. Dad simply sits back as the blood pours in, oblivious to the methods by which it's acquired. Muddled allegory for corporate greed. *AKA: Pura Sangre.* 🗡🗡

1983 98m/C [Luis Ospina Films] Florina Lemaitre, Carlos Mayolo, Humberto Arango, Gilberto Forero; *D:* Luis Ospina; *C:* Ramon Suarez; *M:* Gabriel Ossa, Bernardo Ossa.

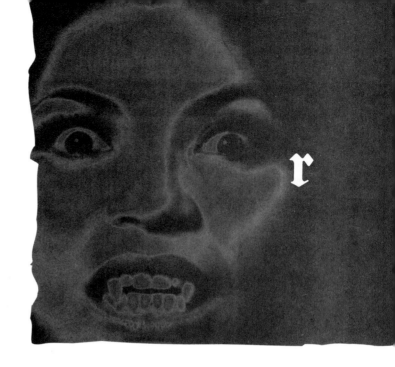

r

Rabid

Marilyn Chambers became famous when she starred in *Behind the Green Door*, one of the most notorious porno flicks of all-time, but not many people realize that she also starred in this film, one of the most memorable splatter movies ever filmed. David Cronenberg's alternative vampire movie, which appeared, interestingly enough, the same year as George Romero's *Martin*, follows the complications faced by young Rose (Chambers) after she has a motorcycle accident. As a result of the skin graft operation, she develops an unusual growth in her arm pit. From that time forward, especially after having sex, a syringe-like appendage appears out of the growth and sucks the blood of her sleeping partners. It takes very little blood, just enough to survive. However, as the incidents multiply, Rose feels compelled to attack people and allow the syringe to take blood just to stay alive. Her victims are in turn infected with a disease resembling rabies that causes them to act out a homicidal mania. When confronted with the reality of what she is doing, Rose cannot believe it. When martial law is declared and orders are given to shoot anyone with the disease, Rose takes a man home with her to see the effects of the disease herself, with disastrous results. A nice change of pace to watch when you get tired of the run-of-the-mill "victims trapped in a castle" vampire movies. *AKA:* Rage. 🎷🎷🎷

1977 (R) 90m/C *CA* [New World Pictures, Cinema Entertainment Enterprises] **Marilyn Chambers**, Frank Moore, Joe Silver; *D:* David Cronenberg; *W:* David Cronenberg. **VHS, Beta** *WAR*

Red and Black

Just as the vampire is an apt metaphor to discuss human relationships, it has also served as a viable vehicle for political comment. In this 1980s Chinese movie, a man is bitten by a Japanese vampire during World War II. The victim manages to impale himself, thus stopping the problem from spreading. Twenty-five years later he is accidentally revived and passes his horrendous condition to the leader

🌙

✝

of the Communist revolution. A brave message for the time. ♫♫♫

1986 ?m/C *D:* Andrew Kam Yeun Wah.

Red Blooded American Girl

Modern rationalist scientific thought tends to treat vampirism as a blood disease, at least on film. In this scifi-horror vein, Dr. John Alcore (Christopher Plummer) has discovered a virus that produces symptoms closely resembling vampirism. Now he, as well as his staff, is infected. He hires scientists Owen Urban (Andrew Stevens) to help discover a cure. Before that cure can be found, Urban and a fellow scientist Paula (Heather Thomas) become infected as well. She goes on a bloody

rampage with Urban in hot pursuit. By now, it's a frantic race to discover the proper antidote. Unfortunately, the pace of the film never quite made it to "frantic." The story was stretched far beyond the time needed to tell it properly and even the actors got bored. Plummer could play (and perhaps did play) the sleazy villain in his sleep. ♫

1990 **(R)** 89m/C *CA* [Prism Entertainment, Syd Cappe, SC Entertainment International, Nicholas Stiliadis] **Christopher Plummer**, **Heather Thomas**, Andrew Stevens, Kim Coates; *D:* David Blyth. **VHS, Beta, LV** *PSM*

Red Lips

Lisa (Michelle Bauer) is an older lesbian who doesn't realize that the love of her life, the

much younger Caroline (Getty Chasun), is also a vampire. By the time Lisa learns Caroline's secret, she is deeply committed to the relationship and will go to any lengths to help her lover. Their life together becomes a series of triangles—Lisa, Caroline, and whoever Caroline's latest victim happens to be. Plenty of bare skin and suggestive situations, but the real fun comes from the biting and the blood, which flows copiously. 🗡🗡

1994 ?m/C Getty Chasun, Michelle (McClellan) Bauer; **D:** Donald Farmer. **VHS** *DRA*

The Reflecting Skin

An intriguing, even disturbing, drama exploring the consciousness of an eight-year-old (Jeremy Cooper) growing up in the 1950s amid insanity, murder, and the specter of radiation sickness. He becomes obsessed with the idea that a young widow (Lindsay Duncan) who lives close by is a vampire after his older brother's blood. Parable for lost innocence or exploitative gore-fest for the arts crowd? Well, it does have exploding frogs. 🗡🗡

1991 116m/C Viggo Mortensen, Lindsay Duncan, Jeremy Cooper; **D:** Philip Ridley; **W:** Philip Ridley; **M:** Nick Bicat. **VHS, LV** *NO*

Requiem for a Vampire

Two women seek refuge in a castle occupied by a sadistic vampire and his female attendants. To no one's surprise, they are attacked by the vampires in several ritualized sadistic and sexual scenes. Like most of director Rollin's vampire epics, *Requiem* contained minimal narrative, a practically non-existent storyline, a series of intense sensual and erotic encounters, (each almost capable of standing independently of the rest) and plenty of horrific atmosphere and sexual arousal. This was all perfectly suited to the limited budget with which he had to work, and provided a transition from the nudie, cutting edge films of the early 1970s, to the more explicit pornographic movies of the present. *AKA:*

Requiem pour un Vampire; Vierges et Vampires; Virgins and Vampires; Caged Virgins; Crazed Vampire. 🗡🗡🗡

1972 ?m/C [ABC, Les Films 13] **Michel De la Salle**, Marie Pierre Castel, Philippe Gaste, Mireille D'Argent; **D:** Jean Rollin; **W:** Jean Rollin; **C:** Renan Polles.

The Return of Count Yorga

Though not as well received as hoped, Count Yorga had been successful enough to justify a sequel. Two bungling detectives, having discovered Yorga's staked out corpse, do the expected and remove it. And as expected, Yorga revives and takes his first meal from his unsuspecting benefactors. Moving from Los Angeles, Yorga finds a new mansion home in San Francisco where he integrates himself into the local culture and cuisine. Yorga turns his attention to Cynthia Nelson (Mariette Hartley), the girlfriend of Dr. Roger Perry, who had dispatched Yorga in the first film. Many vampire fans gave Yorga's return much higher marks than his first appearance. 🗡🗡

1971 (R) 97m/C [American International Pictures (A.I.P.)] **Robert Quarry**, Mariette Hartley, Roger Perry, Yvonne Wilder, Rudy DeLuca, George Macready, Walter Brooke; **D:** Bob Kelljan; **W:** Yvonne Wilder, Bob Kelljan. **VHS** *ORI*

The Return of Dr. X

Many of Bogey's fans would have us forget that he actually appeared in a vampire movie when Warner Brothers decided to grab a little bit of the market Universal had created for vampires and mummies. Earlier in the decade, the studio had outstanding success with an initial Dr. X feature starring Lionel Atwill. In the sequel, Dr. X is called upon to square off against a vampire. The story opens with Walter Barnett (Wayne Morris) discovering the dead body of a famous actress, Angela Merrova (Lya Lys). Soon after the story appears in his paper, she shows up alive, albeit somewhat pale. She sues the newspaper, which results in Barnett joining

"All we want is a chance to live in peace without worrying about someone trying to ram a stake through our hearts."

—Jeremy Capello (Robert Sean Leonard) in *My Best Friend Is a Vampire* (1987).

Vampires Italian Style

While Italian cinema might be better known for its spaghetti Westerns, it was also integral to the rebirth of the horror and vampire film in the 1950s after Universal Studios abandoned the genre in the 1940s. The first Italian vampire movie, *I Vampiri* (also known as *The Devil's Commandment,* 1957), appeared even before Hammer Films' first *Dracula* flick, although it was far less memorable. Today the Italian horror industry is primarily remembered for the contributions director Mario Bava made to the vampire genre. After serving as cameraman for *I Vampiri*, Bava went on to make a number of memorable horror and vampire features. Interestingly enough, the first film he directed—*La Maschera del Demonia* (better known by its English-language title, *Black Sunday,* 1961)—is still considered to be his best thanks to his imaginative use of lights and shadows in creating the film's haunting Gothic imagery

Black Sunday also featured a prominent icon found throughout all of Italian art, fiction, and cinema—the "dangerous female," a woman whose very presence provoked desire in men but caused their destruc-

tion if they dared to approach her. Of course, in the process, the dangerous female was also always destroyed. While casting *Black Sunday*, Bava discovered the hauntingly attractive Barbara Steele, whom he cast as the "dangerous woman" of that film. The collaboration proved a successful one, as Bava and Steele's careers would be linked from that point forward. For the next generation, Steele was the epitome of the horror movie scream queen, never relinquishing that title to the bevy of challengers who came and went in movies released by Hammer Films. Few images in vampire cinema have had more power than that of Steele as the witch Princess Ada in *Black Sunday*, her face mauled by a spiked mask that was pushed into her face at her execution.

In the 1960s, Italian cinema moved into unexplored territory to give the world two homegrown film genres—"Mondo" and "Sexy"—both of which included vampire films. Both genre's relied upon a pseudo-documentary format to titillate audiences with the bizarre, degrading, or forbidden elements of life. The Mondo pictures, launched by *Mondo Cane* in 1961, used an "an-

thropological overlay to explore the fringes of human behavior," while the "Sexy" movies challenged the censorship laws with supposedly true-to-life presentations of various sexual practices and situations. Vampires found their way into both genres as rapist vampires were featured in both *Mondo Keyhole* (1966) and *Sexy Proibitissimo* (1963).

The 1960s were definitely the heyday of Italian vampire cinema. Among the more notable titles were Bava's *Black Sabbath* (1963) with Boris Karloff, *Planet of the Vampires* (1965), and Steele's *Revenge of the Blood Beast*(1966), whose story line harkens back to *Black Sunday* in many respects. By the 1970s, censorship regulations, the consolidation of the Italian film industry into a few large corporations, and the rise of television combined to drive Italian filmmakers out of the horror/vampire business. They had trouble keeping up with the increasingly large doses of sex being added to French and British horror cinema in an attempt to pull moviegoers away from their television sets.

✝ END ✝

the ranks of the unemployed and deciding to vindicate himself. His search leads him to the office of blood specialist Francis Flegg (John Litel), with whom Merrova is spending much of her time. He ties Flegg to a series of murders in which all of the victims had a fairly rare blood type and had previously donated blood at Flegg's hospital. Barnett and a friend investigate and encounter the mysterious Marshall Quesne (Bogart). Flegg had developed a formula to bring humans back to life and tested it on Dr. Maurice Xavier, executed for a murder some years ago (in the original film), and the formerly dead actress. Dr. X goes hunting for the blood he needs and the forces of good and evil head toward a final encounter. Asked later about his blood-sucking role, Bogart was reported to have replied, "If it had been Jack Warner's blood, or Harry's or Pop's, maybe I wouldn't have minded as much. The trouble was, they were drinking mine and I was making this stinking movie." Actually, his only appearance as a vampire yielded a fairly good horror film. Based on a short story, "The Doctor's Secret" by Lee Katz. 🦇🦇🦇

1939 ?m/B [Warner Brothers] **Humphrey Bogart, Lya Lys**, Rosemary Lane, Wayne Morris.

Return of Dracula

An aristocratic Transylvanian nobleman, Dracula's cousin Count Belec (Francis Lederer), moves to a small town in Southern California and assumes the identity of one of his early victims. He finds he has a taste for young females, the closer to the age of the teenagers to whom this movie was aimed the better. After having his toothy way with Jennie (Virginia Vincent), he turns his attention to Rachel (Norma Eberhardt). One of the important transitional films between the Universal era and the still-to-come Hammer color films that would remake the horror genre. Filmed in black and white, with color added for the blood oozing from the staked vampire at the end. Only a few horror film trivia buffs seemed to notice. **AKA: *The Fan-**

tastic *Disappearing Man* and as The Curse of Dracula. 🦇🦇

1958 77m/C Francis Lederer, Norma Eberhardt, Ray Stricklyn, Jimmie Baird; *D:* Paul Landres. **VHS** *MGM, FCT*

Return of the Blind Dead

Second installment of the Spanish trilogy built around a group of medieval Templar Knights who return from the dead. They had originally been executed in the thirteenth century for killing women and using their blood in rituals. They are resurrected as blood-seeking skeletons who are able to locate their victims by sound. During a modern anniversary celebration of their execution, the knights attack a village, where a number of the villagers take refuge in the local Catholic church. Ossorio borrowed some of the very effective scenes of the knights riding off into battle on their horses from the original feature, *Tombs of the Blind Dead*. Followed the next year by *Horror of the Zombies*. **AKA:** *Return of the Evil Dead; El Ataque de los Muertos sin Ojos.* 🦇🦇

Return of the Vampire

After a thirteen year break from Dracula, Lugosi returned to his role in 1944. Well, it wasn't really Dracula, but another Eastern European aristocratic vampire, Armand Tesla. Still, not much of a stretch. During World War II, Tesla was released from his grave by Nazi bombing. Accompanied by a werewolf, he searches for the blood he has been denied in his coffin. He is opposed by Lady Jane Ainsley (Frieda Inescort), who runs an asylum. *Return* was important in the development of the vampire genre for its use of sunlight as a weapon against vampires. Earlier, *Nosferatu* adopted the idea, but very few people ever saw the older silent feature until its re-release in the 1950s. Also, in showing the disintegrative effects of the sun, a wax

Videohound Salutes: Boris Karloff

Boris Karloff, one of the most prominent faces in horror movies for decades, portrayed a vampire only once, and it is likely that only a dedicated fan of horror could name the film.

Karloff launched his career at approximately the same time as Lugosi, but he became famous for his work in the Frankenstein movies instead of in vampire films. Before Universal's 1931 *Frankenstein*, Karloff had appeared in more than 50 silent movies. He followed his star-making performance in *Frankenstein* with equally outstanding work as the *Mummy* and *Dr. Fu Manchu*. Fans could immediately recognize his distinctive voice, which continues to be imitated and parodied in cartoons and comic horror movies even today. Among the more than 100 horror movies in which he starred or co-starred were a few vampire movies—*House of Frankenstein* (1944) and *Isle of the Dead* (1945) come to mind. In his last movie, *The Fear Chamber* (1967), he played a mad scientist working with a vampiric stone that lived off of the fear of females.

Despite those appearances in vampire films, only once did he actually portray a vampire. That one time, however, was a classic. In 1963 he traveled to Italy to work with director Mario Bava on a film version of "The Wurdalak," a nineteenth-century Russian vampire story by Alexei Tolstoy. Karloff played Gorga, the family patriarch who went vampire-hunting and returned a vampire himself. It is an excellent vampire film that is not to be missed.

---

mask of Lugosi was placed over a skull. The melting of the wax is still an effective scene. It was so effective (and horrendous) in the 1940s that the English censors refused to allow it into the theaters, and Columbia had to edit it out of the British version. 🐾🐾

1944 69m/B Bela Lugosi, Frieda Inescort, Nina Foch, Roland Varno, Miles Mander, Matt Willis; **D:** Lew (Louis Friedlander) Landers; **W:** Griffin Jay, Kurt Neumann, Randall Faye; **C:** John Stumar, L.W. O'-Connell; **M:** Nino Castelnuovo. **VHS**

Return of the Wolfman

In this sequel to the brief amateur movie, *Frankenstein Meets Dracula*, Dracula revives Frankenstein's monster, who had been killed in the earlier production. The monster turns on Dracula and leaves the castle. After a short sojourn in the countryside, he returns to the castle where he battles the Wolfman. Followed by *The Revenge of Dracula*. 🐾

1957 ?m/C

Return to Salem's Lot

This rather mundane made-for-TV sequel to Stephen King's novel/movie *Salem's Lot*, features an anthropologist (Michael Moriarty) and his son, who move back to the town of Jerusalem's Lot a decade after the original vampires that infested the town were destroyed. The pair soon learns that the town is overrun again by the nocturnal creatures and their human "drones," who tend to business during the daylight hours while the vampires sleep in their coffins. At first, the chief vampire (Andrew Duggan) seems to be friendly—it turns out that most of the vampires live off of the blood of cattle they raise. However, an elderly Nazi hunter who lives in town makes the anthropologist understand that the vampires must not be allowed to live and multiply. This sequel isn't bad, but it is certainly not the equal of *Salem's Lot* and is even further removed from the terrifying level of the original novel. 🎵🎵

1987 **(R)** **101m/C** [Paul Kurta] Michael Moriarty, Ricky Addison Reed, Samuel Fuller, Andrew Duggan, Evelyn Keyes, Jill Gatsby, June Havoc, Ronee Blakley, James Dixon, David Holbrook; **D:** Larry Cohen; **W:** James Dixon, Larry Cohen. **VHS, Beta** *WAR*

The Revenge of Dracula

In this third independent short (four and a half minutes), following *Frankenstein Meets Dracula* and *Return of the Wolfman*, Dracula (Don Glut) returns to life and begins reviving Frankenstein's monster. In the middle of the process, he grows thirsty, and leaves the castle in search of blood. After killing two people, he returns to castle Frankenstein, trailed by locals who found the bodies of his victims. The revived monster kills the interlopers, but in the process destroys the castle. Followed by the fourth in the series, *The Frankenstein Story.* 🎵

1959 **?m/C** [Don Glut] **Don Glut**, Charles Martinka, Wayne Moretti, Victor Fabian; **D:** Don Glut.

Revenge of Rendezvous

This short feature (five minutes), the sequel to *Rendezvous*, includes very brief clips from old horror movies, including *House of Dracula* and *House of Frankenstein*, in which John Carradine stars as Dracula. 🎵

1975 **?m/C** [Troc Film Corp.] **John Carradine**.

Revenge of the Vampire

In this second of the popular Pontianak series, the vampire (Maria Menado) is revived

and seeks revenge on those who tried to kill her. **AKA:** Dendam Pontianak. 🎵🎵

1957 **?m/C**

The Rider of the Skulls

Consists of three episodes about the adventures of a masked rider. In one story he must battle a vampire. **AKA:** El Charro de las Calaveras. 🎵🎵

1967 **71m/C** *MX* [Azteca] Dagoberto Rodriguez, David Silva, Alicia Caro; **D:** Alfredo Salazar.

Rockula

Three-hundred-years old and still a virgin. Even though this is a comedy, that is no laughing matter. The virginal Ralph's particular curse is to meet the love of his life every 22 years, only to see her destroyed by an evil pirate on Halloween before he can break the spell by bedding her. Now in the midst of the rock subculture, the cycle is repeating and the lovely Mona (Tawny Feré) comes on the scene. Can Ralph do it? Can rock and roll save him? Can you find enough laughs to make it worth 91 minutes of your life? Only if you're a hard-core Bo Diddley fan. 🎵🎵

1990 **(PG-13)** **90m/C** [Cannon Releasing] **Dean Cameron**, Bo Diddley, Tawny Fere, Susan Tyrrell, Thomas Dolby, Toni Basil; **D:** Luca Bercovici; **W:** Luca Bercovici. **VHS, Beta, LV** *MGM, WAR*

Romance of the Vampires

A passionate young vampire cannot find fulfillment in his love quest, and punishes himself by refusing to suck the blood out of his potential victims. A vampire romance thriller. 🎵🎵

1994 **?m/C** Yvonne Yung Hung, Yau Yuet-Ching, Lam Kwok-Bun, Yuen King-Tan; **D:** Ricky Lau Koon-Wai.

"I live off of family money. From Romania."

—female vampire's (Elina Lowensohn) pick up line from *Nadja* (1994).

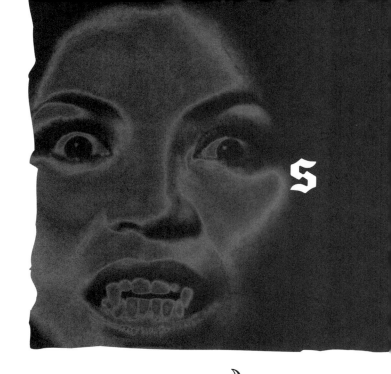

The Saga of the Draculas

Entertaining Spanish vampire film has aging vampire Dracula planing to continue his bloodline through his pregnant niece's unborn child. Berta and her husband go to Dracula's castle, where hubby gets carried away with all of the young female residents. In the meantime, every effort is being made to see to the baby's care and comfort. When Berta discovers that the wine she is being served is in fact blood, she awakens to her situation. A stern, if weird, warning against drinking while pregnant. and later as *Dracula's All Night Orgy*. **AKA:** *La Saga de los Draculas* Dracula Saga; Dracula: The Bloodline Continues...; The Saga of Dracula. ♪

1972 (R) 90m/C *SP* [Profilms, International Amusement Corporation] Narciso Ibanez Menta, Tina Sainz, Tony Isbert, Maria Koski, Cristina Suriani, Helga Line; ***D:*** Leon Klimovsky. **VHS** *SNC*

Salem's Lot

This lengthy made-for-TV adaptation of Stephen King's classic vampire novel has its strengths and weaknesses. On the one hand, it is long enough (three hours) to bring to the screen many of the novel's subplots and complexities. The film also remains true to the book's plot, unlike the movie version of King's *The Shining*, in which the novel's basic understanding of evil was essentially discarded. On the other hand, because the movie had to win the approval of television censors in 1979, many of the incidents that made the book such a horror classic were downplayed or entirely cut out. The basic story concerns writer Ben Mears (David Soul) whose childhood fears of an old house at the edge of town revive after he learns of the mysterious people who have recently moved in. One of the residents, Mr. Straker (James Mason), operates a small shop in town. He combines a certain suave continental manner with a business-like efficiency and a clear disdain for the inhabitants of the small town of Jerusalem's Lot—in many ways, he is the true villain in this story. As Mears and his youthful companion (Mark Petrie) eventually learn, the other, unseen resident of the house is a vampire named Kurt Barlow (Reggie Nalder), who eventually appears looking quite similar to Count Orlok in Murnau's *Nosferatu*. Barlow begins to spread vam-

"Mom, I promise to eat my vegetables." Mr. Barlow (Reggie Nalder) can be very persuasive in *Salem's Lot,* as you can see by the expression of Lance Kerwin.

pirism throughout the peaceful town, rapidly turning it into a ghost town. This of course leads to a stunning final confrontation with Mears and his allies. A sequel, not written by King, *A Return to Salem's Lot,* was produced in 1987. *AKA:* Blood Thirst. 𝄢𝄢𝄢

1979 (PG) 112m/C [Warner Brothers] **Reggie Nalder**, David Soul, James Mason, Lance Kerwin, Bonnie Bedelia, Lew Ayres, Ed Flanders, Elisha Cook Jr., Fred Willard, Kenneth McMillan, Marie Windsor; *D:* Tobe Hooper. **VHS, Beta, LV** *WAR*

Samson vs. the Vampire Women

Santo (or Samson if you're watching a dubbed version) must save his friend's daugh-

ter from a group of female vampires looking for a new queen. Passable entry in the popular series. *AKA: Santo contra Las Mujeres Vampiras. Santo vs. the Vampire Women.* 𝄢𝄢

1961 89m/B MX [Azteca] Santo, Lorena Velasquez, Jaime Fernandez, Maria Duval; *D:* Alfonso Corona Blake. **VHS, Beta** *SNC, HHT*

Santo Against Baron Brakola

At the center of a plot borrowed directly from the movie *Horror of Dracula* is the masked wrestler Santo, who assumes the role usually filled by the vampire hunter Van Helsing to oppose the evil Baron Brakola

(the Mexican Dracula). In this retelling of the Dracula legend, Brakola is intent on turning a young woman into a vampire. At first she is saved by a blood transfusion, but in the end, it is Santo who comes to her rescue to defend her against the evil Baron. *AKA:* El Santo Contra el Baron Brakola. 🗡🗡

1965 ?m/C [Luis Enrique Vergara] Fernando Oses, Susana Robles, Jose Diaz Morales, Santo.

Santo and the Blue Demon vs. Dracula and the Wolfman

Let's get ready to rumble! Picking up the story from *Santo and Dracula's Treasure* (1969), the hunchbacked assistant revives Dracula, who in turn revives the Wolfman. The pair then multiply beyond all reason, requiring two of Mexico's famed masked wrestlers to go against the monsters and their clones in a tag-team battle royale. *AKA:* Santo y Blue Demon contra Dracula y el Hombre Lobo. 🗡🗡

1973 ?m/C [Cinematografica Calderon] **Aldo Monti**, Augustin Martinez Solares, Maria Eugenia San Martin, Santo, Santo; *D:* Miguel M. Delgado.

Santo and the Blue Demon vs. the Monsters

Masked wrestler Santo, who starred in a successful series of movies playing himself, teams up with his wrestling colleague The Blue Demon to confront a variety of monsters brought together by mad scientist Bruno Halder (Carlos Ancira). Included in this monster mash are Dracula (David Avizu), two vampire women (Yolanda Ponce and Elsa Maria Tako), a mummy, and a robot double of the Blue Demon. Marginally better acting than in the WWF. *AKA:* Santo y Blue Demon contra los Monstruos. 🗡🗡

1968 ?m/C [Cinematografica Sotomayor] **David Avizu, Elsa Maria Tako, Yolanda Ponce,** Santo, Blue Demon, Heydi Blue, Jorge Rado; *D:* Gilberto Martinez Solares. *OUP*

Santo en el Tesoro de Dracula

Santo, the masked wrestler and monster-fighting hero goes up against Dracula himself (appearing as Count Alucard). Luisaj (Noelia Noel), a scientist's daughter, uses a time machine to visit the past and is bitten by Dracula. Santo watches these events from a hidden television monitor in his secret headquarters. He follows Luisa in an attempt to locate and destroy Dracula's treasure and, of course, do battle with another masked wrestler working for the villains. Adults usually find the Santo adventures childish, but seem to appreciate the fully mature nude women who so frequently grace the screen. Released in English as *Santo and Dracula's Treasure* and later beefed up by additional nude scenes, was issued as *El Vampiro y El Sexo* and *The Vampire and Sex*. 🗡🗡

1987 90m/C *MX* [Madera] Santo el Enmascarado de Plata, Aldo Monti, Noelia Noel. **VHS, Beta** *MAD*

Santo en la Venganza de las Mujeres Vampiro

In his last adventure of the 1960s, masked wrestler Santo, the bane of evil monsters, must take on the countess Mayra, recently revived by mad scientist Dr. Brancor. She has determined that Santo is the last descendent of the man who impaled her ancestors in Transylvania in the seventeenth century. She gathers an army while Brancor builds a Frankenstein-like monster in preparation for revenge. Walking into the situation is an attractive journalist (Norma Lazareno), whom Santo has to rescue, as if he didn't have enough to worry about. *AKA:* The Vengeance

Vampires for Children

As the popular *Goosebumps* series of books has proved, kids love a scary story, and vampires seem to be among their favorite characters. Several hundred vampire books have been written for children and young adults, so it was inevitable that some would be turned into movies. Actually, once movie studios realized that the average horror movie fan was a teenage male, they began to make movies specifically for teenagers.

Making vampire movies for preteens, however, is a whole different story. Such movies must tone down the scary aspects of the story (as much for the benefit of the parents as the kids) and place the traditional monsters in a safe, humorous setting. By subverting the scary nature of monsters and by turning characters such as Dracula and Frankenstein into lovable playmates, it is hoped that children receive an additional tool to help them deal with bad things in their lives that are very real (abusive parents, bullies at school, etc.). Scary movies aimed at kids also often include inside jokes aimed at parents, who pass on a love of the horror genre to their kids.

Many preschool children have been introduced to vampires through the Public Broadcasting Network's long-running *Sesame Street*, where Count von Count teaches the numbers zero to nine. Sesame Street home videos such as *Sesame Street Presents: Follow that Bird* (1985) and *Count It Higher* (1988) are also available now. *The Muppet Show*, which was aimed at a slightly older audience, also has a number of episodes on video, including a Halloween bash, *Monster Laughs with Vincent Price* (making a rare appearance as a vampire).

Comic monster mashes in the tradition of Abbott and Costello seem ideal for children and Dracula stars in one of the best, *The Night Dracula Saved the World*. As the head of the monster world, Dracula must deal with the demise of Halloween. It seems that The Witch is unhappy with her lot in life and refuses to ride her broom across the moon, a necessary event if Halloween is to begin. Initially she turns a cold shoulder to all of Dracula's pleas, but eventually a child melts her heart and she performs her Halloween duties. Once the day is saved, its time for all of the monsters and children to party, party, party. No true vampire fan would want to miss Dracula in his disco outfit.

Cartoons have also seen their share of vampires. The favorite children's vampire tale, *Bunnicula*, was brought to life as an animated feature in 1987. In that show, the vampire has become a soft lovable housepet who limits his attacks to fruits and vegetables, from which he sucks the juice. His playmates are a talkative dog and intelligent cat who finally befriend him and prepare him for full acceptance by the family. Long before *Bunnicula*, many of the cartoon favorites from the Saturday afternoon movie shorts (Bugs Bunny and Mighty Mouse, for example) had confronted vampires in at least one cartoon.

Post-World War II Japan took graphic art to new heights, and while Japanese animators specialized in superhero stories, they did not neglect vampires altogether. Younger children can now enjoy the adventures of *Astro-Boy*, a popular hero on Japanese television in the 1960s, as he battles vampires in a storyline called the "Vampire Vale." Older kids will enjoy the various adventures of *Princess Miyu*, now compiled in a single video set. Comic book readers of all ages can see the all-time Marvel favorite, *The Tomb of Dracula*, which was brought to the screen in the 1980 Japanimation feature, *Dracula*.

✝ END ✝

of the Vampire Women; La Venganza de las Mujeres Vampiro. 🎵🎵

1969 ?m/C Santo, Aldo Monti, Norma Lazarendo; **D:** Frederick Curiel. **VHS** *OUP*

The Satanic Rites of Dracula

The last of the Christopher Lee *Dracula* movies for Hammer. As with its immediate predecessor, *Dracula AD 1972*, Dracula is living in modern England. He has become a tycoon of sorts who spends his time between his country house and a penthouse apartment. Still up to his nefarious schemes, he is working on the creation of a worldwide plague epidemic. His cohort is Dr. Keely (Freddie Jones) leader of a group of scientists and politicians working to develop a virus capable of destroying the human race. Van Helsing (Peter Cushing), whose daughter has been kidnapped by the vampire fiend, also returns to do battle with his old nemesis. After the *Satanic Rites*, Hammer went on to make one more Dracula movie, *Legend of the Seven Golden Vampires*, with Cushing but sans Lee. It bombed, and Hammer soon followed it into oblivion. *AKA:* Count Dracula and His Vampire Bride. 🎵🎵🎵

1973 88m/C *GB* [Hammer] Christopher Lee, Peter Cushing, Michael Coles, William Franklyn, Freddie Jones, Joanna Lumley, Richard Vernon, Patrick Barr, Barbara Yo Ling; **D:** Alan Gibson. **VHS** *MLB*

Saturday the 14th

Not, as might be thought from the title, a satire on Friday-the-13th type movies, rather a low-budget comic variation on the monster in the old mansion films. A couple (Richard Benjamin, Paula Prentiss) purchase an old house only to discover that they must deal with another couple that also wants the house. Complicating things is the fact that the other couple happen to be vampires (Jeffery Tambor, Nancy Lee). Life in their new home is further complicated by their son, who performs a ritual with a book of black magic that conjures a variety of strange creatures and events into action. Finally, a Van Helsing figure arrives to mess up the situation royally. Not exactly a rousing success, it somehow managed to spawn an even worse sequel, *Saturday the 14th Strikes Back* (1988) 🎵🎵

1981 (PG) 91m/C [Julie Corman] Richard Benjamin, Paula Prentiss, Severn Darden; **D:** Howard R. Cohen; **W:** Howard R. Cohen, Jeff Begun. **VHS, Beta**

Saturday the 14th Strikes Back

Continuing the name, but not the storyline, cast, or characters from the original, this one concerns the invasion of a birthday party by a vampire (Pamela Stonebrook) and her monstrous friends. The monsters have decided that the birthday boy (Jason Presson) should be their new leader. Don't bother. 🎵

1988 91m/C [Pacific Trust] Ray Walston, Avery Schreiber, Patty McCormack, Julianne McNamara, Jason Presson; **D:** Howard R. Cohen; **W:** Howard R. Cohen. **VHS, Beta** *MGM*

The Scars of Dracula

Paralleling the original Dracula in many ways, *Scars* finds a young man, Paul (reminiscent of Jonathan Harker) becoming an unwitting temporary resident at Castle Dracula. He meets Tanya, one of the Count's vampire brides, but their encounter enrages Dracula, who kills them both. Paul's death brings his former girlfriend and brother to the castle to investigate. They are aided in their efforts by a local priest and one of Dracula's servants. Not as well done as its immediate predecessor, *Taste the Blood of Dracula*, but noteworthy for Hammer's successfully increasing the amount of gratuitous violence and nudity. Also released as *Les Cicatrices de Dracula* (French). A novelization by Angus Hall appeared that same year. 🎵🎵🎵

VIDEOHOUND SALUTES: CHRISTOPHER LEE, THE MAN WHO PUT FANGS INTO VAMPIRES:

Many men have donned Dracula's cape through the years, but few have worn it with as much style and panache as Christopher Lee. He was tall, with a commanding presence and sexual magnetism. When he opened his mouth for the first time, Lee displayed a prominent set of fangs ready to penetrate the neck of any sweet young thing that crossed his path. To audiences who watched the series of movies he made for Hammer Films, he was the very personification of the vampire Count Dracula. However, after making *Dracula and Son* in the mid-1970s, Lee swore off playing Dracula, or even doing vampire movies, ever again so he could avoid the typecasting that had destroyed the careers of other horror actors, including the legendary Bela Lugosi. Instead, he went on to play a variety of parts, the best known being the title villain in the James Bond feature *The Man with the Golden Gun*.

Born in 1922, Lee grew to be very tall, a fact that kept him from getting some leading roles but that was perfect for the role that made him a star—playing the Frankenstein monster in Hammer Films *The Curse of Frankenstein* (1957). That film brought together the creative trio of Lee, director Terence Fisher, and fellow actor Peter Cushing for the first time. Lee's portrayal of Dracula in the trio's next project for hammer, *Horror of Dracula* (1958), turned Lee from star into superstar. Lee actually skipped the sequel to *Horror of Dracula* and spent the next years in Italy, where he both affirmed his Italian roots and made a less than spectacular comedy, *Uncle Was a Vampire* (1959). He was finally talked into appearing in additional Hammer Dracula movies beginning in 1965.

Dracula Prince of Darkness (1965) picked up where *Horror of Dracula* left off. Each Hammer film would end with Dracula being dis-

patched in a unique manner, so each sequel would start up from the point of his death and his resurrection. The series created the overall impression that one could temporarily stop a vampire but never totally destroy it. Memorable in this second Dracula outing for Hammer was the insertion of the scene from Stoker's novel that previous Dracula movies had left out, possibly to avoid problems with censors. Lee sliced opened his chest with his fingernail and allowed (forced?) his victim (played by Susan Farmer) to drink. This key scene, now that it had finally been shown on screen, would become a standard part of post-Hammer Dracula movies.

Having largely exhausted the novel in the first two movies, subsequent plots centered upon Dracula's anger at the vampire hunters, especially Van Helsing, and his attempts to seek revenge for their dastardly acts. It is apparent from these later efforts just how powerful Lee's screen presence was. The films' plots centered on Lee, but Hammer was generally unable to pay the fees he commanded and had to strictly limit the number of lines he spoke on camera. Even though Lee was thus limited to various hisses and huffs to show his anger, he still carried the pictures with his commanding presence. Often, he stretched out Dracula's biting opportunities to allow them to stick in the viewer's mind long after they left the theater.

In between the Hammer films, Lee made other movies, and in 1970 he again returned to Europe to make a vampire movie. Spanish B-movie maker Jesus Franco offered him the opportunity to do what he could not do at Hammer—make a more literal portrayal of Dracula in a remake of Stoker's novel. Franco promised faithful adherence to *Dracula*'s story line, and Lee returned to Stoker's descriptions of the Count to rework his screen persona. Lee accomplished his task. His clothing, appearance (down to his growing younger as the movie progressed), and demeanor on screen followed the novel. However, Franco failed to deliver his end of the bargain. After a promising beginning, the movie began to deviate scene by scene from the novel as Franco ran out of money; eventually, the quality of the production disintegrated altogether. While Lee's Hammer films are still much-admired for their entertainment value, Franco's production is of interest only to antiquarians intrigued by Lee or the development of Dracula's image through the century. Fortunately, after Franco, Lee returned for several more Hammer productions.

Now in his seventies, Lee lives in London and continues to travel the world to practice his craft. He has escaped Lugosi's fate and had a long and successful career beyond Dracula movies. However, two decades after his last appearance as the bloodsucking Count, he is still admired by legions of vampire fans as the man who owned the part.

✝ END ✝

1970 **(R)** 96m/C *GB* [Hammer, EMI] Christopher Lee, Jenny Hanley, Dennis Waterman, Wendy Hamilton, Patrick Troughton, Michael Gwynn, Anouska Hempel, Michael Ripper; *D:* Roy Ward Baker; *M:* James Bernard. **VHS, Beta, LV** *REP, MLB*

Scooby-Doo and the Reluctant Werewolf

Cartoon monster mash featuring the cast of the popular *Scooby-Doo* television series. Dracula turns Scooby's pal Shaggy into a werewolf so he can participate in a Transylvanian monster road race. The Frankenstein monster, the mummy, Dr. Jekyll/Mr. Snyde, and Genghis Kong also participate. A delightful farce for Scooby-Doo fans. 🐾🐾🐾

197? 95m/C [Hanna-Barbera Productions] **VHS, Beta, LV** *TTC*

Scream and Scream Again

Detective Superintendent Bellaver (Alfred Marks) investigates a series of murders in which the victims have been drained of blood. A young man with tremendous strength is suspected of the crimes. He is arrested, but escapes by pulling so hard on the cuffs that his hand is severed at the wrist. He leaves it behind and heads for the country mansion of the mysterious Dr. Browning (Vincent Price). The British Prime Minister (Christopher Lee) persuades the police to end their investigation. Browning is revealed to be a surgeon-turned-mad-scientist who has been creating androids from various body parts (including the blood of the murder victim) to produce a new super race. There's also a plot by a foreign country to rule the world through political assassination by the superhumans. Based on a novel by Peter Saxon, *The Disoriented Man.* 🐾🐾🐾

1970 **(PG)** 95m/C *GB* [Max J. Rosenberg, Milton Subotsky, Amicus Productions, American International Pictures (A.I.P.)] Vincent Price, Christopher Lee, Peter Cushing, Judy Huxtable, Alfred Marks, Anthony Newlands, Uta Levka, Judi Bloom, Yutte Stensgaard; *D:* Gordon Hessler. **VHS, Beta** *LIV, VES, ORI*

Scream Blacula Scream

William Marshall revives his role as Blacula/Prince Manuwalde after an occultist uses Blacula's bones in a voodoo ritual. He sets about drinking his way around town until he runs into a voodoo woman (Pam Grier) with whom he falls in love. She, however, cares nothing for him. Inferior to the original, but worth a look for fans. 🐾🐾

1973 **(R)** 96m/C [American International Pictures (A.I.P.)] William Marshall, Don Mitchell, Pam Grier, Michael Conrad, Richard Lawson, Lynne Moody, Janee Michelle, Barbara Rhoades, Bernie Hamilton; *D:* Bob Kelljan. **VHS** *ORI, FCT*

The Screaming Dead

First of three films by prolific director Jesus Franco centered on Frankenstein's monster (vampires do not play an important role in the sequels). In this initial story, the mad Dr. Frankenstein has developed a scheme to destroy the world. Dracula and his vampire brides emerge as his nemesis and thwart his plan. **AKA:** *Dracula vs. Frankenstein, Dracula Prisonnier de Frankenstein; Dracula contra El Dr. Frankenstein.* 🐾🐾

1972 84m/C *SP* [Fenix] Dennis Price, Howard Vernon, Alberto Dalbes, Mary Francis, Genevieve De-

"Is this your wife? What a beautiful neck!"

—Count Orlock (Max Schreck) to Waldermar Hutter in *Nosferatu. Eine Symphonie des Garuens* (1922).

VIDEOHOUND SALUTES: BELA LUGOSI, DRACULA'S PERSONA EXTRAORDINAIRE!

"Damned to immortality" is a fitting epitaph for one of Hollywood's icons. Around the world, Bela Lugosi's face is as familiar as that of Humphrey Bogart or Marilyn Monroe. Everyone can immediately identify the intense gaze, the widow's peak, and the tuxedo and opera cape—the distinguishing elements in Bela Lugosi's portrayal of the vampire Count Dracula.

Lugosi was born in 1882 in a small town in rural Hungary. His real name was Bela Blasko. He deeply disappointed his father by choosing an acting career. Early in the new century he moved to Budapest and began acting in stage productions. In 1917, he made his first film, *The Leopard*. In 1920 he received political asylum in the United States and began to appear on the New York stage. Unable to speak English, he learned his parts phonetically. In 1923 he made his first American movie, *The Silent Command*.

His life changed in 1927 when he was cast in the title role of the Hamilton Deane/John Balderston stage version of Dracula, which opened on Broadway in October 1927. Not the first choice for the part, in hindsight the producers recognized that the Hungarian accent, the slow deliberate delivery of lines, the hand movements, and the eyes, contributed greatly to the play's long successful run on Broadway and then around the country.

In 1930, Universal moved to buy the film rights to Dracula, using Lugosi in their negotiations with Florence Stoker. He was ready to make the jump from stage to screen and thought starring in the play and assisting the studio in the negotiations ensured him the part of Dracula. As he soon found out, Universal had a long list of actors in line ahead of him—John Wray, Conrad Veidt, Ian Keith, William Courtney, Paul Muni, Chester Morris, Joseph Schildkraut. The man director Tod Browning had most wanted to fill the role—Lon Chaney, Sr.—passed away, and one by one the other actors turned the part down for various reasons. Finally, Universal turned to Lugosi. The rest is history.

Lugosi went on to immortality as Dracula, although he actually only played the part once more, in the comedy *Abbott and Costello Meet Frankenstein* (1945). He did play several close variations of the Count, however, and in the end wound up playing parodies of the character. His monumental work in *Dracula*, coupled, some say, with turning down a part in *Frankenstein* the next year, served to typecast him as a horror movie villain. No parts equaled Dracula, and as horror movies declined, so did his fortunes. He wound up an unemployed drug addict, able to find work only with his devoted fan, Ed Wood, Jr. It was Wood who directed Lugosi in his last role, a final parody of Dracula that appeared in the cult classic, *Plan 9 from Outer Space*. Lugosi died a poor and broken man in 1955.

His legacy lives on. The image of the Eastern European aristocrat dressed in formal wear with hair swept straight back has also become the image of the vampire in general. The only element that didn't originate with Lugosi were the fangs, which Christopher Lee added in the 1950s. Throughout this century, the many actors who played Dracula (from John Carradine to Frank Langella) would copy Lugosi with their own.

✝ END ✝

loir, Josianne Gibert, Fernando Bilbao; **D:** Jess (Jesus) Franco. **VHS** *NO*

The 7 Brothers Meet Dracula

Despite creating some of the best vampire movies of all time, by 1974 Hammer Films was suffering diminished success with its vampire films in general and its Dracula films in particular. Desperate for a successful film, Hammer turned to Hong Kong's Shaw Brothers Studio, where very successful martial arts movies were being churned out, and produced this hybrid vampire/martial arts mess. Must've seemed like a good idea to someone at the time. The movie begins in 1904. Cushing, as Van Helsing, travels to China to find Dracula. He is led to a small village were the members of a legendary vampire cult allied to Dracula are terrorizing people. He recruits the help of his Chinese counterpart (David Chaing) and seven other kung-fu experts. Plenty of kung-fu action ensues when the good guys take on the vampire cult. The film failed to save Hammer, which shut down not long after the film was made. Others would later attempt to mix vampires and martial arts and the Gothic and oriental atmospheres, but the task proved as difficult as transplanting vampires to the American West. An announced sequel, *Kali: Devil Bride of Dracula*, was never made. **AKA:** Legend of the Seven Golden Vampires. 🎵🎵

1973 110m/C *GB* [Hammer, Shaw Brothers] Peter Cushing, David Chang, Robin Stewart, Julie Ege; **D:** Roy Ward Baker; **M:** James Bernard. **VHS** *NO*

The Seven Vampires

This muddled, low-budget horror-comedy features a unique approach to vampirism but has little else to recommend it. Set in 1950s Rio de Janeiro, the film features a car-nivorous plant that kills a botanist and seemingly turns his wife into a vampire. We next meet the wife as the star of a cabaret act that she calls the "Seven Female Vampires." And to show how muddled it is, there is another storyline going on at the same time that involves a masked serial killer who leaves his victims drained of blood. **AKA:** As Sette Vampiros. 🎵

1986 ?m/C [Embrafilms] Alvamar Tadei, Andrea Beltrao, Ariel Coelho, Bene Nunes; **D:** Ivan Cardoso.

Sexy Prohibitissimo

Italian sexploitation pseudo-documentary movie purports to tell the history of the strip tease through a series of sketches using professional strippers. In one episode, Dr. Frankenstein brings his monster to life. When the beautiful assistant strips in front of the monster, he breaks the straps binding him and pursues the girl. In a second episode, Dracula decides to delay biting a stripper long enough to watch her act. **AKA:** Sexy Super Interdit; Forbidden Femininity; Sexy Interdit. 🎵

1963 87m/C [Gino Nordini Produzioni] **D:** Marcello Martinelli; **W:** Marcello Martinelli; **C:** Adalberto Albertini.

The She-Beast

Barbara Steele portrays an eighteenth century witch, burned at the stake by angry villagers, who comes back by taking possession of a young woman vacationing in modern Transylvania during the years of Communist rule. She is opposed by Van Helsing (John Karlson), who uses the knowledge gained from defeating Dracula in battling her. Occasionally and unintentionally amusing. Steele only has fifteen minutes of screen time. **AKA:** *La Sorella of Satan. The Sister of Satan.* Il Lago di Satana; The Revenge of the Blood Beast. 🎵🎵

beautiful girl. The girl's true love (Ngai Sing) set out for revenge in an effort to ensure that the girl is favorably reincarnated. There is a cameo appearance by horror veteran Lam Ching-Ying. 🐾🐾

19?? ?m/C **Eric Tsang**, Chan Lung, Ngai Sing, Chung Fa.

Sisters of Satan

The innocent Justine (Susana Kamini) is sent to a monastery where she falls victim to the sinister Alucarda. (No one found that name the least bit suspicious?) Soon the pair are biting each other, attacking the other nuns, and leading a black magic ritual complete with a goat-headed demon orchestrating an orgy. Reminiscent of Ingrid Pitt's famous scene in *Countess Dracula*, the vampire Justine rises naked from a blood-filled coffin. Originally released in Spanish as *Alucarda* and later as *Innocents from Hell*, and as *Alucarda la Hija de las Tinieblas*. 🐾🐾🐾

1975 **(R)** 91m/C MX [Tony Cervi] Claudio Brook, David Silva, Tina Romero, Susana Kamini; **D:** Juan Lopez Moctezuma. **VHS, Beta** ACA, MPI

The Slaughter of the Vampires

A honeymooning couple finds themselves trapped in a castle full of vampires, although it seems neither one can wait until after the honeymoon to break their marriage vows— both the bride and the groom are lured into bed by a seductive bloodsucker. *AKA: La Strage die Vampiri; La Stragi del Vampiri. Curse of the Blood-Ghouls; Curses of the Ghouls.* **Woof!**

1962 81m/C IT [Dino Sant'Ambrogio, Mercury Films International] Walter Brandi, Dieter Eppler, Graziella Granta; **D:** Robert Mauri; **W:** Robert Mauri. **VHS, Beta** SNC

1965 74m/C IT YU [Europix Consolidated] Barbara Steele, Ian Ogilvy, Mel Welles, Lucretia Love; **D:** Michael Reeves. **VHS, Beta** SNC, MPI

Shyly Spirit

The curse placed on a young man (Eric Tsang) leads him to suck the life out of a

Slave of the Vampire

Short sequel to *The Teenage Frankenstein*, in which no vampire appeared. In this one, Dracula and the Wolf Man go mano-a-mano for no apparent reason. 🗡🗡

1959 6m/C [Don Glut] **Victor Fabian**, Don Glut, Wayne Moretti; **D:** Don Glut.

Sleepwalkers

A cat named Klovis proves to be as good a vampire hunter as the legendary Van Helsing in this original vampire tale from Stephen King. The action starts when the Brady family moves to a small town to settle down, but this is definitely not the Brady Bunch we all know and love. Both Mrs. Brady (Alice Krige) and her son Charles (Brian Krause) are a type of demon called a sleepwalker. Normal by day, by night they turn into cats and suck the life force from their victims. Virginal Tanya Robertson (Mädchen Amick) becomes the next target of the Brady's, who seem to be all-powerful. Or so it seems—the heroic Klovis and his feline friends are out to prove otherwise. *AKA:* Stephen King's Sleepwalkers. 🗡🗡

1992 (R) 91m/C [Columbia Pictures] Brian Krause, Madchen Amick, Alice Krige, Jim Haynie, Cindy Pickett, Lyman Ward, Ron Perlman; **Cameos:** Dan Martin, Glenn Shadix, Joe Dante, John Landis, Clive Barker, Tobe Hooper, Stephen King, Mark Hamill; **D:** Mick Garris; **W:** Stephen King. **VHS, LV** *COL*

Son of Dracula

In this late-coming sequel to the Universal classic, a stranger named Alucard is invited to America by a Southern belle obsessed with eternal life. It is actually Dracula himself, not his son, who wreaks havoc in this spine-tingling chiller. *AKA:* Young Dracula. 🗡🗡🗡

1943 80m/B [Universal] Lon Chaney Jr., Evelyn Ankers, Frank Craven, Robert Paige, Louise Allbrit-

ton, J. Edward Bromberg, Samuel S. Hinds; **D:** Robert Siodmak. **VHS, Beta, LV** *MCA*

Son of Dracula

On this less than coherent horror comedy/musical, Dracula's musical male offspring, Count Down (Harry Nilsson), travels to the netherworld, ostensibly to become its ruler. His dominion includes a variety of monstrous types, including Count Frankenstein and his monster. The Count makes common cause with Van Helsing (Dennis Price), both to rid himself of his vampirism and to destroy the netherworld. Ringo Starr makes a less than stellar appearance as Merlin the Magician, and cameos by rock musicians Peter Frampton, Keith Moon, and John Bonham don't even help. It probably sounded much better on paper. *AKA:* Count Downe, Son of Dracula; Young Dracula. 🗡🗡

1973 90m/C [Apple Films] **Harry Nilsson**, Dennis Price, Ringo Starr, Freddie Jones, Peter Frampton, John Bonham, Keith Moon; **D:** Freddie Francis; **W:** Jay Fairbanks.

Sorority House Vampires

A sorority goes to a secluded cabin in the woods for their new member initiations ceremonies. Once there, they encounter Count Vlad (Robert Bucholz). 🗡🗡

1991 ?m/C Robert Bucholz, Natalie Bondurant, Eugenie Bondurant, Rachel Wolkow; **D:** Geoffrey de Valois.

Spermula

A softcore French science fiction vampire film in which a group of sexy female vampires from outer space land at a luxurious castle on Earth. These space vixens differ from the average vampire, though—they live

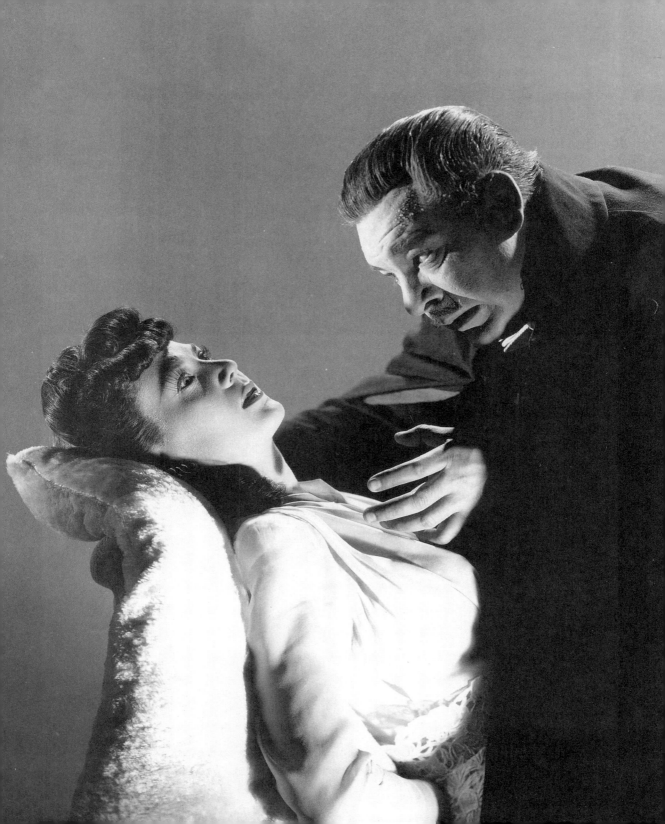

off sperm instead of blood. Udo Kier portrays a handsome young man who develops a relationship with the luscious leading vampire (Dayle Haddon). 🎵🎵🎵

1976 88m/C Dayle Haddon, Udo Kier, Georges Geret, Ginette LeClerc, Susannah Djain; **D:** Charles Matton; **W:** Charles Matton; **C:** Jean-Jacques Flori; **M:** Jose Bartel.

Spooks Run Wild

It's on several vampire filmographies, but even as a pseudo-vampire flick its status is dubious. The East Side Kids were a successful screen commodity, so why not take them off the streets and pair them with Bela Lugosi in a supernatural setting, maybe an old mansion in the countryside? Lugosi portrays Nardo, a strange man who lives with Luigi, his midget assistant (Angelo Rositto). He dresses in evening clothes and cape (like Dracula) and travels with coffins. The East Side Boys are on a vacation arranged for underprivileged youth. They suspect the mysterious Nardo of being the Monster. A Van Helsing imitation appears in the person of Professor Van Grosch (Dennis Morgan). Lugosi's presence, coupled with the vampire trappings, gets this one in on a technicality. 🎵🎵🎵

1941 64m/B [Monogram] Huntz Hall, Leo Gorcey, Bobby Jordan, Sammy Morrison, Dave O'Brien, Dennis Moore, Bela Lugosi; **D:** Phil Rosen; **W:** Carl Foreman. **VHS, Beta** *NOS, SNC, VYY*

Star Virgin

In the distant future, a robot is attempting to explain sex to the last surviving female human. To do this he shows her a series of vignettes from the past, one of which features a young couple forced to stay at an old castle after their car breaks down. Of course

we all know what follows in that old plot line—the owner of the castle is a vampire! 🎵

1979 ?m/C [Linus Gator]

Stephen King's The Tommyknockers

Another of King's creepy tales, adapted for TV. Bobbi (Helgenberger) and Gard (Smits) live in the small town of Haven, Maine (actually filmed on New Zealand's North Island). She's an aspiring writer; he's a fading poet with a drinking problem and a metal plate in his head (this is important). Walking in the woods, Bobbi stumbles over a long-buried spaceship which begins to take possession of the townspeople—their eyes shine green, their teeth fall out, and they act out their (often violent) fantasies—all but Gard. The whole thing's more silly than scary. The title comes from an old children's rhyme. **AKA:** The Tommyknockers. 🎵🎵🎵

1993 (R) 120m/C Jimmy Smits, Marg Helgenberger, Joanna Cassidy, E.G. Marshall, Traci Lords, John Ashton, Allyce Beasley, Cliff DeYoung, Robert Carradine, Leon Woods, Paul McIver; **D:** John Power; **W:** Lawrence D. Cohen. **VHS, LV** *VMK, TWV*

Strange Love of the Vampires

A young woman (Emma Cohen) falls in love with an aristocrat (Carlos Ballesteros) after their enjoyable one night stand. Afterwards, she believes that he is calling out to her, so she makes haste to his standard-issue mysterious castle home. Unfortunately for her, it is inhabited by (Surprise!) vampires, among them her former lover. Her arrival provides an excuse for some gratuitous sex, which is brought to an abrupt end by the gratuitous

Son of Dracula: "C'mon, you can't be dead, all I did was look at ya." Lon Chaney's Count Alucard has struck again.

They did the mash, they did the monster mash!

Success does strange things to those who experience it. Universal Studios, threatened with closure as the effects of the Great Depression reverberated through the country, finally found success in Bela Lugosi's *Dracula* (1931). They repeated that success before the year was out with Boris Karloff's *Frankenstein* (1931), and then followed it with *White Zombie* (1932), *The Mummy* (1932) and finally *The Wolf Man* (1941). Those wonderful monsters pumped new life into the studio, so the studio sought as many ways as possible to perpetuate their successes. One way was through sequel's—*Dracula's Daughter* (1936), *The Son of Dracula* (1943), *The Bride of Frankenstein* (1935), *Son of Frankenstein* (1939), *The Mummy's Hand* (1940), are just some of the films pumped out by Universal.

Once the sequels were exhausted, it appeared that the monster party might be over. Luckily for the studio, one of its bright young executives had a sudden flash of inspiration—what would happen if the different monsters actually met each other in a movie? After all, Universal had four successful monsters, all of whom had passed through death and come back

for another movie. If one was good, two should be better, and four would be even better yet. Thus, the type of movie known as the "monster mash" born. The first foray into the new genre—*Frankenstein meets the Wolfman* (1942)—starred Karloff and Lugosi and featured only two monsters. In it, the Wolf Man turned to Dr. Frankenstein for a cure, but wound up battling the Frankenstein monster.

The first monster mash to feature all four monsters originated in a projected sequel to *Frankenstein Meets the Wolfman* that would have been called *Wolfman vs. Dracula*. Lugosi was set to play Dracula. However, the plans for that movie quickly fell apart. Karloff signed to do two more movies, and it turned out that the second one, the *House of Frankenstein* (1944), subverted the Lugosi movie that was still in the planning stage. *House of Frankenstein* became the first flick to feature all of the Universal characters and also had a mad scientist thrown in for good measure; John Carradine assumed the role of Dracula. After that film was released, negotiations to finally make *Wolfman vs. Dracula* resumed but were unproductive. That movie was eventually killed altogether and replaced

by a sequel *to House of Frankenstein* that was called *House of Dracula* (1945). Again Carradine portrayed Dracula. The monster mash formula played well for a film or two, but it was difficult to continue the plot. How many times can a mad scientist attempt to turn the monsters into normal people? Under the demands of the monster mash story lines, the monsters began to lose their individual identities that had made them so memorable to so many audiences.

What next for the movie monsters? The monster theme seemed to be exhausted, but Universal had one more trick up its sleeve. Instead of playing it straight, the studio decided to add a little comedy to the monster mix. Thus was born a series of Abbott and Costello movies in which they spoofed horror themes. Only the first film in the series—*Abbott and Costello Meet Frankenstein* (1949)—featured the familiar Universal monsters (in fact Universal abandoned the horror genre after this film), but the movie was successful enough to allow the comedy duo to make several other monster films. Subsequent appearances featured the Invisible Man (1951), Dr. Jekyll and Mr. Hyde (1952), and the Mummy

(1955). The comedic twist given to the monsters would be successfully revived in the mid-1960s in two television series, the *Addams Family* and *The Munsters*.

Since Universal ran their monsters into the ground and seemingly exhausted every format in which the creatures could appear, the only real attempts to bring all of the monsters together have been in productions aimed at children and teenagers. These include a puppet movie, *Mad Monster Party?* (1966), that included a Lugosi-like Dracula and a Karloff-like Frankenstein's monster; and *The Night Dracula Saved the World* (1979), in which the monsters united to preserve the annual celebration of Halloween. Another film, *Transylvania 6-5000* (1985), is best understood and appreciated when viewed as a comedic monster mash for the younger set.

The temptation to bring the monsters together, at least two of them if not all four, has resurfaced from time to time. Some, like *Dracula vs. Frankenstein*(1969), were unmitigated disasters, but others, such as *Howling VI: The Freaks* (1990), exhibited thoughtful creativity.

✝ **END** ✝

violence of angry villagers attacking the castle. *AKA:* El Extrano Amor de los vampiros; La Noche de los Vampiros; Los Vampiros Tambien Duerman; Night of the Walking Dead. 𝄞𝄞

1974 91m/C [Richard Films] **Carlos Ballestros**, Emma Cohen, Barta Barry, Vicky Lusson, Raphael Hernandez, Roberto Carmardiel; *D:* Leon Klimovsky; *W:* Juan Jose Daza, Carlos Pumares, Juan Jose Porto; *C:* Miguel Mila.

Subspecies

In the first horror movie shot in post-Ceausescu Transylvania, a creative new version of the vampire is revealed. The story revolves around a stone known as a bloodstone, which supposedly contains the blood of saints. Legend has it that if a vampire drinks from the stone, he or she can be sustained without drinking the blood of living victims. In flashback several centuries ago, King Vladimir (Angus Scrimm) is killed with a silver sword wielded by his son Radu (Anders Hove), an evil and evil-looking being. In a scene that would be redone to great effect by Francis Ford Coppola in his version of *Dracula* a year later, Radu licks the blood from the blade. The story now jumps to the present. Radu turns his attention to three American tourists, Lillian, Mara, and Michelle (Michelle McBridge, Trina Movila, and Laura Tate). In spite of having the bloodstone from which to drink, Radu goes after the women and succeeds in turning the first two into vampires like himself. As he is approaching the third, his more handsome brother Stefan (Michael Watson) intervenes

and protects her. The stage is set for the final conflict. One of the better vampire movies of the 1990s, it spawned two sequels, *Bloodstone: Subspecies II* (1993) and *Bloodlust: Subspecies III* (1995). 𝄞𝄞𝄞

1990 (R) 90m/C [Full Moon Entertainment] **Anders Hove**, Laura Tate, Michael Watson, Michelle McBride, Irina Movila, Angus Scrimm; *D:* Ted Nicolaou. **VHS, LV, 8mm** *PAR, BTV*

Sundown

A blend of Western and vampire genres that director Hickox pulls off thanks to a good story and plenty of humor. It seems that Dracula (David Carradine) has grown tired of the old biting and bloodsucking routine and created an "artificial blood" synthesizer that allows vampires to live without killing humans. Armed with this machine he forms the town of Purgatory, where vampires lead a fairly "normal" life. In fact, with the help of sunscreen, shade, and wide-brim hats, the creatures of the night can even go out into the sun. Turns out that some vampires miss the old days, however, and would rather go back to terrorizing humans. A group of rebellious vampires led by Shane (Maxwell Caufield) and Jefferson (John Ireland) organize a gang to attack Dracula and the townsfolk, which leads to an old-fashioned free-for-all shootout at high noon between the forces of good and evil. 𝄞𝄞𝄞

1991 (R) 104m/C [Vestron Pictures] David Carradine, Bruce Campbell, Deborah Foreman, Maxwell Caulfield, Morgan Brittany; *D:* Anthony Hickox. **VHS** *VES*

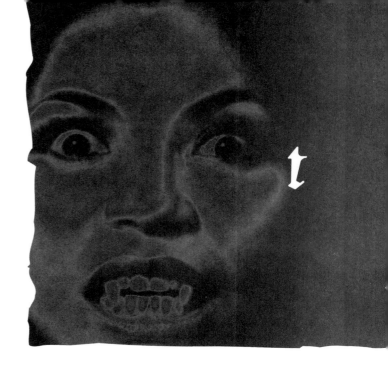

Tale of a Vampire

Alex, a very old vampire, spends much of his time in the local library. One day, a new employee named Anne appears at the library; Alex is convinced that Anne is the reincarnation of his nineteenth-century lover. Loosely based on Edgar Allen Poe's "Annabel Lee", this stylish and atmospheric film unfortunately moves at a very slow pace and lacks the bite that all good vampire movies sport. *AKA: A Tale of Vampire.* 🦇🦇

1992 (R) 93m/C *GB* Julian Sands, Kenneth Cranham, Suzanna Hamilton; *D:* Shimako Sato; *W:* Jane Corbett, Shimako Sato; *M:* Julian Joseph. VHS *VMK*

Tales from the Crypt Presents Bordello of Blood

Detective Rafe Guttman (Miller) is on the case of a Bible thumper's (Eleniak) missing brother (Feldman). The trail leads him to a unique establishment, a brothel presided over by vampire queen Lilith (Everhart), whose clients all wind up dead (but probably with smiles on their faces), and the strange Reverend Current (Sarandon, who made a fine vampire himself in "Fright Night"). Crypt Keeper's second big screen outing showcases Miller's slant on the leading man gig and serves up campy fun with the blood. *AKA:* Bordello of Blood. 🦇🦇

1996 (R) 87m/C [Gilbert Adler] **Angie Everhart,** Dennis Miller, Chris Sarandon, Corey Feldman, Erika Eleniak; *D:* Gilbert Adler; *W:* Gilbert Adler, A.L. Katz; *C:* Tom Priestley; *M:* Chris Boardman. VHS *NYR*

Tales from the Darkside, Vol. 4

Five scary new episodes from the popular TV show. Includes Stephen King's "Sorry, Right Number," about a woman who receives a phone call from her future self. 🦇🦇

19?? 100m/C Jeff Conaway, Deborah Harry, Paul Dooley, John Friedler; *D:* Theodore Gershuny; *W:*

BLOODSUCKERS FROM SOUTH OF THE BORDER

Given Mexico's reputation for generating some of the worst of the worst in horror films, it is hard to imagine that it played a pioneering role in the film world. However, its film industry actually dates back to the 1890s, when Salvador Toscano Barragan first began traveling through his homeland documenting its culture. In the years following World War I, movie theaters became increasingly popular, and in 1919, the first Mexican feature length film was released. Mexico then became the center of the Latin American cinema world.

During the silent film era, the international distribution of films was relatively easy; only the dialogue cards needed to be changed from country to country. With the arrival of sound in films, more creative measures had to be taken. Universal took the lead among Hollywood studios in producing sound films for the Spanish-speaking and in 1931 decided to make a Spanish-language version of Dracula that was shot on the same set as the English-language version. Each evening after the English cast completed its shooting, a Spanish crew moved in and began filming. In the end, many people felt the Spanish version was superior to Tod Browning's better-known English version. In any case, Universal's *Dracula* staring Carlos Villarias and Lupita Tovar was a great success in Mexico and profoundly influenced later vampire films.

After World War II, Mexican filmmakers were among those who discovered that teenagers loved to be scared. For several decades thereafter, Mexican cinema featured a steady stream of vampire movies. Mexico's first vampire movie, *El Vampiro* (*The Vampire*), released in 1957, was also one of its finest. Starring German Robles as the suave Count Lavud, it demonstrated the influence of Carlos Villarias's Dracula. Director Fernando Mendez could have used Mexico's own lively vampire folk traditions as the inspiration for the Lavud character, but instead he turned to Villarias as his role model. Count Lavud is little-known outside of vampire circles today, but he was one of the strongest influences on Christopher Lee's now-famous portrayal of Dracula that was released just a year later.

In spite of its commendable beginnings, Mexico justly deserves its reputation for grinding out low-quality vampire movies. Cost-cutting rules that governed Mexican films are at least partly to blame for the poor quality of the movies. In order to keep costs down, movies were shot as a series of shorts for release in Mexico. Then, at a later date, three of the shorts would be edited together into a feature-length movie for release to foreign markets, primarily the United States.

King of the Mexican horror B-movies was a unique fellow by the name of Rodolfo Gizmán Huerta, who spent much of his adult life as one of the masked wrestlers who were very popular in Mexico for years. He was known by his ring name of Santo. Through the 1960s and 1970s, Santo starred in four movies a year in which he defeated a wide variety of monsters, including female vampires in *Santo Conta las Mujeres Vampiro* (1962) and the Lugosi-like Baron Brakola (1965).

At the same time Santo was grinding out his steady stream of formula fare, veteran (and by this point, aging) actor John Carradine traveled south of the border and ended up making some of the worst movies of his long career. In 1968, Carradine competed directly for Santo's wrestling audience in *The Vampires* (*Las Vampiras*), in which he played the leader of a group of female vampires opposed by a pair of wrestlers, Mil Mascaras and Maria Duval. Treated almost like a stage prop, the mono-lingual Carradine spoke only one line.

Mexican filmmakers largely abandoned vampire movies in the early 1980s. Then, without warning in 1992, the film world was shocked by the release of the Mexican film *Cronos*, one of the most innovative of the new breed of vampire movies. The award-winning tale of alchemy, occultism, and vampirism built around the bloodthirsty Cronos device is not to be missed by vampire fans.

✝ END ✝

Stephen King, Michael McDowell, Theodore Gershuny. **VHS** *WOV*

A Taste of Blood

Independent film by famed gore director Herschell Gordon Lewis begins as the youthful John Stone (Bill Rodgers) receives a package from England containing two bottles of slivovitz, the very strong brandy made in Transylvania. He is also given instructions to use the brandy for a toast to an unnamed long-dead ancestor. Soon, Stone's habits begin to change; most importantly, he becomes nocturnal. He decides to track down the sender of the slivovitz and, while in England, discovers that he is a descendent of Count Dracula. Returning to America, he becomes a full-fledged vampire and starts to take revenge on the family of the people who killed Dracula. His actions alert Dr. Howard Helsing (Otto Schlesinger), setting up the showdown between the descendent of the vampire hunter and the descendent of the vampire. A most interesting variation on the vampire tale. *AKA:* The Secret of Dr. Alucard. *♫♫*

1966 120m/C Bill Rogers, Elizabeth Wilkinson, Thomas Wood, Otto Schlesinger; *D:* Herschell Gordon Lewis; *W:* Donald Stanford; *C:* Andy Romanoff.

Taste the Blood of Dracula

In this sequel to *Dracula Has Risen from His Grave*, the action shifts to Victorian England, where three gentlemen involve themselves somewhat unwittingly in the nefarious plot of Lord Courtley (Ralph Bates). To assist Dracula in again rising from his grave, he enlists their help in obtaining Dracula's ring and cloak, and a vial of red powder. Searching for a treasure, the three kill Lord Courtley just as he is attempting to bring Dracula back to life. Successfully resurrected, Dracula began to work his revenge on the three men through their offspring, who he attacks and sends to kill their parents. Dracula further assaulted Victorian family values by turning the

two young daughters into passionate objects of sensuality. Christopher Lee (as Dracula) was paid well, but given little to do as the rest of the cast carried the action. Less than a year later, Hammer followed up with *The Scars of Dracula.* *♫♫♫*

1970 (PG) 91m/C *GB* [Hammer House of Horror, Warner Brothers] Christopher Lee, Ralph Bates, Geoffrey Keen, Gwen Watford, Linda Hayden, John Carson, Peter Sallis, Isla Blair, Martin Jarvis, Roy Kinnear; *D:* Peter Sasdy; *M:* James Bernard. **VHS** *WAR*

Teen Vamp

Murphy Gilcrease (Beau Bishop), a nerdish high school kid, is bitten by a prostitute who just happens to be a vampire. He comes out of the experience not only having lost his virginity, but also miraculously transformed into a very cool adolescent. He is opposed by a vampire-hunting priest portrayed by Clu Gulager (what is he doing here?). This low budget effort suffers from a very predictable storyline, amateurish acting, and poor photography. *AKA: Murphy Gilcrease, Teenage Vampire.* **Woof!**

1988 87m/C Clu Gulager, Karen Carlson, Angela Brown; *D:* Samuel Bradford. **VHS, Beta** *VTR, NWV*

Tender Dracula, or The Confessions of a Bloodsucker

In this comedy, McGregor (Peter Cushing) is a maturing actor who has specialized in horror movies, including those of the vampire genre. Hoping to escape being typecast, he petitions his producer to get out of horror and into more mainstream films. The producer responds by staging several fake murders as part of a scheme to convince McGregor to return to his work in horror films. Originally released in French as *Tendre Dracula ou les Confessions d'un Buveur de Sang* with Jean Rochefort dubbing Cushing's

voice. *AKA:* Confessions of a Bloodsucker; Tender Dracula, Vampire; Tendre Dracula ou les Confessions d'un Buveur de Sang. 🩸🩸🩸

1974 86m/C [Renn Productions] **Peter Cushing**, Jean-Louis Trintignant, Bernard Menez, Miou-Miou, Alida Valli, Nathalie Courval, Stephane Shandour; *D:* Alain Robbe-Grillet; *W:* Alain Robbe-Grillet, Justin Lenoir, Harold Brav; *C:* Jean-Jacques Tarbes, Karl Heinz Schafer.

Tenderness of Wolves

German filmmakers, who had earlier found inspiration in the career of serial killer Peter Kurten, finally discovered another famous German serial killer, Fritz Haarman, whose criminal activity, like Kurten's, had vampiric overtones. The homosexual Haarman picked up young men off the street and invited them to his home. Most of the time, he limited his activities to sex, but several times a year, he also killed them. Then, on occasion, he bit them and drank their blood. *AKA:* Die Zartlichkeit der Wolfe. 🩸🩸

1973 87m/C [Tango Film] **Kurt Raab**, Jeff Roden, Wolfgang Schenck, Rainer Werner Fassbinder, Margit Castensen; *D:* Ulli Lommel.

Terror Creatures from the Grave

Unfaithful wife is visited by medieval plague victims, at her husband's behest. Should've been much better. *AKA:* Cinque Tombe per un Medium. 🩸

1966 85m/C IT [International Entertainment Corporation] Barbara Steele, Riccardo Garrone, Walter Brandi; *D:* Ralph Zucker. **VHS** SNC

Terror in the Crypt

This represents the only time that Christopher Lee played a part in a movie inspired by "Carmilla," the classic vampire tale by Sheri-dan Le Fanu. An evil housekeeper calls forth the spirit of Mircalla (in Le Fanu's world vampires are always referred to by an anagram of their name), an ancestor of the present-day Count Ludwig von Karnstein (Lee). Mircalla launches an attack against the Karnstein family, which fights back against the bloodsucker. Even with Lee's notable presence, this black-and-white version of the Le Fanu story pales when compared to the full-color productions from Hammer Studios that were also released in the 1960s. *AKA:* La Cripta e l'Incubo; La Maldicion de los Karnsteins; The Karnstein Curse; The Crypt of the Vampire; The Vampire's Crypt; Karnstein, the Crypt and the Nightmare; Curse of the Karnsteins. 🩸🩸

1962 84m/B [Hispamer Film] **Christopher Lee**, Andriana Ambesi, Ursula Davis, Jose Campos, Vera Valmont, Nela Conjiu, Jose Villasante; *D:* Camillo Mastrocinque; *W:* Ernesto Gastaldi, Bruno Valeri, Jose Monter, Maria del Carmen; *C:* Giuseppe Aquari, Julio Ortas; *M:* Carlo Savina.

Theatre of Death

Top-notch thriller that features a series of vampire-like murders at the Grand Guignol Theatre of Death in Paris. As the body count grows, playwright Phillipe Darvas (Christopher Lee), who possesses hypnotic powers, emerges as the prime suspect, but there are plenty of twists and turns while the police inspector (Ivor Dean) and a forensic specialist (Julian Glover) track down the real killer. *AKA:* Blood Fiend; *Female Fiend.* 🩸🩸🩸

1967 90m/C [Hemisphere Productions] Christopher Lee, Lelia Goldoni, Julian Glover, Evelyn Laye, Jenny Till, Ivor Dean; *D:* Samuel Gallu. **VHS, Beta** *REP,* SNC

They've Changed Faces

Creative modern adaptation of the Dracula story imagines the vampire (Adolfo Celi) as the leader of a modern automobile manufacturing company. He runs the company as a

From the movies to television: Dark Shadows is only the beginning

Vampire films first became popular on the big screen, with bloodsucking villains becoming a regular treat for the Saturday matinee crowd. However, once the television was invented, many people saw their first vampire movie from the comfort of their own homes, curled up on the living room couch on a Friday night watching a creature-feature television show in the 1950s. Many more saw their first vampire after rushing home from school in the early 1970s to tune into *Dark Shadows*, the groundbreaking vampire soap opera. Since that time, vampires have been a regular feature on the luminous box that sits in nearly every house in America. Thanks to the emergence of the made-for-television movie, the birth of the VCR and the spread of home videos, and the rapid growth of cable television, vampire fans have been able to witness the spilling of plenty of fresh blood over the years.

The developing relationship between the vampire and boob tube goes back almost to the birth of TV itself. People began staying home instead of visiting the local theater, but they wanted some of the same programs they could find at the theater. Vampire movies like *Dracula* (1931) found new life when they were released for late-night viewing on television in the 1950s, whetting the public's desire for horror films on television. At the end of the 1960s, the unheard of occurred when a failing soap opera called *Dark Shadows* added a vampire named Barnabas Collins to its cast of characters. Suddenly, the show was transformed into the highest-rated show on daytime television. Producer/director Dan Curtis somewhat reluctantly recognized that the vampire was the centerpiece of the show and in 1970 gathered the cast to shoot the first of two spin-off movies (*House of Dark Shadows*).

The next year Curtis launched a fruitful collaboration with writer Richard Matheson when the two produced *Night Stalker*, a vampire movie that became the highest-rated television movie to date. Curtis and Matheson next turned to the Dracula legend. Using Bram Stoker's novel as a starting point, the pair became the first to cinematically incorporate the legend of Prince Vlad Tepes into the Dracula story. Using the watershed book *In Search of Dracula* (by Raymond McNally and Radu Florescu) as their guide, Curtis and Matheson used the historical information on fifteenth-century ruler Tepes to answer many of the unanswered questions in Stoker's novel. The result was the 1974 mad-for-television version of Dracula that starred Jack Palance as a very sinister Dracula. A few years later, Curtis also produced Matheson's story, "No Such Thing as a Vampire" as an episode in a horror anthology called *Dead of Night* (1977).

Curtis has also done some excellent work for the small screen that had nothing to do with vampires (the mini-series *Winds of War* for example), but he has continued to draw on the vampire theme throughout his career. Most recently in 1991, Curtis brought *Dark Shadows* back to television as a prime-time series. Unfortunately, the show did not perform well in the ratings and was canceled after its first season. This was due in part to just plain bad timing. The show appeared just as the Gulf War between Iraq and the United States and its allies broke out. Known as the first televised war, the Gulf conflict proved to be too much competition for Dark Shadows and several other shows.

Dark Shadows continues to live on, however. Barnabas Collins has proven to be a very persistent bloodsucker, especially with the ladies. Throughout the 1990s, the episodes of both the original series and the 1991 revival series have become available on video. A whole new series of *Dark Shadows* anthologies (*Best of Barnabas, Dark Shadows: Vampires and Ghosts, Dark Shadows Bloopers, Dark Shadows Scariest Moments*) featuring the show's more memorable scenes have been issued on video.

Even before *Dark Shadows* made its mark, several other television vampires had touched the heart of America. From *The Munsters*, there was Grandpa Munster (whom we eventually learned was really Dracu-

la) and Herman Munster's beloved wife, Lily. And of course there was that witch of a vamp, Morticia Addams, from the *Addams Family*. Refusing to die when their two-year runs on TV ended, both *The Munsters* and the *Addams Family* spawned several made-for-TV movies. The latter show also was the subject of two big-screen releases—*The Addams Family* (1991) and *Addams Family Values* (1993).

In recent years, television has brought us other immortal bloodsuckers. Detective and "good" vampire Nick Knight (Rick Springfield) made his first appearance in a made-for-TV movie aired in the summer of 1989. Several years later, with his lair changed from Los Angeles to Toronto, Knight (now played by Geraint Wyn Davies) returned in a Canadian television series called *Forever Knight*, which was syndicated in the United States. After two years of growing popularity, the series moved to A&E, the American cable network. Unfortunately, the A&E producers completely misunderstood the dynamics that had

made the show such a hit; they removed two of the key stars and downplayed the role of Lecoix (Nigel Bennett), Knight's constant vampire antagonist. The revised show never enjoyed the success of its Canadian original.

Despite the failure of that cable effort, the cable genre proved an important boon for vampire fans. With more and more movie channels popping up every year, the demand for movies to fill programming slots grew rapidly. Vampire films benefitted from this need just as much as other popular genres. As mentioned, VCRs and home video have also made a dramatic impact on the number of vampires on television. Many of the new vampire movies have been produced by independent directors using semi-professional and amateur actors. Having been cut out of the distribution system supplying product for theaters, independent moviemakers have flocked to video as a means of supplying their films directly to consumers.

✝ END ✝

FAMOUS ONE-TIME COUNT DRACULAS

Jack Palance *Dracula* (1973)

Legendary TV producer Dan Curtis (of *Dark Shadows* and *The Night Stalker* fame) casts this actor more famous for his screen presence as a heavy in the title role of one of the first remakes of Bram Stoker's classic book. But in this made for tv version of Dracula, Palance's usual viciousness was kept to a minimum and Palance portrayed a lovesick Dracula looking for his love he lost four hundred years ago. He finally sees the image of long ago bride in Lucy Westenra. Palance returned the romanticism not recently seen in the prior Lugosi and Lee Dracula films.

Louis Jourdan *Count Dracula* (1978)

In a lengthy BBC production which was originally broadcast as a miniseries for PBS, French actor Louis Jourdan took the role and was the first to introduce Dracula as a rich, aristocratic and sensual creature. This *Count Dracula* was famous also for chillingly recreating Stroker's scene of Jonathan Harker witnessing Dracula crawling down the side walls of his castle. Even though sexuality was emphasize heavily in this version, and women did swoon after being bit, your rarely saw a fang in this Dracula, since they played up the drama and tension.

Frank Langella *Dracula* (1979)

Following in Lugosi's footsteps, Langella originated his role in the 1978 Tony award-winning Broadway play of Dracula and then made the transgression to film. Ironically, the play received more laurels than John Badham's adaptation. Langella's Dracula did become famous for having his shirt unbuttoned the most times and oozing sensuality to Kate Nelligan's Lucy and becoming a love and blood thirsty opponent to Sir Laurence Oliver's Van Helsing. But unlike Lugosi, Langella was able to walk away from his role of Dracula and work steadily in supporting roles in feature films.

Gary Oldman *Bram Stoker's Dracula* (1992)

This chameleon like British actor's range includes Sid Vicious, Beethoven and now Count Dracula. This lavish and star studded version of the classic not only further exemplified Oldman's versatility, but put director Francis Ford Coppola back on the map with a commercial success. Many critics disagreed with Coppola's claim that his film was closely adapted to the original novel, but it did provide some unique background information on how Count Dracula came into being from a once mighty warrior Vlad the Impaler to a man cursed after the loss of his love who was reincarnated into Wynona Ryder's Mina. With Oldman's Dracula, you got to see the many forms that Dracula was known to take, an aged man, a bat and a sex starved wolf.

feudal lord whose power is now in the form of capital, not land and he now has employees rather than the serfs. Don't ask about the health plan. He summons a young man (Giuliano Disperati) to his mansion to offer him a post as a company director. To get the job, however, he must be amenable to sucking the life out of the employees. The young man refuses and leads a revolt against Dracula and his undead middle-management minions. *AKA:* Hanno Cambiato Faccia. 🦇🦇

1971 ?m/C [Garigliano Films] **Adolfo Celi**, Geraldine Hooper, Giuliano Disperati; *D:* Corrado Farina.

The Thing

In this very first science fiction vampire movie, a flying saucer containing an alien (James Arness) crashes in the Artic. A research team recovers the body and takes it back to their installation, where it is thawed out. Unfortunately for the scientists, it comes to life as an eight-foot vegetable monster (would you believe a carrot) that needs a constant supply of blood in order to germinate its seeds and create the next generation of creatures. The relatively small and very isolated research station becomes the battleground between the scientists, the military, and the creature, which seems to be impervious to bullets or the freezing cold. We won't reveal the outcome, but in his next life the vampire carrot became a sheriff in the Old West. Fast-paced and suspenseful creature feature. Based upon *Who Goes There?* by John W. Campbell. Also released as *The Thing from Another World* and available in a colorized version. A 1982 remake lost most of the vampiric content. *AKA:* The Thing From Another World. 🦇🦇🦇

1951 87m/B [Howard Hawks, RKO] James Arness, Kenneth Tobey, Margaret Sheridan, Dewey Martin; *D:* Christian Nyby, Howard Hawks; *W:* Charles Lederer; *M:* Dimitri Tiomkin. **VHS, Beta, LV** *MED, TTC, MLB*

Think Dirty

A comedy in which Marty Feldman, in his first starring role, portrays an advertising executive prone to daydreams. In one of his fantasies he becomes a vampire. *AKA:* Every Home Should Have One; *Marty Feldman, Vampire!* 🦇🦇

1970 (R) 93m/C *GB* [Bob Maurice] **Marty Feldman**, Judy Cornwell, Shelley Berman; *D:* Jim Clark. **VHS, Beta** *COL*

Thirst

A secret cult/society abducts a young woman (Chatal Contouri) and takes her to an isolated area of Australia where they have established a modern scientific facility, a psychiatric ward. The members of the secret group believe that the girl is a descendent of their founder, Countess Elizabeth Bathory, and hence is destined to become their leader. Patients at this secret facility are systematically drained of their blood which is put in milk bottles later to meet the needs of the vampiric staff . Well, it could happen! You can measure your paranoid component by your willingness to suspend belief. 🦇🦇

1987 (R) 96m/C [New Line Cinema] David Hemmings, Henry Silva, Chantal Contouri; *D:* Rod Hardy. **VHS, Beta** *MED*

The Thirsty Dead

John Constantine plays the king of a jungle tribe that kidnaps beautiful young women. The women's blood is drained to keep him young and healthy. The crux of the story concerns a young actress whom Constantine abducts and invites to share his throne. In order to assume her queenly post, she must join in the sacrifices and the subsequent blood drinking. Wretchedness abounds. *AKA:* The Blood Cult of Shangri-La; Blood Hunt. **Woof!**

1974 (PG) 90m/C *PH* [International Amusement Corporation] John Considine, Jennifer Billingsley, Judith McConnell, Fredricka Meyers, Tani Phelps Guthrie; *D:* Terry Becker. **VHS, Beta** *NO*

To Die for

Dracula/Vlad Tepish (Brendan Hughes), who has moved to Los Angeles in search of a new home and a new life, meets and falls in love with a real estate agent named Kate (Amanda Wyss), who happens to resemble a woman he killed several centuries ago. The plot thickens when another vampire (Steve Bond) arrives in L.A.; turns out he bears a grudge against Dracula for killing that same woman. The vampiric love triangle leads to a nasty final confrontation between the two macho supernatural creatures of the night. Vlad's adventures are continued in *To Die For II.* 𝄞𝄞𝄞

1989 **(R)** 99m/C [Skouras Pictures, Arrowhead Entertainment] Brendan Hughes, Scott Jacoby, Duane Jones, Steve Bond, Sydney Walsh, Amanda Wyss, Ava Fabian; **D:** Deran Sarafian; **M:** Cliff Eidelman. **VHS, Beta, LV** *ACA*

To Die for 2: Son of Darkness

This sequel to *To Die For* finds our "hero" Dracula/Vlad Tepish (now portrayed by Michael Praed) leaving Los Angeles to become a doctor working the graveyard shift at a hospital, where he has access to a supply of blood. One night while he's working, a woman brings in her adopted son, complaining that he stays up all night making noise. Vlad (who now goes by the name Max Schrenk, a clever tribute to the actor who played the lead role in the 1922 silent vampire classic, *Nosferatu*) immediately recognizes that he is the child's real father. This realization sets off a chain of events that leads to the return of the evil vampire known as Tom, who was supposedly killed in the first movie. Another bloody confrontation ensues. In one notable scene, Tom captures Jane, a vampire friend of Vlad's, and kills her by handcuffing her to a tree facing the rising sun. This sequel rivals the original as an enjoyable vampire horror tale. 𝄞𝄞𝄞

1991 **(R)** 95m/C [Vidmark Entertainment] Rosalind Allen, Steve Bond, Scott Jacoby, Michael Praed, Jay Underwood, Amanda Wyss, Remy O'Neill; **D:** David F. Price. **VHS** *VMK*

To Sleep with a Vampire

A color remake of the classic black-and-white vampire film *Dance of the Damned.* A thousand-year-old vampire (Scott Valentine) chooses Nina (Charlie Spradling), a down-and-out young woman, as his victim. Before he kills her, he offers to spare her life for a

few hours if she will tell him about sunlight, the memory of which has faded from his mind. A very good movie when considered in its own right; however, it pales in comparison to the earlier version, which was one of the finest vampire movies ever made. 𝄞𝄞𝄞

1992 **(R)** 90m/C [Roger Corman] Scott Valentine, Charlie Spradling, Richard Zobel, Ingrid Vold, Stephanie Hardy; **D:** Adam Friedman. **VHS** *NHO*

Tom Thumb and Little Red Riding Hood vs. the Monsters

A gruesome fairy tale for the kiddies set in a haunted forest. Little Red Riding Hood (Maria Garcia), Tom Thumb, and their forest friends must contend with an evil witch and her crew of monsters, including a fang-wielding black-robed vampire. **AKA:** y Pulgareito contra los Monstruos; Caperucita. 𝄞𝄞

1962 90m/C [Azteca] Maria Garcia, Jose Elias Moreno, Cesareo Quesades; **D:** Robert Rodriguez; **W:** Robert Rodriguez.

Tomb

Vampire and mummy themes mix in this low budget production as a pair of fortune-seekers enter an ancient Egyptian tomb and unknowingly awaken the vengeful, sadistic, and vampiric Princess Nefratis (Michelle Bauer). She can't rest without her treasures and she comes to America in search of them. Along the way to doing in the thieves with her magical powers, she stops to feed one girl to a bed of serpents. Carradine appears as an egyptologist, one of his better parts during those last years of his life, in which he was free from any expectation of playing another aging vampire. Based on a Bram Stoker story. 𝄞𝄞

1986 106m/C Cameron Mitchell, John Carradine, Sybil Danning, Richard Hench, Michelle (McClellan) Bauer; **D:** Fred Olen Ray; **C:** Paul Elliott. **VHS, Beta** *TWE*

Tombs of the Blind Dead

Blinded by crows for using human sacrifice in the thirteenth century, zombies rise from the grave to wreak havoc upon 20th-century Spaniards. Atmospheric chiller was extremely popular in Europe and spawned three sequels. The sequels, also on video, are "Return of the Evil Dead" and "Horror of the Zombies." *AKA:* The Blind Dead; La Noche dell Terror Ciego. 𝄢𝄢𝄢

1972 (PG) 86m/C *SP PT* [Hallmark] Caesar Burner, Lone Fleming, Helen Harp; *D:* Armando de Ossorio. **VHS, Beta** *NO*

Torture Chamber of Dr. Sadism

Loosely inspired by Edgar Allan Poe's short story, "The Pit and the Pendulum." Count Regula (Christopher Lee) has killed twelve virgins in his medieval dungeon torture chamber. But is caught, beheaded, and drawn and quartered before getting to lucky number thirteen. Forty years later the Count returns, ready to claim his thirteenth victim (Karin Dor), the daughter of his earlier intended victim. He also goes after Roger Monte Elise (Lex Barker), the son of Reinhard von Mairienberg, the prosecuting attorney at his trial. A fine example of the inverse relationship between the quality of a movie and the number of titles under which it was released. *AKA:* The Snake Pit and the Pendulum, Blood Demon, The Torture Room. Blood Demon; Castle of the Walking Dead; Die Schlangengrube und das Pendel. 𝄢𝄢𝄢

1969 120m/C *GE* [Hemisphere Productions] **Christopher Lee**, Karin Dor, Lex Barker, Carl Lange, Vladimir Medar, Christiane Rucker, Dieter Eppler; *D:* Harald Reinl. **VHS, Beta**

Tower of the Devil

According to legend, somewhere in the far reaches of the Philippine jungle there lives a pregnant woman who survives on the blood of lizards. The leader of a cult of vampires (Ramon D'Salva) wants her help in creating a new generation of vampire children. The vampires eventually find the woman after defeating a pack of angry werewolves, and then things get really weird—acts of God, earthquakes, and a vampire child are just some of the oddities. *AKA:* Tore ng Diyablo. 𝄢𝄢

1969 ?m/C **Ramon D'Salva**, Jimmy Morato, Pilar Pilapil, Rodolfo Garcia; *D:* Lauro Pacheco.

Track of the Vampire

Antonio Sordi is an artist possessed by a vampire ancestor who kills women he lures to his studio or finds on the streets of Venice, California. After killing them, he arranges their bodies in grotesque positions as models for his artwork. The finished product, painted with various shades of red, are designated "dead, red nudes." Sordi then finishes the job by dunking his victim's bodies in wax—or at least he thinks that's the end of things. Turns out his victim's have a final surprise in store for their killer. Producer Roger Corman fired original director Jack Hill and turned the project over to Stephanie Rothman, one of the first female directors to work on horror movies. Though the finished product is a hodge podge of Hill's footage, some scenes from a Yugoslavian film, and Rothman's work, it is a credible and intriguing film. *AKA:* Blood Bath. 𝄢𝄢

1966 80m/B *YU* [American International Pictures (A.I.P.)] William Campbell, Jonathan Haze, Sid Haig, Marissa Mathes, Lori Saunders, Sandra Knight; *D:* Stephanie Rothman, Jack Hill. **VHS** *SNC, GNS*

Transylvania 6-5000

In this attempt to capitalize on the success of *Love at First Bite* (1979) and *Once Bitten*

(1985), two klutzy tabloid reporters travel to modern day Transylvania to investigate reports that Frankenstein's monster has been sighted. It seems, however, that Transylvania is no longer the home of supernatural beings, but rather nothing more than a tourist trap. As a result, the reports of various creatures roaming the countryside, including that of the aforementioned Frankenstein and a seductive vampiress named Odette (Geena Davis), turn out to have very mundane explanations. *Transylvania 6-5000* could have turned out to be a delightful farce, but a disconnected storyline and hasty production led to a disjointed, pointless collection of a few funny moments held together by inactivity. ♫♫♪

1985 (PG) 93m/C [Mace Neufeld] **Geena Davis**, Jeff Goldblum, Joseph Bologna, Ed Begley Jr., Carol Kane, John Byner, Jeffrey Jones, Norman Fell; *D:* Rudy DeLuca; *W:* Rudy DeLuca. **VHS, Beta, LV** *VTR, NWV*

Transylvania Twist

Dexter Ward's uncle is a persistent librarian. He directs Dexter to locate the ancient *Book of Ulthar*, which is valued for its supposed ability to raise the Devil. Dexter teams up with Marissa Orlok, the neice of the last person to borrow the book, and travels to Castle Orlok, home of Marissa's uncle, the vampire Byron Orlok. (It is interesting to note that Orlok is the name given to the Dracula-like character in 1922's classic silent vampire movie, *Nosferatu*) The duo is also aided in their search for the book by a descendent of the original vampire hunter Dr. Van Helsing. Director Wynorski and his boss Roger Corman poked fun at a number of horror movies in this flick and also shamelessly included scenes from Corman's Edgar Allen Poe films. Cameos from the likes of Forest Ackerman, scream queen Brinke Stevens, and Boris Karloff spice things up. H.P. Lovecraft fans will also recognize the homage this movie pays to the master horror writer. ♫♪

1989 (PG-13) 90m/C [Concorde] Robert Vaughn, Teri Copley, Steve Altman, Ace Mask, Angus Scrimm, Jay Robinson, Brinke Stevens; *D:* Jim Wynorski; *W:* R.J. Robertson. **VHS, Beta** *MGM*

Twins of Evil

Real-life sisters Madeleine and Mary Collinson play the twins Frieda and Maria Geldhorn (respectively) in this third part of the Hammer Carmilla trilogy. The pair arrive at the home of their uncle Gustav Weil (Peter Cushing) a puritanical religious fanatic. Meanwhile, at nearby Karnstein castle, the current head of the vampire-infested family (Damien Thomas) revives his ancestor Carmilla/Mircalla (Katya Wyeth). By way of thanks, she introduces him to the joys of vampirism. He in turn enjoys his new life so much that he seems to bite everyone he meets, including the voluptuous Madeleine. The rise of a new vampire menace trumpets a call to action for Uncle Gustav, as the leader of a witchcraft fighting group called the Brotherhood. This might be a case of the cure being worse than the disease, but the audience has a good time watching the action as the battle between good and evil rages. The increasing emphasis on beautiful scantily-clad young women at Hammer was emphasized by the Collinson sisters, who seem to have auditioned for their parts by posing as the October 1970 *Playboy* centerfold, the magazine's first set of twins. Their accent (they are Maltese) was so thick that their lines in the movies were dubbed during the final stages of production. One of the finer Hammer productions, released just prior to the studio's fall. ♫♫♫

1971 86m/C *GB* [Hammer, Universal] **Madeleine Collinson, Damien Thomas, Katya Wyeth**, Mary Collinson, Peter Cushing, Kathleen Byron, Dennis Price, David Warbeck, Maggie Wright, Luan Peters, Kristen Lindholm, Judy Matheson; *D:* John Hough. **VHS, Beta** *MLB*

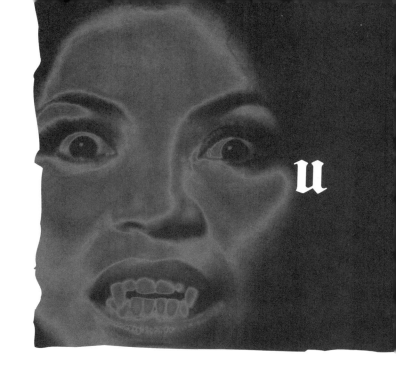

Ultimate Vampire

In this last of the original Mr. Vampire series, the priest with one eyebrow (Lam Ching-Ying returns to fight the hopping vampires. He also has to contend with the Hell Police, four unintelligible zombie cops, and a ghost woman. Definitely worth a look. 🦴🦴🦴

1991 ?m/C Lam Ching-ying, Chin Siu Ho, Carrie Ng Ka-Lai, Wong Chi-Yeung; **D:** Lau Wai-Keung.

Uncle Was a Vampire

Fresh from the success of *Horror of Dracula*, Christopher Lee chose this Italian comedy as his next vampire film (seen by most as a parody of Hammer's Count Dracula). Lee plays Baron Rodrigo, a vampire who pays a visit to his nephew Baron Osvaldo Lambertenghi's (Renato Rascal) castle only to find that it has been turned into a hotel and that his nephew has been relegated to the role of porter. Baron Rodrigo is of course upset by this turn of events, but it seems that he can't keep his eyes off the female guests long enough to help his nephew. Upset by this slight, Osvaldo tries to kill his uncle, but his attempt fails and he is instead turned into a vampire by Rodrigo. The rest of the film deals with the apparent troubles caused by being an eligible vampire bachelor in a hotel full of beautiful women. The years have not been kind to this lame comedy, as even the few laughs it originally provoked now fall flat. **AKA:** *Tempi Duri Pet I Vampiri; Hard Time for Vampires.* 🦴🦴

1959 ?m/C Christopher Lee, Kay Fisher. **VHS** *SNC, OUP*

Understudy:
The Graveyard Shift 2

Death is never final in a vampire movie, so it is no surprise that the vampire from the first *Graveyard Shift*, Stephen Tsepes (Silvio Oliviero), is back from the dead in this sequel. Now an actor instead of a cab driver,

Tsepes has the starring role in a low-budget movie about a vampire who plays snooker. While the original film was a tolerable vampire story, part two is ruined by a slow pace that eventually drags the viewer into a hopeless state of boredom. 🩸🩸

1988 (R) 88m/C [Virgin] Wendy Gazelle, Mark Soper, Silvio Oliviero; **D:** Gerard Ciccoritti. **VHS, Beta, LV** *NO*

The Unearthing

An unwanted pregnancy seems to find a happy solution when a woman decides to marry the heir to a wealthy estate and pass off her child as his. Only the family has some very strange tastes, including a taste for the blood of the unborn. Based on a Filipino vampire legend. 🩸

1993 (R) 83m/C [Wyre Martin, Barry Poltermann, Young American Films, Purple Onion Productions] Norman Moses, Tina Ona Paukstelis; **D:** Wyre Martin, Barry Poltermann; **W:** Wyre Martin, Barry Poltermann. **VHS, LV** *PSM*

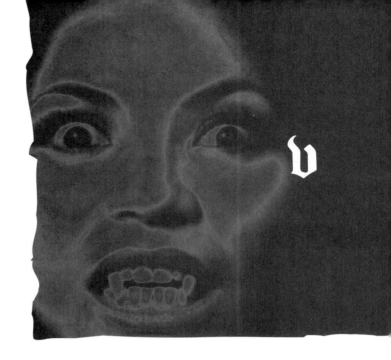

Valerie and the Week of Wonders

In this award-winning film, dream world and reality mix in a complex fashion for Valerie (Jaroslava Schallerová), a thirteen-year-old girl who lives with her grandmother. In one of her daydreams, her grandmother becomes a vampire in order to regain her youth. She is tried for witchcraft but is protected by a set of magic earrings. Based on a story by V. Nezval. *AKA:* Valerie a Tyden Divu. 🗡🗡🗡

1969 ?m/C Helena Anyzkova, Jaroslava Schallerova; ***D:*** Jaromil Jires.

Valley of the Zombies

Ormand Murks (Ian Keith), an undertaker, returns from the dead but needs constant infusions of fresh blood to stay alive. Plenty of scenes of Murks in a black cloak stalking innocent townsfolk, but little additional action until the final confrontation. 🗡🗡▽

1945 ?m/B [Republic Pictures] **Ian Keith**, Robert Livingston, Adrian Booth, Thomas E. Jackson.

Vamp

A fairly well-known but muddled effort that can't decide if it wants to be a horror film or a comedy—in the end it succeeds in being neither. Three college freshmen, hoping to earn the attention needed to get into their favorite fraternity, travel to the seedy part of a nearby city in search of a stripper for a campus party. Taking in the show at the After Dark Club, the boys soon realize that the club's owner Katrina (Grace Jones) and all of the dancers are in fact vampires. A couple of the boys realize that important point a little too late and end up joining the undead, while the third teams up with his girlfriend (who happened to be working at the club) to fight off the vampire horde. *Vamp* is memorable for a Grace Jones dance performance, but little else due to the comedy/horror identity crisis. 🗡🗡

1986 (R) 93m/C [New World Pictures] **Grace Jones,** Chris Makepeace, Robert Rusler, Gedde Watanabe;

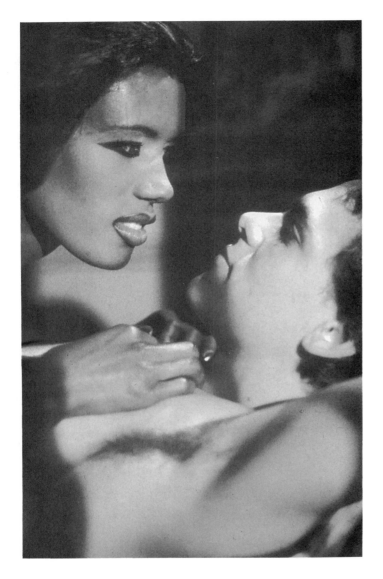

starred Christopher Lee. The main part of the film is shown without dialogue and seems to deal with the problem of how to present a gothic villain in the modern world. In the closing scene, Lee describes Dracula's death and reads the corresponding passage from the novel. **AKA:** Cuadecuc. ♫♫

1970 ?m/C Christopher Lee, Herbert Lom; **D:** Pedro Portabella.

The Vampire

Thinking he is just taking a couple of aspirin, Dr. Paul Beecher (John Beal) instead takes some pills that include ingredients derived from a vampire bat. The result? Instead of having his headache cured, Beacher turns into a nocturnal, scaly vampire-like monster. From that point the plot becomes rather predictable, with the monster attacking people and his actions leading to a final confrontation with the forces of good. **AKA:** It's Always Darkest Before the Dawn; Mark of the Vampire. ♫♫

1957 ?m/B [United Artists] **John Beal**, Coleen Gray, Kenneth Tobey, Lydia Reed.

The Vampire

Drawing on other classic vampire films (1922's *Nosferatu* and 1931's *Dracula*), German Robles created a new vampire character—Count Lavud—in what would become one of the classic Mexican vampire movies of all time. Count Karol de Lavud, a Hungarian, moves to Mexico and purchases some land. Once there, he proceeds to vampirize the inhabitants, especially Maria Teresa (Alicia Montoya). As Teresa is being buried, her neice Marta (Ariadna Welter) and physician Enrique (Abel Salazar) arrrive and are attacked by Lavud, who kidnaps Marta. Enrique recovers and pursues Lavud through the underground crypts of his castle. He is aided by Teresa, who comes back from the grave to assist the doctor and protect her niece at crucial moments. A stirring final confrontation

Vamp: I'm not wearing too much make-up for you, am I?

D: Richard Wenk; **M:** Jonathan Elias. **VHS, Beta, LV** *NWV, VTR*

Vampir

An experimental underground documentary made during the shooting of *El Conde Dracula*, Jesus Franco's version of Dracula that

cements this film's position as a well-done, low-budget movie that featured capable special effects for the era. Released in United States in 1968. **AKA:** El Vampiro, The Lurking Vampire, Mark of the Vampire. 🗡🗡🗡🗡

1957 95m/B MX [K. Gordon Murray] Abel Salazar, Ariadne Welter, German Robles, Carmen Montejo, Jose Luis Jimenez; **D:** Fernando Mendez. **VHS** SNC

The Vampire

Maria Menado is transformed from a repulsive hunchbacked creature into a beautiful young woman through magic. A short time later her husband is bitten by a poisonous snake and she sucks the wound to save him from the venom. The unfortunate result is that she becomes a vampire, called a pontianak in Malaysian folklore. The movie proved so popular that it led to no less than five sequels: Dendam Pontianak (1957), Sumpah Pontianak (The Vampire's Curse, 1958), Anak Pontianak (1958), Pontianaka Kembali (The Vampire Returns, 1963), and Pontianak Gua Musang (The Vampire of the Cave, 1964). The series was never widely circulated in the West. **AKA:** Pontianak. 🗡🗡

1957 ?m/B [Keris] **Maria Menado**, Salmah Ahmed, Dollah Serewak.

Vampire

Anton Voytek (Richard Lynch), handsome millionaire playboy and centuries old vampire, is living the high (un)life in San Francisco. There aren't many vampire hunters around, so he basically does what he pleases. His lifestyle is threatened by the appearance of an efficient and obstinate pair of Van Helsings, in the form of Harry Kilcoyne (E. G. Marshall) and John Rawlins (Jason Miller). Made for television. 🗡🗡

1979 120m/C [MTM Enterprises] **Richard Lynch**, E.G. Marshall, Jason Miller, Kathryn Harrold, Barrie Youngfellow, Michael Tucker, Jessica Walter; **D:** E.W. Swackhamer; **W:** Steven Bochco, Michael Kozoll; **C:** Dennis Dalzell; **M:** Fred Karlin.

Vampire and the Ballerina

This Italian quickie draws on the familiar plot of unwitting people being driven to the door of a old castle inhabited by supernatural terror. In this case, two young ballerinas choose the castle over an evening out-of-doors in a storm. If only they had known that a vampire countess and equally sinister vampire servant own the castle. The long night, made even longer by meaningless scenes of people walking around the local forests, comes to an end with the vampires being destroyed in the sunshine. **AKA:** L'Amante del Vampiro; The Vampire's Lover; The Dancer and the Vampire. 🗡🗡

1963 86m/C [ACIF Consorzio] **Walter Brandi**, Aldo Piga, Helene Remy, Tina Gloriani, Tina Gloriani, Isarco Ravaioli, John Turner; **D:** Renato Polselli; **W:** Ernesto Gastaldi; **C:** Angelo Baistrocchi.

Vampire at Midnight

A vampire serial killer is stalking modern Los Angeles. A policeman assigned to the case is taken off when his partner becomes victim number eleven. He can't break away that easily, however, since his girlfriend is becoming rather attached to Dr. Radcoff, a hypnotherapist and major suspect in the case. A good mystery that keeps its secret hidden to the end. Also includes plenty of gratuitous sex. 🗡🗡

1988 93m/C [Skouras] **Gustav Vintas**, Jason Williams, Jeanie Moore, Christina Whitaker, Leslie Milne; **D:** Gregory McClatchy. **VHS, Beta** FOX

The Vampire Bat

Low-budget imitation of the Universal Studios horror productions was better than it

> "Tonight I will take Niki away. Her soul will wander the night and you will never find where her body rests."
>
> —Armand Tesla (Bela Lugosi). *The Return of the Vampire* (1944).

should have been, thanks in part to stellar performances from Lionel Atwell and Dwight Frye. Dr. Otto Von Neoman (Atwell) is a scientist working in an obscure Balkan village. His experiments require blood, which he is taking from local residents. He also is spreading the cover story that a real vampire is loose in the community, when in fact his henchman Emil Borst (Robert Frazier) is roaming around the countryside dressed in a flowing cloak. A slightly mad barkeeper (Frye) provides a convenient suspect. Viewed today, *Vampire Bat* seems a very dated, obvious attempt to exploit the monster movie craze started by Universal. At the time, however, it did well for Majestic. 🦇🦇

1932 69m/B [Majestic] Lionel Atwill, Fay Wray, Melvyn Douglas, Dwight Frye, Maude Eburne, George E. Stone; **D:** Frank Strayer. **VHS, Beta** *VYY, SNC, WFV*

Vampire Centerfold

This low budget sequel to *Vampire Conspiracy*, replaces the innocent sorority sisters of the first film with an "innocent" young cheerleader (Elaine Juliette Williamson) who is bound and determined to make it as an actress. When she heads to California for her big career break, she is cast in a vampire movie. Much to her chagrin, she soon finds out that the cast of the film consists primarily of a coven of actresses (led by Tanya Qualls and Jasmine Jeans) who turn into sex-obsessed vampires each evening when the sun goes down. 🦇🦇

1996 ?m/C Tanya Qualls, Jasmine Jean, Elaine Juliette Williamson; **D:** Geoffrey de Valois.

Vampire Circus

Not initially a financial success, but now seen as one of the best of the Hammer vampire movies, *Vampire Circus* begins with the staking of vampire Count Mitterhaus at the hands of villagers angered by the count's feasting from the local children. Following the opening credits, the story shifts to the village which is cut off from the rest of the world due to the plague hitting the area. Into this hapless town comes the Circus of Nights. Only gradually revealed is the fact that the circus performers are vampires with the ability to change shapes and that the company is led by Emil (Anthony Corban) a cousin of the deceased count. The performers entertain the villagers with their shape-changing (trapeze artists becoming bats in midair being the most memorable), invite their attention to a magical mirror, and ultimately turn on them for their blood. Ultimately, the villagers must rise up again to slay the resurrected Count and bring the circus to an end. The sex and nudity which tested the British censors in 1972 appears rather tame by contemporary standards. 🦇🦇🦇

1971 (R) 84m/C GB [Hammer] Adrienne Corri, Laurence Payne, Thorley Walters, John Moulder-Brown, Lynne Frederick, Elizabeth Seal, Anthony Corlan, Richard Owens, Domini Blythe, David Prowse; **D:** Robert W. Young. **VHS** *FRG, MLB*

The Vampire Conspiracy

Headed by billionaire vampire Rupert Keaton, an alien alliance has conceived of a fiendishly sinister conspiracy—they will seduce young and innocent sorority girls using hi-tech cybersex and virtual reality and then breed the girls to create a superior race of vampires. After a pair of investigators uncover the plot, they join with Lisa Kilpatrick and her sorority sisters in the battle against the evil and inhuman plan. An adult erotic dark comedy. 🦇🦇

1994 ?m/C Mihaella Stoicova, Jasmine Jean, Heather LeMire, Anastasia Alexander, Leigh Hunt; **D:** Geoffrey de Valois.

Vampire : "Wow, I guess I shouldn't have had that second bowl of chili." Thinks millionare vampire Richard Lynch as he airs out his hiding place.

Vampire Cop

A policeman (Ed Cannon) who also happens to be a vampire has a unique method of fighting the drug war—he vampirizes the dealers. His antagonist is a reporter (Melissa Moore) who tries to stop him. Together can they stop the bad guys and find true love? (The latter part might be tough since the cop happens to sleep hanging upside down like a bat instead of in a bed.) ♫♫

1990 (R) 89m/C [Donald Farmer, Panorama Entertainment] Melissa Moore, Ed Cannon, Terence Jenkins. **VHS** *ATL*

Vampire Dracula Comes to Kobe

Following the suggestion in the Dan Curtis production of *Dracula* (1973), others began to play on the theme of the resemblance of one of Dracula's modern victims to his original love of several centuries ago. In this Japanese variation on the *Dracula* story, a modern-day Dracula discovers that a woman living in Kobe is the reincarnation of his former lover. *AKA:* Evil Make Beautiful Women; Kyuketsuki Dorakyura Kobe Ni Arawaru: Akuma Wa Onna Utsukushiku Suru. ♫♫

1979 84m/C [Toei/Asahi Communications] **Masumi Okada**, Kei Taguichi.

Vampire Family

Borrows some of the same misplaced-monster ideas as the Addams Family and the Munsters. A modern-day vampire family in Hong Kong must learn the proper etiquette to get along in today's world. Delightful comedy from the Hong Kong cinema assembly lines. ♫♫♫

1993 ?m/C Eric Tsang, Sandra Ng Kwun-Yu, Jimmy Lin; **D:** Eric Tsang.

The Vampire for Two

Vampire farce in which an aristocratic German vampire, Baron von Rosenthal (Fernando Gomez), and his family, attack two guest workers (Morales and Lopez Vazquez) from Spain. It's all (somewhat successfully) played for laughs. ♫♫

1965 85m/C [Bravo Murillo] **Fernando Gomez**, Trini Alonzo, Morales Vazques, Gracita Morales, J. Lopez Vazquez; **D:** Pedro Lazanga Sabater; **W:** Lazanga Sabater, Jose Maria Palacio; **C:** Eloy Molla.

The Vampire Girls

John Carradine starred, but claimed little creative input, in this Mexican travesty. He was the only person in the film who did not speak Spanish—he learned just enough to repeat in Spanish a famous line he had created once while playing Dracula on stage: "If I am alive, what am I doing here? On the other hand, if I'm dead, why do I have to wee-wee?" For most of the movie, he simply stood around, imprisoned in a cell. While he did that, the rest of the plot carried on around him. Countess Dracula assembled a group of vampire women to rescue him, but they were opposed by Mils Mascaras (literally "Thousand Masks"), one of the famous masked wrestlers-turned-actor of Mexico. *AKA:* Las Vampiras. ♫

1968 ?m/C [Luis Enrique Vergara] **John Carradine**, Pedro Armendariz Jr., Mil Mascaras, Maria Duval; **D:** Frederick Curiel.

The Vampire Happening

A bland attempt as a nudie vampire film drawing inspiration from Jean Rollin's suc-

John Carradine was a staple of the horror genre, specializing in vampire flicks.

cessful French films and Roman Polanski's *Fearless Vampire Hunters* (1971), *The Vampire Happening* featured the beautiful Pai Dagermark, its only asset, as a woman who looks like her vampire grandmother and who then begins to act like a member of the family. Ferdy Mayne revives his vampiric role from the Polanski film, but cannot help a weak story line and repetitious sex scenes. The movie just never happens. *Gebissen Wird nur Nichts Happening der Vampire.* ♫

1971 (R) 90m/C *GE* Ferdinand "Ferdy" Mayne; *D:* Freddie Francis. **VHS, Beta** *NO*

The Vampire Hookers

Looking for some female companionship while on leave, some sailors think they've gotten lucky when they run into a group of accommodating women at a local bar. Bad luck for the sailors, however—turns out the women are vampires sent out into the night by their leader and head vampire, Richmond Reed (an aging John Carradine). The women lure the men back to their home beneath the local graveyard, where a series of confrontations takes place after the men finally realize the danger they are in. Carradine did no credit to his long career with this boring and amateurish production, one of a series of similar vampire catastrophes he made in the 1970s. *AKA:* Cemetery Girls; Sensuous Vampires; Night of the Bloodsuckers; Twice Bitten. ♫

1978 (R) 82m/C *PH* [Capricorn Films] John Carradine, Bruce Fairbairn, Trey Wilson, Karen Stride, Lenka Novak, Katie Dolan, Lex Winter; *D:* Cirio H. Santiago. **VHS, Beta** *NO*

Vampire Hunter D

An impressive Japanimation film, based on *Vampire Hunter D* by Hideyuki Kikuchi, aimed at an adult audience. In 12,090 CE,

earth has been overrun by vampires. When Count Magus Lee bites homesteader Doris Lang, a vampire hunter known only as "D" (but reminiscent of Clint Eastwood's "man with no name") comes riding in on his cyborg horse to right the wrong. To save Doris, he enters the vampire's castle, where he encounters a variety of horrors that includes a large golem and a cat made of mist that draws his blood but is unaffected by any weapons. His most formidable foes are three snake women who drain his life force and leave him near death. Only then, while at death's door, can D explore his own true nature and find the power he needs to rescue Doris. The storyline of this futuristic vampire tale is more than adequate, but it is the graphic art and dazzling visual presentation that are the real highlights of this fine example of the unique Japanese animation. ♫♫♫♫

1985 80m/C *JP* **VHS** *STP, TPV*

Vampire in Brooklyn

Reminiscent of the early blaxploitation vampire flicks of the 1970s, this vampire comedy features comedian Eddie Murphy as Maximillian, a member of a West Indian vampire race, the Nosferatu. He travels to New York city to find Rita Veder (Angela Bassett), a New York police detective who is unaware that she is the descendant of vampires. The plot revolves around Maximillian's attempts to put the bite on Rita, but subplots involving a budding romantic attraction betweeen Rita and her partner Warren (Allen Payne) and Rita's growing awareness of her vampire ancestry manage to muddle things up. This disjointed marriage of horror and comedy is neither Murphy's nor director Wes Craven's best effort, but not their worst either. ♫♫♫

1995 (R) 103m/C [Mark Lipsky, Eddie Murphy] Eddie Murphy, Angela Bassett, Kadeem Hardison, Allen Payne, Zakes Mokae, John Witherspoon; *D:*

Vampire in Brooklyn: "Maybe if I use hypnosis, they'll come see my movies." ponders a ghoulish Eddie Murphy in *Vampire in Brooklyn.*

Wes Craven; *W:* Charles Murphy, Christopher Parker, Michael Lucker; *C:* Mark Irwin; *M:* J. Peter Robinson. **VHS** *PAR*

A Vampire in Paradise

Noster Abi (Farid Chopel) is an escapee from a mental institution who believes he is a vampire. Dressed in a cape and artificial fangs, he moves around Paris biting innocent and unsuspecting people. However, he falls in love with a young French girl (Laure Marsac) and begins to hang around outside her window. When she begins to speak Arabic (Abi's native language) even though she has never studied it, her parents send for an African exorcist to save her. 🎜🎜

1992 ?m/C **Farid Chopel**, Laure Marsac; *D:* Abdelkrim Bahoul.

Vampire in Venice

Klaus Kinski again assumes the role of a Nosferatu-like Dracula who is given new life by a band of gypsies. He travels to Venice, where he falls in love with a beautiful virgin. There is only one problem, however—if she should ever return his love, he would be destroyed. Meanwhile, a vampire hunter (Christopher Plummer) following Dracula doesn't want to wait for true love to run its course—he wants to destroy the vampire immediately. The only drama in this slow-moving film is what will kill Dracula—true love

or his mortal enemy. *AKA:* Nosferatu a Venezia; Vampires in Venice. 🦇🦇

1988 ?m/C [Reteitalia, Vestron] **Klaus Kinski**, Christopher Plummer, Donald Pleasence, Barbara DeRossi; *D:* Augusto Caminito.

Vampire Journals

Vampire in present-day Eastern Europe chronicles his centuries of bloodletting. 🦇🦇

1996 (R) ?m/C VHS *FLL*

Vampire Knights

Three vicious female vampires roam the modern Transylvania countryside doing their bloody best to quench their thirst on the people of a small town. They are opposed by a TV horror movie host (Daniel M. Peterson) assisted by a member of the club he founded, "The Vampire Knights," which is dedicated to protecting mortals from the vampires and wiping out the bloodsucking plague. 🦇🦇🦇

1987 ?m/C Daniel M. Peterson, Robin Rochelle, Thomas Kingsley; *D:* Daniel M. Peterson.

The Vampire Lovers

With *The Vampire Lovers*, Hammer Films created the most faithful screen adaptation of Sheridan Le Fanu's classic tale of "Carmilla," the story of a female vampire's lust for others of her kind. Though many decades old, Carmilla holds her age well and has no problem luring young females into her clutches. Mircalla (according to Le Fanu, vampires use anagrams of their name) Karnstein, a young female vampire, attacks other young women, much to the consternation of their older male protectors (owners?) and lovers. Mircalla appears on the scene from her having survived the destruction of the rest of her family at the hands of vampire hunter Baron Hartog (por-

trayed by Douglas Wilmer). Now, some years later, she works her way into the home of General Spielsdorf (Peter Cushing) who unwittingly offers complete access to his daughter Laura, (Pippa Steele). Hammer, experimenting with the ever-increasing openness of the British censors, provides some memorable scenes of the semi-clad antics of the two women. Carmilla then moves on to attack other members of the household and that of neighbor Roger Morton's daughter Emma (Madeleine Smith). Slowly the General becomes aware of what is occurring and he teams with Hartog to track Carmilla and dispatch her with stake and sword. *The Vampire Lovers* was the best of the Hammer Carmilla trilogy, which included the far inferior *Lust of a Vampire* (1970) but concluded on a higher note with *Twins of Evil* (1971). 🦇🦇🦇🦇

1970 (R) 91m/C *GB* [Hammer, American International, American International Pictures (A.I.P.)] Ingrid Pitt, Pippa Steele, Madeleine Smith, Peter Cushing, George Cole, Dawn Addams, Kate O'Mara, Ferdinand "Ferdy" Mayne; *D:* Roy Ward Baker. **VHS, Beta** *ORI, MLB*

Vampire Man

In Japan's second go at a vampire film, director Nakagawa tries a comedic approach. A vampire (Shigeru Amachi) kidnaps the wife of an atomic scientist and carries her to his subterranean lair. This sword-wielding vampire has a unique problem: he can't stand the light of the moon. *AKA:* Onna Kyuketsuki; The Male Vampire; The Female Vampire; Vampire Woman. 🦇🦇

1959 81m/B Shigeru Amachi, Yoko Mihara, Kienosuke Wade, Nobuo Nakagawa; *W:* Shin Nakazawa, Katsuyoshi Nakatsu; *C:* Yoshimi Hirano.

Vampire Moth

This very first Japanese vampire movie was included in a series of films collectively titled Kaidan Eiga (ghost stories). A series of murders has occurred and the only clues are teeth marks on the victims' necks and a moth with a bloodstained mouth. Like *London*

Ingrid Pitt

Born Natasha Petrovana in 1943 on a train headed for a Polish concentration camp, little would indicate that this woman would become a frightening yet seductive femme fatale. But a name change and years later, Ingrid Pitt became well known as the quintessential female vampire as film studio Hammer branched off into a more sensual side of vampirism. After starting out on the stage Ingrid Pitt gradually made the leap into film with a Spanish horror entry entitled *The Sound of Horror* (1965). She switched gears with a supporting role in the action caper *Where Eagles Dare* (1969) where she caught the eye of Hammer producer Jimmy Carreras who immediately signed her up with the studio. Pitt became an international star with Hammer films. Beginning with *The Vampire Lovers* (1970) which was based on the Carmilla short story, it was the first Hammer film to feature nudity as Pitt's vampire seduces the local girls in a European village. The film was shocking due to its lesbian love scenes and popular enough for Hammer to unleash Pitt in another vampire film based on the horrifying life of Countess Elizabeth Bathory. Hammer decided to top itself with this "true" story of mass murderer Bathory who believed that she could sustain everlasting youth and beauty by bathing in virginal blood. Blood is aplenty as Pitt's Countess seduces and slaughters her female prey. After her two legendary portrayals of femme fatales, Pitt made one last comedic appearance as a voluptuous vamp in the horror anthology *The House that Dripped Blood*. Feeling a tad bit typecasted, Pitt retired from her scream queen image and sought refuge in television in the late '70s, but resurfaced in supporting roles as a hooker in such B movies as *Wild Geese II* (1985) and *Transmutations* (1985).

✝ *After Midnight* and *Mark of the Vampire*, *Kyuketsuki Ga* turns out to be a pseudo-vampire story. Director Nakagawa would return to the vampire theme in 1959 with a real vampire in *Onna Kyuketsuki*. **AKA:** Kyuketsuki Ga. ◿◿

1956 88m/B [Toho] Ryo Ikebe, Akio Kobori, Asami Kuji, Kinuto Ito; **D:** Nobuo Nakagawa.

Vampire of the Cave

In this last outing for the beautiful Malaysian vampire (Maria Menado), she resides in a cave. Sixth of the Pontianak series from Keris. Sequel to *Pontianaka Kembali*. **AKA:** Pontianak Gua Musang. ◿◿

1964 ?m/C [Keris] Suraya Haron, Ghazali Sumantri, Malek Siamat; **D:** B.N. Rao.

The Vampire of the Highway

In order to claim his inheritance, and where have we heard this story before, Count Oblensky and his significant other must spend a night in the family home, the castle of the Von Winninger family. The Count is the last descendent. The castle is said to still be the haunt of Baron von Winninger, a vampire. The vampire is very real, and has a habit (a repetitiously boring habit) of quenching his thirst from the necks of naked young females. This Spanish film set in Germany's Black Forest features uninspired acting, an undernourished plot, and a finished product fit only for the undead. **AKA:** El Vampiro de la Autopista; The Vampire of Castle Frankenstein; The Horrible Sexy Vampire. ◿◿

1969 ?m/C Valdemar Wohlfahrt, Patricia Loran, Luis Induni; **D:** Jose Luis (Delavena) Madrid.

The Vampire of the Opera

An early Italian sexploitation movie with a very predictable plot. The opera house replaces the castle as the site for an unsuspecting group's encounter with terror. A team of actors takes over an unused opera house only to find their attention drawn to its mysterious atmosphere. A stranger, the vampire Stefano makes an appearance and lures one of the female cast members (Vittoria Prada)

into his lair in the dark basement. He has fallen in love with Prada who he sees as the reincarnation of his lost love. When she finally returns, she is a vampire who begins to attack the remainder of the cast, the various biting sessions occurring in various stages of undress. To keep the evil contained, the vampires and opera house is destroyed in a fire. The plot was loosely based on the *Phantom of the Opera* by Gaston Leroux. *AKA:* Il Vampiro dell'Opera; Il Mostro dell'Opera; The Monster of the Opera. 🗡🗡🗡

1961 80m/B [NIF] **Giuseppe Addobati**, Mark Marian, Barbara Howard, Catla Cavelli, Vittoria Prada; *D:* Renato Polselli; *W:* Renato Polselli.

The Vampire People

Philippine star Ronald Remy stars as Marco, an aristocrat who hopes to save his dying girlfriend by kidnapping her twin sister and stealing her heart and blood. With the help of an odd cast of characters (including a hunchback dwarf and a bat), Marco travels to a small town to carry out his nefarious scheme. He succeeds in putting the local townsfolk under his control, but his plot is challenged by a passing stranger, who battles Marco in a final confrontation. *AKA:* The Blood Drinkers. 🗡🗡

1966 (PG) 79m/C PH [Cirio H. Santiago, Hemisphere Productions] Ronald Remy, Amalia Fuentes, Eddie Fernandez, Eva Montez; *D:* Gerardo (Gerry) De Leon. **VHS, Beta** *SNC*

Vampire Princess Miyu

A Japanimation feature film with English subtitles. Features four episodes from a popular Japanese series in which the spiritualist Himiko Se pursues the enigmatic vampire and *shinma* (a god/demon) Princess Miyu and her servant Larva. The first of the four episodes, "Unearthly Kyoto," is set during a vampire epidemic in Kyoto. There, Himiko comes to the assistance of Aiko, a young girl

in a trancelike coma who has been possessed by an evil *shinma* named Raen. As Himiko seeks a solution, Princess Miyu and Larva drive Raen into the darkness, while Himiko decides he must seek out the mysterious pair. Further episodes pit Miyu against other *shinma*. In episode three, "Fragile Armor," Miyu must gain Himiko's assistance to save Larva, and in return tells Himiko the story of the beginning of her relationship with the servant, who first awakened her vampiric nature. In the end, Miyu's mission is to return all the *shinma* presently active on earth to the sleep state from which they have escaped. 🗡🗡🗡

1990 60m/C JP [Japanese] **VHS, LV** *ANI, FCT, INJ*

Vampire Raiders— Ninja Queen

Evil ninjas are plotting to infiltrate the hotel industry and are opposed by good ninjas. 🗡🗡

1989 90m/C Agnes Chan, Chris Petersen; *D:* Bruce Lambert. **VHS** *TWE*

The Vampire Returns

After several years break, the beautiful vampire (Maria Menado) returns to the series to wreak havoc on her neighborhood. Fifth of the Pontianak series. *AKA:* Pontianak Kembali. 🗡🗡

1963 ?m/C [Keris] **Maria Menado**, Malik Selamat; *D:* Ramon Estella.

Vampire Trailer Park

A two-hundred-year-old former plantation owner (Patrick Moran) and his Aunt Hattie move into a Florida trailer park where they have a new diet awaiting them. When they snack on an elderly grandmother, her grandson, an epileptic psychic (Blake Pickett), goes vampire hunting. Assisted by a drunken Sherlock Holmes type (Robert Shurtz), he

Ingrid Pitt personified the seductive power of the female vampire for Hammer.

concentrates his search in the local topless bars. Definitely as bad as it sounds. 🦴🦴

1991 ?m/C **Patrick Moran**, Robert Shurtz, Blake Pickett, Bentley Little; **D:** Steve Latshaw.

Vampire Vixens from Venus

Three hideous drug smuggling aliens transform themselves into bodacious babes on earth so they can get what they came for. Seems their drug fix is derived from the life essence of men and they plan to get as much as they can. 🦴

1994 90m/C Michelle (McClellan) Bauer, Charlie Callas. **VHS** *SHR*

Vampire vs. Vampire

Lam Ching Ying, the vampire-fighting Taoist priest with one eyebrow, directed and starred in this very different tale. A western-style vampire comes to China and opposes the priest's power. The Chinese hopping vampires take offense. 🦴🦴🦴

1989 ?m/C Lam Ching-ying, Lui Fong, Billy Lau; **D:** Lam Ching-ying.

Vampire Woman

In one of the earliest and best of the Hong Kong vampire flicks, director Li Tie appears to have turned to Sherlock Holmes "Sussex

Vampire" adventure as the vehicle to carry his indictment of the pre-revolutionary Chinese feudal system. A young mother finds herself victimized by her husband's family. One night, someone is seen sucking blood from the baby. A medium was called in to locate the perpetrator which turned out to be the mother. Her sentence was being buried alive. Too late to save her, the truth is revealed. The sister of the woman's husband had become the target of a former boyfriend. He had killed her husband and set out to destroy the entire family. Along the way he had poisoned the baby. The mother had been sucking the blood, but had been doing so for the purpose of getting the poison out of the child's body. *AKA:* Xi Xuefu. 🗡🗡

1962 ?m/B [Zhong Lian] **Bai Yang**, Zhang Houyou, Huang Manli; *D:* Li Tie.

Vampirella

Comic book heroine Vampirella finally makes it to the screen in this made-for-cable science fiction/horror/superhero action film. Though aimed primarily at the comic book's teenage readers, this film from director Jim Wynorski does a credible job of translating Forrest Ackerman's sexy bad girl to the motion picture format. She's a different sort of vampire for this generation—she hisses, bares her fangs, assumes an attack mode, and, rather than shrink from a threat, she attacks full-on. With little money for special effects, the writers came up with a better than average story (complete with some special James Bond-like weapons, including a vampire-destroying Sun gun). Having killed those who would imprison him on his home planet of Drakulon, serial killer and vampire Vlad and his companions Traax, Demos, and Sallah travel across the galaxy to Earth. Vampirella, determined to avenge the death of her planet's leaders and the only father she has ever known, follows the vampire but is stranded on Mars for centuries when her ship crashes. Without her there to stop them, Vlad and his cronies spread vampirism throughout the world and plot to take over the world.

She is rescued by a space probe and finally arrives on Earth, where she meets Adan Van Helsing (Richard Joseph Paul) and Operation PURGE (the salute to The Man from U.N.C.L.E. is not missed), a paramilitary anti-vampire organization he heads. She must convince van Helsing and his associates that she is a "good" vampire and together they must defeat Vlad, who is armed with the latest technology. 🗡🗡🗡

1996 ?m/C [New Horizons Corporation, Concorde, Sunset Films] **Talisa Soto**, **Roger Daltrey**, **Tom Deters**, **Cirnna Harney**, **Brian Bloom**, Richard Joseph Paul; *D:* Jim Wynorski.

Vampires

Madeline, a widow, presides over Abadon, a private school in Connecticut, where she uses a machine created by her late husband to attain immortality. The only problem is that it uses the life energy of her students, and in the process, kills them. A year after its original release, *Vampires* was combined with another film, *Fright Night* (no relation to the 1985 Chris Sarandon vehicle), also directed by Len Anthony, and released in 1989 as *Abadon*. Al Lewis (Grampa on *The Munsters*) is featured as an investigator. 🗡🗡

1988 ?m/C Jackie James, Orly Benyair, Robin Michaels; *D:* Len Anthony.

Vampires

Looks to unravel the culture of the undead. 🗡🗡

1995 50m/C [A&E (Arts & Entertainment) Network] **VHS** *NEW*

Vampires and Other Stereotypes

In spite of its name, vampires are a small part of this otherwise well-done independent horror flick. Two cops, a businessman, his

daughter, and several of her friends are trapped in an abandoned building that is also a gateway to an alternative realm. As it turns out, the father has made a deal with some demonic creatures to give them his daughter. They want her for breeding purposes and he wants wealth from a successful business. Vampires are among the creatures who show up at the gateway to wreak havoc, but they are among the lesser demons featured. 🗡🗡🗡

1992 ?m/C Wendy Bednarz, Bill White, Suzanne Scott, Ed Hubbard, Rick Poli; **D:** Kevin J. Lindenmuth. **VHS** *DRA*

Vampire's Breakfast

A reporter launches an investigation of a se-

ries of murders only slowly to realize that the killer is a vampire. 🗡🗡

1986 ?m/C Emily Chu, Andrew Jackson, Wong Man; **D:** Wong Chun.

The Vampire's Coffin

A sequel to *The Vampire* (1957), one of the better Mexican vampire movies. At the close of the first movie, the evil vampire Count Lavud was dead, staked through the heart. Dr. Enrique who struck the death blow, took the body to his laboratory to study, but once there, one of his assistants removes the offending object from the vampire's heart. Lavud takes up residence in a wax museum, where he encounters Maria Teresa (Alicia

Montoya), who he had terrorized in the first film. Enrique finally tracks Lavud to the museum, where a final confrontation ensues. While *The Vampire* proved an important film standing behind the Hammer films, this sequel sinks to mediocrity. *AKA:* El Ataud Del Vampiro; El Ataud Del Coffin. 🎭🎭🎭

1958 86m/B MX [K. Gordon Murray] Abel Salazar, Ariadne Welter, German Robles; *D:* Fernando Mendez. **VHS** *SNC*

Vampire's Curse

In her third outing, the pontianak vampire (Maria Menado) has help from a variety of other Malaysian ghosts and monsters. *AKA:* Sumpah Pontianak. 🎭🎭

1958 ?m/B [Keris] Maria Menado.

A Vampire's Dream

This early contribution to the vampire genre comes from Brazil and tells the tale of Dr. Pan, who is given two options by Death—die or become a vampire. He chooses the latter and then sets out on a fantastic power trip, taking over his town by biting a number of local leaders. Only a brave young couple can stop Dr. Pan...or can they? *AKA:* Um Sonho de Vampiros. 🎭🎭

1970 ?m/C Ankito, **Irma Alvarez**, Janet Chermont, Sonelio Costa, Augusto Maia Filho; *D:* Ibere Cavalcanti.

The Vampire's Ghost

This film is significant because it represents the only attempt ever made to create a movie based on John Polidori's story "The Vampyre," which was written in 1819 and is considered to be the original modern vampire story. The movie tells the story of Webb Fallon (John Abbott), a vampire whose wanderings have led him to the west coast of Africa in the 1940s, where he operates a nightclub as a cover for his large-scale criminal empire. Like Polidori's original character, Lord Ruthven, Fallon is able to walk around in the daytime, and if harnessed can be revived by moonlight, but most of the original Polidori plot and peculiarities are lost. 🎭🎭

1945 59m/B [Republic] John Abbott, Peggy Stewart; *D:* Lesley Selander. **VHS** *NOS, DVT, HEG*

Vampires in Havana

Surprising product out of Castro's Cuba is an animated feature film set in the country's capital in the 1930s. A group of Mafia elites, themselves vampires, have heard rumors of a new product, Vampisol, which allows vampires to move about in the daylight and lead what is otherwise a perfectly normal life. Joseph, a young carefree trumpet player, and nephew of the inventor, has used the product all of his life and doesn't even know he's a vampire. Various factions fight for control of the product, with Joseph caught in the middle. *AKA:* Vampiros in la Habana. 🎭🎭🎭

1986 ?m/C *D:* Juan Padron; *V:* Frank Gonzalez, Manuel Marin, Irela Bravo.

Vampire's Kiss

Falsely marketed as a comedy, *Vampire's Kiss* is an intense drama about a man (Nicolas Cage) who becomes obsessed with the idea that a woman he met one evening in a nightclub is a vampire who is slowly draining him and transforming him into a vampire. As the man's fixation on the vampire causes his condition to deteriorate, he must fight for his sanity. His breakdown has a drastic affect on one of his employees (Maria Conchita Alonso)—he begins to make unreasonable demands on her and, in the end, attacks her in an attempt to force her to shoot him. 🎭🎭🎭

1988 (R) 103m/C [Hemdale Films] Nicolas Cage, Elizabeth Ashley, Jennifer Beals, Maria Conchita Alonso, Kasi Lemmons, Bob Lujan, Jennifer Lundy; *D:* Robert Bierman; *C:* Stefan Czapsky; *M:* Colin Towns. **VHS, Beta, LV** *HBO*

Vampire's Kiss

Not to be confused with the 1989 mainstream movie starring Nicolas Cage, this adult erotic film features Count Dupree, a vampire (Jonathan Morgan) dressed as Dracula who shows up at a costume party put on by a writer of vampire fiction named Anna Price (Nikki Dahl). In the midst of the party, Anna is drawn to the vampire, and their sexual union is topped off when he bites her and she sucks blood from his finger. The next day, Anna is in her backyard when the gardener cuts his finger and she goes after his blood. She realizes she must be changing into a vampire, so she hires a private detective to locate the mysterious stranger. He finds the Count, who almost killed him in a plane crash, and manages to dispatch him with a stake through the heart. Anna is left to pursue her blood drinking as further inspiration for her writing. Not a great storyline, but far better than most X-rated vampire movies in that it actually has a plot and some interesting special effects. The sex scenes were later rearranged and featured in an interactive CD game of the same name. 🗡🗡🗡

1992 ?m/C **Jonathan Morgan**, Nikki Dahl, Rebecca Wild, Rebecca Bardot; *D:* Scotty Fox.

Vampires Settle on Police Camp

Stars a bunch of young martial arts students as rookie cops battling the ever-present hop-

ping vampires. Low-budget action flick used as a proving ground for the young, aspiring thespians. ♫♫

1988 ?m/C D: Kamm Yoo Tu.

Vampirisme

A 12-minute comedy/parody short showing vampires going about their day-to-day lives. Includes a baby vampire getting his daily supply of nourishment from his mother. ♫♫

1967 ?m/C [Films du Cosmos] Jean-Pierre Bouyxou, Michel Beaune, Alain Le Bris; **D:** Patrice Duvic.

Vamps

Reminiscent of Grace Jones' club in *Vamp*, Vamps is a strip club owned and operated by Tasha (Jenny Wallace) and two other dancing female vampires, Randi (Amber Newman) and Tabitha. If a customer gets out of line, the waitresses just treat him as their next meal. The plot thickens when the innocent Heather (Jennifer Huss) starts to work at the club in order to pay for school. While she is troubled by the job, she gains strength from a young priest (Paul Morris) who is also attracted to Heather but able (at least for a while) to curb his desires. Trouble begins when Tasha decides she is attracted to Heather—the dual challenge of making Heather her own and battling the priest for Heather's body and soul is too much for her to resist. This reasonably good B-movie features Lorissa McComas in a cameo as the Vampire Queen in a dream sequence. ♫♫

1996 ?m/C Lorissa McComas, Amber Newman, Jenny Wallace, Stacy Sparks, Paul Morris, Jennifer Huss; **D:** Michael D. Fox, Mark Burchett. **VHS** *EII*

Vampyr

Dreyer's classic portrays a hazy, dreamlike world full of chilling visions from the point of view of a young man who believes him-

self surrounded by vampires and who dreams of his own burial in a most disturbing way. Evil lurks around every corner as camera angles, light and shadow sometimes overwhelm plot. A high point in horror films based on a collection of horror stories by Sheridan le Fanu. In German with English subtitles. *AKA:* Vampyr, Ou L'Etrang e Aventure De David Gray; Vampyr, Der Traum Des David Gray; Not Against the Flesh; Castle of Doom; The Strange Adventure of David Gray; The Vampire. ♫♫♫♫

1931 75m/B *GE* [Tobis Klangfilm, Carl Dreyer] Julien West, Sybille Schmitz, Harriet Gerard, Maurice Schutz; **D:** Carl Theodor Dreyer; **W:** Carl Theodor Dreyer; **M:** Wolfgang Zeller. **VHS, Beta** *VYY, NOS, SNC*

The Vampyr

Uncut version of the BBC musical production about a lustful vampire. Text sets present-day lyrics to the 1827 opera by Heinrich Marschner. Vampire Ripley (Ebrahim) has just been set free in London after having been trapped in an underground tomb for 200 years. Unless he puts the bite on three lovely ladies within three days he will be condemned to eternal damnation. Everyone gets to sing in the nude. Surreally amusing. ♫♫

1992 115m/C *GB* [BBC (British Broadcasting Corporation)] Omar Ebrahim, Willemijn Van Gent, Fiona O'Neill, Sally-Ann Shepherdson. **VHS** *FOX*

Vampyre

A town is infested by a group of vampires led by a vampiress (Kathy Seyler) in this independent, low-budget quickie. As the vampires go about their bloody feeding, a hero emerges to fight them. By the end, you almost hope the vampires win the battle, since they are the only ones providing any entertainment in this slow-paced film. ♫

1990 ?m/C [Panorama Entertainment] **Cathy Seyler,** Randy Scott Rozler, John Brent, Greg Boggia; **D:** Bruce G. Hallenbeck.

"I am here because this is a young and virile race, not dry and decadent like ours. You have what I want, what I need, what I must have!"

—Dracula (Lon Chaney Jr.) rationalizes his move to America in *Son of Dracula* (1943).

The Velvet
Vampire: "Oh, good
I didn't break a
nail." Century old
vampire Diane Le
Fanu (Celeste
Yarnall) surmises
the dagger in hand
is a minor
flesh wound.

244

VAMPIRES on VIDEO

Vampyres

A low-budget British film that's considered a classic among vampire aficionados, *Vampyres'* tale of love, sex, and death is told in such blunt and explicit terms that it still effectively shocks and disturbs viewers. Fran (Marianne Morris) and Mariam (Anulka) portray two attractive women who are killed during their lovemaking by a man, but return as siren-like vampires who lure victims, primarily men, to their castle abode. Each evening they indulge in an orgy of sex and blood drinking that literally leaves the victims drained of all life force. Their routine is challenged, however, when one of the vampires falls in love with Ted, a handsome young stranger. His ordeal, carried over several nights, leaves him in an increasingly depleted state and he leaves in hopes of reaching the local hospital. A couple attempts to assist him, but are overtaken by the vampires. While the couple is being killed, however, enough time passes that the young man can escape in the approaching dawn. *AKA:* Vampyres, Daughters of Dracula; Blood Hunger; Satan's Daughters. 🗡🗡🗡

1974 (R) 90m/C *GB* [Cambist] Marianne Morris, Anulka, Murray Brown, Brian Deacon, Sally Faulkner; **D:** Joseph Larraz. **VHS, Beta** *NO*

Vault of Horror

A horror anthology of five stories, one of which, "Midnight Mess," is a vampire tale. A murderer stumbles into a restauraunt that caters exclusively to vampires. Deciding that standard menu offerings such as "bloodclot soup" are getting a little old, the vampires attack the murderer to add a little fresh blood to the menu. *AKA:* Tales from the Crypt II. 🎵🎵

1973 (R) 86m/C *GB* [Max J. Rosenberg, Milton Subotsky, Metromedia Producers Corporation, Amicus Productions, Cinerama] Terry-Thomas, Curt Jurgens, Glynis Johns, Dawn Addams, Daniel Massey, Tom Baker, Michael Craig, Anna Massey, Denholm Elliott; *D:* Roy Ward Baker; *W:* Milton Subotsky. **VHS, Beta** *MED*

The Velvet Vampire

Its pure California as a sexy young vampiress (whose name derives from the writer of the first prominent piece of literature featuring a female vamp) attempts to seduce a couple (Sherry Miles and Michael Blodgett) she has invited to visit her desert home. Le Fanu (portrayed by Celeste Yarnell) quenches her thirst as opportunity allows while showing the couple around the neighborhood. She sinks her teeth into the husband while a snake does likewise to the wife. The husband is left behind while Yarnell saves the wife by sucking the poisonous blood out of her. In the end the new widow catches on to the vampire's aim and escapes to Los Angeles. Le Fanu follows and must be killed as the wife uses crosses to force her into the sunlight. Producer Roger Corman gave young director Stephanie Rothman her career break at a time when female directors were hard to find in Hollywood. Her influence is best seen in the action between the vampire and her female victim. *AKA:* Cemetary Girls; Through the Looking Glass. 🎵🎵

1971 (R) 82m/C [New World Pictures] Michael Blodgett, Sherry Miles, Celeste Yarnall, Gene Shane, Jerry Daniels, Sandy Ward, Paul Prokop, Chris Woodley, Robert Tessier; *D:* Stephanie Rothman. **VHS, Beta, LV**

Vengeful Vampire Girl

Director Kim In Soo puts a vampiric twist to a traditional Korean folk tale in this story which begins with the violent rape of a young woman by a wealthy medieval aristocrat. She makes her defiance of the violation evident in her suicide. While being raped she bites off her tongue and bleeds to death. She becomes a vampire and a decade later is released from her grave by some grave robbers who open her tomb. He begins to reek revenge, but finally turns up against the son of the man who raped her who has learned a secret method of dispatching vampires (I'll never tell) from a knowledgeable priest. This rare Korean foray into the vampire realm has been received by Western audiences as a rare curiosity. Originally released in Korean as *Huphyokwi Yanyo.* 🎵🎵🎵

1981 ?m/C [Han Jin Enterprise] Choi Bong, Chong Hi Jung; *D:* Kim In Soo.

Vincent Price's Dracula

Though noted as an actor in horror movies, Vincent Price rarely played a vampire or appeared in vampire movies. He was, however, one of the most knowledgeable and admired of horror movie personalities. This documentary explores the life of the real Dracula, Vlad Tepes of Romania, with film clips from the region. Highlights Dracula's many screen incarnations through excerpts from some classic vampire movies. Also included is footage from the 1979 Canadian documentary *Count Dracula: The True Story. AKA:* Dracula-The Great Undead. 🎵🎵🎵

1982 ?m/C [M&M Film Productions, Ltd., Atlantis Films] Vincent Price; *D:* John Miller.

The Vineyard

A scientist who also functions as a sorcerer (James Hong) lures out-of-work actors and actresses to his isolated island residence, where he kills them in order to maintain his youthful appearance. Gory, bloody, and unfortunately predictable, although it does feature some inventive scenes (such as one in which a woman regurgitates a mouthful of spiders). 🎵

Videohound salutes: Vincent Price

For many horror film fans, Vincent Price is synonymous with scary movies. With his distinctive voice and stare, Price created any number of memorable characters during his nearly five decade career. However, much like fellow horror film legend Boris Karloff, Price only portrayed a vampire on film on one occasion in a little-known film.

Price's career began in England in the 1930s, but he became both a star and identified with horror after appearing in the *House of Wax* (1953), one of the more popular 3-D movies released in the 1950s. During the 1960s, his fame increased even more when he starred in a series of Edgar Allan Poe movies made by Roger Corman.

Most memorable were *The Fall of the House of Usher* (1960), 1961's *The Pit and the Pendulum* (with scream queen Barbara Steele), *Tomb of Ligeia* (1964), and *Masque of the Red Death* (1965).

Like Karloff, Price did star in a few vampire movies in non-vampire roles. By far the most notable was *The Last Man on Earth* (1964), in which he played a vampire hunter in the movie version of Richard Matheson's apocalyptic vampire novella, *I Am Legend*. He portrayed a mad scientist in *Scream and Scream Again* (1970), also starring Christopher Lee and Peter Cushing, and a horror star in *The Madhouse* (1974). And in 1982, he narrated a documentary on Vlad Tepes and the image of the vampire in the hour-long *Vincent Price's Dracula*. But when did he actually play a vampire?

Well, we have to mention that television appearance on the 1960s sitcom *F-Troop*. Then, some years later he appeared on *The Muppet Show* and briefly donned fangs for a vampiric give-and-take with Kermit the Frog (strictly for the younger set). The episode was released on video in 1994 as *The Muppet Show: Monster Laughs with Vincent Price*. Those were just warm-ups, however, for his one and only screen appearance as a vampire. In 1985, he appeared in a movie called *The Monster Club*, which was an anthology of Ronald Chetwynd-Hayes' short stories. The stories were tied together by a conversation held in the Club between Chetwynd-Hayes, played by John Carradine, and the vampire Erasmus, played by Price.

One can only wonder how the vampire's image could have been changed had Price lent his considerable talents to its portrayal more often.

1989 (R) 95m/C [Northstar Entertainment, Vineyard Partners Ltd.] James Hong, Karen Witter, Michael Wong; **D:** James Hong, Bill Rice. **VHS, Beta, LV** *VTR, NWV*

Vlad Tepes

In the early 1970s, historians concluded that the fictional character of Count Dracula was based on the real-life leader Prince Vlad Tepes of Wallachia, who was called Dracula after his father, Prince Vlad Dracul (Vlad of the Dragon). This historical drama tells the true story of Prince Vlad Tepes, who led Wallachia from 1456 to 1462 (he briefly ruled the country two other times, also). During that time he attempted to create a national state in Wallachia (southern Romania) and to break the power of the boyars (feudal lords) and the German Transylvanians who controlled much of the regional economy. He

also fought the Turks and is credited with turning back an occupation army sent by the ever-expanding Ottoman Empire. This film was put out by a group of Romanians who hoped to discredit the link between Vlad Tepes and the bloodthirsty Count Dracula. Instead, this and other similar documentaries created more interest in the story and pointed out the many similarities between the fictional Dracula and the real Vlad. 🗡🗡🗡

1978 ?m/C [Romaniafilm-Animafilm] Stefan Sileanu, Ernest Maftei, Emanoil Petrut, Teofil Vilcu; **D:** Dorui Nastase.

Voodoo Heartbeat

A group of spies are after a voodoo serum that will keep them youthful forever. Instead it turns them into bloodsucking deviants. Producer Molina doubles as an unkept Elvis look-alike in this low budget feature shot in Las Vegas. The voodoo motif looks to be an excuse to show a group of scantily clad young women acting out alleged voodoo rituals. A failure on many levels. 🗡🗡

1972 88m/C [TWI Productions] **R. Molina**, Philip Ahn, Ern Dugo; **D:** Charles Nizet.

"Count Alucard
is immortal.
Through him I
attained
immortality.
Through me,
you'll do
the same."

—Katherine Caldwell (Louise Albritton) in *Son of Dracula* (1943).

W

Wanda Does Transylvania

Jane is flat broke. Her attorney suggests bankruptcy, but Jane is willing to do almost anything to avoid that alternative. This being an adult erotic picture, she then proceeds to show her attorney the extent to which she is committed to recovering financially. Duly impressed, the attorney proposes a solution. Jane assumes the identity of a young heiress client of his who has died before claiming her inheritance. Jane will assume Wanda's identity and go to Transylvania where some papers need to be signed, and claim the inheritance. Once in Transylvania she must work her way through various people in order to get to the Countess, the person whose signature she must attain. 🐾🐾

Waxwork

A horror/comedy in which Mark (Zach Galligan), Sarah (Deborah Foreman) and four college classmates accept an invitation to a spe-cial preview of a wax museum opening in their town. All of the sets at the museum depict scenes of well-known incidents, crimes, or otherwise gory events. Conveniently, amid the eighteen scenes, six are missing figures of the victims. Tension mounts as one by one the students are lured into the scenes when the characters in those scenes come to life. Among the evil characters they must fight off is Dracula (Miles O'Keefe). A final confrontation featuring Patrick Macnee leading the charge against the creatures from his wheelchair is not to be missed. The sequel, *Waxworks II*, has even less vampire content. 🐾🐾

1988 (R) 97m/C [Vestron Pictures] Zach Galligan, Deborah Foreman, Michelle Johnson, Dana Ashbrook, Miles O'Keeffe, Patrick Macnee, David Warner; **D:** Anthony Hickox; **M:** Roger Bellon. **VHS, Beta, LV** *LIV, VES*

Waxwork 2: Lost in Time

A delightful and entertaining fantasy (rather than horror) movie that begins with the fire that consumes the museum at the end of

RENFIELD: DRACULA'S FRIEND

Maybe you have to be a little mad to love a vampire, especially if the vampire is Dracula. In Bram Stoker's novel, the character of Renfield was first introduced to vampire fans as an inmate in Dr. Seward's asylum. He had been locked up because of his very weird behavior, especially his desire to eat living creatures, from insects to birds and cats. His behavior gave clues to understanding the essential nature of vampirism—he had some kind of mysterious connection to Dracula and was the first to sense his presence in England. Later, he unwittingly supplied Dracula's enemies with vital information.

As Dracula has become the stereotypical vampire, so has Renfield come to represent the human servant that a vampire needs to carry out his work in the daylight and to protect him while he sleeps in his coffin. Just as vampires must have blood, they must also have a Renfield. As an asylum inmate, Renfield represents an attempt to explain vampirism through modern psychological interpretations instead of supernatural ones.

Stoker saw no reason to ever answer the many questions surrounding the origin of Renfield's illness or his special attachment to Dracula. However, in 1931 when Universal brought the Dracula play by Hamilton Deane and John L. Balderston to the screen, screenwriter Louis Bloomfield expanded the part of Renfield and in the process offered an explanation of Renfield's illness. He sent Renfield, not Jonathan Harker, to Transylvania for the initial encounter with Dracula and his three mysterious female companions. He did not become a vampire, but the encounter drove him mad and forged his special bond with Dracula. Many filmmakers have since shown that Stoker's story can easily be told on film without Renfield (for example, in the 1973 Dracula with Jack Palance).

The role of Renfield in Universal's 1931 production was handled by Dwight Frye. Frye's performance was a memorable one—he freely moved back and forth between apparent sanity and an obsessive interest in the insects and animals that he ate, all the while professing his undying loyalty to his master. Frye's almost manic presence brought Renfield to life for the many people who had missed the performances of Bernard H. Jukes and others who had assumed the role in the stage productions. Frye's interpretation was so good that at times he stole the audience's attention away from Bela Lugosi's Dracula.

Over the decades, Renfield has been treated many different ways by screenwriters and directors. Frye's well-known performance cried out for parody, and no one did it better than Arte Johnson in Love at First Bite (1979). More serious attempts to portray Renfield were offered by Tony Haygarth in Dracula (1979) and by Tom Waits in Francis Ford Coppola's production of Bram Stoker's Dracula (1992). Though not as frantic as Frye's performance, Waits's intensity earned favorable audience and critical reactions.

There have been several noteworthy Renfield-like characters in recent films, including James Mason's as Richard Straker in 'Salem's Lot (1979), and Willie Loomis, who served Barnabas Collins on the television show Dark Shadows. Recently, John Witherspoon created a delightful Renfield-like character in the African-American version of Dracula starring Eddie Murphy, Vampire in Brooklyn (1995).

✝ END ✝

Waxworks. Mark (Zach Gilligan) and Sarah (Monika Schnarre) manage to escape the fire, but so does a single hand from one of the evil creatures that inhabited the museum. The disembodied hand follows Sarah home and eventually kills her father; Sarah is charged with his murder when no one believes her story about the hand. To prove her innocence, she and Mark must journey into numerous fantasy worlds where they become a part of the action unfolding there. The only vampire action comes near the end of the film when Mark and Sarah find themselves in the final scene from the 1922 vampire movie *Nosferatu*, just before Count Orlock is destroyed by the sun's rays. Drew Barrymore appears briefly as Orlock's victim. Other cameos include Juliet Mills, David Carradine, Patrick Macnee (briefly reviving his role from the first movie), and John Ireland,. 🗡🗡🗡

1991 (R) 104m/C [Electric Pictures] Zach Gilligan, Alexander Godunov, Bruce Campbell, Michael Des Barres, Monika Schnarre; **D:** Anthony Hickox. **VHS** *LIV*

The Werewolf vs. the Vampire Woman

In his continuing series as the reluctant werewolf Count Waldemar Daninsky, Paul Naschy occasionally encounters a vampire, in this case the Countess Waldessa (played by Patty Shepard). In the beginning, Daninsky is revived by the extraction of the silver bullet which had previous dispatched him. He rewards the doctors who bring him back to life by killing them. He settles into a lonely existence, fortunately, that loneliness is broken by the arrival of two young females on a quest to find the tomb of Countess Waldessa. Daninsky joins their quest as he wishes to retrieve the silver cross by which the countess was supposedly impaled. When the girls find the body, one accidentally cuts herself and the blood drips on the Countess' face (shade of Mario Bava's *Black Sunday* 1960) and the countess revives. She

bites one of the girls and kidnaps the other for use in a witchcraft ritual on Walpurgis Night. As with many Slavic vampires, the countess is also a witch. In the end Daninsky rescues the surviving young woman, but true to the curse placed upon him, she also kills him. One of the best of the Daninsky series. **AKA:** *Shadow of the Werewolf, Blood Moon, Night of Walpurgis,* and *La Noche de Walpurgis.* 🗡🗡

1970 (R) 82m/C *SP GE* [Ellman International] Paul Naschy, Gaby Fuchs, Barbara Capell, Patty Shepard, Valerie Samarine, Julio Pena, Andres Resino; **D:** Leon Klimovsky. **VHS** *SNC, HEG*

Who Is Afraid of Dracula

Count Dracula (Edmond Purdom) and his vampire sister Countess Oniria (Ania Pieroni)decide to sell the family castle in this horror comedy. Real estate salesman Fracchia (Paolo Villaggio) does his best to find a buyer. His best hope for a sale is a near-sighted boob (Gigi Reder). Just when Fracchia can smell his commission, Frankenstein's monster and some zombies show up to muddy the waters. **AKA:** *Fracchia contro Dracula; Fracchia vs. Dracula.* 🗡🗡

1985 ?m/C *Edmund Purdom,* Paolo Villaggio, Gigi Reder, Ania Pieroni, Neri Parenti; **D:** Neri Parenti.

The Wicked

The Australian outback can be every bit as cut off from the rest of the world as a European gothic castle. So Lucy, Bronco, and Nick discover when their car breaks down near the community of Yarralumala. The town turns out to be the residence of Sir Alfred Terminus, aristocratic Australian vampire, and his bloodsucking relatives, who invite the trio tourists to dinner. The setting is changed, but you've seen it all before. **AKA:** *Outback Vampires.* 🗡🗡

1989 87m/C Brett Cumo, Richard Morgan, Angela Kennedy, Maggie Blinco, John Doyle; **D:** Colin Eggleston. **VHS** *HMD*

"Come to me and live forever. Young forever. Strong as the night. Strong as eternity. Stronger than death!"

—The vampire Jefferson (John Ireland) in *Sundown: Vampires in Retreat* (1990).

VIDEOHOUND SALUTES: ANNE RICE

When Anne Rice's bestselling novel *Interview with the Vampire* finally made it to the screen in 1994, it ended a 15-year struggle for the popular author, who has been credited as a major force in the contemporary revival of interest in vampires. Rice enjoyed some success when the novel was originally released in 1976. It went through several printings and was picked up by book clubs. Paramount bought a 10-year film option, and all seemed well. She moved on to other projects and waited for the movie to be made.

Rice had long dreamed of having Rutger Hauer play the lead role of Lestat the vampire. However, as Hauer aged and became too old for the part, Paramount sat on the project. Rice worked on several other projects, including the Sleeping Beauty erotic novels that she wrote under a pseudonym, before she returned to the vampire world in 1985 and produced by far the best novel on the subject, *The Vampire Lestat.* That novel provoked an immediate response among vampire aficionados—even more so than *Interview with the Vampire*, Lestat stands out as one of the catalysts in the current

movement that has seen the nocturnal creatures reach new heights of popularity.

However, Paramount continued to sit on the film option, doing nothing before it finally ran out in 1986. Reclaiming the film rights, Rice sold them to Lorimer, along with the rights to *The Vampire Lestat* (1985) and the third novel in what had become The Vampire Chronicles, *The Queen of the Damned* (1988). Lorimer's only act, however, was to pass the rights to Warner Brothers, who in turn passed them to Geffen Pictures, Inc.

Finally Geffen Pictures took action. A script was produced and Neil Jordan selected as the director. Vampire fans everywhere, especially Rice, were overjoyed. Then disaster struck. David Geffen announced that he had signed Tom Cruise to play Lestat. Cruise had received an Academy Award nomination for his performance in *Born on the Fourth of July*, but the roles he had played had all portrayed basic, almost stereotypical, heterosexual males. Could an actor of his popularity play the villainous Lestat and allow the underlying homosexual theme of the book to survive? Rice was furious.

She claimed she had the right to veto leading cast members, but discovered that that right had been lost as the film was being passed from studio to studio. She then started a public protest campaign and called upon her fans to boycott the movie. He lack of faith in Cruise's ability to portray the undead creature Lestat was absolute.

Then, just before the film was released at Halloween in 1994, she was allowed a private screening. Suddenly, all of her anger and doubts dissolved. She admitted that she had been wrong about Cruise. He had pulled it off. He was Lestat. But by then the "damage" had been done. The controversy had played into the hands of the studio publicists and had fueled interest in the film as the media had a field day with the story. *Interview with the Vampire* was assured an international audience and quickly became one of the highest grossing films of the year. Now fans can live in anticipation that *The Vampire Lestat* will make it to the screen before Cruise becomes too old to revive his role one more time.

✝ END ✝

Winter with Dracula

Travelogue of Romania which mentions Vlad Tepes, the real Dracula. For Dracula fans, its major asset is its brevity. 🦇🦇

1971 30m/C

Witchcraft 3: The Kiss of Death

This entertaining tale of good magician vs. very bad vampire features a convoluted plot but plenty of action. It seems that defense attorney William Spanner (Charles Solomon) has lots of tension in his life—an ambitious prosecuting attorney he must battle in court and a girlfriend who wants more of his time and attention are just two of the problems he faces. Little does he know that his troubles have just begun. Along comes the vampire Louis (Dominic Luciano), who has the power to suck the life out of people with his kiss, and his fawning associate Roxy (Leana Hall) to really make Spanner's life interesting. When Louis kills the prosecuting attorney and attempts to seduce his girlfriend, Spanner turns to the mysterious Rev. Jondular for assistance in his battle against Louis. Jondular helps Spanner unlock the magical power he has always had inside him, a power that will help him in his final confrontation with the vampire. 🦇🦇

1990 (R) 85m/C [Vista Street Ent., Academy Entertainment] Charles Solomon, Lisa Toothman, William L. Baker, Lena Hall; **D:** R.L. Tillmanns. **VHS** *ACA*

Witchcraft 7: Judgement Hour

Modern-day defense attorney and everyday magician William Spanner (David Byrnes) must again square off against vampires in this seventh installment of the popular occult series. He enlists the aid of two cops, Lutz (Alisa Christensen) and Graner (John Cragen)

to bring down the evil vampire Martin (Loren Schmalle) and his sex-starved female demonic cohorts. 🦇🦇

1995 (R) 91m/C [Michael Feifer, Vista Street Ent.] David Byrnes, April Breneman, Alisa Christensen, John Cragen, Loren Schmalle; **D:** Michael Paul Girard; **W:** Peter Fleming; **C:** Denis Maloney; **M:** Miriam Cutler. **VHS** *APX*

Witches, Vampires & Zombies

A creepy look at the real world of monsters and black magic, plus the history of voodoo, witchcraft and other occult sciences. 🦇🦇

1988 40m/C [Simitar] **VHS** *NO*

Wolnyoui Han

This vampire tale draws on Korean folklore and is set in a medieval village. A young girl becomes possessed by an evil spirit in the form of a white cat (cats are traditionally associated with vampires in Asian cultures). She is later turned into a vampire who seeks revenge from the villagers who had betrayed her. 🦇🦇🦇

1980 ?m/C [Han Jin Enterprise] Chin Bong Chin, Huh Chin.

The World of Abbott & Costello

Compilation of clips from the series of eighteen films done by the comedy team while at Universal. Includes brief scenes from *Abbott and Costello Meet Frankenstein*, in which Bela Lugosi appears as Dracula. If you want this one just for the vampire, you'd be better served by checking out the original. Still worth a look without the vampires. 🦇🦇

1964 75m/B Bud Abbott, Lou Costello. **VHS** *MCA*

World of Dracula

Feature-length movie comprised of all ten episodes of the "Curse of Dracula" segment of the TV series *Cliffhangers*. Dracula (Michael Nouri) teaches Eastern European history in a San Francisco college, where he recruits new blood. His nemesis is Abraham Van Helsing's grandson Kurt (Stephen Johnson). A shorter version, *Curse of Dracula* was made from the first four episodes of the show (see separate entry). ♫♫♫

1979 ?m/C [NBC, et al.] **Michael Nouri**, Stephen Johnson, Carol Baxter, Antoinette Stella, Bever-Leigh Banfield, Louise Sorel.

World of the Vampires

Building on the understanding of the sensitive hearing ability of vampire bats, the 1959 Mexican film *Nostradamus and the Destroyer of Monsters* introduced the use of sound to destroy vampires. That twist is copied in the *World of the Vampires* which opens with the vampire Sergio Sotubai (played by Guillermo Murray) playing an organ made of bones while his vampire colleagues attack the occupants of a jeep and capture a young woman. As it turns out, the vampire is out to revenge a wrong done his family by that of a professor Kolman, who has two lovely young nieces. Blocking his plans is occultist Rodolfo (Mauricio Graces) who arrives on the scene just as Sotubai is about to put the bite on one of the young women. He first launches an attack by playing on the vampire's organ, but Sotubai protected himself with earplugs. He finally has to be dispatched by falling into a pit full of wooden stakes. The interestingly different story was unfortunately about the only highlight of this otherwise poorly produced movie. **AKA:** *El Mundo de los Vampiros.* ♫♫

1960 75m/B *MX* [American International Pictures (A.I.P.)] Mauricio Garces, Erna Martha Bauman, Silvia Fournier, Guillermo Murray; **D:** Alfonso Corona Blake. **VHS, Beta** *SNC, HHT, MAD*

Wrestling Women vs. the Aztec Mummy

The Aztec Mummy emerged as a character in Mexican cinema in 1957, in a film variously titled *La Momia Azteca* or *Attack of the Mayan Mummy*. In the original story, a Dr. Almada attempts to prove his theories concerning reincarnation by hypnotizing and regressing his lover Flor to a past life (a scenario inspired by the Bridey Murphy episode in the United States). She turned out to be an Aztec maiden named Xochitl who was killed and entombed for having an illicit relationship with a warrior. The warrior, Popoca, was killed and his body placed near his lover's in order to protect the valuable bracelet and amulet buried with her body. When Almada and his assistant steal the jewelry, Popoca comes back to life as the Mummy. A minor vampiric element is added when the Mummy is held in check by a crucifix, in the manner of the European vampire hunters. Hardly pausing for a breath, Director Rafael Portillo produced two sequels in a matter of weeks, *La Maldición de la Monia Azteca* and *La Momia vs el Robot Humano*. Shortly after the original Aztec Mummy films, director Rena Cardona, Jr. revived the Mummy for a fourth outing, in this case fighting a group of female wrestlers. During the course of the ongoing battle, the Mummy turns into a vampire bat, thus earning a place in this volume. **AKA:** *Las Luchadoras Contra La Momia; Rock and Roll Wrestling Women vs. The Aztec Mummy.* ♫♫

1959 88m/C *MX* [Mexican] Lorena Velasquez, Armando Silvestre; **D:** Rene Cardona Sr. **VHS, Beta** *SNC, RHI, HHT*

Young Jonathan Dracula

Delightful comedic reflection on the Dracula story picks up after the death of the Count. One of Van Helsing's descendants has become mayor of the town near Castle Dracula. He intends to acquire the castle and turn it into a tourist attraction. Standing in his way is Jonathan Dracula (Carlos Benpar), a student of vampirology at the University of Venice. Jonathan returns to Transylvania to hear the reading of the will and acquire his inheritance. Along with meeting Mina and Lucy (characters in the original novel), he foils the schemes of the mayor with the help of Renfield, the faithful family servant. *AKA:* El Jovencito Dracula. 🎞🎞🎞

1975 95m/C [Carlos Benpar (Carlos Benito Parra), Los Films del Mediterraneo] Carlos (Carlos Benito Parra) Benpar, Susanna Estrada, Victor Israel, Marina Ferri, Veronica Miriel, Norma Kerr; *D:* Carlos (Carlos Benito Parra) Benpar, Jorge Gigo; *W:* Carlos (Carlos Benito Parra) Benpar, Jose Domenech, Patricio Raoran; *C:* Tomas Pladevall.

Zoltan ... Hound of Dracula

One of the Hound's favorites, for fairly obvious reasons, it's a little better than the title would indicate, but not by much. In 1970s Romania, military war games uncover the vault where Dracula is buried. Before the coffins can be burned, a soldier foolishly unstakes two of the corpses, bringing them to life and costing him his own life. At least the soldier doesn't unleash the Count himself—instead, he frees the vampire's equally bloodthirsty dog Zoltan, along with a "fractional lamia," a strange creature who serves the vampires (the lamia can move in the daylight and locate victims). Like any good dog, poor Zoltan needs a master, so the pair of undead creatures sets sail for Los Angeles in search of Michael Drake, the last member of the Dracula family. Drake and his family take off on vacation, and apparently so did the screenwriter, since the movie runs out of steam at this point. Slow-moving, and totally implausible to boot. Based on a novel by Ken Johnson. **AKA:** Dracula's Dog. ⚔⚔

1978 85m/C [Albert Band, Frank Perilli, Crown International] Michael Pataki, Reggie Nalder, Jose Ferrer; **D:** Albert Band; **W:** Frank Ray Perilli; **M:** Andrew Belling. **VHS, Beta** *REP, VCI, FCT*

Zombie Brigade

A low-budget feature in which the mayor of a small isolated town in the Australian Outback blows up a monument to Vietnam veterans. That evening, an army of the undead (they're called zombies but act like vampires), go on a killing spree in the village. ⚔⚔

1988 ?m/C

Vampire Connections

So you've seen all the movies, or there's one you haven't been able to find in your area. There are other people out there with these very same concerns. This guide provides you with some ways to contact them. It lists vampire web sites (many with e-mail addresses and links), vampire organizations, and independent periodicals devoted to all things vampire. Happy hunting!

WEB SITES

Arica's Vampire Page
http://www.geocities.com/Paris/1598/
Includes photos from current vampire films and has an interactive Dracula movie.

Australian Vampire Information Association
http://www.necronomi.com/projects/darkdesire/
A resource for any vampire enthusiast.

B-Movie Theater
http://www.b-movie.com/
Order those hard to find horror and vampire movies here along with other movie merchandise.

The Bela Lugosi Homepage
http://www.isisnet.com/tournier/lugosi.htm
Dedicated to the man who put Dracula on the map in the Hollywood history books.

Bites
http://www.gremlins.com/weird_werx/bites.html
Hey, if you would like to order a bust of Peter Cushing or masks of various alien creatures, this your place.

Bloodlust
http://www.ozemail.com.au/~jswjon/

Page devoted to the one Australian vampire film that was banned in Britain.

Bram Stoker's Dracula Collection
http://www.screamqueen.com/dracula.htm
Order figurines, models and masks from the hit 1992 film.

The Cabinet of Dr. Casey
http://www.cat.pdx.edu/~caseyh/horror/index.
  html
Has some gory graphics from such vampire classics as Fright Night, The Hunger *and* Innocent Blood.

Chad McQuay Web Page
http://www-scf.usc.edu/~mcquay/
Women, witches, movies and vampires.

Classic Universal Monsters
http://www-leland.stanford.edu/~krouse/
  monsters.htm
Order the original horror classics such as Dracula (1931) *and* Dracula's Daughter *from the studio that pioneered in horrifying audiences.*

Christopher Lee
http://xray.chm.bris.ac.uk:8000/naj/lee.html
Presents a biography of this actor.

Cult Film Page
http://sepnet.com:80/rcramer/index.htm
Order classic horror films from such actors as John Carradine, Lon Chaney, Jr. Roger Corman, Peter Cushing, Christopher Lee and Bela Lugosi.

Darkness On the Edge of Town
http://home.interhop.net/~ve3aqh/dark.htm
Connects you to everything associated with vampirism.

Do A Blood Count
http://www.swellstuff.com/Ken/Pages/Vampire.
  html
Film fan rates his top vampire films.

Dracula
http://www.kiss.com/richter/dracula/dindex.htm
Features the entire stage production of the play Dracula.

Dracula and Frankenstein
http://www.frii.com/~gnat/movies/censorship/6.
  html
Explains how Dracula and Frankenstein made it to the silver screen.

Dracula Triple-Face
http://idibbs.com/bus/gemstone/bdh03.htm

Shows photos of the three forms Dracula (Gary Oldman) takes in Francis Ford Coppola's film Bram Stoker's Dracula.

Dracula's Homepage
http://www.ucs.mun.ca/~emiller/
Includes information on all the Dracula conventions and rates all Dracula films using a fang system.

Following Dracula's Steps
http://indis.ici.ro/romania/tourism/drachome.
  html
Chronicles Dracula's history in film and in literature.

From Dusk Till Dawn
http://www.hooked.net/users/cpatubo/fdtd.html
Web page for fans of the Tarantino film.

Hammer House
http://www.futurenet.co.uk/,sairwas,perkele,/
  netmag/hammer/
Details all the Hammer classics beginning with Dracula: Prince of Darkness.

Haunted Verdun Manor
http://www.webcom.com/verdun/welcome.html
Cruise through a virtual haunted house loaded with werewolves and vampires.

Horror Poster Archive
http://www.cat.pdx.edu/~caseyh/horror/poster/
A photo gallery for several popular horror films including vampire films.

InterVamp
http://www.xs4all.nl/~intrvamp/main.htm
Enter the world of the undead and link up to other sites pertaining to vampire music, Dark Shadows *and Anne Rice.*

Interview With The Vampire
http://home.earthlink.net/~delker/interview.html
Includes the script and photos of the film.

Judy's Dark Shadows Page
http://www.epix.net/~jphill/shadows.html
Avid fan Judy places great depth into this classic vampire series. Includes episode summaries and a photo gallery.

Khi's Vampire Page
http://www.cs.uit.no/~ingunne/1vampire/
  vampire.html
Offers vamp links which includes Hammer House of Horror and the online version of Bram Stoker's book Dracula.

Killers, Rogues, Vampires and Fish: Lesbianism in Film
http://www.geocities.com/WestHollywood/6271/
Lists and reviews films on lesbianism and its relation to vampirism..

Kindred: The Embrace
http://www.kindredemb.com/
Webpage devoted to the short-lived Fox series.

Lair of the Vampiress
http://members.aol.com/ckarnstein/index.html
Highlights films and actresses who have portrayed vampires in movies. Also has film reviews of several vampire films.

Memnoch's Lair
http://users.atcon.com/~memnoch/
Devoted to Anne Rice and other vampire literature.

Nosferatu, the Vampire
http://www.webzone1.co.uk/www/phantom/nosfera2.htm
Site forum for the musical version of the classic vampire film.

October Funhouse
http://www.scifi.com/sforiginals/funhouse/hammer.html
Lists when all Hammer Films will be shown on network television.

The Official Anne Rice Page
http://www.annerice.com/
Information on the author, upcoming titles and books tours.

Pam Keesey's Daughters of Darkness
http://www1.minn.net/~pkeesey/
Writer of several horror novels dedicates her website to female vampires with film stills from their various movies. Also includes general vampire information.

Peter Cushing
http://xray.chm.bris.ac.uk:8000/naj/cushing.html
Dedicated to the famed British horror legend.

Pitt of Horror
http://www.webworld.co.uk/mall/PittOfHorror/
Dedicated to Countess Dracula a.k.a. Ingrid Pitt and tells how you can be in your own horror movie.

Rhino's Guide to Hammer House
http://village.vossnet.co.uk/r/rhino/hammer.htm
Features the famous film studio's films, from vampires to werewolves.
Also has a photo gallery of poster art.

Sabretooth Home Page
http://www.sabretooth.com/
Order vampire paraphernalia (fangs and contact lenses) that's similar to the real thing in Interview With The Vampire and The Lost Boys.

Sinister Cinema
http://www.cinemaweb.com/sinister/cushing.html
Lists all the films of Peter Cushing and how to order them.

Theatre des Vampires
http://users.aol.com/mishian/nosferatu/TdV.html
Features information on Anne Rice.

Tod Browning
http://www.cs.monash.edu.au/~pringle/silent/ssotm/Jun96/
The director of the first film adaption of Dracula is given tribute with biographical information as well as a filmography.

Transylvanian Society of Dracula Canadian Chapter
http://www.ccn.cs.dal.ca/Recreation/TSD/tsdhompg.html
Has convention information on Dracula's centennial celebration and links to other vampy sites.

Vampire: The Senate of Hamburg
http://www.lynet.de/~vampire/vampire.htm
The official vampire page of Hamburg, Germany.

Vampire Darkness
http://www.ualberta.ca/~dtzatzov/knight.htm
Spotlights the recently canceled late night show Forever Knight and outlines the lives of various characters on the show as well as vampire characters as Lestat, Louis, Claudia and Armand from Interview With The Vampire.

Vampire Duck Page
http://www.cs.utk.edu/~ghenry/vampired.html
Check out some photo stills from various films and look at some video clips.

Vampire Female Scrapbook
http://www.necronomi.com/projects/darkdesire/
Offers photo stills of female vampires in film and in comic books.

Connections

The Vampire Film

http://members.aol.com/indiabc/private/vfilmo.
    htm

A filmography list of many vampire films, including foreign ones. Only includes cast members, running time and production company.

The Vampires of Anne Rice

http://users.aol.com/venturello/vampengmain.
    htm

Chronicles the author's characters she herself have chronicled and has clips from the film In-terview With the Vampire.

Vampiress Visions

http://members.aol.com/ckarnstein/images.html

Offers reviews and photos from films with a female perspective on vampirism.

The Vampyre Music Homepage

http://www.cs.clemson.edu/~kec/vampyre.html

Lists vampire movies and information on their soundtracks.

VAMPYRES Film List

http://www.netaxs.com/~elmo/vamp-mov.html

Lists almost every vampire film made.

Vlad III's Vampyres Only

http://www.vampyre/index.htm

Contains lots of general Vampire info, plus some notes and images specifically Rice-related. Lots of book and movie reviews and an excellent selection of links too.

William Simmons Page

http://mustuweb.mnsfld.edu/users/simmonsw/
    home.htm

Offers links to other vampire web sites.

NORTH AMERICAN VAMPIRE ORGANIZATIONS

Anne Rice's Vampire Lestat Fan Club

PO Box 58277
New Orleans, LA 70158-8277
Publishes Anne Rice's Vampire Lestat Fan Club Newsletter.

Bite Me in the Coffin Not the Closet Fan Club

c/o Jeff Flaster
72 Sarah Lane
Middletown, NY 10940

The Camarilla

8314 Greenwood Ave., N.

PO Box 2859
Seattle, WA 98103
Publishes Requiem.

Cheeky Devil Vampire Research Inc.

c/o L. E. Elliott, Director
PO Box 7633
Abilene, TX 79608-7633

Children of the Night

c/o Thomas J. Strauch
9200 S. Avers Avenue
Evergreen Park, IL 60602

Club Vampire

c/o Riyn Gray
1764 Lugonia
Ste. 104, #223
Redlands, CA 92374
Publishes Fresh Blood.

Communion

c/o Lament
628 Woodlawn Road
Steens, MS 39766

Count Dracula Fan Club

29 Washington Square West
Penthouse North
New York, NY 10011
Publishes Bites and Pieces, Count Dracula Fan Club News-Journal, Letterzine, Undead Undu-lations.

Dynamite Fan Club

PO Box 30443
Cleveland, OH 44130
Publishes Dynamite Fan Club Horror Newsletter.

P. N. Elrod Fan Club

c/o Jackie Black
1201 Byrd, #39
Tishomingo, OK 73460
Publishes P.N. Elrod Fan Club Newsletter.

Elvira Fan Club

14755 Ventura Blvd., #1-710
Sherman Oaks, CA 91403
Publishes The Elvira Examiner.

The Fang Gang

PO Box 273895
Tampa, FL 33688-3895

Forever Knight Fan Club

c/o Lora Haines
PO Box 1108
Boston, MA 02103-1108
Publishes Feeding Frenzy.

Gothic Society of Canada
465 Queen Street West
Toronto, ON
Canada M5V 2AG
Publishes Gothic Society of Canada Newsletter.

Loyalists of the Vampire Realm
c/o Lucinda
PO Box 6975
Beverly Hills, CA 90212-6975

Midnight to Midnight: A Writer's Circle for Vampires and Werewolves
The High Mistress
c/o Karen Dove
11 North Avenue
Mt. Clemens, MI 48043

Miss Lucy Westenra Society of the Undead
c/o H. Lewis Sanders
125 Taylor Street
Jackson, TN 38302

The Munsters & The Addams Family Fan Club
c/o Louis Wendruck
PO Box 69A04
West Hollywood, CA 99969

Nigel Bennett Fan Club
c/o Star Urioste
25055 Copa del Oro, #104
Hawyard, CA 94545-2573

Nocturnal Ecstacy Vampire Coven
c/o Darlene Daniels
PO Box 147
Palo Heights, IL 60463-0147

Nosferatu Society of Vampire Fans
PO Box 2
McKean, PA 16426-0002
Publishes Nosferatu Society of Vampire Fans Newsletter.

The Official Geraint Wyn Fan Club
c/o Rosemary Shad
4133 Glendale Rd.
Woodbridge, VA 22193

Order of the Vampyre
c/o Temple of Set
PO Box 470307
San Francisco, CA 91470

Quincey P. Morris Dracula Society
c/o Charlotte Simpson
PO Box 381
Ocean Gate, NJ 08740

Realm of the Vampire
PO Box 517
Metairie, LA 70004-0517
Publishes Realm of the Vampire Newsletter.

Screem in the Dark Fan Club
c/o Screem Jam Productions
PO Box 138300
Chicago, IL 60613
Publishes Screem in the Dark Newsletter.

Secret Order of the Undead
c/o T. J. Teer
155 East "C" Street, Suite 323
Upland, CA 91786
Publishes S.O.UND Newsletter.

Shadows of the Night
PO Box 17006
Rochester, NY 14617

Temple of the Vampire
PO Box 3582
Lacey, WA 98503
Publishes Bloodlines: the Vampire Temple Journal *and* Life Force: the International Vampire Forum.

Vampire Information Exchange
c/o Eric Held
PO Box 328
Brooklyn, NY 11229-0328

Vampire Research Center
PO Box 252
Elmhurst, NY 11373

Vampire Studies
PO Box 151
Berwyn, IL 60412

The Vampire's Vault
Suite 3H
One Fifth Avenue
New York, NY 10003

Vampires, Werewolves, Ghosts & Other Such Thngs that Go Bump in the Night
PO Box 6975
Beverly Hills, CA 90212-6975

Vampirism Research Institute
PO Box 20167
Seattle, WA 98111
Publishes Journal of Modern Vampirism.

Van Helsing Society
PO Box 602088
Cleveland, OH 44102

Connections

INDEPENDENT VAMPIRE PERIODICALS

Bathory Palace
c/o Laure
1610 SW 3rd
Topeka, KS 66606-1215

Bloodreams
c/o Kelly Gunter Atlas
1312 West 43rd Street
N. Little Rock, AR 72118

Bloodlines
Danis the Dark Productions
305 Hahani Street, #296
Kailua, HI 96734

Cemetary Gates
4336 Byesville Blvd.
Dayton, OH 45431

Children of Darkness
c/o Dracula Field
6224 Edgewater Drive
Falls Church, VA 22041

The Circle of Twins
c/o Alexa Danceny
Route 4, Box 304H
Savannah, TN 38372

Dark Terrors
c/o Avelon
Ventor Ice, St. Ives
Cornwall TR25 1DY
United Kingdom

Dyad: The Vampire Stories
c/o MKASHEF Enterprises
PO Box 368
Poway, CA 92074-0368

Elegia Magazine
c/o Marie Buckner
3116 Porter Lane
Ventura, CA 93003

Elvira
c/o Kevin Hayward, Editor
3 Farm Rd.
Old Woking, Surrey GU22 9HL
England

Exquisite Corpse
5320 N. Central Avenue
Indianapolis, IN 46220

Good Guys Wear Fangs
c/o Mary Ann B. McKinnon, Editor

254 Blunk Avenue
Plymouth, MI 48170

Gothica
c/o Susan M. Jenssen
98 Union St., Apt. 4
Brewer, ME 04412

International Vampire
c/o Rob Brautigam
Galileiplantsoen 90-1
1098NC Amsterdam
The Netherlands

Journal of Vampirology
c/o John Vellutini
PO Box 881631
San Francisco, CA 94188-1631

Kiss of Death
c/o Darcie Blaszak
1616 Wasserman Court
Virginia Beach, VA 23454

Knight Beat
c/o Special Services Unltd.
8601-A W. Cermak Rd.
North Riverside, IL 60546

Knightly Tales
c/o Jessica Daigneault
PO Box 334
Lisbon Falls, ME 04252

Necro
1648 W. Hazelhurst
Ferndale, MI 48220

Necropolis
c/o Chad Savage
PO Box 77693
San Francisco, CA 94107

Nightlore
PO Box 8148
Mobile, AL 36689

Nightmist
c/o Tammy Pond
PO Box 17006
Rochester, NY 14617

Night's Children —Not Exactly Human
c/o Wendy Snow-Lang
PO Box 5010, Ste. 115
Salem, MA 01970

On the Wings of the Knight
c/o Ann & Bill Hupe
916 Lamb Road
Mason, MI 48854-9445

Onyx
c/o Mark Williams
PO Box 137
Uniontown, OH 44685

Perfect Darkness
c/o M. Perkins
530 S. Flood
Norman, OK 73069

Prisoners of the Night
MKASHEF Enterprises
PO Box 688
Yucca Valley, CA 92286-0688

The Raven
c/o Amy Hull and Paula Sanders
603 W. Walnut
Carbondale, IL 62901

Rouge et Noir
c/o Meg Thompson
Preternatural Productions
PO Box 786
Fort Huachuca, AZ 85613

The Secret Life
c/o Alisa Kester
PO Box 1512
Mt. Vernon, WA 98273

Shadowdance
c/o Michelle Belanger
PO Box 474
Hinckley, OH 44233

Terra-X
34159 Gem Circle
N. Ridgeville, OH 44039

This Evil on Earth
PO Box 616
Hawthorne, NJ 075-7

Vampire Archives
c/o Jule Ghoul
2926 W. Leland
Chicago, IL 60625-3716

The Vampire Journal
Baker Street Publications
PO Box 994
Metarie, LA 70004

Vampire Junction
c/o C. Cosner
505 NW 13th St.
Gainesville, FL 32601

The Vampire Quarterly
c/o Susan M. Garrett
142 Sunvalley Drive
Toms River, NJ 08753

Vamps
c/o de Lioncourt
PO Box 21067
Seattle, WA 98111

Wicked Mystic
c/o Andre Scheluchin
PO Box 3087
Astoria, NY 11103

Connections

Alternate Titles

Vampire movies, like vampires themselves, are known by many names and are often foreign. In an effort to help identify the movies that are out there, by whatever name you know them, we've included (at no additional charge!) this handy Alternate Titles index. The alternate title of a movie is followed by the title under which it's listed.

Blood Demon *See* Torture Chamber of Dr. Sadism (1969)

The Blood Drinkers *See* The Vampire People (1966)

Blood Fiend *See* Theatre of Death (1967)

Blood for Dracula *See* Andy Warhol's Dracula (1974)

Blood Hunger *See* Vampyres (1974)

Blood is My Heritage *See* Blood of Dracula (1957)

Blood Moon *See* The Werewolf vs. the Vampire Woman (1970)

Blood of Frankenstein *See* Dracula vs. Frankenstein (1971)

Blood of the Vampires *See* Curse of the Vampires (1970)

The Blood Suckers *See* Alien Massacre (1967)

The Blood Suckers *See* Dr. Terror's House of Horrors (1965)

Blood Thirst *See* Salem's Lot (1979)

Bloodthirsty Eyes *See* Lake of Dracula (1971)

Bordello of Blood *See* Tales from the Crypt Presents Bordello of Blood (1996)

Bram Stoker's Count Dracula *See* Count Dracula (1971)

Caged Virgins *See* Requiem for a Vampire (1972)

Cake of Blood *See* Blood Pie (1971)

Capuexita y Pulgareito contra los Monstruos *See* Tom Thumb and Little Red Riding Hood vs. the Monsters (1962)

Carne de Tu Carne *See* Flesh of Your Flesh (1984)

The Case of the Smiling Stiffs *See* The Case of the Full Moon Murders (1974)

Castle of Doom *See* Vampyr (1931)

Castle of Terror *See* Castle of Blood (1964)

Castle of the Walking Dead *See* Torture Chamber of Dr. Sadism (1969)

Cemetary Girls *See* The Vampire Hookers (1978)

Cemetary Girls *See* The Velvet Vampire (1971)

Ceremonia Sangrienta *See* The Legend of Blood Castle (1972)

Chabelo y Pepito contra los Monstruos *See* Pepito y Chabelo vs. los Monstruos (1973)

Chamber of Fear *See* The Fear Chamber (1967)

Chi O Suu Bara *See* The Evil of Dracula (1975)

Chi O Suu Me *See* Lake of Dracula (1971)

Chi O Suu Ningyo *See* Night of the Vampire (1970)

Coffin of Terror *See* Castle of Blood (1964)

Confessions of a Bloodsucker *See* Tender Dracula, or The Confessions of a Bloodsucker (1974)

Contes Immoraux *See* Immoral Tales (1974)

Count Downe, Son of Dracula *See* Son of Dracula (1973)

Count Dracula and His Vampire Bride *See* The Satanic Rites of Dracula (1973)

Count Dracula's Great Love *See* Dracula's Great Love (1972)

Crazed Vampire *See* Requiem for a Vampire (1972)

Creatures of Evil *See* Curse of the Vampires (1970)

Creatures of the Prehistoric Planet *See* Horror of the Blood Monsters (1970)

Creatures of the Red Planet *See* Horror of the Blood Monsters (1970)

The Crypt of the Vampire *See* Terror in the Crypt (1962)

Cuadecuc *See* Vampir (1970)

Curse of Dark Shadows *See* Night of Dark Shadows (1971)

The Curse of Dracula *See* Return of Dracula (1958)

Curse of the Blood-Ghouls *See* The Slaughter of the Vampires (1962)

Curse of the Karnsteins *See* Terror in the Crypt (1962)

Curse of the Vampire *See* Anak Pontianak (1958)

Curses of the Ghouls *See* The Slaughter of the Vampires (1962)

Dance of the Vampires *See* The Fearless Vampire Killers (1967)

Danza Macabra *See* Castle of Blood (1964)

De Vampier van New York *See* Love After Death (1969)

Dead of Night *See* Deathdream (1972)

Deathshead Vampire *See* Blood Beast Terror (1967)

The Demon Lover *See* The Body Beneath (1970)

The Demon Planet *See* Planet of the Vampires (1965)

Dendam Pontianak *See* Revenge of the Vampire (1957)

Dentro il Cimitrio *See* Graveyard Disturbance (1987)

Der Fluch Der Gruenen Augen *See* Cave of the Living Dead (1965)

Desire the Vampire *See* I, Desire (1982)

Die Schlangengrube und das Pendel *See* Torture Chamber of Dr. Sadism (1969)

Die Zartlichkeit der Wolfe *See* Tenderness of Wolves (1973)

Dr. Breedlove, or How I Learned to Stop Worrying and Love *See* Kiss Me Quick! (1964)

Dr. Terror's Gallery of Horrors *See* Alien Massacre (1967)

Doctors Wear Scarlet *See* The Bloodsuckers (1970)

Double Possession *See* Black Vampire (1973)

Dracula *See* Bram Stoker's Dracula (1992)

Dracula *See* The Horror of Dracula (1958)

Dracula 71 *See* Count Dracula (1971)

Dracula Contra Frankenstein *See* Dracula vs. Frankenstein (1971)

Dracula in Brianza *See* Il Cavaliere Costante Nicosia Demoniaco Ovvero (1975)

Dracula in the Provinces *See* Il Cavaliere Costante Nicosia Demoniaco Ovvero (1975)

Dracula Pere et Fils *See* Dracula & Son (1976)

Dracula Saga *See* The Saga of the Draculas (1972)

Dracula: The Bloodline Continues... *See* The Saga of the Draculas (1972)

Dracula-The Great Undead *See* Vincent Price's Dracula (1982)

Dracula vs. Frankenstein *See* The Screaming Dead (1972)

Dracula's Castle *See* Blood of Dracula's Castle (1969)

Dracula's Dog *See* Zoltan...Hound of Dracula (1978)

Dracula's Lust for Blood *See* Lake of Dracula (1971)

Dracula's Virgin Lovers *See* Dracula's Great Love (1972)

Dragon vs. Vampire *See* Dragon Against Vampire (1984)

Drakula Istanbulda *See* Drakula in Istanbul (1953)

Dugong Vampira *See* Curse of the Vampires (1970)

El Allido del Diablo *See* Howl of the Devil (1972)

El Ataud Del Coffin *See* The Vampire's Coffin (1958)

El Ataud Del Vampiro *See* The Vampire's Coffin (1958)

El Baul Macabro *See* The Macabre Trunk (1936)

El Castillo se los Monstruos *See* Castle of the Monsters (1958)

El Charro de las Calaveras *See* The Rider of the Skulls (1967)

El Conde Dracula *See* Count Dracula (1971)

El Extrano Amor de los vampiros *See* Strange Love of the Vampires (1974)

El Imperio de Dracula *See* The Empire of Dracula (1967)

El Jovencito Dracula *See* Young Jonathan Dracula (1975)

El Retorno de la Walpurgis *See* Curse of the Devil (1973)

El Santo Contra el Baron Brakola *See* Santo Against Baron Brakola (1965)

El Signo del Vampiro *See* Lesbian Vampires The Heiress of Dracula (1971)

El Vampiro Aechecha *See* The Lurking Vampire (1962)

El Vampiro de la Autopista *See* The Vampire of the Highway (1969)

Ercole al Centro Della Terra *See* Hercules in the Haunted World (1964)

Et Mourir de Plaisir *See* Blood and Roses (1961)

Every Home Should Have One *See* Think Dirty (1970)

The Faceless Monsters *See* Nightmare Castle (1965)

The Female Butcher *See* The Legend of Blood Castle (1972)

The Female Vampire *See* Vampire Man (1959)

A Filha de Dracula *See* Daughter of Dracula (1972)

A Filha de Dracula *See* Dracula's Daughter (1971)

The Flesh Creatures *See* Horror of the Blood Monsters (1970)

Flesh Creatures of the Red Planet *See* Horror of the Blood Monsters (1970)

Forbidden Femininity *See* Sexy Prohibitissimo (1963)

Fracchia contro Dracula *See* Who Is Afraid of Dracula (1985)

Fracchia vs. Dracula *See* Who Is Afraid of Dracula (1985)

Frankenstein, El Vampiro, y Cia *See* Frankenstein, the Vampire and Co. (1961)

Frankenstein, El Vampiro y Compania *See* Frankenstein, the Vampire and Co. (1961)

The Freak From Suckweasel Mountain *See* Geek Maggot Bingo (1983)

Gallery of Horror *See* Alien Massacre (1967)

Ganja and Hess *See* Black Vampire (1973)

Garu, the Mad Monk *See* Guru, the Mad Monk (1970)

Genie of Darkness *See* Nostradamus and the Genie of Darkness (1960)

The Ghastly Orgies of Count Dracula *See* Horrible Orgies of Count Dracula (1973)

The Giant Leeches *See* Attack of the Giant Leeches (1959)

Glump *See* Please Don't Eat My Mother (1972)

Goke, Body Snatcher from Hell *See* Body Snatcher from Hell (1969)

Goke the Vampire *See* Body Snatcher from Hell (1969)

Gran Amore del Conde Dracula *See* Dracula's Great Love (1972)

Grave Robbers from Outer Space *See* Plan 9 from Outer Space (1956)

The Grip of the Vampire *See* Curse of the Undead (1959)

Hand of Night *See* Beast of Morocco (1966)

Alternate Titles

Hanno Cambiato Faccia *See* They've Changed Faces (1971)

Hell's Creatures *See* Frankenstein's Bloody Terror (1968)

The Heritage of Dracula *See* Lesbian Vampires The Heiress of Dracula (1971)

The Horrible Sexy Vampire *See* The Vampire of the Highway (1969)

Horror Convention *See* Nightmare in Blood (1975)

Horror Creatures of the Prehistoric Planet *See* Horror of the Blood Monsters (1970)

Hungry Pets *See* Please Don't Eat My Mother (1972)

Huphyokwi Yanyo *See* Vengeful Vampire Girl (1981)

I Tre Volti della Paura *See* Black Sabbath (1964)

I, Vampiri *See* The Devil's Commandment (1956)

Il Castello de Morti Vivi *See* Castle of the Living Dead (1964)

Il Lago di Satana *See* The She-Beast (1965)

Il Mostro dell'Opera *See* The Vampire of the Opera (1961)

Il Vampiro dell'Opera *See* The Vampire of the Opera (1961)

Incense For the Damned *See* The Bloodsuckers (1970)

Insomnie *See* Insomnia (1963)

The Invisible Killer *See* Curse of the Undead (1959)

It Lives By Night *See* The Bat People (1974)

It! The Vampire From Beyond Space *See* It! The Terror from Beyond Space (1958)

It's Always Darkest Before the Dawn *See* The Vampire (1957)

Jonathan, le Dernier Combat contre les Vampires *See* Jonathan (1970)

Jonathan, Vampire Sterben Nicht *See* Jonathan (1970)

The Karnstein Curse *See* Terror in the Crypt (1962)

Karnstein, the Crypt and the Nightmare *See* Terror in the Crypt (1962)

Khorda *See* The Deathmaster (1971)

Killer Bats *See* The Devil Bat (1941)

The Killing Box *See* The Ghost Brigade (1993)

Kiss of Evil *See* Kiss of the Vampire (1962)

Kronos *See* Captain Kronos: Vampire Hunter (1974)

Kyuketsu Dukorosen *See* Living Skeleton (1968)

Kyuketsuki Dorakyura Kobe Ni Arawaru: Akuma Wa Onna Utsukushiku Suru *See* Vampire Dracula Comes to Kobe; Evil Make Woman Beautiful (1979)

Kyuketsuki Ga *See* The Vampire Moth (1956)

Kyuketsuki Ga *See* Vampire Moth (1956)

Kyuketsuki Gokemidoro *See* Body Snatcher from Hell (1969)

La Camara Del Terror *See* The Fear Chamber (1967)

La Casa Embrujada *See* The Curse of the Crying Woman (1961)

La Cripta e l'Incubo *See* Terror in the Crypt (1962)

La Fille de Dracula *See* Daughter of Dracula (1972)

La Hija de Dracula *See* Daughter of Dracula (1972)

La Hija de Dracula *See* Dracula's Daughter (1971)

La Huella Macabra *See* The Macabre Mark (1962)

La Invasion de los Muertos *See* Invasion of the Dead (1972)

La Invasion de Los Vampiros *See* Invasion of the Vampires (1961)

La Llamada del Vampiro *See* The Curse of the Vampyr (1971)

La Maldicion de a Llorona *See* The Curse of the Crying Woman (1961)

La Maldicion de los Karnsteins *See* Terror in the Crypt (1962)

La Marca del Hombre Lobo *See* Frankenstein's Bloody Terror (1968)

La Marca del Muerto *See* Creature of the Walking Dead (1960)

La Morte Vivante *See* The Living Dead Girl (1982)

La Nipote del Vampiro *See* Fangs of the Living Dead (1968)

La Noche de los Diablos *See* Night of the Devils (1971)

La Noche de los Vampiros *See* Strange Love of the Vampires (1974)

La Noche dell Terror Ciego *See* Tombs of the Blind Dead (1972)

La Notte dei Diavoli *See* Night of the Devils (1971)

La Novia Esangentada *See* The Blood Spattered Bride (1972)

La Sangre de Nostradamus *See* Blood of Nostradamus (1960)

La Venganza de las Mujeres Vampiro *See* Santo en la Venganza de las Mujeres Vampiro (1969)

The Lady Dracula *See* Lemora, Lady Dracula (1973)

Las Mujeres de Dracula *See* The Empire of Dracula (1967)

Las Vampiras *See* The Vampire Girls (1968)

Last Rites *See* Dracula's Last Rites (1979)

Le Rouge aux Levres *See* Daughters of Darkness (1971)

Le Teur Invisible *See* Curse of the Undead (1959)

Le Vampire de New York *See* Love After Death (1969)

Legend of the Seven Golden Vampires *See* The 7 Brothers Meet Dracula (1973)

The Legendary Curse of Lemora *See* Lemora, Lady Dracula (1973)

Les Femmes Vampires *See* La Reine des Vampires (1968)

Les Griffes du Vampire *See* Curse of the Undead (1959)

Les Vampires en Ont Ras le Bol *See* Blood Relations (1977)

Lesbian Vampires *See* Lesbian Vampires The Heiress of Dracula (1971)

Los Vampiros Tambien Duerman *See* Strange Love of the Vampires (1974)

Love at First Gulp *See* Dracula Exotica (1981)

Lovers From Beyond the Tomb *See* Nightmare Castle (1965)

L'Ultimo Uomo Della Terra *See* The Last Man on Earth (1964)

Lust of the Vampires *See* The Devil's Commandment (1956)

The Male Vampire *See* Vampire Man (1959)

Malenka, the Vampire *See* Fangs of the Living Dead (1968)

Mark of the Beast *See* Curse of the Undead (1959)

Mark of the Vampire *See* The Vampire (1957)

Mark of the Vampire *See* The Vampire (1957)

Mark of the West *See* Curse of the Undead (1959)

The Mark of the Wolfman *See* Frankenstein's Bloody Terror (1968)

The Master of the Dungeon *See* Guess What Happened to Count Dracula? (1970)

The Monster of the Opera *See* The Vampire of the Opera (1961)

The Monsters Demolisher *See* Nostradamus and the Destroyer of Monsters (1962)

Mosquito deer Scheander *See* Bloodlust (1970)

Mother Riley Meets the Vampire *See* My Son, the Vampire (1952)

Mr. Vampire *See* Magic Cop (1989)

Nacht Wenn Dracula Erwacht *See* Count Dracula (1971)

The Naked Temptress *See* The Naked Witch (1964)

Naked Vampire *See* La Vampire Nue (1969)

New Mr. Vampire II *See* One Eyebrow Priest (1987)

The Niece of the Vampire *See* Fangs of the Living Dead (1968)

Night of the Bloodsuckers *See* The Vampire Hookers (1978)

Night of the Doomed *See* Nightmare Castle (1965)

Night of the Walking Dead *See* Strange Love of the Vampires (1974)

Night Walk *See* Deathdream (1972)

The Nights of Dracula *See* Count Dracula (1971)

Nocturna, Granddaughter of Dracula *See* Nocturna (1979)

Nosferat, A Symphony of Horror *See* Nosferatu (1922)

Nosferatu, A Symphony of Terror *See* Nosferatu (1922)

Nosferatu a Venezia *See* Vampire in Venice (1988)

Nosferatu, Eine Symphonie des Grauens *See* Nosferatu (1922)

Nosferatu: Phantom der Nacht *See* Nosferatu the Vampyre (1979)

Nosferatu, The Vampire *See* Nosferatu (1922)

Nostradamus y el Destructor de Monstruos *See* Nostradamus and the Destroyer of Monsters (1962)

Nostradamus y el Genio de las Tinieblas *See* Nostradamus and the Genie of Darkness (1960)

Not Against the Flesh *See* Vampyr (1931)

Nude Vampire *See* La Vampire Nue (1969)

Old Drac *See* Old Dracula (1975)

Old Mother Riley Meets the Vampire *See* My Son, the Vampire (1952)

Onna Kyuketsuki *See* Vampire Man (1959)

Pardon Me, Your Teeth are in My Neck *See* The Fearless Vampire Killers (1967)

Pastel de Sangre *See* Blood Pie (1971)

Pastel de Sangre *See* Cake of Blood (1972)

Pontianak *See* The Vampire (1957)

Pontianak Gua Musang *See* Vampire of the Cave (1964)

Pontianak Kembali *See* The Vampire Returns (1963)

Pura Sangre *See* Pure Blood (1983)

Queen of Blood *See* Planet of Blood (1966)

Queen of the Vampires *See* La Reine des Vampires (1968)

Rage *See* Rabid (1977)

The Rape of the Vampire *See* La Reine des Vampires (1968)

Reincarnation of Isabel *See* Horrible Orgies of Count Dracula (1973)

Requiem pour un Vampire *See* Requiem for a Vampire (1972)

Return from the Past *See* Alien Massacre (1967)

The Revenge of Dracula *See* Dracula vs. Frankenstein (1971)

Alternate Titles

The Revenge of the Blood Beast *See* The She-Beast (1965)

Riti Magie Nere e Segret Ogre del Trecento *See* Horrible Orgies of Count Dracula (1973)

The Saga of Dracula *See* The Saga of the Draculas (1972)

Sangre de Virgenes *See* Blood of the Virgins (1968)

Santo y Blue Demon contra Dracula y el Hombre Lobo *See* Santo and the Blue Demon vs. Dracula and the Wolfman (1973)

Santo y Blue Demon contra los Monstruos *See* Santo and the Blue Demon vs. the Monsters (1968)

Satan's Daughters *See* Vampyres (1974)

Satellite of Blood *See* First Man into Space (1959)

The Secret of Dr. Alucard *See* A Taste of Blood (1966)

Seed of Terror *See* Grave of the Vampire (1972)

Sensuous Vampires *See* The Vampire Hookers (1978)

Sex and the Vampire *See* La Reine des Vampires (1968)

Sex and the Vampire *See* Le Frisson des Vampires (1970)

Sex on the Groove Tube *See* The Case of the Full Moon Murders (1974)

Sexy Interdit *See* Sexy Prohibitissimo (1963)

Sexy Super Interdit *See* Sexy Prohibitissimo (1963)

She Demons of the Swamp *See* Attack of the Giant Leeches (1959)

Shudder of the Vampire *See* Le Frisson des Vampires (1970)

The Sign of the Vampire *See* Lesbian Vampires The Heiress of Dracula (1971)

Sinfonia del Mas Alla *See* The Empire of Dracula (1967)

The Sleep of the Dead *See* The Inn of the Flying Dragon (1981)

Son of the Vampire *See* Anak Pontianak (1958)

Space Mission of the Lost Planet *See* Horror of the Blood Monsters (1970)

Space Mutants *See* Planet of the Vampires (1965)

Stephen King's Sleepwalkers *See* Sleepwalkers (1992)

The Strange Adventure of David Gray *See* Vampyr (1931)

The Strange Adventures of Jonathan Harker *See* Lesbian Vampires The Heiress of Dracula (1971)

Subspecies 2 *See* Bloodstone: Subspecies 2 (1992)

Subspecies 3 *See* Bloodlust: Subspecies 3 (1993)

Sumpah Pontianak *See* Vampire's Curse (1958)

Tales from the Crypt II *See* Vault of Horror (1973)

Tender Dracula, Vampire *See* Tender Dracula, or The Confessions of a Bloodsucker (1974)

Tendre Dracula ou les Confessions d'un Buveur de Sang *See* Tender Dracula, or The Confessions of a Bloodsucker (1974)

Terreur dans l'Espace *See* Planet of the Vampires (1965)

Terror in Space *See* Planet of the Vampires (1965)

Terror of the Vampires *See* Le Frisson des Vampires (1970)

They're Coming to Get You *See* Dracula vs. Frankenstein (1971)

The Thing From Another World *See* The Thing (1951)

Three Immoral Women *See* Immoral Tales (1974)

Through the Looking Glass *See* The Velvet Vampire (1971)

To Love a Vampire *See* Lust for a Vampire (1971)

The Tommyknockers *See* Stephen King's The Tommyknockers (1993)

Tore ng Diyablo *See* Tower of the Devil (1969)

Torture Zone *See* The Fear Chamber (1967)

Twice Bitten *See* The Vampire Hookers (1978)

L'Ultima Predadel Vampiro *See* Playgirls and the Vampire (1960)

Um Sonho de Vampiros *See* A Vampire's Dream (1970)

Upir z Feratu *See* Ferat Vampire (1982)

Valerie a Tyden Divu *See* Valerie and the Week of Wonders (1969)

Vampira *See* Old Dracula (1975)

The Vampire *See* Vampyr (1931)

The Vampire and the Robot *See* My Son, the Vampire (1952)

The Vampire-Beast Craves Blood *See* Blood Beast Terror (1967)

Vampire Men of the Lost Planet *See* Horror of the Blood Monsters (1970)

The Vampire of Castle Frankenstein *See* The Vampire of the Highway (1969)

The Vampire of Dr. Dracula *See* Frankenstein's Bloody Terror (1968)

The Vampire of New York *See* Love After Death (1969)

Vampire Over London *See* My Son, the Vampire (1952)

Vampire Woman *See* Vampire Man (1959)

The Vampire's Crypt *See* Terror in the Crypt (1962)

Vampires in Venice *See* Vampire in Venice (1988)

The Vampire's Lover *See* Vampire and the Ballerina (1963)

The Vampire's Niece *See* Fangs of the Living Dead (1968)

Vampire's Night Orgy *See* Orgy of the Vampires (1973)

The Vampire's Thrill *See* Le Frisson des Vampires (1970)

Vampiros in la Habana *See* Vampires in Havana (1986)

Vampyr, Der Traum Des David Gray *See* Vampyr (1931)

Vampyr, Ou L'Etrang e Aventure De David Gray *See* Vampyr (1931)

Vampyres, Daughters of Dracula *See* Vampyres (1974)

Vampyros Lesbos Die Erbin des Dracula *See* Lesbian Vampires The Heiress of Dracula (1971)

Veil of Blood *See* The Devil's Plaything (1973)

The Vengeance of the Vampire Women *See* Santo en la Venganza de las Mujeres Vampiro (1969)

The Veteran *See* Deathdream (1972)

Vierges et Vampires *See* Requiem for a Vampire (1972)

Virgins and Vampires *See* Requiem for a Vampire (1972)

Wicked Wife *See* Curse of the Wicked Wife (1984)

The Wolfman of Count Dracula *See* Frankenstein's Bloody Terror (1968)

The Worst Crime of All *See* Mondo Keyhole (1968)

Xi Xuefu *See* Vampire Woman (1962)

Young Dracula *See* Andy Warhol's Dracula (1974)

Young Dracula *See* Son of Dracula (1943)

Young Dracula *See* Son of Dracula (1973)

Yureiyashiki no Kyofu-Cho Wo Sun Ningyo *See* Night of the Vampire (1970)

Alternate Titles

Cast Index

The Cast Index lists all actors and actresses credited in the main review section, alphabetically by last name. They are listed in first-name-first, last-name-last format. Do not panic. We meant to do that.

Robin Altman
The Gong Show Movie '80

Steve Altman
Transylvania Twist '89

Aurora Alvarado
Nostradamus and the
Destroyer of Monsters
'62
Nostradamus and the
Genie of Darkness '60

Enrique Garcia Alvarez
Invasion of the Vampires
'61

Andriana Ambesi
Fangs of the Living Dead
'68
Terror in the Crypt '62

Heather Ames
Blood of Dracula '57

Madchen Amick
Sleepwalkers '92

Suzy Amis
Nadja '95

John Amplas
Martin '77

Anet Anatelle
The Malibu Beach
Vampires '91

Donna Anders
Count Yorga, Vampire '70

Isa Anderson
Night Angel '90

Rona Anderson
Devils of Darkness '65

Susy Anderson
Black Sabbath '64

Tina Anderson
Blood Freak '72

Annie Andersson
Le Vampire du
Dusseldorf '64

Starr Andreeff
Dance of the Damned
'88

Hector Andremar
Capulina contra Los
Monstros '72
Capulina contra Los
Vampiros '72

Simon Andrew
The Blood Spattered
Bride '72
Night of the Sorcerers '70

Barry Andrews
Dracula Has Risen from
the Grave '68

Angelyne
The Malibu Beach
Vampires '91

Philip Anglim
Haunted Summer '88

Evelyn Ankers
Son of Dracula '43

Michael Ansara
It's Alive '74

Lysette Anthony
Dark Shadows
Resurrected The Video
'95
Dracula: Dead and
Loving It '95

Anulka
Vampyres '74

Helena Anyzkova
Valerie and the Week of
Wonders '69

Noel Appleby
My Grandpa is a Vampire
'92

Angel Aranda
Planet of the Vampires
'65

Humberto Arango
Pure Blood '83

Dawn Archibald
The Bad Sister '83

Mary Arden
Blood and Black Lace '64

George Ardisson
Hercules in the Haunted
World '64

Rosita Arenas
The Curse of the Crying
Woman '61

Eddi Arent
Lady Dracula '77

Pedro Armendariz, Jr.
The Vampire Girls '68

James Arness
The Thing '51

Alice Arno
The Loves of Irina '80s

Eduardo Arozamena
Dracula (Spanish Version)
'31

David Arquette
Buffy the Vampire Slayer
'92

Patricia Arquette
Ed Wood '94

Dana Ashbrook
Waxwork '88

Linda Ashby
Night Angel '90

Elizabeth Ashley
Vampire's Kiss '88

John Ashton
Stephen King's The
Tommyknockers '93

Gregoire Aslan
Blood Relations '77
Paris When It Sizzles '64

Fred Astaire
Paris When It Sizzles '64

Thomas Astan
Jonathan '70

John Astin
Halloween with the
Addams Family '79
Night Life '90

Christopher Atkins
Dracula Rising '93

Malcolm Atterbury
Blood of Dracula '57

Lionel Atwill
The Horror of It All '91
House of Dracula '45
House of Frankenstein
'44
The Vampire Bat '32

Lenore Aubert
Abbott and Costello Meet
Frankenstein '49

Mischa Auer
Condemned to Live '35

Amadeus August
Love Vampire Style '70

Ewa Aulin
The Legend of Blood
Castle '72

Lew Ayres
Salem's Lot '79

Richard Backus
Deathdream '72

Jimmie Baird
Return of Dracula '58

Tom Baker
Vault of Horror '73

William L. Baker
Witchcraft 3: The Kiss of
Death '90

Nicholas Ball
Lifeforce '85

Vincent Ball
Blood of the Vampire '58

Maxine Ballantyne
Lemora, Lady Dracula
'73

Thomas Balltore
Once Bitten '85

Anne Bancroft
Dracula: Dead and
Loving It '95

Bever-Leigh Banfield
Curse of Dracula '79
World of Dracula '79

Christine Baranski
Addams Family Values
'93

Jered Barclay
Howling 6: The Freaks
'90

Joan Barclay
The Corpse Vanishes '42

Roy Barcroft
Billy the Kid Versus
Dracula '66

Rebecca Bardot
Vampire's Kiss '92

Lex Barker
Torture Chamber of Dr.
Sadism '69

Steve Barkett
Dark Universe '93

Vince Barnett
The Corpse Vanishes '42

Elizabeth Barondes
Not of This Earth '96

Carina Barone
The Living Dead Girl '82

Patrick Barr
The Satanic Rites of
Dracula '73

Paula Barr
Casual Relations '73

Jean-Louis Barrault
Chappaqua '65

Cast Index

To Die for 2: Son of
Darkness '91

Eugenie Bondurant
Sorority House Vampires
'91

Natalie Bondurant
Sorority House Vampires
'91

Nai Bonet
Nocturna '79

Choi Bong
Vengeful Vampire Girl
'81

Pat Boone
Horror of it All '63

Adrian Booth
Valley of the Zombies '45

Milan Borich
My Grandpa is a Vampire
'92

Lucia Bose
The Legend of Blood
Castle '72

Jean-Pierre Bouyxou
Vampirisme '67

David Bowie
The Hunger '83

Judi Bowker
Count Dracula '78

Guy Boyd
Body Double '84

Kim Braden
Bloodsuckers from Outer
Space '83

Stephen Bradley
Disciple of Death '72

**Francisco (Frank)
Brana**
Crypt of the Living Dead
'73

Neville Brand
Evils of the Night '85

Walter Brandi
The Slaughter of the
Vampires '62
Terror Creatures from the
Grave '66

Marie Breillat
Dracula & Son '76

April Breneman
Witchcraft 7: Judgement
Hour '95

John Brent
Vampyre '90

Bernard Bresslaw
Old Dracula '75

Jana Brezkova
Ferat Vampire '82

Shane Briant
Captain Kronos: Vampire
Hunter '74

Morgan Brittany
Sundown '91

Mark Brock
The Bride's Initiation '76

J. Edward Bromberg
Son of Dracula '43

Claudio Brook
Cronos '94
Sisters of Satan '75

Hillary Brooke
Crime Doctor's Courage
'45

Paul Brooke
The Lair of the White
Worm '88

Walter Brooke
The Return of Count
Yorga '71

Christopher Brooks
Alabama's Ghost '72

Mel Brooks
Dracula: Dead and
Loving It '95

Victor Brooks
Devils of Darkness '65

Angela Brown
Teen Vamp '88

Edmund Brown
The Man in Half Moon
Street '44

Murray Brown
Vampyres '74

Steve Brown
Darkness '92

Walter Brown
Dracula: Prince of
Darkness '65

Dora Bryan
My Son, the Vampire '52

Yvette Buchanan
The Malibu Beach
Vampires '91

Christine Buchegger
Lady Dracula '77

Robert Burgos
The Naked Witch '64

Caesar Burner
Tombs of the Blind Dead
'72

Mark Burns
Count Dracula '78

William S. Burroughs
Chappaqua '65

LeVar Burton
The Midnight Hour '86

Raymond Bussieres
Paris When It Sizzles '64

Ulrike Butz
The Devil's Plaything '73

Lando Buzzanca
Il Cavaliere Costante
Nicosia Demoniaco
Ovvero '75

John Byner
Transylvania 6-5000 '85

Gabriel Byrne
Gothic '87
The Keep '83

David Byrnes
Witchcraft 7: Judgement
Hour '95

Kathleen Byron
Twins of Evil '71

Libby Caculus
Dracula, The Dirty Old
Man '69

Sid Caesar
Munster's Revenge '81

Nicolas Cage
Vampire's Kiss '88

Rita Calderon
Horrible Orgies of Count
Dracula '73

Paul Calderone
The Addiction '95

Charlie Callas
Vampire Vixens from
Venus '94

Dean Cameron
Rockula '90

Bill Campbell
Bram Stoker's Dracula
'92

Bruce Campbell
Sundown '91
Waxwork 2: Lost in Time
'91

William Campbell
Track of the Vampire '66

Jose Campos
Terror in the Crypt '62

Rafael Campos
The Astro-Zombies '67

Gianna Maria Canale
The Devil's
Commandment '56
Evil's Commandment '56

John Candy
Little Shop of Horrors '86

Ed Cannon
Vampire Cop '90

Peter Capaldi
The Lair of the White
Worm '88

Barbara Capell
The Werewolf vs. the
Vampire Woman '70

Capulina
Capulina contra Los
Monstros '72
Capulina contra Los
Vampiros '72

Rene Cardona, Jr.
The Macabre Trunk '36

John Cardos
Blood of Dracula's Castle
'69

Harry Carey, Jr.
Billy the Kid Versus
Dracula '66

MacDonald Carey
It's Alive 3: Island of the
Alive '87

Lynn Carlin
Deathdream '72

Mary Carlisle
Dead Men Walk '43

Karen Carlson
Teen Vamp '88

Veronica Carlson
Dracula Has Risen from
the Grave '68
Old Dracula '75

Roberto Carmardiel
Strange Love of the
Vampires '74

Cast Index

Michael Colyar
Jugular Wine: A Vampire Odyssey '94

Jeff Conaway
Elvira, Mistress of the Dark '88
Tales from the Darkside, Vol. 4

Barry Concula
Dracula Bites the Big Apple '79

Nela Conjiu
Terror in the Crypt '62

Carol Connors
The Bride's Initiation '76

Michael Conrad
Scream Blacula Scream '73

John Considine
The Thirsty Dead '74

Eddie Constantine
Blood Relations '77
It's Alive 2: It Lives Again '78

Chantal Contouri
Thirst '87

Vangelis Contronis
Dracula Tan Exarchia '83

Jackie Coogan
Halloween with the Addams Family '79

Elisha Cook, Jr.
Salem's Lot '79

Jackie Cooper
Chosen Survivors '74
Hollywood on Parade '34

Jeremy Cooper
The Reflecting Skin '91

Teri Copley
Transylvania Twist '89

Gretchen Corbett
Let's Scare Jessica to Death '71

Harry H. Corbett
Carry On Screaming '66

Ellen Corby
Bowery Boys Meet the Monsters '54

Alex Cord
Chosen Survivors '74

Wendell Corey
The Astro-Zombies '67

Anthony Corlan
Vampire Circus '71

Judy Cornwell
Think Dirty '70

Adrienne Corri
Madhouse '74
Vampire Circus '71

Lloyd Corrigan
Bowery Boys Meet the Monsters '54
Crime Doctor's Courage '45

Ray Corrigan
It! The Terror from Beyond Space '58

Bud Cort
Hysterical '83

Valentina Cortese
Il Cavaliere Costante Nicosia Demoniaco Ovvero '75

Jesse Corti
Nightlife '90

Sonelio Costa
A Vampire's Dream '70

Lou Costello
Abbott and Costello Meet Frankenstein '49
The World of Abbott & Costello '64

Chuck Courtney
Billy the Kid Versus Dracula '66

Nathalie Courval
Tender Dracula, or The Confessions of a Bloodsucker '74

Jerome Cowan
Crime Doctor's Courage '45

Noel Coward
Paris When It Sizzles '64

John Cragen
Witchcraft 7: Judgement Hour '95

Michael Craig
Vault of Horror '73

Grant Cramer
Killer Klowns from Outer Space '88

Marc Cramer
Isle of the Dead '45

Barbara Crampton
Body Double '84

Kenneth Cranham
Tale of a Vampire '92

Frank Craven
Son of Dracula '43

Galaxy Craze
Nadja '95

Francis Creighton
The Malibu Beach Vampires '91

Barry Crocker
Barry McKenzie Holds His Own '74

Eve Crosby
Blood '73

Ben Cross
Nightlife '90

Kathleen Crowley
Curse of the Undead '59

Dana Culliver
Blood Freak '72

Joseph Culp
The Arrival '90

Brett Cumo
The Wicked '89

Sean S. Cunningham
The Case of the Full Moon Murders '74

Gordon Currie
Blood & Donuts '96

Althea Currier
Kiss Me Quick! '64

Tony Curtis
Paris When It Sizzles '64

Joan Cusack
Addams Family Values '93

Peter Cushing
Blood Beast Terror '67
The Bloodsuckers '70
The Brides of Dracula '60
Dr. Terror's House of Horrors '65
Dracula A.D. 1972 '72
The Horror of Dracula '58
The House that Dripped Blood '71
Madhouse '74
The Satanic Rites of Dracula '73
Scream and Scream Again '70

The 7 Brothers Meet Dracula '73
Twins of Evil '71
The Vampire Lovers '70

Miriam Cyr
Gothic '87

Howard da Silva
M '51

Maryam D'Abo
Nightlife '90

Willem Dafoe
The Hunger '83

Alan Dahl
Casual Relations '73

Nikki Dahl
Vampire's Kiss '92

Robert Dalban
Blood Relations '77

Alberto Dalbes
Daughter of Dracula '72
Dracula's Daughter '71
The Screaming Dead '72

Jim Dale
Carry On Screaming '66

Joe Dallesandro
Andy Warhol's Dracula '74

Eileen Daly
Demonsoul '94

Mark Damon
Black Sabbath '64
Crypt of the Living Dead '73
Devil's Wedding Night '73

Cliff Dance
Demon Queen '80s

Carlo D'Angelo
The Devil's Commandment '56

Jennifer Daniel
Kiss of the Vampire '62

Emma Danieli
The Last Man on Earth '64

David Mason Daniels
One Dark Night '82

Jerry Daniels
The Velvet Vampire '71

Cast Index

Roy Dotrice
Carmilla '89

Angela Douglas
Carry On Screaming '66

Melvyn Douglas
The Vampire Bat '32

John Doyle
The Wicked '89

Maxine Doyle
Condemned to Live '35

Shannon Doyle
Kingdom of the Vampire
'91

Claudia Drake
Face of Marble '46

Louise Dresser
Dracula/Garden of Eden
'28

Lieux Dressler
Grave of the Vampire '72

Ellen Drew
Isle of the Dead '45

Ramon D'Salva
Batman Fights Dracula
'67

Denice Duff
Bloodlust: Subspecies 3
'93
Bloodstone: Subspecies 2
'92

Jacques Dufilho
Nosferatu the Vampyre
'79

Andrew Duggan
It's Alive '74
It's Alive 2: It Lives Again
'78
Return to Salem's Lot '87

Ern Dugo
Voodoo Heartbeat '72

Lindsay Duncan
The Reflecting Skin '91

Jean Durand
Le Frisson des Vampires
'70

Roger Dutoit
Le Vampire du
Dusseldorf '64

Maria Duval
Samson vs. the Vampire
Women '61
The Vampire Girls '68

Peter Dvorsky
The Kiss '88

Valentine Dyall
Horror of it All '63

Carlos East
The Fear Chamber '67

Norma Eberhardt
Return of Dracula '58

Omar Ebrahim
The Vampyr '92

Maude Eburne
The Vampire Bat '32

Louis Edmonds
The Best of Dark
Shadows '60s

Bill Edwards
First Man into Space '59

Julie Ege
The 7 Brothers Meet
Dracula '73

Anatoly Egorov
Father, Santa Claus Has
Died '92

Anthony Eisley
Dracula vs. Frankenstein
'71

Anita Ekberg
Fangs of the Living Dead
'68

Britt Ekland
Beverly Hills Vamp '88
The Monster Club '85

Erika Eleniak
Tales from the Crypt
Presents Bordello of
Blood '96

Sandor Eles
Countess Dracula '70

Evangelina Elizondo
Castle of the Monsters
'58

Denholm Elliott
The House that Dripped
Blood '71
Vault of Horror '73

Laura Ellis
Bloodsuckers from Outer
Space '83

Michael Elphick
I Bought a Vampire
Motorcycle '90

Cary Elwes
Bram Stoker's Dracula
'92

Karrie Emerson
Evils of the Night '85

Jesse Emery
Chillers '88

Sanae Emi
Lake of Dracula '71

Michael Emmet
Attack of the Giant
Leeches '59

Dieter Eppler
The Slaughter of the
Vampires '62
Torture Chamber of Dr.
Sadism '69

Kathryn Erbe
The Addiction '95

Roberto Escalada
El Vampiro Negro '53

Luis Escobar
Buenas Noches, Senor
Monstruo '82

Emmanuelle Escourrou
The Evil Within '94

Paul Esser
Daughters of Darkness
'71

Joe Estevez
Dark Universe '93

Susanna Estrada
Young Jonathan Dracula
'75

Pierre Etaix
Insomnia '63

Rafael Etienne
Invasion of the Vampires
'61

Jake Euker
Darkness '92

Art Evans
Mom '89

Clifford Evans
Kiss of the Vampire '62

Mitch Evans
Alien Massacre '67

Robin Evans
One Dark Night '82

Angie Everhart
Tales from the Crypt
Presents Bordello of
Blood '96

Barbara Ewing
Dracula Has Risen from
the Grave '68

Chung Fa
Shyly Spirit

Ava Fabian
To Die for '89

Victor Fabian
The Revenge of Dracula
'59

Bruce Fairbairn
The Vampire Hookers '78

Edie Falco
The Addiction '95

Fay Falcon
Curse of the Devil '73

Mary Fanaro
Demon Queen '80s

Lu Fang
Kung Fu Vampire Buster

Sergio Fantoni
Atom Age Vampire '61

Antonio Fargas
Howling 6: The Freaks
'90

Suzan Farmer
Dracula: Prince of
Darkness '65

Sharon Farrell
It's Alive '74

**Rainer Werner
Fassbinder**
Tenderness of Wolves '73

Chung Fat
Close Encounters of the
Spooky Kind '80

Sally Faulkner
Vampyres '74

Melinda Fee
Fade to Black '80

Corey Feldman
The Lost Boys '87
Tales from the Crypt
Presents Bordello of
Blood '96

Norman Fell
Transylvania 6-5000 '85

Cast Index

Valerie Gaunt
The Horror of Dracula
'58

Cassandra Gaviola
The Black Room '82

Wendy Gazelle
Understudy: The
Graveyard Shift 2 '88

Karl Geary
Nadja '95

Mary-Louise Gemmill
Project Vampire '93

Minnie Gentry
Def by Temptation '90

Roger Gentry
Alien Massacre '67

Gil Gerard
Buck Rogers in the 25th
Century: Space
Vampire '80

Harriet Gerard
Vampyr '31

Georges Geret
Spermula '76

Gaia Germani
Castle of the Living Dead
'64

Jami Gertz
The Lost Boys '87

Paul Gibboneyy
Cafe Flesh '82

Matyclock Gibbs
The Bad Sister '83

Josianne Gibert
The Screaming Dead '72

Leslie Gilb
Lemora, Lady Dracula
'73

Timo Gilbert
Darkness '92

Walter Giller
Lady Dracula '77

James Gillis
Dracula Sucks '79

Teresa Gimpera
Crypt of the Living Dead
'73
Night of the Devils '71

Hermione Gingold
Munster, Go Home! '66

Allen Ginsberg
Chappaqua '65

Domiziana Giordano
Interview with the
Vampire '94

Maria Giovannini
Playgirls and the Vampire
'60

Russell Gleason
Condemned to Live '35

Montgomery Glenn
Castle of Blood '64

Scott Glenn
The Keep '83

Tina Gloriani
Vampire and the
Ballerina '63

Gloriella
Capulina contra Los
Monstros '72
Capulina contra Los
Vampiros '72

Julian Glover
Theatre of Death '67

Don Glut
Frankenstein Meets
Dracula '57
Slave of the Vampire '59

Justin Gocke
My Grandpa is a Vampire
'92

Hector Godoy
Bring Me the Vampire '61

Alexander Godunov
Waxwork 2: Lost in Time
'91

Jeff Goldblum
Transylvania 6-5000 '85

Lelia Goldoni
Theatre of Death '67

Jenette Goldstein
Near Dark '87

Bernard Gorcey
Bowery Boys Meet the
Monsters '54

Leo Gorcey
Bowery Boys Meet the
Monsters '54
Spooks Run Wild '41

Bruce Gordon
Curse of the Undead '59

Colin Gordon
The Body Beneath '70

Rachel Gordon
I Married a Vampire '87

Michael Gothard
Lifeforce '85

Michael Gough
The Horror of Dracula
'58

Andre Gower
The Monster Squad '87

Gerrit Graham
It's Alive 3: Island of the
Alive '87

Alexander Granach
Dracula/Garden of Eden
'28
Nosferatu '22

Beverly Grant
Batman Dracula '64

Hugh Grant
The Lair of the White
Worm '88

Richard E. Grant
Bram Stoker's Dracula
'92

Graziella Granta
The Slaughter of the
Vampires '62

Carole Gray
Devils of Darkness '65

Coleen Gray
The Leech Woman '59
The Vampire '57

Erin Gray
Buck Rogers in the 25th
Century: Space
Vampire '80

Nigel Green
Countess Dracula '70

Daniel Greene
Elvira, Mistress of the
Dark '88

Ellen Greene
Little Shop of Horrors '86

Dabbs Greer
It! The Terror from
Beyond Space '58

Gregory A. Greer
Midnight Kiss '93

Robert Gregory
The Devil's Mistress '68

Nan Grey
Dracula's Daughter '36

Pam Grier
Scream Blacula Scream
'73

Corine Griffith
Dracula/Garden of Eden
'28

Melanie Griffith
Body Double '84

Eva Grimaldi
La Maschera del
Demonio '90

Scott Grimes
Night Life '90

Randy Grinter, Jr.
Blood Freak '72

**William Donald
Grollman**
Bongo Wolf's Revenge
'70

Willard Gross
Creature of the Walking
Dead '60

Gustav Grundgens
M '31

Carmen Guerrero
Dracula (Spanish Version)
'31

David Guerrero
Flesh of Your Flesh '84

Christopher Guest
Little Shop of Horrors '86

Nicholas Guest
Night Hunter '95

Wandisa Guida
The Devil's
Commandment '56

Jean-Francois Guillotte
The Evil Within '94

Gukar
Jaws of the Jungle '36

Clu Gulager
The Mystery of Dracula's
Castle '73
Teen Vamp '88

Bill Gunn
Black Vampire '73

Alizia Gur
Beast of Morocco '66

Cast Index

Geraldine Hooper
They've Changed Faces '71

Kaitlyn Hooper
Addams Family Values '93

Kristen Hooper
Addams Family Values '93

Anthony Hopkins
Bram Stoker's Dracula '92

Bo Hopkins
Blood Ties '92

Dennis Hopper
Planet of Blood '66

Hedda Hopper
Dracula's Daughter '36

Cathy Horlan
Body Snatcher from Hell '69

Deborah Horlen
Legacy of Satan '73

Nicholas Hormann
Buck Rogers in the 25th Century: Space Vampire '80

Chien Hsiao Hou
Kung Fu Vampire Buster

Zhang Houyou
Vampire Woman '62

Adrian Hoven
Cave of the Living Dead '65

Barbara Howard
The Vampire of the Opera '61

Vanessa Howard
Blood Beast Terror '67

John Hoyt
Curse of the Undead '59

Wong Tsu Hsien
A Chinese Ghost Story '87

Ed Hubbard
Vampires and Other Stereotypes '92

Brett Hudson
Hysterical '83

Mark Hudson
Hysterical '83

Rochelle Hudson
Alien Massacre '67

William Hudson
Hysterical '83

Barnard Hughes
The Lost Boys '87

Brendan Hughes
Howling 6: The Freaks '90
To Die for '89

Heather Hughes
Blood Freak '72

Helen Hughes
Incubus '82

Ricky Hui
Mr. Vampire '86
Mr. Vampire II '86
Mr. Vampire III '87

Barry Humphries
Barry McKenzie Holds His Own '74

Leigh Hunt
The Vampire Conspiracy '94

Marsha Hunt
Dracula A.D. 1972 '72

Martita Hunt
The Brides of Dracula '60

Tanna Hunter
Invasion of the Blood Farmers '72

Jennifer Huss
Vamps '96

Anjelica Huston
The Addams Family '91
Addams Family Values '93

Lauren Hutton
Once Bitten '85

Judy Huxtable
Scream and Scream Again '70

Scott Hylands
Fools '70

Ryo Ikebe
Vampire Moth '56

Michael Imperioli
The Addiction '95

Luis Induni
The Vampire of the Highway '69

Frieda Inescort
Return of the Vampire '44

Ciccio Ingrassia
Il Cavaliere Costante Nicosia Demoniaco Ovvero '75

John Ireland
Incubus '82

Shaun Irons
Jugular Wine: A Vampire Odyssey '94

Tony Isbert
The Saga of the Draculas '72

Hikari Ishida
My Soul Is Slashed '92

Neal Israel
It's Alive 3: Island of the Alive '87

Victor Israel
Young Jonathan Dracula '75

Judith Isral
Guru, the Mad Monk '70

Kinuto Ito
Vampire Moth '56

Yunosuke Ito
The Evil of Dracula '75

Dana Ivey
The Addams Family '91
Addams Family Values '93

Andrew Jackson
Vampire's Breakfast '86

Freda Jackson
The Brides of Dracula '60

Kate Jackson
The Best of Dark Shadows '60s
Night of Dark Shadows '71

Leonard Jackson
Black Vampire '73

Samuel L. Jackson
Def by Temptation '90

Thomas E. Jackson
Face of Marble '46
Valley of the Zombies '45

Scott Jacoby
To Die for '89
To Die for 2: Son of Darkness '91

Richard Jaeckel
Chosen Survivors '74

Brion James
Mom '89

John James
The Devil Bat's Daughter '46

Georges Jamin
Daughters of Darkness '71

Walter Janovitz
Billy the Kid Versus Dracula '66

Horst Janson
Captain Kronos: Vampire Hunter '74

Martin Jarvis
Taste the Blood of Dracula '70

Jose Jasso
Frankenstein, the Vampire and Co. '61

Barbara Jefford
Lust for a Vampire '71

Terence Jenkins
Vampire Cop '90

Jean Jennings
The Case of the Full Moon Murders '74

Paul Craig Jennings
Invasion of the Blood Farmers '72

Jose Luis Jimenez
The Vampire '57

Glynis Johns
Mrs. Amworth '73
Vault of Horror '73

Stratford Johns
The Lair of the White Worm '88

Arte Johnson
Love at First Bite '79

Craig Johnson
Dawn '90

Laura Johnson
Nick Knight '80s

Michael Johnson
Lust for a Vampire '71

Michelle Johnson
Blood Ties '92
Waxwork '88

Cast Index

Brian Knudson
Project Vampire '93

Hideo Ko
Body Snatcher from Hell '69

Akio Kobori
Vampire Moth '56

Scott Kolden
The Mystery of Dracula's Castle '73

Ricky Hui Koon-Ying
Mr. Vampire 1992 '92

Karen Kopins
Once Bitten '85

Harvey Korman
Dracula: Dead and Loving It '95

Julia Koschka
Alraune '52

Sylva Koscina
Il Cavaliere Costante Nicosia Demoniaco Ovvero '75

Maria Koski
The Saga of the Draculas '72

Ljudmila Kozlovskava
Father, Santa Claus Has Died '92

Brian Krause
Sleepwalkers '92

Alice Krige
Haunted Summer '88
Sleepwalkers '92

Sylvia Kristel
Dracula's Widow '88

Henry Kruger
Castle of Blood '64

Otto Kruger
Dracula's Daughter '36

David Krumholtz
Addams Family Values '93

Asami Kuji
Vampire Moth '56

Manjeet Kular
Bandh Darwaza '90

Kelley Kunicki
Gore-Met Zombie Chef From Hell '87

Kunita
Bandh Darwaza '90

Toshio Kurosawa
The Evil of Dracula '75

Yuko Kusunoki
Body Snatcher from Hell '69

Mimi Kuzyk
The Kiss '88

Lam Kwok-Bun
Romance of the Vampires '94

Rosemary La Planche
The Devil Bat's Daughter '46

Ronald Lacey
Disciple of Death '72

Skip Lackey
Once Bitten '85

Beatriz Lacy
The Curse of the Vampyr '71

Walter Laderigast
Nosferatu the Vampyre '79

Gina Laforteza
Drakula in Istanbul '53
Drakulita '69

Brigitte Lahie
Fascination '79

Loletta Lee Lai-Chun
The Musical Vampire '90

Debra Lamb
Beverly Hills Vamp '88

Molly Lamont
The Devil Bat's Daughter '46

Zohra Lampert
Let's Scare Jessica to Death '71

Martin Landau
Ed Wood '94

Inge Landgut
M '31

Marla Landi
First Man into Space '59

John Landon
Guess What Happened to Count Dracula? '70

Laurene Landon
It's Alive 3: Island of the Alive '87

Gerard Landry
Anemia '86

Rosemary Lane
The Return of Dr. X '39

Judith Lang
Count Yorga, Vampire '70

Carl Lange
Torture Chamber of Dr. Sadism '69

Frank Langella
Dracula '79

Paul Langton
It! The Terror from Beyond Space '58

Anthony LaPaglia
Innocent Blood '92

Philip Latham
Dracula: Prince of Darkness '65

Billy Lau
Vampire vs. Vampire '89

Richard Lawson
Scream Blacula Scream '73

Evelyn Laye
Theatre of Death '67

Norma Lazarendo
Santo en la Venganza de las Mujeres Vampiro '69

Becky Le Beau
The Malibu Beach Vampires '91

Alain Le Bris
Vampirisme '67

Ginette LeClerc
Spermula '76

Francis Lederer
Return of Dracula '58

Bryarly Lee
The Naked Witch '64

Christopher Lee
Castle of the Living Dead '64
Count Dracula '71
Dr. Terror's House of Horrors '65
Dracula & Son '76
Dracula Has Risen from the Grave '68

Hercules in the Haunted World '64
The Horror of Dracula '58
The House that Dripped Blood '71
The Satanic Rites of Dracula '73
The Scars of Dracula '70
Scream and Scream Again '70
Taste the Blood of Dracula '70
Theatre of Death '67
Uncle Was a Vampire '59
Vampir '70

Lito Legaspi
Drakula in Istanbul '53

Suzanna Leigh
Lust for a Vampire '71

Jean-Marie Lemaire
Fascination '79

Florina Lemaitre
Pure Blood '83

Maurice Lemaitre
La Vampire Nue '69

Heather LeMire
The Vampire Conspiracy '94

Kasi Lemmons
Vampire's Kiss '88

Phillippe LeRoy
Castle of the Living Dead '64

John Leslie
Dracula Sucks '79

Ly Letrong
La Vampire Nue '69

Bernard Letrou
La Reine des Vampires '68
Le Viol du Vampire '67

Tony Leung
A Chinese Ghost Story III '91

Uta Levka
Scream and Scream Again '70

Al Lewis
My Grandpa is a Vampire '92

Charlotte Lewis
Embrace of the Vampire '95

Cast Index

Huang Manli
Vampire Woman '62

David Manners
Dracula '31

Alan Manson
Let's Scare Jessica to Death '71

Evi Marandi
Planet of the Vampires '65

Fredric March
Hollywood on Parade '34

Mark Marian
The Vampire of the Opera '61

Lisa Marie
Ed Wood '94

Richard "Cheech" Marin
From Dusk Till Dawn '95

Lia Marino
Bloodthirsty '92

Alfred Marks
Scream and Scream Again '70

John Marley
Deathdream '72
It's Alive 2: It Lives Again '78

Florence Marly
Planet of Blood '66

Laure Marsac
A Vampire in Paradise '92

Carol Marsh
The Horror of Dracula '58

E.G. Marshall
Stephen King's The Tommyknockers '93
Vampire '79

Mike Marshall
The Living Dead Girl '82

William Marshall
Scream Blacula Scream '73

K.C. Martel
Munster's Revenge '81

Dewey Martin
The Thing '51

Dick Martin
The Maltese Bippy '69

George Martin
The Bloodsuckers '67

Helen Martin
Night Angel '90

Maribel Martin
The Blood Spattered Bride '72

Olivier Martin
La Vampire Nue '69

Steve Martin
Little Shop of Horrors '86

Strother Martin
Nightwing '79

Vincent Martin
Les Charlots contre Dracula '80

Elsa Martinelli
Blood and Roses '61

Raul Martinez Solares
Chanoc contra el Tigre y el Vampiro '71

Charles Martinka
The Revenge of Dracula '59

Lea Martino
Graveyard Disturbance '87

Alan Marx
Gore-Met Zombie Chef From Hell '87

Mil Mascaras
The Vampire Girls '68

Mil Maschras
Los Vampiros de Coyoacan '73

Ace Mask
Not of This Earth '88
Transylvania Twist '89

James Mason
Salem's Lot '79

Anna Massey
Vault of Horror '73

Daniel Massey
Vault of Horror '73

Marissa Mathes
Track of the Vampire '66

Judy Matheson
Twins of Evil '71

Michelle Matheson
Howling 6: The Freaks '90

Kerwin Mathews
Nightmare in Blood '75

Kayo Matsuo
Night of the Vampire '70

Kikko Matsuoka
Living Skeleton '68

Francis Matthews
Dracula: Prince of Darkness '65

Maria May
Cake of Blood '72

Marta May
Blood Pie '71

Mathilda May
Lifeforce '85

John Maynard
Dark Universe '93

Ferdinand "Ferdy" Mayne
The Fearless Vampire Killers '67
The Vampire Happening '71
The Vampire Lovers '70

Carlos Mayolo
Pure Blood '83

Marianne McAndrew
The Bat People '74

Michelle McBride
Subspecies '90

Kevin McCarthy
The Midnight Hour '86

Edie McClurg
Elvira, Mistress of the Dark '88

Judith McConnell
The Thirsty Dead '74

Patty McCormack
Saturday the 14th Strikes Back '88

Winston McDonald
Bloodthirsty '92

Jo McDonnel
Munster's Revenge '81

Mary McDonough
Mom '89

Roddy McDowall
Carmilla '89
Fright Night '85
Fright Night 2 '88

Darren McGavin
Night Stalker '72
The Night Stalker: Two Tales of Terror '74

Vonetta McGee
Blacula '72

Charles McGraw
Night Stalker '72

Stephen McHattie
Deadly Love '95

Paul McIver
Stephen King's The Tommyknockers '93

Susan McIver
Doctor Dracula '80

Maxine McKendry
Andy Warhol's Dracula '74

Kenneth McMillan
Salem's Lot '79

Mercedes McNab
Addams Family Values '93

Kevin McNally
The Bad Sister '83

Julianne McNamara
Saturday the 14th Strikes Back '88

Vladimir Medar
Torture Chamber of Dr. Sadism '69

Ralph Meeker
Night Stalker '72

Maria Menado
Vampire's Curse '58

Bernard Menez
Dracula & Son '76
Tender Dracula, or The Confessions of a Bloodsucker '74

Narciso Ibanez Menta
The Saga of the Draculas '72

Nicole Mentz
Bloodscent '94

Jiri Menzel
Ferat Vampire '82

Michele Mercier
Black Sabbath '64

Judi Meredith
Planet of Blood '66

Cast Index

Jimmy Murphy
Curse of the Undead '59

Michael Murphy
Count Yorga, Vampire '70

Bill Murray
Ed Wood '94
Little Shop of Horrors '86

Guillermo Murray
The Macabre Mark '62
World of the Vampires '60

Ornella Muti
Leonor '75

Jim Myers
Ed Wood '94

Michael Nader
Nick Knight '80s

Maite Nahyr
Le Nosferat ou les Eaux Glacees du Calcul Egoiste '74

J. Carrol Naish
Dracula vs. Frankenstein '71
House of Frankenstein '44

Nobuo Nakagawa
Vampire Man '59

Atsuo Nakamura
Night of the Vampire '70

Kichiemon Nakamura
Kuroneko '68

Akira Nakao
Night of the Vampire '70

Reggie Nalder
Salem's Lot '79
Zoltan...Hound of Dracula '78

Nicole Nancel
Le Frisson des Vampires '70

Paul Naschy
Buenas Noches, Senor Monstruo '82
The Craving '80
Curse of the Devil '73
Dracula vs. Frankenstein '69
Dracula's Great Love '72
Frankenstein's Bloody Terror '68
The Werewolf vs. the Vampire Woman '70

Myron Natwick
Project Vampire '93

David Naughton
I, Desire '82

Christopher Neame
Dracula A.D. 1972 '72

Kate Nelligan
Dracula '79

John Allen Nelson
Killer Klowns from Outer Space '88

Constantin Nepo
La Bonne Dame '66

Rosalba (Sara Bay) Neri
Devil's Wedding Night '73

Jack Neubeck
Invasion of the Blood Farmers '72

Anthony Newlands
Scream and Scream Again '70

Julie Newmar
Evils of the Night '85
Hysterical '83

Sandra Ng Kwun-Yu
Vampire Family '93

Denise Nicholas
Blacula '72

Britt Nichols
Dracula's Daughter '71

Darcy Nichols
Cafe Flesh '82

Ivy Nicholson
Batman Dracula '64

Jack Nicholson
Little Shop of Horrors '60

Leslie Nielsen
Dracula: Dead and Loving It '95

Yvonne Nielson
Blood Thirst '65

NiXan
Crazy Safari '90

Amanda Noar
I Bought a Vampire Motorcycle '90

Noelia Noel
Santo en el Tesoro de Dracula '87

Piero Nomi
La Maschera del Demonio '90

Tom Noonan
The Monster Squad '87

Manuel Noriega
The Macabre Trunk '36

Barry Norton
Dracula (Spanish Version) '31

Lenka Novak
The Vampire Hookers '78

Bene Nunes
The Seven Vampires '86

Bill Nunn
Def by Temptation '90

Simon Oakland
Night Stalker '72
The Night Stalker: Two Tales of Terror '74

Dave O'Brien
The Devil Bat '41
Spooks Run Wild '41

Kevin J. O'Connor
Let's Scare Jessica to Death '71

Tim O'Connor
Buck Rogers in the 25th Century: Space Vampire '80

Martha O'Driscoll
House of Dracula '45

Ken Ogaka
My Soul Is Slashed '92

Ian Ogilvy
The She-Beast '65

Masumi Okada
Living Skeleton '68

Miles O'Keeffe
Waxwork '88

Laurence Olivier
Dracula '79

Silvio Oliviero
Graveyard Shift '87
Understudy: The Graveyard Shift 2 '88

Kate O'Mara
The Vampire Lovers '70

Fiona O'Neill
The Vampyr '92

Michael O'Neill
Gore-Met Zombie Chef From Hell '87

Remy O'Neill
To Die for 2: Son of Darkness '91

Cyril O'Reilly
Dance of the Damned '88

Carlos Orellana
Castle of the Monsters '58

Per Oscarsson
The Inn of the Flying Dragon '81

Fernando Oses
Santo Against Baron Brakola '65

Consuelo Osorio
Drakula in Istanbul '53

Carlos Otero
Blood Pie '71

Daniele Ouimet
Daughters of Darkness '71

Michelle Owens
Midnight Kiss '93

Richard Owens
Vampire Circus '71

Catherine Oxenberg
The Lair of the White Worm '88

Tom Pace
The Astro-Zombies '67

Robert Paige
Son of Dracula '43

Jack Palance
Dracula '73

Nelly Panizza
El Vampiro Negro '53

Yannis Panousis
Dracula Tan Exarchia '83

Helen Papas
Graveyard Shift '87

Marisa Paredes
Blood Pie '71
Cake of Blood '72

Neri Parenti
Who Is Afraid of Dracula '85

Cast Index

Wolfgang Preiss
Cave of the Living Dead '65

Paula Prentiss
Saturday the 14th '81

E. Kerrigan Prescott
Alabama's Ghost '72

Jason Presson
Saturday the 14th Strikes Back '88

Kelly Preston
From Dusk Till Dawn '95

Amelle Prevost
Les Charlots contre Dracula '80

Dennis Price
Horror of it All '63
Lesbian Vampires The Heiress of Dracula '71
The Screaming Dead '72
Son of Dracula '73
Twins of Evil '71

Vincent Price
The Horror of It All '91
The Last Man on Earth '64
Madhouse '74
The Monster Club '85
Scream and Scream Again '70
Vincent Price's Dracula '82

Andrew Prine
Crypt of the Living Dead '73

Juergen Prochnow
The Keep '83

Paul Prokop
The Velvet Vampire '71

Robert Prosky
The Keep '83

David Proval
Innocent Blood '92

David Prowse
Vampire Circus '71

Harrison Pruett
Embrace of the Vampire '95

Rolo Puente
Blood of the Virgins '68

Monty Pyke
Lemora, Lady Dracula '73

Natasha Pyne
Madhouse '74

Lee Hyoung Pyo
Dracula Rises from the Coffin '82

Iain Quarrier
The Fearless Vampire Killers '67

Robert Quarry
Madhouse '74

Cesareo Quesades
Tom Thumb and Little Red Riding Hood vs. the Monsters '62

Linnea Quigley
The Black Room '82

Fons Rademakers
Daughters of Darkness '71

Jorge Rado
Santo and the Blue Demon vs. the Monsters '68

Park Yang Rae
Dracula Rises from the Coffin '82

William Ragsdale
Fright Night '85
Fright Night 2 '88

Umberto Raho
Night of the Devils '71

Steve Railsback
Lifeforce '85

Tulsi Ramay
The Case of the Full Moon Murders '74

Martin Ramos
Pepito y Chabelo vs. los Monstruos '73

James Randall
Deafula '75

Jane Randolph
Abbott and Costello Meet Frankenstein '49

Thalmus Rasulala
Blacula '72

Basil Rathbone
The Magic Sword '62
Planet of Blood '66

Andrea Rau
Daughters of Darkness '71

Isarco Ravaioli
Vampire and the Ballerina '63

Mike Raven
Disciple of Death '72

Aldo Ray
Evils of the Night '85

Charles Ray
Dracula/Garden of Eden '28

Rosa Ray
Face of Marble '46

Paula Raymond
Blood of Dracula's Castle '69

Stephen Rea
Interview with the Vampire '94

Alex Rebar
Incredible Melting Man '77

Gigi Reder
Who Is Afraid of Dracula '85

Lydia Reed
The Vampire '57

Ricky Addison Reed
Return to Salem's Lot '87

Tracy Reed
Devils of Darkness '65

Harry Reems
The Case of the Full Moon Murders '74

Elizabeth Rees
Dawn '90

Keanu Reeves
Bram Stoker's Dracula '92

Regaliz
Buenas Noches, Senor Monstruo '82

Duncan Regehr
The Monster Squad '87

Fiona Reid
Blood & Donuts '96

Erika Remberg
Cave of the Living Dead '65

Helene Remy
Vampire and the Ballerina '63

Ronald Remy
The Vampire People '66

Michael Rennie
Dracula vs. Frankenstein '69

Eva Renzi
Love Vampire Style '70

Andres Resino
The Werewolf vs. the Vampire Woman '70

Arthur Resley
The Devil's Mistress '68

Robert Reynolds
Daughter of Darkness '89

David Reynoso
Invasion of the Vampires '61

Barbara Rhoades
Scream Blacula Scream '73

Susan Rhodes
The Girl with the Hungry Eyes '94

Christina Ricci
The Addams Family '91
Addams Family Values '93

John Richard
Orgy of the Vampires '73

John Richardson
Black Sunday '60

Natasha Richardson
Gothic '87

Don Rickles
Innocent Blood '92

Beatrice Ring
Graveyard Disturbance '87

Michael Ripper
Dracula Has Risen from the Grave '68
The Scars of Dracula '70

Marie-France Risier
Le Vampire du Dusseldorf '64

George Riviere
Castle of Blood '64

Alfredo Rizzo
Playgirls and the Vampire '60

Jason Robards, Jr.
Fools '70

Cast Index

Camille Saviola
Nightlife '90

Lauro Sawaya
O Macabro Dr. Scivano '71

John Saxon
The Arrival '90
From Dusk Till Dawn '95
Planet of Blood '66

Jaroslava Schallerova
Valerie and the Week of Wonders '69

Wolfgang Schenck
Tenderness of Wolves '73

Otto Schlesinger
A Taste of Blood '66

Loren Schmalle
Witchcraft 7: Judgement Hour '95

Sybille Schmitz
Vampyr '31

Monika Schnarre
Waxwork 2: Lost in Time '91

Bonnie Schneider
Mama Dracula '80

Maria Schneider
Mama Dracula '80

Max Schreck
Dracula/Garden of Eden '28

Avery Schreiber
Saturday the 14th Strikes Back '88

Greta Schroeder
Nosferatu '22

Reinhold Schuenzel
The Man in Half Moon Street '44

Maurice Schutz
Vampyr '31

Gioia Maria Scila
Anemia '86

Yvonne Scio
Dinner with the Vampire '88

Annabella Sciorra
The Addiction '95

Cherie Scott
Dark Universe '93

Jay Scott
Grave of the Vampire '72

Kathryn Leigh Scott
Best of Barnabas '90
House of Dark Shadows '70

Robert Scott
Crime Doctor's Courage '45

Suzanne Scott
Vampires and Other Stereotypes '92

Angus Scrimm
Subspecies '90
Transylvania Twist '89

Elizabeth Seal
Vampire Circus '71

Seka
Dracula Sucks '79

Malik Selamat
The Vampire Returns '63

David Selby
Best of Barnabas '90
The Best of Dark Shadows '60s
Night of Dark Shadows '71

Dean Selmier
The Blood Spattered Bride '72

Serena
Dracula Sucks '79

Dollah Serewak
The Vampire '57

Delphine Seyrig
Daughters of Darkness '71

Glenn Shadix
Nightlife '90

Tamara Shanath
Cronos '94

Stephane Shandour
Tender Dracula, or The Confessions of a Bloodsucker '74

Gene Shane
The Velvet Vampire '71

Marie Sharp
Cafe Flesh '82

Dick Shawn
Love at First Bite '79

Robert Shayne
Face of Marble '46

Martin Sheen
The Ghost Brigade '93

Barbara Shelley
Blood of the Vampire '58
Dracula: Prince of Darkness '65

Deborah Shelton
Body Double '84

Jack Shepard
Count Dracula '78

Patty Shepard
Crypt of the Living Dead '73
Curse of the Devil '73
Dracula vs. Frankenstein '69
The Werewolf vs. the Vampire Woman '70

W. Morgan Shepherd
Elvira, Mistress of the Dark '88

Sally-Ann Shepherdson
The Vampyr '92

Margaret Sheridan
The Thing '51

Arthur Shields
The Daughter of Dr. Jekyll '57

Stanley Fung Shui-Fan
The Musical Vampire '90

Robert Shurtz
Vampire Trailer Park '91

Malek Siamat
Vampire of the Cave '64

Michael Siegel
Killer Klowns from Outer Space '88

Stefan Sileanu
Vlad Tepes '78

David Silva
The Rider of the Skulls '67
Sisters of Satan '75

Henry Silva
Thirst '87

Maria Silva
Curse of the Devil '73

Joe Silver
Rabid '77

Armando Silvestre
Wrestling Women vs. the Aztec Mummy '59

Jean Simmons
Dark Shadows Resurrected The Video '95

Joan Sims
Carry On Screaming '66

Frank Sinatra
Paris When It Sizzles '64

Ngai Sing
Shyly Spirit

Rocco Sisto
Innocent Blood '92

Chin Siu Ho
Mr. Vampire 1992 '92
Ultimate Vampire '91

Jackie Skarvellis
The Body Beneath '70

Ines Skorpio
The Curse of the Vampyr '71

Ione Skye
Carmilla '89

Christian Slater
Interview with the Vampire '94

Cheryl "Rainbeaux" Smith
Incredible Melting Man '77
Lemora, Lady Dracula '73

Kent Smith
Night Stalker '72

Madeleine Smith
The Vampire Lovers '70

Melanie Smith
Night Hunter '95

Shawn Smith
It! The Terror from Beyond Space '58

Sis Smith
Casual Relations '73

William Smith
Grave of the Vampire '72

Jimmy Smits
Stephen King's The Tommyknockers '93

Cast Index

Kei Taguichi
Vampire Dracula Comes
to Kobe; Evil Make
Woman Beautiful '79

Melissa Tait
Jonathan of the Night '87

Choei Takahashi
Lake of Dracula '71

Masay Takahashi
Body Snatcher from Hell
'69

Gloria Talbot
The Leech Woman '59

Lyle Talbot
Plan 9 from Outer Space
'56

Nita Talbot
Frightmare '81

Gloria Talbott
The Daughter of Dr.
Jekyll '57

Russ Tamblyn
Dracula vs. Frankenstein
'71

Quentin Tarantino
From Dusk Till Dawn '95

Candece Tarpley
Black Vampire '73

Laura Tate
Subspecies '90

Sharon Tate
The Fearless Vampire
Killers '67

Jack Taylor
The Loves of Irina '80s
Night of the Sorcerers '70
Orgy of the Vampires '73

Lili Taylor
The Addiction '95

Teeto
Jaws of the Jungle '36

Phillip Terry
The Leech Woman '59

Terry-Thomas
Vault of Horror '73

Robert Tessier
The Velvet Vampire '71

N. Tgelev
Morning Star '62

**Gregory Lech
Thaddeus**
Graveyard Disturbance
'87

Roy Thinnes
Dark Shadows
Resurrected The Video
'95

Tim Thomerson
Fade to Black '80
Near Dark '87

Marshall Thompson
First Man into Space '59
It! The Terror from
Beyond Space '58

Jenny Till
Theatre of Death '67

Meg Tilly
Carmilla '89
One Dark Night '82

Charles Tingwell
Dracula: Prince of
Darkness '65

Bently Tittle
Dark Universe '93

Kenneth Tobey
The Thing '51
The Vampire '57

George Todd
Creature of the Walking
Dead '60

Marilyn Tokuda
The Jitters '88

Renato Tontini
The Devil's
Commandment '56

Lisa Toothman
Witchcraft 3: The Kiss of
Death '90

Roland Topor
Nosferatu the Vampyre
'79

Eddie Torrente
Men of Action Meet the
Women of Dracula '69

Lupita Tovar
Dracula (Spanish Version)
'31

Stacy Travis
Dracula Rising '93

Danny Trejo
From Dusk Till Dawn '95

Jean-Louis Trintignant
Tender Dracula, or The
Confessions of a
Bloodsucker '74

Patrick Troughton
The Scars of Dracula '70

Eric Tsang
Vampire Family '93

Michael Tucker
Vampire '79

Isaac Turner
The Girl with the Hungry
Eyes '94

John Turner
Vampire and the
Ballerina '63

Susan Tyrrell
Rockula '90

Julian Ugarte
Blood Pie '71
Fangs of the Living Dead
'68

Liv Ullmann
Leonor '75

Ellen Umlauf
Bloodlust '70

Jay Underwood
To Die for 2: Son of
Darkness '91

Annette Vadim
Blood and Roses '61

German Valdes
Chanoc contra el Tigre y
el Vampiro '71

Paloma Valdes
Le Vampire du
Dusseldorf '64

Manuel Valdez
Frankenstein, the
Vampire and Co. '61

Scott Valentine
To Sleep with a Vampire
'92

Kitty Vallacher
Grave of the Vampire '72

Riccardo Valle
The Awful Dr. Orlof '62

Alida Valli
Tender Dracula, or The
Confessions of a
Bloodsucker '74

Vera Valmont
Terror in the Crypt '62

Vampira
Plan 9 from Outer Space
'56

John Van Eyssen
The Horror of Dracula
'58

Willemijn Van Gent
The Vampyr '92

Dick Van Patten
The Midnight Hour '86

Edward Van Sloan
Dracula '31
Dracula's Daughter '36

Joaquin Vargas
Bring Me the Vampire '61

Reg Varney
Go for a Take '72

Roland Varno
Return of the Vampire '44

Dante Varona
Men of Action Meet the
Women of Dracula '69

Romeo Vasquez
Curse of the Vampires '70

Paris Vaughan
Buffy the Vampire Slayer
'92

Robert Vaughn
Transylvania Twist '89

Morales Vazques
The Vampire for Two '65

J. Lopez Vazquez
The Vampire for Two '65

Bruno Ve Sota
Attack of the Giant
Leeches '59
Creature of the Walking
Dead '60

Lorena Velasquez
Samson vs. the Vampire
Women '61
Wrestling Women vs. the
Aztec Mummy '59

Wanda Ventham
Blood Beast Terror '67
Captain Kronos: Vampire
Hunter '74

Harley Venton
Blood Ties '92

Cast Index

Kenneth Williams
Carry On Screaming '66

Oren Williams
The Devil's Mistress '68

Elaine Juliette Williamson
Vampire Centerfold '96

Fred Williamson
From Dusk Till Dawn '95

Julia Willis
Guru, the Mad Monk '70

Matt Willis
Return of the Vampire '44

Noel Willman
Kiss of the Vampire '62

Don "The Dragon" Wilson
Night Hunter '95

Elizabeth Wilson
The Addams Family '91

Katherine Wilson
Deafula '75

Paul Wilson
My Best Friend Is a Vampire '88

Roger Wilson
The Ghost Brigade '93

Trey Wilson
The Vampire Hookers '78

Marie Windsor
Salem's Lot '79

Robert Winston
Blood Thirst '65

Alex Winter
Haunted Summer '88

Lex Winter
The Vampire Hookers '78

Estelle Winwood
The Magic Sword '62

Billy Wirth
The Lost Boys '87

Ray Wise
The Ghost Brigade '93

John Witherspoon
Vampire in Brooklyn '95

Karen Witter
The Vineyard '89

David Wohl
Chillers '88

Valdemar Wohlfahrt
The Vampire of the Highway '69

Jim Wolfe
Chillers '88

Frank Wolff
The Awful Dr. Orlof '62

Donald Wolfit
Blood of the Vampire '58

Rachel Wolkow
Sorority House Vampires '91

Joey Wong
A Chinese Ghost Story III '91

Michael Wong
The Vineyard '89

Thomas Wood
A Taste of Blood '66

Chris Woodley
The Velvet Vampire '71

Leon Woods
Stephen King's The Tommyknockers '93

Robert S. Woods
Deadly Love '95

Edward Woodward
The Bloodsuckers '70

Jimmy Workman
The Addams Family '91
Addams Family Values '93

Fay Wray
The Vampire Bat '32

Jenny Wright
Near Dark '87

Maggie Wright
Twins of Evil '71

Maris Wrixon
Face of Marble '46

Amanda Wyss
To Die for '89
To Die for 2: Son of Darkness '91

Rossana Yanni
Fangs of the Living Dead '68

Celeste Yarnall
The Velvet Vampire '71

Amy Yasbeck
Dracula: Dead and Loving It '95

Narumi Yaseda
My Soul Is Slashed '92

Lam Ching Ying
Close Encounters of the Spooky Kind '80

Barbara Yo Ling
The Satanic Rites of Dracula '73

Michael York
Not of This Earth '96

Teruo Yoshida
Body Snatcher from Hell '69

David Young
Mary, Mary, Bloody Mary '76

James Young
Bloodlust '92

Nedrick Young
Dead Men Walk '43

Ray Young
Blood of Dracula's Castle '69

Barrie Youngfellow
Nightmare in Blood '75
Vampire '79

Sandra Ng Kwun Yu
Mr. Vampire 1992 '92

Yau Yuet-Ching
Romance of the Vampires '94

Yvonne Yung Hung
Romance of the Vampires '94

Grace Zabriskie
Blood Ties '92

John Zacherle
Geek Maggot Bingo '83

Moon Zappa
Heartstopper '92

Nestor Zavarce
The Lurking Vampire '62

Richard Zobel
To Sleep with a Vampire '92

Olga Zubarry
El Vampiro Negro '53

George Zucco
Dead Men Walk '43
House of Frankenstein '44

Dianik Zurakowska
Frankenstein's Bloody Terror '68
Orgy of the Vampires '73

Director Index

This index lists all directors credited in the main review section. As in the cast index, they are listed alphabetically by last name. Some might also appear in the cast index, if you're inclined to look for them there (and even if you aren't!).

Face of Marble '46

Gabrielle Beaumont
Carmilla '89

Terry Becker
The Thirsty Dead '74

Earl Bellamy
Munster, Go Home! '66

Jack Bender
The Midnight Hour '86

Joel Bender
Midnight Kiss '93

Carlos (Carlos Benito Parra) Benpar
Young Jonathan Dracula '75

Luca Bercovici
Rockula '90

Bruce Beresford
Barry McKenzie Holds His Own '74

Michael Bergmann
My Lovely Monster '91

Edward L. Bernds
Bowery Boys Meet the Monsters '54

Robert Bierman
Vampire's Kiss '88

Kathryn Bigelow
Near Dark '87

Richard Blackburn
Lemora, Lady Dracula '73

Alfonso Corona Blake
Samson vs. the Vampire Women '61
World of the Vampires '60

David Blyth
My Grandpa is a Vampire '92
Red Blooded American Girl '90

James Bond, III
Def by Temptation '90

J.R. Bookwalter
Kingdom of the Vampire '91

Harry Booth
Go for a Take '72

Walerian Borowczyk
Immoral Tales '74

Daniel Boyd
Chillers '88

Samuel Bradford
Teen Vamp '88

Mel Brooks
Dracula: Dead and Loving It '95

Tod Browning
Dracula '31
Mark of the Vampire '35

Juan Bunuel
Leonor '75

Mark Burchett
Vamps '96

Tim Burton
Ed Wood '94

Rosalvo Cacador
O Macabro Dr. Scivano '71

Edward L. Cahn
It! The Terror from Beyond Space '58

Raul Calhado
O Macabro Dr. Scivano '71

Augusto Caminito
Vampire in Venice '88

Dirk Campbell
I Bought a Vampire Motorcycle '90

Rene Cardona, Sr.
Wrestling Women vs. the Aztec Mummy '59

Rene Cardona, Jr.
Capulina contra Los Monstros '72
Capulina contra Los Vampiros '72

Ivan Cardoso
The Seven Vampires '86

Henry Cass
Blood of the Vampire '58

Ibere Cavalcanti
A Vampire's Dream '70

L. Chang-Xu
Devil's Vindeta '86

Henry S. Chen
Mixed Up '85

Mason Ching
One Eyebrow Priest '87

Siu-Tung Ching
A Chinese Ghost Story III '91

Lam Ching-ying
Vampire vs. Vampire '89

Stephen Chiodo
Killer Klowns from Outer Space '88

Yam Chun-Lu
First Vampire in China '90

Wong Chun
Vampire's Breakfast '86

Gerard Ciccoritti
Graveyard Shift '87
Understudy: The Graveyard Shift 2 '88

Bob (Benjamin) Clark
Deathdream '72

Jim Clark
Madhouse '74
Think Dirty '70

Alan Clarke
Billy the Kid and the Green Blaze Vampire '85

Brian Clemens
Captain Kronos: Vampire Hunter '74

Glenn Coburn
Bloodsuckers from Outer Space '83

Howard R. Cohen
Saturday the 14th '81
Saturday the 14th Strikes Back '88

Larry Cohen
It's Alive '74
It's Alive 2: It Lives Again '78
It's Alive 3: Island of the Alive '87
Return to Salem's Lot '87

Lance Comfort
Devils of Darkness '65

Christopher Coppola
Dracula's Widow '88

Francis Ford Coppola
Bram Stoker's Dracula '92

Roger Corman
Little Shop of Horrors '60
Not of this Earth '57

Frederic Corte
Creature of the Walking Dead '60

William Crain
Blacula '72

Wes Craven
Vampire in Brooklyn '95

Francis Creighton
The Malibu Beach Vampires '91

David Cronenberg
Rabid '77

Frederick Curiel
Blood of Nostradamus '60
Curse of Nostradamus '60
The Empire of Dracula '67
Genie of Darkness '60
The Monster Demolisher '60
Nostradamus and the Destroyer of Monsters '62
Nostradamus and the Genie of Darkness '60
Santo en la Venganza de las Mujeres Vampiro '69
The Vampire Girls '68

Dan Curtis
The Best of Dark Shadows 2 '90s
Dark Shadows Resurrected The Video '95
Dracula '73
House of Dark Shadows '70
Night of Dark Shadows '71

Holly Dale
Blood & Donuts '96

Gerard Damiano
Legacy of Satan '73

Ray Danton
Crypt of the Living Dead '73
The Deathmaster '71

Manny Davis
Gandy Goose in Ghosttown '44

Anthony (Antonio Margheriti) Dawson
Castle of Blood '64

Robert Day
First Man into Space '59

Director Index

Brad Grinter
Blood Freak '72

Allan Grunewald
Nightmare Castle '65

Bill Gunn
Black Vampire '73

Bruce G. Hallenbeck
Fangs! '92
Vampyre '90

John Hancock
Let's Scare Jessica to Death '71

Rod Hardy
Thirst '87

Curtis Harrington
Planet of Blood '66

Robert Hartford-Davis
The Bloodsuckers '70

Steve Hawkes
Blood Freak '72

Howard Hawks
The Thing '51

John Hayes
Grave of the Vampire '72

Juraj Herz
Ferat Vampire '82

Werner Herzog
Nosferatu the Vampyre '79

Gordon Hessler
Scream and Scream Again '70

David L. Hewitt
Alien Massacre '67

Jean Hewitt
Blood of Dracula's Castle '69

Jon Hewitt
Bloodlust '92

George Hickenlooper
The Ghost Brigade '93

Anthony Hickox
Sundown '91
Waxwork '88
Waxwork 2: Lost in Time '91

Jack Hill
The Fear Chamber '67
Track of the Vampire '66

Arthur Hiller
Nightwing '79

Lambert Hillyer
Dracula's Daughter '36

Fredric Hobbs
Alabama's Ghost '72

Tom Holland
Fright Night '85

James Hong
The Vineyard '89

Tobe Hooper
Lifeforce '85
Salem's Lot '79

Robert Hossein
Le Vampire du Dusseldorf '64

John Hough
Incubus '82
Twins of Evil '71

V.V. Dachin Hsu
Pale Blood '91

Jimmy Huston
My Best Friend Is a Vampire '88

Juan Ibanez
The Fear Chamber '67

Jon Jacobs
The Girl with the Hungry Eyes '94

Rick Jacobson
Night Hunter '95

Jerry Jameson
The Bat People '74

Jaromil Jires
Valerie and the Week of Wonders '69

Niall Johnson
Dawn '90

Leif Jonker
Darkness '92

Neil Jordan
Interview with the Vampire '94

George Joseph
Horror of the Blood Monsters '70

Hung Kam-Bo
Close Encounters of the Spooky Kind 2 '89

Shusuke Kaneko
My Soul Is Slashed '92

Saka Kawamura
My Soul Is Slashed '92

Fran Rubel Kazui
Buffy the Vampire Slayer '92

Bob Kelljan
Count Yorga, Vampire '70
The Return of Count Yorga '71
Scream Blacula Scream '73

J.D. Kendis
Jaws of the Jungle '36

Elisar C. Kennedy
Demonsoul '94

Erle C. Kenton
House of Dracula '45
House of Frankenstein '44

Wong King-Fang
Curse of the Wicked Wife '84

Leon Klimovsky
Orgy of the Vampires '73
The Saga of the Draculas '72
Strange Love of the Vampires '74
The Werewolf vs. the Vampire Woman '70

Ricky Lau Koon-Wai
Romance of the Vampires '94

Bernard L. Kowalski
Attack of the Giant Leeches '59

Viktor Kubal
Krvava Pani '81

Harry Kumel
Daughters of Darkness '71

John Lamb
Mondo Keyhole '68

Bruce Lambert
Ninja, the Violent Sorcerer '86
Vampire Raiders—Ninja Queen '89

Lew (Louis Friedlander) Landers
Return of the Vampire '44

John Landis
Coming Soon '83
Innocent Blood '92

Paul Landres
Return of Dracula '58

Fritz Lang
M '31

Joseph Larraz
Vampyres '74

Steve Latshaw
Dark Universe '93
Vampire Trailer Park '91

Jeff Lau
Haunted Cop Shop II '86

Norman Law
Ninja Vampire Busters '89

Pedro Lazanga Sabater
The Vampire for Two '65

Q. Xen Lee
Doctor Vampire '91

Yongmin Lee
The Bad Flower '61

Lionel Leung
Dragon Against Vampire '84

Herschell Gordon Lewis
A Taste of Blood '66

Kevin J. Lindenmuth
Addicted to Murder '95
Vampires and Other Stereotypes '92

Wim Linder
Blood Relations '77

Ulli Lommel
Tenderness of Wolves '73

Jose Luis (Delavena) Madrid
The Vampire of the Highway '69

Albert Magnoli
Atom Age Vampire '61

Rosangela Maldonado
A Deusa de Marmore Escrava do Diabo '78

Michael Mann
The Keep '83

Artemio Marquez
Men of Action Meet the Women of Dracula '69

Philip Marshak
Dracula Sucks '79

Wyre Martin
The Unearthing '93

Marcello Martinelli
Sexy Prohibitissimo '63

Director
Index

Alain Robak
The Evil Within '94

Alain Robbe–Grillet
Tender Dracula, or The Confessions of a Bloodsucker '74

Mark Robson
Isle of the Dead '45

Robert Rodriguez
From Dusk Till Dawn '95

Robert Rodriquez
Tom Thumb and Little Red Riding Hood vs. the Monsters '62

Sutton Roley
Chosen Survivors '74

Jean Rollin
Fascination '79
La Reine des Vampires '68
La Vampire Nue '69
Le Frisson des Vampires '70
Le Viol du Vampire '67
Requiem for a Vampire '72

Jean Marie Rollin
The Living Dead Girl '82

George A. Romero
Martin '77

Conrad Rooks
Chappaqua '65

Phil Rosen
Spooks Run Wild '41

Stephanie Rothman
Track of the Vampire '66
The Velvet Vampire '71

Katt Shea Ruben
Dance of the Damned '88

Ken Russell
Gothic '87
The Lair of the White Worm '88

Marti Rustam
Evils of the Night '85

William Sachs
Incredible Melting Man '77

Alfredo Salazar
The Rider of the Skulls '67

Sidney Salkow
The Last Man on Earth '64

Jimmy Sangster
Lust for a Vampire '71

Cirio H. Santiago
The Vampire Hookers '78

Deran Sarafian
To Die for '89

Joe Sarno
The Devil's Plaything '73

Peter Sasdy
Countess Dracula '70
Taste the Blood of Dracula '70

Hajime Sato
Body Snatcher from Hell '69

Shimako Sato
Tale of a Vampire '92

Philip Saville
Count Dracula '78

Stephen Sayadian
Cafe Flesh '82

David Schmoeller
The Arrival '90

Joel Schumacher
The Lost Boys '87

Tony Scott
The Hunger '83

Lesley Selander
The Vampire's Ghost '45

Vernon Sewell
Blood Beast Terror '67

Don Sharp
Kiss of the Vampire '62

George Sherman
Crime Doctor's Courage '45

Kaneto Shindo
Kuroneko '68

Takako Shira
Elusive Song of the Vampire '87

Jacqueline Sieger
Jugular Wine: A Vampire Odyssey '94
La Reine des Vampires '68

James Signorelli
Elvira, Mistress of the Dark '88

Lynn Silver
Ghost Stories: Graveyard Thriller '86

Robert Siodmak
Son of Dracula '43

Stanley Siu
Ninja Vampire Busters '89

Gilberto Martinez Solares
Chanoc contra el Tigre y el Vampiro '71
Santo and the Blue Demon vs. the Monsters '68

Julian Soler
Castle of the Monsters '58

Paul Solvay
Devil's Wedding Night '73

Barry Sonnenfeld
The Addams Family '91
Addams Family Values '93

Kim In Soo
Vengeful Vampire Girl '81

John Stanley
Nightmare in Blood '75

Duncan Stewart
The Bride's Initiation '76

Larry Stewart
Buck Rogers in the 25th Century: Space Vampire '80

John Stone
Count It Higher '88

Howard Storm
Once Bitten '85

Frank Strayer
Condemned to Live '35
The Vampire Bat '32

Herbert L. Strock
Blood of Dracula '57

Dave Stuckey
Lugosi the Forgotten King '85

E.W. Swackhamer
Vampire '79

Don Swan
Gore-Met Zombie Chef From Hell '87

Boris Szulzinger
Mama Dracula '80

Harry Tampa
Nocturna '79

Daniel Taplitz
Nightlife '90

Gerald Thomas
Carry On Screaming '66

Paul Thomas
Out for Blood '90

Li Tie
Vampire Woman '62

Roman Tikhomirov
Morning Star '62

R.L. Tillmanns
Witchcraft 3: The Kiss of Death '90

Eric Tsang
Vampire Family '93

Kamm Yoo Tu
Vampires Settle on Police Camp '88

Ching Siu Tung
A Chinese Ghost Story '87

Edgar G. Ulmer
The Daughter of Dr. Jekyll '57

Roger Vadim
Blood and Roses '61

Marijan Vajda
Bloodlust '70

Jose Maria Valles
Blood Pie '71
Cake of Blood '72

Norman Thaddeus Vane
The Black Room '82
Frightmare '81

Emilio Vieyra
Blood of the Virgins '68

Akos Von Rathony
Cave of the Living Dead '65

Ernst R. von Theumer
The Bloodsuckers '67

Andrew Kam Yeun Wah
Red and Black '86

Director Index

Category List

Listed below are subjects by which we categorize the videos reviewed in this book, with definitions for these sometimes bizarre classifications. Following this "Category List" is, appropriately enough, a "Category Index," which puts all these categories to good use.

Abbott & Costello They show up in the craziest places with the craziest people.

Action Adventure Sometimes blood isn't enough; you need explosions and gunplay, too.

Adapted from a Book Movies that borrowed their plots from real writers and actually gave them credit for it. You might be surprised at some on the list—run right out to the library. See also *Books to Film.*

Adapted from a Cartoon Movies that borrowed their plots from real cartoonists.

Adapted from a Comic Strip Same thing but in print media.

Adapted from a Fairy Tale Same thing, from a story designed to make kids behave.

Adapted from a Play or Musical Same thing, originally live.

Adapted from a Story Same thing but usually shorter.

Adapted from an Opera Same thing, but the fat lady sings.

Adapted from Television Same thing, with commercials.

Adapted from the Radio Same thing but with added visuals.

Adolescence see *Hell High School; Teen Angst*

Advertising Bloodsuckers who sell you stuff you don't need.

Africa In and around the Dark Continent.

African America Vampires in the 'Hood.

Alien Beings—Benign Friendly well-meaning space visitors. See also *Alien Beings—Vicious*.

Alien Beings—Vicious Not-so-friendly, and, well, *mean* space visitors, often bent on turning Earth's population into a buffet. See also *Alien Beings—Benign*.

Animals see *Cats; Dogs; Killer Apes; Killer Birds; Killer Cats; Monkeying Around*

Animation & Cartoons Includes cartoons, stop-motion puppets, Anime. You know, Saturday morning stuff.

Anthology More than one story per movie. Now how much would you pay?

Archaeology see *Big Digs*

Art & Artists They wear black and they brood about their cursed existence. Sound familiar?

Australia see *Down Under*

Australian Movies produced in the land Down Under.

Automobiles see *Fast Cars*

Avant-Garde Either "Before-Their-Time" genius or mere pretension? You make the call.

B/W & Color Combos Toto, I don't think we're in Transylvania anymore.

BBC TV Productions British couch-potato imports.

Babysitting Taking care of someone else's kids.

Ballet Gotta stay on your toes!

Bathroom Scenes Try not to get caught with your pants down.

Behind the Scenes Take a look backstage. You never know what you'll find.

Belgian Movies produced in Belgium. They *do* make things besides waffles, ya know.

Big Digs Movies featuring archaeologists—most of whom end up as vampire chow.

Big Ideas Philosophy, ideology, and other navel-gazing pursuits.

Bikers It's not a gang. It's a club!

Billy the Kid Western outlaw who happens upon the strangest people.

Bisexuality Doubles your chances for a date on Saturday night.

Black Comedy Movies featuring biting or despairing humor that makes you feel guilty for laughing. See also *Comedy; Satire & Parody*.

Blaxploitation '70s remakes of horror classics with African-American casts and storylines.

Bloody Mayhem Expanded scenes of arterial explosions of both human and non-human blood, usually for consumption.

Books to Film: Stephen King Prolific scream-to-screen meister.

Books to Film: Edgar Allan Poe Romantic master of the macabre.

Books to Film: Anne Rice Took a few years to get to the big screen. Raised some Hell once she did.

Books to Film: Bram Stoker The mother lode. Three stories have kept thousands of Hollywood typewriters clicking for almost 100 years.

Boom! Really big explosions to go with the buckets of blood.

The Bowery Boys The Dead End Kids get into a different kind of trouble.

Brazilian Movies produced in Brazil.

Bringing Up Baby Precocious children—usually with odd eating habits.

British Movies with an English accent because they were produced in England.

Buddhism Far Eastern religion with plenty of bald heads and vampire-fighting power to go around.

Buddies Bud and Lou are always there to help each other in and out of trouble.

Campus Capers School spirit tends to lose its positive connotations. See also *Hell High School*.

Canada Good day, and welcome to the movies set in the Great White North.

Canadian Hey! What about the ones produced up there, too?

Cannibalism "Why don't you come on up for a bite?" and other non-vegetarian scenarios.

Carnivals & Circuses There's a reason the 'Chamber of Horrors' is only a nickel.

Carry On Low-brow British humor series.

Cats The Hound only grudgingly approves of these movies.

Chases Like a road trip but faster. See also *Road Trip*.

Cheerleaders Gimme a V! Gimme an A! Gimme an M! Gimme a P!

Childhood Visions Stories dominated by the kid point of view. Can you say child psychologist?

China Big country in Asia? Lots of people? Communist oppression? C'mon, I know you've heard of it.

Chinese Movies produced in China (or Taiwan, or Hong Kong).

Circuses see *Carnivals & Circuses*

Civil War Oxymoron Alert! Undead Yanks vs. Zombie Rebs.

Classic Horror Bela Lugosi, Christopher Lee, Peter Cushing, Boris Karloff, John Carradine, piercing screams, spooky houses. See also *Supernatural Horror*.

Classics Quality scares not to be missed.

Clowns Junior's right. Clowns are to be feared.

Cold Spots Frostbite isn't the only thing to watch out for.

Cold War see *Red Scare*

Comedy Funny stuff generally lacking in drama. See also *Black Comedy; Genre Spoofs; Horror Comedy; Satire & Parody*.

Comedy Anthologies Lots of funny different stuff in one place.

Comedy Drama Funny stuff with serious junk going on.

Contemporary Noir Dark and moody in a modern setting.

Cops The long arm (and sometimes teeth) of the law. Let's be careful out there. See also *Detectives*.

Corporate Shenanigans Profit-hunting bloodsuckers wreak havoc on the world. World usually wreaks back.

Creepy Houses Big, old, creaky, filled with cobwebs. If someone dares you to spend the night, don,'t!

Crime & Criminals Non-supernatural bad guys and girls. See also *Fugitives*.

Crop Dusters Strange things are happening down on the farm.

Cuban Movies produced a mere 90 miles from our shores!

Cult Items Recognized by a (usually) small but devoted audience as genius for quirky (or just plain bad) acting, writing, directing, or F/X.

Cults People with glazed expressions, no money, and an aggressive recruitment program. Usually entails a change in dietary habits.

Death & the Afterlife Dead people, undead people, walking dead people, and other dead issues.

Demons & Wizards Mystics whose powers are generally not beneficial to those around them.

Dental Mayhem Mr. Dracula, I think those wisdom teeth might be impacted.

Detectives Clue-happy but often grizzled and cynical. See also *Cops; Feds*.

Devils Sources of all evil. Not to be trusted in contract negotiations.

Disease of the Week You should really have that looked at...urk!

Disney Animated Movies Mickey! Donald! What are you guys doing in this book?

Disney Family Movies Scary movies designed specifically not to scare the kiddies.

Doctors & Nurses Refuse the elective surgery. Even if you're HMO does cover it, you'll pay for it in the end.

Documentary Typically a serious examination of an issue or idea, these generally cover Vlad Tepes, Transylvanian history, and celluloid vampires.

Down Under Australia and New Zealand have their share of vampires, too.

Dracula Would't be much of a book without the big man, would it?

Dragons Fire-breathing lizards, usually from the Middle Ages.

Drama Something serious is going on here.

Dream Girls Devils Girls, Vampire Vixens, and other male fantasies.

Drugs see *Pill Poppin'*

Dutch Movies produced in the Netherlands.

Emerging Viruses New improved versions of stuff that can kill you.

Erotic Thrillers Plenty of sex, but remember to pay attention to that plot.

Evil Doctors Now, this may hurt a bit.

Exploitation As in, exploiting the audience's taste for over-the-top sex, blood, and mayhem.

Extraordinary Pairings One of these things is not like the other...

Fairs & Expositions Step right up, folks! See oddities of all kinds!

Family Ties You can't pick your family.

Family Viewing Fun and safe for the whole family, even little Timmy.

Fantasy This is what happens when screenwriters are able to remember their stuffed-peppers-induced dreams.

Feds Men and women of the Bureau, the Agency, the Shop, or any national police organization with an acronym and a dress code. See also *Detectives; I Spy*.

Femme Fatale She done him and him and him wrong. See also *Wonder Women*.

Filipino Movies produced in the Philippines.

Film History Remembers the times when Black & White was the only game in town.

Film Stars Movies about the stars of movies.

Filmmaking What do these guys do for their $20 million?

Flower Children The Sixties didn't die, they just fell asleep.

Folklore & Mythology Age-old tales handed down

Category List

from generation to generation. Now generally regarded as plot points.

4 Bones Here it is! The creme de la creme!

France European country with the Eiffel Tower, snooty waiters, and sexy vampiresses.

Frankenstein Well known guy with bolts in his neck.

Friendship see *Buddies*

French Movies produced in France.

Front Page Hard-boiled reporters, skeptical editors, high-profile murder cases, huge headlines.

Funerals You might wanna check that body again before you close the lid.

Gambling You bet your life.

Gays Homosexual themes.

Gender Bending Boys will be girls—and vice versa.

Genre Spoofs Skewed looks at film genres. See also *Comedy; Satire & Parody.*

German Movies produced in Germany.

Germany Vampires along the Rhine.

Ghosts, Ghouls, & Goblins Apparitions with attitude.

Grand Hotel Check out time is strictly enforced.

Great Britain Werewolves of London aren't the only creatures of the night to look out for.

Great Death Scenes If you gotta go, go with style.

Greek Movies produced in Greece.

Growing Older Not generally a problem for vampires.

Hammer Films: Horror British studio is the first word in quality vampire flicks.

Hearts! Unpleasant scenes involving the ticker.

Hell High School Isn't that redundant? See also *Campus Capers; Teen Angst.*

Hercules Ancient strongman with a flair for heroics

Historical Drama Based (usually loosely) on actual historical events or personages.

Home Alone Are you sure you're alone?

Hong Kong Movies produced in Hong Kong— chop-socky capital of the world.

Horror Anthology More scares for your rental dollar.

Horror Comedy Laughing all the way to the grave. See also *Black Comedy; Comedy; Genre Spoofs; Satire & Parody.*

Hunted! Prey for a day. See also *Survival.*

Horse Racing Playing the ponies.

Immigration Green cards, Ellis Island, looking for a new start.

Incest It's like kissin' yer sister, only worse.

Indian Movies produced in India.

Island Fare Generally inhabited by blood-drinking cults or mad scientists.

Italian Movies produced in Italy.

Japanese Movies produced in the Land of the Rising Sun. Sorry, no Godzillas here.

Japanimation Japanese cartoons. Usually violent and complex.

Jungle Stories Blood cults, wild animals, oppressive heat. Next year we're going to the Grand Canyon.

Killer Apes They think they're King Kong on the Planet of the Apes.

Kidnapped! Taken against your will.

Killer Beasts They're mad as hell, and they're not gonna take it anymore.

Killer Bugs Creepy crawly things get feisty.

Killer Cars Recalls would be futile.

Killer Dogs The Hound thinks they got a bad rap.

Killer Plants Including foliage, fruits, and fungi.

Killer Rodents Mickey's evil twins.

King of Beasts (Dogs) Did you really expect me to say lions?

Korean Movies produced in Korea.

L.A. The City of Angels gets a few visits from the dark side.

Lesbians Women who don't need men to have a good time.

London Hey, with all this fog here, this would be a good setting for a scary movie!

Mad Scientists Mutant things for mutant living.

Made for Television see *TV Movies; TV Pilot Movies; TV Series*

Magic Hocus pocus, often with an evil intent. See also *Sword & Sorcery.*

Marriage In this case, marriage really *can* be forever.

Martial Arts Everybody Was Kung Fu Fighting.

Medieval Romps Dirty peasants, deodorized kings and queens, and knights in shining armor.

Meltdown Or, how I learned to stop worrying and love the bomb.

Men in Prison Guys behind bars.

Metamorphosis Ch-ch-ch-changes.

Mexican Movies produced south of the border.

Mistaken Identity Hey, aren't you...?

Monsters, General You know, the basics: Frankenstein, mummies, vampires, werewolves, Zombies

Motor Vehicle Dept. Your mileage may vary. See also *Bikers; Killer Cars.*

Mummies Withered folks wrapped in toilet paper.

Music I wanna rock and roll all night...

Musical Comedy Sing along with the funny stuff.

Musicals More singing, but no intentional laughs.

Nazis & Other Paramilitary Slugs The *real* jack-booted government thugs. See also *Nazi Zombies; World War II.*

New York, New York Creatures of the night take a bite outta the Big Apple.

Nifty '50s When everything was great, if you don't count McCarthyism, the Korean War, the Cold War...

Nightclubs The name alone just screams 'vampire hangout.'

Nuclear Disaster see *Meltdown*

Nuns & Priests Have 'em on the speed-dial if you're going up against any vampires.

Occult Magic, spells, curses, devil worship. Vampires are usually pretty well-versed in this sort of thing.

Oldest Profession Prostitutes. They keep the same hours, so it makes since for vampires to seek them out as victims and/or companions.

Opera Large people singing in foreign languages for long stretches of time.

Organized Crime They also prey on and feed off the weak.

Outtakes & Bloopers Oops. We weren't rolling there, were we?

Parenthood Because I said so, that's why!

Paris The City of Lights. I thought vampires didn't like light.

Period Piece Costume epics, or evocative of a certain time and place—think Victorian England.

Phobias! You know, maybe those fears aren't so irrational, after all.

Phone Terror And we're not just talking about long-distance commercials, either.

Pill Poppin' Consumption of drugs, mostly illegal or in extra-large doses.

Pittsburgh Three rivers, one city.

Politics Republicans and Democrats fighting over how to run the government. Insert vampire joke here.

Pool Just a tip. Cue sticks are made of wood.

Pornography Genre where disrobing = plot and moaning = dialogue. No kids allowed.

Portuguese Movies produced in Portugal.

Post Apocalypse No more convenience stores.

Pregnant Pauses And baby makes...a mess!

Producers: Roger Corman/ New World You can tell how much he likes an idea by how many times he remakes it.

Production Problems When bad things happen to good (and not-so-good) movies.

Psycho-Thrillers It's all in your mind.

Psychotics/Sociopaths Stay outta their way!

Pure Ego Vehicles Why? Because they can.

Rape Movies usually deal with the aftermath, the victims, and their revenge.

Red Scare For vampires it means a blood shortage.

Religion Not real popular among vampires.

Renegade Body Parts Hands, fingers, eyes, brains, and other appendages with a life of their own.

Revealing Swimwear Minimum amounts of fabric, copious amounts of flesh.

Revenge It's a strong motivator, and a dish best served cold.

Road Trip Rollin' down the highway...preferably in a vehicle.

Robots & Androids Danger, Will Robinson!

Rock Stars on Film But can they act?

Role Reversal Switching identities for fun and profit.

Romanian Movies produced in Drac's backyard.

Romantic Drama Will Dracula find love with Lucy?

Romantic Triangles Will Dracula find love with Lucy or Mina?

Russian Movies produced in Russia.

Sail Away "Gilligan, little buddy!"

San Francisco City by the Bay where people keep leaving their hearts.

Sanity Check Inmates running the asylum; also deviant states of mind. See also *Shrinks.*

Satanism Speak of the devil.

Satire & Parody Biting social comment or genre spoofs. See also *Black Comedy; Comedy; Genre Spoofs; Horror Comedy.*

School Daze Don't go in the cafeteria.

Sci Fi Imagining the future, or the present if engineers ran the world.

Screwball Comedy Snappy banter, outrageous situations.

Category List

Sea Critter Attack Monsters from the deep, in the large economy size.

Serial Killers Killing in bulk.

Serials Flicks rationed out a little at a time, once a week. Designed to keep your parents coming back.

Sex & Sexuality Focus is on lust, for better or worse.

Sexploitation Softcore epics usually lacking in plot but not skin.

Showbiz Comedies Funny stuff about the entertainment industry.

Showbiz Thrillers Hollywood whodunits.

Shrinks As in head shrinkers (psychiatrists, not witch doctors). See also *Sanity Check*.

Shutterbugs Photographers—another group vampires aren't too thrilled with.

Silent Films Often employing a very rudimentary means of subtitling.

Silent Horror/Fantasy Classics The best of the early scares.

Space Operas Going where no vampire has gone before.

Spanish Movies produced in Spain.

Special F/X Extravaganzas The blood doesn't look like ketchup.

Special F/X Extravaganzas: Make-Up Faces only a mother could love.

Special F/X Wizards: Rick Baker *The Incredible Melting Man* and *Star Wars,* all in the same year.

Special F/X Wizards: Tom Savini Jumped in front of the camera in *From Dusk Till Dawn.*

Special F/X Wizards: Dick Smith Helped *Dark Shadows* make the jump to feature films.

Speculation The truth is out there.

Spies & Espionage Cloak and dagger stuff, or is it cape and stake?

Strippers Scantily-clad women make good vampires—or their victims.

Summer Camp Let's send the kids to Camp Runamok this year.

Superheroes Men and women of extraordinary strength and/or abilities wearing silly-looking costumes.

Supernatural Comedies It's unexplained, but it's funny.

Supernatural Horror Forces from beyond terrorize those who are here.

Supernatural Martial Arts Chop-socky vampire hunting.

Supernatural Westerns Get outta town by sun-up, pardner.

Survival Nobody said it was going to be easy.

Swashbucklers Rope-swinging, sword-fighting, (sometimes) seafaring action.

Sword & Sandal See Arnold Schwartzenegger's early career. Ancient mythology plays a big role.

Taiwanese Movies made in Taiwan.

Technology—Rampant Machines wreak havoc—messily.

Teen Angst Adolescent anxieties become even more angst-ridden with a loss of blood. See also *Hell High School.*

Television see *TV Movies; TV Pilot Movies; TV Series*

This is Your Life Biography and autobiography.

3-D Flicks Movies requiring special glasses that often cause headaches (watching the movies without the glasses can sometimes cause headaches as well).

Time Travel Fast forward or reverse. See also *Rescue Missions Involving Time Travel.*

Torrid Love Scenes Steaming up the screen in a fit of passion.

Trash The dregs. May have unintentionally humorous moments.

Trees & Forests If the hills aren't alive, then the woods definitely are.

Troma Films Low-brow fare from the Barons of Bad Taste.

True Stories Approximations of real-life events, often significantly fictionalized for the screen.

Turkish Movies produced in Turkey.

TV Movies First shown on broadcast, cable, or foreign television before hitting your VCR. See also *BBC TV Productions.*

TV Pilot Movies Some made it to the small screen on a weekly basis; some did not.

TV Series Your favorite vampire shows that are available on video.

Twins Just because they were born at the same time, doesn't necessarily mean they get along.

Unexplained Phenomena Ummm, it's hard to define.

Universal Studios' Classic Horror Without them (and their various descendants), this would be an awfully small book.

Up All Night The action picks up after the sun goes down.

Vacations Not as relaxing as they're cracked up to be.

Vampire Babes The fairer sex bares its fangs.

Vampire Spoof Tongue-in-cheek bloodsuckers.

Variety Like 'potpourri' on *Jeopardy*—who knows what'll be there.

Venice The canal city in Italy, not the beach in Cali.

Vietnam War It was all over the news in the '60s.

Viva Las Vegas Perfect place for vampires. If you're in the casinos, you can't tell if it's day or night.

Voodoo Haitian religion usually involves zombies, curses, and other unpleasantness.

War Between the Sexes Men and women battle for supremacy...or at least a slight advantage.

Wedding Hell Marriages that don't start off on the right foot. Or claw. Or whatever.

Werewolves During the full moon, things can get a little hairy.

Westerns They don't even have indoor plumbing, and you want 'em to deal with vampires?

Wild Kingdom Those amazing animals.

Witchcraft Magic used by scary-looking old women for nefarious purposes.

Women Impressive women and less-than-impressive women.

Wonder Women Sorry, no Lynda Carter.

Woofs! Those pics not even rating a half a bone.

World War II The second "war to end all wars."

Wrestling And you thought Hulk Hogan was weird.

Writers Tortured souls who put pen to paper when not putting bottle to lips. Hobbies include dying young and penniless of tuberculosis.

Yugoslavian Movies produced in what used to be Yugoslavia.

Yuppie Nightmares Oh no! The Beemer's scratched!

Zombie Soldiers Undead GIs who don't know the war is over.

Zombies Astro zombies, government zombies (same diff), vampire zombies, voodoo zombies—we got all kinds.

Category List

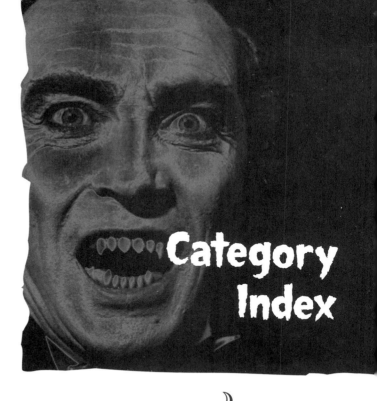

Category
Index

Being a faithful VideoHound reader, by now you are no doubt familiar with the idea of a category index. This one helps you identify themes these movies have in common besides vampires.

Category Index

House of Dracula
House of Frankenstein
The House that Dripped
  Blood
The Hunger
Invasion of the Vampires
Isle of the Dead
The Lair of the White
  Worm
The Legend of Blood
  Castle
Lemora, Lady Dracula
Mark of the Vampire
Martin
Night of Dark Shadows
Nosferatu
Son of Dracula
The Vampire
The Vampire Bat
The Vampire People
The Vampire's Coffin
The Vampire's Ghost
Vampyr
The Werewolf vs. the
  Vampire Woman

Classics
Bowery Boys Meet the
  Monsters
Condemned to Live
Dracula
M
Mark of the Vampire
Nosferatu
The Thing
Vampyr

Clowns
See also Carnivals &
  Circuses
Killer Klowns from Outer
  Space

Cold Spots
The Thing

Cold War *See* Red
Scare

Comedy
See also Black Comedy;
  Comedy Drama; Horror
  Comedy; Musical
  Comedy; Satire &
  Parody; Screwball
  Comedy; Slapstick
  Comedy
Because the Dawn
Blood Relations
Buffy the Vampire Slayer
Capulina contra Los
  Monstros
The Case of the Full
  Moon Murders
Ed Wood
Go for a Take
Halloween with the
  Addams Family

Il Cavaliere Costante
  Nicosia Demoniaco
  Ovvero
The Ketchup Vampires
Kung Fu Vampire Buster
Les Charlots contre
  Dracula
The Malibu Beach
  Vampires
Pepito y Chabelo vs. los
  Monstruos
Please Don't Eat My
  Mother
A Polish Vampire in
  Burbank
Rockula
Think Dirty
The Vampire Conspiracy
Vampire Family
Vampire Man

Comedy Anthologies
See also Comedy
The World of Abbott &
  Costello

Comedy Drama
See also Black Comedy;
  Comedy
The Mark of Lilith

Contemporary Noir
Body Double

Cops
See also Detectives
Blood Relations
Deadly Love
Ghost Punting
Haunted Cop Shop I
Haunted Cop Shop II
Innocent Blood
Kingdom of the Vampire
Magic Cop
Vampire at Midnight
Vampire Cop
Vampire in Brooklyn
Vampires Settle on Police
  Camp

Corporate
Shenanigans
See also Advertising
Dracula Rises from the
  Coffin
Il Cavaliere Costante
  Nicosia Demoniaco
  Ovvero
My Soul Is Slashed
Pure Blood
They've Changed Faces

Creepy Houses
See also Horror
The Bloodsuckers
Castle of Blood
Castle of the Living Dead
Close Encounters of the
  Spooky Kind

The Curse of the Vampyr
Drakulita
Fright Night
Ghost Punting
The House that Dripped
  Blood
Lake of Dracula
The Maltese Bippy
Salem's Lot

Crime & Criminals
See also Organized
  Crime; Serial Killers
Body Double
The Devil's
  Commandment
From Dusk Till Dawn
Go for a Take

Crop Dusters
Bloodsuckers from Outer
  Space

Cuban
Vampires in Havana

Cult Items
Andy Warhol's Dracula
Billy the Kid Versus
  Dracula
Ed Wood
The Fearless Vampire
  Killers
Geek Maggot Bingo
The Hunger
Little Shop of Horrors
Martin
Plan 9 from Outer Space
Please Don't Eat My
  Mother
The Thing

Cults
See also Occult; Satanism
The Bloodsuckers
Doctor Dracula
Invasion of the Blood
  Farmers
Kiss of the Vampire
La Vampire Nue
Lemora, Lady Dracula
The 7 Brothers Meet
  Dracula
Thirst
The Thirsty Dead
Tower of the Devil

Czech
Ferat Vampire

Deafness
Deafula

Death & the Afterlife
See also Funerals;
  Ghosts, Ghouls, &
  Goblins; Great Death
  Scenes; Occult
Blood of the Vampire

Frightmare
Graveyard Disturbance
The Midnight Hour
Nightmare Castle
A Vampire's Dream
The Vampire's Ghost

Demons & Wizards
See also Occult
Bloodlust: Subspecies 3
Bloodstone: Subspecies 2
Incubus
The Nine Demons
Tower of the Devil
Vampires and Other
  Stereotypes

Dental Mayhem
See also Doctors &
  Nurses; Evil Doctors
Little Shop of Horrors

Detectives
See also Cops; Feds
Carry On Screaming
Cave of the Living Dead
Kathavai Thatteeya
  Mohni Paye
Nick Knight
Tales from the Crypt
  Presents Bordello of
  Blood

Devils
Night of the Vampire

Disease of the Week
See also Emerging Viruses
Incredible Melting Man
Isle of the Dead
The Last Man on Earth
Rabid
Terror Creatures from the
  Grave

Disney Animated
Movies
Mickey's Gala Premier

Disney Family Movies
The Mystery of Dracula's
  Castle

Doctors & Nurses
See also Dental Mayhem;
  Disease of the Week;
  Emerging Viruses; Evil
  Doctors; Sanity Check;
  Shrinks
Blood Relations
Crime Doctor's Courage
The Curse of the Vampyr
Dr. Terror's House of
  Horrors
Doctor Vampire
Legacy of Satan
Living Skeleton
The Macabre Trunk

The Man in Half Moon
Street
Night of the Devils
The Return of Dr. X
The Vampire
A Vampire's Dream

Documentary
Bram Stoker's Whitby
Dracula: A Cinematic
Scrapbook
The Dracula Business
Dracula: Fact or Fiction
Dracula in the Movies
Dracula: The Great
Undead
Fangs!
The Horror of It All
Lugosi the Forgotten King
Vampires
Vincent Price's Dracula

Dogs
See King of Beasts (Dogs)

Down Under
Zombie Brigade

Dracula
Abbott and Costello Meet
Frankenstein
The Bad Flower
Batman Dracula
Bela Lugosi Scrapbook
Blood of Dracula
Blood of Dracula's Castle
Bram Stoker's Dracula
The Bride's Initiation
The Brides of Dracula
Chappaqua
Count Dracula
Count Dracula
Curse of Dracula
Dracula
Dracula: A Cinematic
Scrapbook
Dracula & Son
Dracula: Dead and
Loving It
Dracula/Garden of Eden
Dracula Has Risen from
the Grave
Dracula Rising
Dracula (Spanish Version)
Dracula Sucks
Dracula: The Ballet
Dracula, The Dirty Old
Man
Dracula: The Great
Undead
Dracula: Up in Harlem
Dracula vs. Frankenstein
Dracula's Daughter
Dracula's Great Love
Dracula's Last Rites
Dracula's Widow
Frankenstein Meets
Dracula
Hello Dracula

The Horror of Dracula
House of Dracula
House of Frankenstein
Hysterical
Invasion of the Dead
The Jail Break
Jonathan
Les Charlots contre
Dracula
Love at First Bite
The Mad Love Life of a
Hot Vampire
Mickey's Gala Premier
Mondo Keyhole
The Monster Squad
Nocturna
Old Dracula
Return of Dracula
Return of the Wolfman
The Revenge of Dracula
Santo and the Blue
Demon vs. the
Monsters
The Satanic Rites of
Dracula
The Scars of Dracula
The Screaming Dead
Slave of the Vampire
Son of Dracula
Son of Dracula
Taste the Blood of
Dracula
They've Changed Faces
To Die for
Transylvania 6-5000
Vampir
Vampire Circus
Vampire Dracula Comes
to Kobe; Evil Make
Woman Beautiful
Vampire in Venice
Vincent Price's Dracula
Waxwork
Who Is Afraid of Dracula
Winter with Dracula
World of Dracula
Young Jonathan Dracula
Zoltan...Hound of
Dracula

Dragons
See also Medieval Romps
The Magic Sword

Drama
See also Comedy Drama;
Historical Drama;
Romantic Drama
Blood Ties
Leonor
Nadja
The Reflecting Skin

Dream Girls
Blood of the Virgins
Dracula: Dead and
Loving It
The Vampire Conspiracy

Vampire Vixens from
Venus
Vampire's Kiss

Drugs
See Pill Poppin'

Dutch
Blood Relations

Eating
See Cannibalism

Emerging Viruses
See also Disease of the
Week
Bloodthirsty

Erotic Thrillers
See also Sex & Sexuality
Embrace of the Vampire

Evil Doctors
See also Doctors &
Nurses; Mad Scientists
The Awful Dr. Orlof
Dr. Terror's House of
Horrors

Experimental
See Avant-Garde

Exploitation
See also Sexploitation
Devil's Wedding Night

Extraordinary
Pairings
Abbott and Costello Meet
Frankenstein
Billy the Kid and the
Green Blaze Vampire
Billy the Kid Versus
Dracula
Dracula vs. Frankenstein
Wrestling Women vs. the
Aztec Mummy

Fairs & Expositions
See also Carnivals &
Circuses
Howling 6: The Freaks

Family Ties
See also Parenthood
The Addams Family
Addams Family Values
Blood Ties
The Body Beneath
Curse of the Vampires
Dead Men Walk
Dracula A.D. 1972
Dracula's Daughter
The Empire of Dracula
Fangs of the Living Dead
Father, Santa Claus Has
Died
Flesh of Your Flesh
From Dusk Till Dawn

Grave of the Vampire
Halloween with the
Addams Family
Here Come the Munsters
Horror of it All
The Kiss
Kuroneko
La Reine des Vampires
Lake of Dracula
Les Charlots contre
Dracula
The Lost Boys
Muster, Go Home!
My Grandpa is a Vampire
My Soul Is Slashed
The Mystery of Dracula's
Castle
Nadja
Night of the Devils
Pure Blood
Terror in the Crypt
To Die for 2: Son of
Darkness
Valerie and the Week of
Wonders
Vampire Family
The Vampire for Two
The Vampire of the
Highway
Vampire Trailer Park
Vampire Woman
Vampires and Other
Stereotypes
Who Is Afraid of Dracula

Family Viewing
See also Animation &
Cartoons; Fantasy
The Magic Sword
The Mystery of Dracula's
Castle
Scooby-Doo and the
Reluctant Werewolf

Fantasy
See also Animation &
Cartoons
Hercules in the Haunted
World
La Bonne Dame

Farming
See Crop Dusters

Fast Cars
See also Motor Vehicle
Dept.
Dragstrip Dracula

Feds
See also Detectives; Spies
& Espionage
Dracula Exotica

Feminism
See Women; Wonder
Women

Category Index

Vlad Tepes

Home Alone
See also Childhood Visions
The Monster Squad

Homosexuality
See Bisexuality; Gays; Lesbians

Hong Kong
A Chinese Ghost Story III
Close Encounters of the Spooky Kind
Close Encounters of the Spooky Kind 2
Crazy Safari
Devil's Vindeta
Doctor Vampire
Dragon Against Vampire
First Vampire in China
Ghost Punting
Haunted Cop Shop I
Haunted Cop Shop II
Magic Cop
Mr. Vampire 1992
The Musical Vampire
Ninja Vampire Busters
One Eyebrow Priest
Romance of the Vampires
Shyly Spirit
Ultimate Vampire
Vampire Family
Vampire vs. Vampire
Vampire Woman
Vampires Settle on Police Camp

Hopping Vampires
The Close Encounter of the Vampire
Close Encounters of the Spooky Kind
Close Encounters of the Spooky Kind 2
Crazy Safari
Mr. Vampire 1992
The Musical Vampire
One Eyebrow Priest
Ultimate Vampire
Vampire vs. Vampire
Vampires Settle on Police Camp

Horror Anthologies
Alien Massacre
Dr. Terror's House of Horrors
Ghost Stories: Graveyard Thriller
The House that Dripped Blood
The Monster Club
Tales from the Darkside, Vol. 4
Vault of Horror

Horror Comedy
Andy Warhol's Dracula
Billy the Kid Versus Dracula
Blood & Donuts
Bowery Boys Meet the Monsters
Carry On Screaming
Castle of the Monsters
The Close Encounter of the Vampire
Crazy Safari
Dracula & Son
Dracula Blows His Cool
Dracula: Dead and Loving It
Dracula: Up in Harlem
Drakulita
Elvira, Mistress of the Dark
Face of Marble
The Fearless Vampire Killers
Gore-Met Zombie Chef From Hell
Horroritual
Hysterical
I Bought a Vampire Motorcycle
I Married a Vampire
The Ketchup Vampires
Killer Klowns from Outer Space
Lady Dracula
Little Shop of Horrors
The Maltese Bippy
Mama Dracula
Mr. Vampire
Mr. Vampire II
Mr. Vampire III
Mr. Vampire IV
Mom
My Grandpa is a Vampire
My Son, the Vampire
Near Dark
Nightlife
Nocturna
Old Dracula
Once Bitten
Saturday the 14th
Saturday the 14th Strikes Back
The Seven Vampires
Spooks Run Wild
Tales from the Crypt Presents Bordello of Blood
Vamp
The Vampire Happening
Vampire in Brooklyn
Young Jonathan Dracula

Horse Racing
See Gambling

Immigration
Goliath and the Vampires

Incest
See also Family Ties
Flesh of Your Flesh

Indian
Bandh Darwaza
Kathavai Thatteeya Mohni Paye

Island Fare
Counter Destroyer
Lesbian Vampires The Heiress of Dracula

Italian
Andy Warhol's Dracula
Anemia
Atom Age Vampire
Black Sabbath
Black Sunday
Blood and Black Lace
Castle of Blood
Castle of the Living Dead
Count Dracula
Cry of the Vampire
Daughters of Darkness
Dinner with the Vampire
Dracula vs. Frankenstein
Evil's Commandment
Fangs of the Living Dead
Goliath and the Vampires
Graveyard Shift
Hercules in the Haunted World
Il Cavaliere Costante Nicosia Demoniaco Ovvero La Maschera del Demonio
The Last Man on Earth
The Legend of Blood Castle
Leonor
Nightmare Castle
Orgy of the Vampires
Planet of the Vampires
Playgirls and the Vampire
Sexy Prohibitissimo
The She-Beast
The Slaughter of the Vampires
Terror Creatures from the Grave
Vampire and the Ballerina
Vampire in Venice
The Vampire of the Opera
Who Is Afraid of Dracula

Jail
See Men in Prison

Japanese
Body Snatcher from Hell
Cyber City Oedo 808: Data 3
Dracula
The Evil of Dracula

Kuroneko
Lake of Dracula
Living Skeleton
My Soul Is Slashed
Night of the Vampire
Vampire Dracula Comes to Kobe; Evil Make Woman Beautiful
Vampire Hunter D
Vampire Man
The Vampire Moth
Vampire Moth
Vampire Princess Miyu

Japanimation
See also Animation & Cartoons
Cyber City Oedo 808: Data 3
Vampire Princess Miyu

Journalism
See Front Page

Jungle Stories
Crazy Safari
Jaws of the Jungle
The Thirsty Dead
Tower of the Devil

Kidnapped!
The Body Beneath
The Bride's Initiation
Vampire Man

Killer Beasts
See also Killer Dogs; Killer Rodents
Attack of the Giant Leeches
Bunnicula: Vampire Rabbit
The Devil Bat
The Devil Bat's Daughter
Nightwing
Sleepwalkers
Subspecies

Killer Bugs
Blood Beast Terror
The Lair of the White Worm

Killer Dogs
See also King of Beasts (Dogs)
Face of Marble
Zoltan...Hound of Dracula

Killer Plants
Blood
The Bloodsuckers
Dr. Terror's House of Horrors
Little Shop of Horrors
Please Don't Eat My Mother
The Seven Vampires

Category Index

Dracula Tan Exarchia

Musical Comedy
See also Musicals
Buenas Noches, Senor
Monstruo
Little Shop of Horrors
Son of Dracula

Musicals
See also Musical Comedy
The Vampyr

Mystery & Suspense
See also Psycho-Thriller
Body Double
The Corpse Vanishes
Mrs. Amworth
Night Angel
Nightwing
Tale of a Vampire
The Vampire Moth

**Nazis & Other
Paramilitary Slugs**
See also Germany; World
War II
The Keep
Scream and Scream
Again

New Orleans
Interview with the
Vampire

New York, New York
The Addiction
Because the Dawn
Blood
Dracula Bites the Big
Apple
The Hunger
Jonathan of the Night
Love After Death
Love at First Bite
Nadja
Night Owl
Vampire in Brooklyn

New Zealand
See Down Under

Newspapers
See Front Page

Nifty '50s
The Reflecting Skin

Nightclubs
Dracula Blows His Cool

Ninjitsu
See Martial Arts

Nuclear Disaster
See Meltdown

Nuns & Priests
See also Religion

Crazy Safari
The Devil's Plaything
Guru, the Mad Monk
Mr. Vampire 1992
The Musical Vampire
One Eyebrow Priest
Sisters of Satan
Ultimate Vampire
Vampire vs. Vampire
Vamps

Occult
See also Demons &
Wizards; Satanism;
Witchcraft
Alabama's Ghost
Curse of Nostradamus
The Curse of the Crying
Woman
Curse of the Devil
The Devil's Mistress
Dracula: The Great
Undead
Frankenstein's Bloody
Terror
Genie of Darkness
Invasion of the Blood
Farmers
The Kiss
Leonor
Mrs. Amworth
The Monster Demolisher
The Night Stalker: Two
Tales of Terror
Ninja, the Violent
Sorcerer
Tales from the Darkside,
Vol. 4
Terror Creatures from the
Grave
Torture Chamber of Dr.
Sadism
Witches, Vampires &
Zombies

Oceans
See Sea Critter Attack

Oldest Profession
Beverly Hills Vamp
Doctor Vampire
I, Desire
The Vampire Hookers

Opera
See also Musicals
The Vampire of the
Opera

Organized Crime
See also Crime &
Criminals
Blood & Donuts
Innocent Blood
Vampires in Havana

Outtakes & Bloopers
Bela Lugosi Scrapbook

Dark Shadows: Behind
the Scenes
Dark Shadows Bloopers

Painting
See Art & Artists

Parenthood
See also Bringing Up
Baby; Monster Moms
Addams Family Values
Mom

Paris
See also France
The Devil's
Commandment
Paris When It Sizzles
Theatre of Death
A Vampire in Paradise

Period Piece
See also Historical
Drama; Medieval
Romps
The Awful Dr. Orlof
Bram Stoker's Dracula
Gothic
Haunted Summer
Interview with the
Vampire
Kuroneko
Vampires in Havana

Phobias!
Body Double

Phone Terror
Black Sabbath
Tales from the Darkside,
Vol. 4

Photography
See Shutterbugs

Pill Poppin'
Blood Freak
Chappaqua
Ed Wood
Gothic
Haunted Summer
Red Blooded American
Girl
The Vampire

Pittsburgh
Innocent Blood

Politics
Anemia
Flesh of Your Flesh
Le Nosferat ou les Eaux
Glacees du Calcul
Egoiste
Red and Black

Pool
See also Gambling
Billy the Kid and the
Green Blaze Vampire

Pornography
See also Sex & Sexuality;
Sexploitation
Bloodscent
The Body Beneath
Body Double
The Bride's Initiation
Cafe Flesh
The Case of the Full
Moon Murders
The Devil's Plaything
Immoral Tales
Lesbian Vampires The
Heiress of Dracula
Love Vampire Style
The Mad Love Life of a
Hot Vampire
Mondo Keyhole
Out for Blood
Spermula
The Vampire Conspiracy
Vampire's Kiss
Wanda Does
Transylvania

Portuguese
Dracula's Daughter
Tombs of the Blind Dead

Post Apocalypse
See also Technology-
Rampant
The Last Man on Earth

Pregnant Pauses
See also Bringing Up
Baby
Dawn
Tower of the Devil
The Unearthing

Prison
See Men in Prison

**Producers: Roger
Corman/New World**
Attack of the Giant
Leeches
Little Shop of Horrors
Not of This Earth

**Producers: Val
Lewton**
Isle of the Dead

Production Problems
Vampire in Brooklyn

Prostitutes
See Oldest Profession

Psychiatry
See Shrinks

Psycho-Thriller
See also Mystery &
Suspense
Deadly Love
M

Category
Index

Psychotics/ Sociopaths
Fade to Black
From Dusk Till Dawn
A Vampire in Paradise

Pure Ego Vehicles
See also Rock Stars on
  Film
Vampire in Brooklyn

Rape
It's Alive
Night of the Vampire
Vengeful Vampire Girl

Red Scare
The She-Beast

Religion
See also Buddhism; Nuns
  & Priests
The Addiction
Bloodlust
Def by Temptation
Tales from the Crypt
  Presents Bordello of
  Blood

Renegade Body Parts
See also Horror
The Addams Family
Addams Family Values
Waxwork 2: Lost in Time

Revealing Swimwear
Blood of Dracula's Castle
The Malibu Beach
  Vampires

Revenge
Bandh Darwaza
Black Sunday
Curse of the Devil
Darkness
The Devil's Mistress
Dr. Terror's House of
  Horrors
The Empire of Dracula
Frightmare
The Girl with the Hungry
  Eyes
Grave of the Vampire
The Jitters
La Maschera del
  Demonio
Living Skeleton
Love After Death
My Soul Is Slashed
The Naked Witch
Night Hunter
Night of the Vampire
Nightmare Castle
The Nine Demons
Revenge of the Vampire
The She-Beast
Shyly Spirit
A Taste of Blood

Taste the Blood of
  Dracula
Terror Creatures from the
  Grave
Tombs of the Blind Dead
Torture Chamber of Dr.
  Sadism
Vengeful Vampire Girl
Wolnyoui Han

Road Trip
See also Bikers; Chases;
  Fast Cars; Motor
  Vehicle Dept.
From Dusk Till Dawn

Robots & Androids
See also Technology-
  Rampant
The Astro-Zombies
Star Virgin

Rock Stars on Film
See also Pure Ego
  Vehicles
The Hunger
Son of Dracula

Role Reversal
See also Gender Bending
Blood of Dracula
Paris When It Sizzles

Romance
See Romantic Drama;
  Romantic Triangles

Romanian
Vlad Tepes

Romantic Drama
Fools

Romantic Triangles
Red Lips

Russian
Father, Santa Claus Has
  Died
Morning Star

Sail Away
See also Sea Critter
  Attack
Living Skeleton

San Francisco
Fools
Nightmare in Blood
Vampire

Sanity Check
See also Doctors &
  Nurses; Shrinks
The Devil Bat
The Devil Bat's Daughter
Let's Scare Jessica to
  Death
Pale Blood
Vampire's Kiss

Satanism
See also Demons &
  Wizards; Devils;
  Occult
Black Sunday
The Bloodsuckers
The Devil's Mistress
Disciple of Death
Horrible Orgies of Count
  Dracula
La Vampire Nue
Legacy of Satan
Leonor
The Satanic Rites of
  Dracula
Sisters of Satan
Tombs of the Blind Dead
Witchcraft 3: The Kiss of
  Death

Satire & Parody
See also Black Comedy;
  Comedy; Genre Spoofs
Andy Warhol's Dracula
Anemia
Barry McKenzie Holds
  His Own
Dracula: Dead and
  Loving It
Dracula Sucks
Flesh of Your Flesh
Geek Maggot Bingo
I Married a Vampire
Le Nosferat ou les Eaux
  Glacees du Calcul
  Egoiste
Mad Monster Party
My Best Friend Is a
  Vampire
My Lovely Monster
Nocturna
Transylvania 6-5000

School Daze
See also Campus Capers;
  Hell High School
The Evil of Dracula
Vampires

Sci Fi
See also Fantasy
The Arrival
The Astro-Zombies
Attack of the Giant
  Leeches
Buck Rogers in the 25th
  Century: Space
  Vampire
Cafe Flesh
A Chinese Ghost Story
Cyber City Oedo 808:
  Data 3
Dark Universe
First Man into Space
Grampa's Sci-Fi Hits
Incredible Melting Man
It! The Terror from
  Beyond Space
Kiss Me Quick!

Lifeforce
Not of this Earth
Not of This Earth
Plan 9 from Outer Space
Planet of Blood
Planet of the Vampires
Scream and Scream
  Again
Spermula
Star Virgin
The Thing
Vampire Vixens from
  Venus
Vampirella
Waxwork 2: Lost in Time

Screwball Comedy
See also Comedy;
  Slapstick Comedy
Munster's Revenge
Teen Vamp

Sea Critter Attack
See also Killer Beasts
Attack of the Giant
  Leeches

Serial Killers
See also Crime &
  Criminals
Addams Family Values
Addicted to Murder
The Awful Dr. Orlof
Deadly Love
El Vampiro Negro
Le Vampire du
  Dusseldorf
M
M
Night Owl
Pale Blood
The Seven Vampires
Tenderness of Wolves
Vampirella

Serials
Blood of Nostradamus
Curse of Nostradamus
Genie of Darkness
The Monster Demolisher

Sex & Sexuality
See also Erotic Thrillers;
  Pornography;
  Sexploitation
Andy Warhol's Dracula
The Black Room
Body Double
Bram Stoker's Dracula
Devil's Wedding Night
Dracula Exotica
Dracula Sucks
Elvira, Mistress of the
  Dark
Embrace of the Vampire
Evils of the Night
Fascination
Gothic

Il Cavaliere Costante
  Nicosia Demoniaco
  Ovvero
Incubus
Le Frisson des Vampires
Lifeforce
The Loves of Irina
Sisters of Satan
Star Virgin
Strange Love of the
  Vampires
To Sleep with a Vampire
Twins of Evil

Sexploitation
See also Erotic Thrillers;
  Exploitation
The Body Beneath
The Bride's Initiation
Cafe Flesh
The Case of the Full
  Moon Murders
The Devil's Plaything
Devil's Wedding Night
Dracula Exotica
Dracula Sucks
Dracula, The Dirty Old
  Man
La Reine des Vampires
Lesbian Vampires The
  Heiress of Dracula
Love Vampire Style
The Mad Love Life of a
  Hot Vampire
Mondo Keyhole
Out for Blood
Playgirls and the Vampire
Please Don't Eat My
  Mother
Requiem for a Vampire
Sexy Prohibitissimo
Spermula
The Vampire Conspiracy
The Vampire Hookers
The Vampire of the
  Opera
Vampire's Kiss
Wanda Does
  Transylvania
Witchcraft 3: The Kiss of
  Death

Ships
See Sail Away

Showbiz Comedies
The Gong Show Movie
Tender Dracula, or The
  Confessions of a
  Bloodsucker

Showbiz Thrillers
Guess What Happened to
  Count Dracula?

Shrinks
See also Doctors &
  Nurses
Demonsoul

Love Vampire Style

Shutterbugs
See also Front Page
Because the Dawn

Silent Films
See also Silent
  Horror/Fantasy Classics
Dracula/Garden of Eden
Nosferatu

Silent Horror/
Fantasy Classics
See also Silent Films
Nosferatu
Vampyr

Sixties
See Flower Children

Slapstick Comedy
See also Comedy;
  Screwball Comedy
Abbott and Costello Meet
  Frankenstein
Bowery Boys Meet the
  Monsters
Frankenstein, the
  Vampire and Co.

Space Operas
See also Alien Beings—
  Benign; Alien Beings—
  Vicious
Lifeforce
Planet of the Vampires

Spanish
The Blood Spattered
  Bride
Buenas Noches, Senor
  Monstruo
Cake of Blood
Count Dracula
Curse of the Devil
The Curse of the Vampyr
Daughter of Dracula
Dracula vs. Frankenstein
Dracula's Great Love
Fangs of the Living Dead
Frankenstein's Bloody
  Terror
The Legend of Blood
  Castle
Leonor
Lesbian Vampires The
  Heiress of Dracula
Nostradamus and the
  Destroyer of Monsters
Nostradamus and the
  Genie of Darkness
Orgy of the Vampires
The Saga of the Draculas
The Screaming Dead
Tombs of the Blind Dead
The Vampire of the
  Highway

The Werewolf vs. the
  Vampire Woman

Special FX
Extravaganzas
Lifeforce

Special FX
Extravaganzas:
Make-Up
Vampire in Brooklyn

Special FX Wizards:
Rick Baker
Incredible Melting Man
It's Alive

Special FX Wizards:
Tom Savini
Deathdream
Martin

Special FX Wizards:
Dick Smith
House of Dark Shadows

Speculation
In Search of Dracula

Spies & Espionage
See also Feds
Voodoo Heartbeat

Strippers
From Dusk Till Dawn
Sexy Prohibitissimo
Vamps

Summer Camp
Addams Family Values
Evils of the Night

Super Heroes
Batman Fights Dracula
Vampirella

Supernatural
Comedies
See also Comedy
My Best Friend Is a
  Vampire
Rockula
Saturday the 14th
Saturday the 14th Strikes
  Back
Spooks Run Wild

Supernatural Horror
See also Classic Horror;
  Horror
Alabama's Ghost
Children of the Night
The Curse of the Crying
  Woman
The Daughter of Dr.
  Jekyll
Deathdream
Def by Temptation

Devil's Wedding Night
Disciple of Death
Dr. Terror's House of
  Horrors
Embrace of the Vampire
From Dusk Till Dawn
The Ghost Brigade
Ghost Stories: Graveyard
  Thriller
Horror of the Blood
  Monsters
Howling 6: The Freaks
Invasion of the Blood
  Farmers
The Kiss
The Last Man on Earth
Let's Scare Jessica to
  Death
Los Vampiros de
  Coyoacan
The Loves of Irina
Lust for a Vampire
Mary, Mary, Bloody Mary
The Monster Demolisher
Moon Legend
Near Dark
Night Life
Night of the Sorcerers
The Night Stalker: Two
  Tales of Terror
Nightmare Castle
Nightmare in Blood
Orgy of the Vampires
Terror Creatures from the
  Grave

Supernatural Martial
Arts
Kung Fu Vampire Buster
Magic Cop
Ninja, the Violent
  Sorcerer
Ninja Vampire Busters
The 7 Brothers Meet
  Dracula
Vampire Raiders—Ninja
  Queen

Supernatural
Westerns
Billy the Kid and the
  Green Blaze Vampire
Billy the Kid Versus
  Dracula
The Devil's Mistress
Sundown

Survival
See also Post Apocalypse
Chosen Survivors

Swashbucklers
See also Action
  Adventure; Medieval
  Romps
Captain Kronos: Vampire
  Hunter

Category
Index

Swedish
The Inn of the Flying
Dragon

Sword & Sandal
Hercules in the Haunted
World

Taiwanese
Elusive Song of the
Vampire
Ghostly Mouth-to-Mouth
Resusitation

Technology-Rampant
See also Robots &
Androids
Munster's Revenge

Teen Angst
See also Hell High
School
Buffy the Vampire Slayer
Dracula A.D. 1972
Evils of the Night
Graveyard Disturbance
I Was a Teenage Vampire
The Lost Boys
Mixed Up
My Best Friend Is a
Vampire
Night Life
One Dark Night
Rockula
Valerie and the Week of
Wonders

Television
See TV Movies; TV Pilot
Movies; TV Series

This is Your Life
Anne Rice: Birth of the
Vampire
Chappaqua
Ed Wood
Gothic
Haunted Summer
Lugosi the Forgotten King
Vincent Price's Dracula
Vlad Tepes

3-D Flicks
Frankenstein's Bloody
Terror

Time Travel
The Arrival
Dark Shadows 1840
Flashback
Night of Dark Shadows
Waxwork 2: Lost in Time

Toilets
See Bathroom Scenes

Torrid Love Scenes
See also Sex & Sexuality;
Sexploitation

Body Double
Bram Stoker's Dracula

**Transvestites &
Transsexuals**
See Gender Bending

Trash
Alien Massacre
Andy Warhol's Dracula
The Astro-Zombies
Attack of the Giant
Leeches
Blood Freak
Crypt of the Living Dead
Dracula vs. Frankenstein
Gore-Met Zombie Chef
From Hell
Heartstopper
Kung Fu Vampire Buster
Plan 9 from Outer Space
Please Don't Eat My
Mother
Saturday the 14th Strikes
Back
Vampire Vixens from
Venus

Trees & Forests
A Chinese Ghost Story III
Sorority House Vampires
Tom Thumb and Little
Red Riding Hood vs.
the Monsters

Troma Films
I Married a Vampire

True Stories
See also This is Your Life
Ed Wood
The Legend of Blood
Castle

Turkish
Drakula in Istanbul

TV Movies
Blood Ties
Buck Rogers in the 25th
Century: Space
Vampire
Carmilla
Count Dracula
Deadly Love
Dracula
Graveyard Disturbance
Halloween with the
Addams Family
Here Come the Munsters
I, Desire
The Midnight Hour
Munster's Revenge
Munster, Go Home!
The Mystery of Dracula's
Castle
Night of Dark Shadows
Night Stalker

The Night Stalker: Two
Tales of Terror
Nightlife
Stephen King's The
Tommyknockers
Vampire
Vampirella

TV Pilot Movies
Nick Knight

TV Series
Best of Barnabas
The Best of Dark
Shadows
The Best of Dark
Shadows 2
Curse of Dracula
Dark Shadows 1840
Flashback
Dark Shadows: Behind
the Scenes
Dark Shadows Bloopers
Dark Shadows
Resurrected The Video
Dark Shadows' Scariest
Moments
Dark Shadows: Vampires
& Ghosts
Dark Shadows 25th
Anniversary
World of Dracula

Twins
See also Family Ties
Curse of the Wicked Wife
Devil's Wedding Night
Twins of Evil

UFOs
See Alien Beings—
Benign; Alien Beings—
Vicious; Space Operas

Underground
See Avant-Garde

**Unexplained
Phenomena**
The Night Stalker: Two
Tales of Terror
Salem's Lot

**Universal Studios'
Classic Horror**
Abbott and Costello Meet
Frankenstein
Dracula
Dracula (Spanish Version)
Dracula's Daughter
House of Dracula
House of Frankenstein
Son of Dracula

Up All Night
See also Vampire Babes
Blood & Donuts
Fascination
From Dusk Till Dawn

Vacations
Devils of Darkness
My Grandpa is a Vampire

Vampire Babes
See also Up All Night
Addicted to Murder
The Addiction
Alraune
The Bad Sister
Because the Dawn
Bloodlust
Bloodscent
The Brides of Dracula
Buffy the Vampire Slayer
Captain Kronos: Vampire
Hunter
The Case of the Full
Moon Murders
Countess Dracula
The Craving
Crypt of the Living Dead
The Curse of the Vampyr
Daughter of Dracula
Daughters of Darkness
Demon Queen
Demonsoul
A Deusa de Marmore
Escrava do Diabo
Devil's Vindeta
Doctor Vampire
Dracula's Daughter
Dracula's Daughter
Drakulita
Dungeon Master
Fangs of the Living Dead
The Fearless Vampire
Killers
Fright Night
From Dusk Till Dawn
Ghost Punting
The Girl with the Hungry
Eyes
I, Desire
The Inn of the Flying
Dragon
Insomnia
Interview with the
Vampire
The Kiss
Krvava Pani
La Maschera del
Demonio
La Vampire Nue
Lady Dracula
Lemora, Lady Dracula
Lesbian Vampires The
Heiress of Dracula
The Living Dead Girl
Lust for a Vampire
The Mad Love Life of a
Hot Vampire
Mary, Mary, Bloody Mary
Men of Action Meet the
Women of Dracula
Moon Legend
Nadja
Night of the Sorcerers
Nightlife

Old Dracula
Once Bitten
Out for Blood
Playgirls and the Vampire
Red Lips
The Return of Dr. X
Revenge of the Vampire
Santo and the Blue
    Demon vs. the
    Monsters
Santo en la Venganza de
    las Mujeres Vampiro
Sorority House Vampires
Spermula
Tales from the Crypt
    Presents Bordello of
    Blood
Terror in the Crypt
Twins of Evil
Vamp
The Vampire
Vampire and the
    Ballerina
Vampire Centerfold
The Vampire Conspiracy
The Vampire Girls
Vampire Knights
The Vampire Lovers
Vampire of the Cave
The Vampire of the
    Opera
Vampire Princess Miyu
The Vampire Returns
Vampirella
Vampire's Kiss
Vamps
Vampyre
Vampyres
The Velvet Vampire
Vengeful Vampire Girl
Wanda Does
    Transylvania

Vampire Spoof
See also Horror Comedy
Andy Warhol's Dracula
Beverly Hills Vamp
Buenas Noches, Senor
    Monstruo
Buffy the Vampire Slayer
Casual Relations
Dracula & Son
Dracula Blows His Cool
Dracula: Dead and
    Loving It
Dracula Sucks
Dracula, The Dirty Old
    Man
Dracula: Up in Harlem
Dracula vs. Frankenstein
The Fearless Vampire
    Killers
Gore-Met Zombie Chef
    From Hell
I Married a Vampire
Kiss Me Quick!
Kung Fu Vampire Buster
Love at First Bite

The Malibu Beach
    Vampires
Mr. Vampire
Mr. Vampire II
Mr. Vampire III
Mr. Vampire IV
My Best Friend Is a
    Vampire
My Grandpa is a Vampire
Near Dark
Once Bitten
A Polish Vampire in
    Burbank
Rockula
Son of Dracula
Teen Vamp
Vamp
The Vampire for Two
The Vampire Happening
Vampirisme
Who Is Afraid of Dracula

Variety
Hollywood on Parade

Venice
Vampire in Venice

Vietnam War
Deathdream

Viva Las Vegas!
See also Gambling
Night Stalker

Voodoo
See also Occult
Dr. Terror's House of
    Horrors
O Macabro Dr. Scivano
Scream Blacula Scream
Theatre of Death
Voodoo Heartbeat

War Between the
Sexes
See also Marriage
The Thing

Wedding Hell
See also Marriage
Black Vampire
The Blood Spattered
    Bride
The Brides Wore Blood

Werewolves
See also Metamorphosis
Blood of Dracula's Castle
Capulina contra Los
    Monstros
The Craving
Curse of the Devil
Dr. Terror's House of
    Horrors
Dracula vs. Frankenstein
House of Frankenstein
Howling 6: The Freaks
The Monster Squad

Pepito y Chabelo vs. los
    Monstruos
Return of the Wolfman
Santo and the Blue
    Demon vs. Dracula and
    the Wolfman
Scooby-Doo and the
    Reluctant Werewolf
Slave of the Vampire
Tower of the Devil
The Werewolf vs. the
    Vampire Woman

Westerns
Curse of the Undead
The Devil's Mistress

Wild Kingdom
See also Cats; Killer
    Beasts; Killer Bugs;
    King of Beasts (Dogs);
    Sea Critter Attack
Attack of the Mutant
    Roadkill and the
    Vampyer Zombies from
    Beyond the Grave
Vampire Circus

Witchcraft
See also Demons &
    Wizards; Occult
Black Sunday
The Curse of the Crying
    Woman
Curse of the Devil
Horrible Orgies of Count
    Dracula
The Naked Witch
The She-Beast
Valerie and the Week of
    Wonders
The Werewolf vs. the
    Vampire Woman
Witchcraft 3: The Kiss of
    Death
Witchcraft 7: Judgement
    Hour
Witches, Vampires &
    Zombies

Women
See also Dream Girls;
    Femme Fatale; Wonder
    Women
Anne Rice: Birth of the
    Vampire
Because the Dawn
Dry Kisses Only
The Legend of Blood
    Castle
Samson vs. the Vampire
    Women

Wonder Women
See also Dream Girls
Buffy the Vampire Slayer
Wrestling Women vs. the
    Aztec Mummy

Woofs!
Alien Massacre
The Astro-Zombies
Atom Age Vampire
Blood Freak
Bloodsuckers from Outer
    Space
The Brides Wore Blood
Cave of the Living Dead
Crypt of the Living Dead
Devil's Wedding Night
Dracula: Up in Harlem
Dracula vs. Frankenstein
Dracula's Great Love
Dracula's Last Rites
The Evil Within
Fade to Black
The Fear Chamber
Gore-Met Zombie Chef
    From Hell
Halloween with the
    Addams Family
Horror of the Blood
    Monsters
Incredible Melting Man
Incubus
Invasion of the Blood
    Farmers
It's Alive 2: It Lives Again
Kung Fu Vampire Buster
Mama Dracula
Mom
Night of Dark Shadows
Night of the Sorcerers
Nocturna
Plan 9 from Outer Space
Please Don't Eat My
    Mother
The Slaughter of the
    Vampires
The Thirsty Dead
Vampire Raiders—Ninja
    Queen
World of the Vampires
Wrestling Women vs. the
    Aztec Mummy

World War II
The Reflecting Skin

Wrestling
Chanoc contra el Tigre y
    el Vampiro
Invasion of the Dead
Los Vampiros de
    Coyoacan
Men of Action Meet the
    Women of Dracula
Santo Against Baron
    Brakola
Santo and the Blue
    Demon vs. Dracula and
    the Wolfman
Santo and the Blue
    Demon vs. the
    Monsters
Santo en la Venganza de
    las Mujeres Vampiro
The Vampire Girls

**Category
Index**

327

VAMPIRES on VIDEO

Wrestling Women vs. the
Aztec Mummy

Writers
See also This is Your Life
Gothic
Haunted Summer
Vampire's Kiss

Yugoslavian
Cave of the Living Dead
The She-Beast
Track of the Vampire

Yuppie Nightmares
Addams Family Values
The Malibu Beach
Vampires

Zombie Soldiers
See also Zombies
Deathdream
Scream and Scream
Again

Zombies
See also Death & the
Afterlife; Ghosts,

Ghouls, & Goblins;
Zombie Soldiers
Alien Massacre
The Astro-Zombies
Attack of the Mutant
Roadkill and the
Vampyer Zombies from
Beyond the Grave
Close Encounters of the
Spooky Kind 2
Counter Destroyer
Creature of the Walking
Dead
Deathdream

The Ghost Brigade
Goliath and the Vampires
Isle of the Dead
The Jitters
Night Life
Plan 9 from Outer Space
Tombs of the Blind Dead
Ultimate Vampire
Valley of the Zombies
The Vampire's Ghost
Who Is Afraid of Dracula
Witches, Vampires &
Zombies
Zombie Brigade

Distributor List

The following explains the three-letter codes at the end of each entry. Those are distributor codes, letting you know where you can find that particular video. Turn the page and you will find a Distributor Guide, which provides contact information for these distributors.

ACA—Academy Entertainment, Inc.

AHV—Active Home Video

AIP—A.I.P. Home Video, Inc.

ANI—AnimEigo Inc.

AOV—Admit One Video

APD—Applause Productions, Inc.

APX—A-PIX Entertainment Inc.

ATL—Atlas Entertainment Corporation

BAR—Barr Films

BTV—Baker & Taylor Video

CAB—Cable Films & Video

CAN—Cannon Video

CCB—Critics' Choice Video, Inc.

CDV—Television International

CNG—Congress Entertainment, Ltd.

CNM—Cinemacabre Video

COL—Columbia Tristar Home Video

CPM—Central Park Media/U.S. Manga Corps

DRA—Draculina

DVT—Discount Video Tapes, Inc.

EII—EI Independent Cinema

FCT—Facets Multimedia, Inc.

FHE—Family Home Entertainment

FLL—Full Moon Home Video

FOX—CBS/Fox Video

FRG—Fright Video

FRH—Fries Home Video

FUS—Fusion Video

FXV—FoxVideo

GEM—Video Gems

GKK—Goodtimes Entertainment

GLV—German Language Video Center

GNS—21st Genesis Home Video

GPV—Grapevine Video

GVV—Glenn Video Vistas, Ltd.

HBO—HBO Home Video

HEG—Horizon Entertainment

HHT—Hollywood Home Theatre

HMD—Hemdale Home Video

HMK—Hallmark Home Entertainment

HMV—Home Vision Cinema

IHF—International Historic Films, Inc. (IHF)

IME—Image Entertainment

INJ—Ingram International Films

JEF—JEF Films, Inc.

JFK—Just for Kids Home Video

KAR—Karol Video

KIV—Kino on Video

LCA—Modern Curriculum Press - MCP

LIV—Live Entertainment

LOO—Loonic Video

LSV—LSVideo, Inc.

MAD—Madera Cinevideo

MED—Media Home Entertainment

MGI—Monarich Group, Inc.

MGM—MGM/UA Home Entertainment

MLB—Mike LeBell's Video

MON—Monterey Home Video

MOV—Movies Unlimited

MPI—MPI Home Video

MRV—Moore Video

MSP—Modern Sound Pictures, Inc.

MTH—MTI Home Video

MVD—Music Video Distributors

MWF— Monday/Wednesday/Friday Video

NEW—New Video Group

NHO—New Horizons Home Video

NOS—Nostalgia Family Video

NWV—New World Entertainment

NYR—Not Yet Released

ORI—Orion Home Video

OUP—Outre Products

PAR—Paramount Home Video

PGV—Polygram Video (PV)

PMS—Professional Media Service Corp.

PSM—Prism Entertainment

PYR—Pyramid Film & Video

REP—Republic Pictures Home Video

RHI—Rhino Home Video

RXM—Rex #Miller

SGE—Amsell Entertainment

SHR—Shanachie Entertainment

SMW—Something Weird Video

SNC—Sinister Cinema

STP—Streamline Pictures

TEM—Tempe Video

TIM—Timeless Video Inc.

TLF—Time-Life Video and Television

TOU—Buena Vista Home Video

TPV—Tapeworm Video Distributors

TRI—Triboro Entertainment Group

TTC—Turner Home Entertainment Company

TWE—Trans-World Entertainment

TWV—Time Warner Viewer's Edge

UAV—UAV Corporation

UNI—Unicorn Video, Inc.

USH—Universal Studios Home Video

VCD—Video City Productions/Distributing

VCI—VCI Home Video

VCN—Video Connection

VDB—Video Data Bank

VDM—Video Dimensions

VEC—Valencia Entertainment Corp.

VES—Vestron Video

VHE—VCII Home Entertainment, Inc.

VMK—Vidmark Entertainment

VSM—Video Search of Miami

VTR—Anchor Bay

VYY—Video Yesteryear

WAR—Warner Home Video, Inc.

WFV—Western Media Systems

WMM—Women Make Movies

WOV—Worldvision Home Video, Inc.

Distributor Guide

The following lists contact information for the distributors cited in the main review section. Those listing with the code **OM** are on moratorium, and are no longer available to retailers. Although older copies may be floating around. Entries with the code **NO** aren't currently distributed.

A-PIX ENTERTAINMENT INC.
(APX)
500 5th Ave., 46th Fl.
New York, NY 10110
212-764-7171

ACADEMY ENTERTAINMENT
(ACA)
9250 Wilshire Blvd., Ste. 400
Beverly Hills, CA 90212
Fax: 310-275-2195

ACTIVE HOME VIDEO (AHV)
12121 Wilshire Blvd., No. 401
Los Angeles, CA 90025
310-447-6131
800-824-6109
Fax: 310-207-0411

ADMIT ONE VIDEO (AOV)
PO Box 66, Sta. O
Toronto, ON, Canada M4A 2M8
416-463-5714
Fax: 416-463-5714

A.I.P. HOME VIDEO, INC.
(AIP)
10726 McCune Ave.
Los Angeles, CA 90034
Fax: 213-559-8849

AMSELL ENTERTAINMENT
(SGE)
12001 Ventura Pl., 4th Fl., Ste. 404
Studio City, CA 91604
818-766-8500
Fax: 818-766-7873

ANCHOR BAY (VTR)
500 Kirts Blvd.
Troy, MI 48084
810-362-9660
800-786-8777
Fax: 810-362-4454

ANIMEIGO INC. (ANI)
PO Box 989
Wilmington, NC 28402-0989
910-251-1850
800-242-6463
Fax: 910-763-2376

APPLAUSE PRODUCTIONS,
INC. (APD)
85 Longview Rd.
Port Washington, NY 11050
516-883-2825
800-278-7326
Fax: 516-883-7460

ATLAS ENTERTAINMENT
CORPORATION (ATL)
1 Jocama Blvd., Ste. 2E
Old Bridge, NJ 08857
908-591-1155
Fax: 908-591-0660

BAKER & TAYLOR VIDEO
(BTV)
501 S. Gladiolus
Momence, IL 60954
815-472-2444
800-775-2300
Fax: 800-775-3500

BARR FILMS (BAR)
12801 Schabarum
Irwindale, CA 91706
818-338-7878
800-234-7878
Fax: 818-814-2672

BUENA VISTA HOME VIDEO
(TOU)
350 S. Buena Vista St.
Burbank, CA 91521-7145
818-562-3568

CABLE FILMS & VIDEO (CAB)
Country Club Sta.
PO Box 7171
Kansas City, MO 64113
816-362-2804
800-514-2804
Fax: 816-341-7365

CANNON VIDEO (CAN)
PO Box 17198
Beverly Hills, CA 90290
310-772-7765

CBS/FOX VIDEO (FOX)
PO Box 900
Beverly Hills, CA 90213
562-373-4800
800-800-2369
Fax: 562-373-4803

**CENTRAL PARK MEDIA/U.S.
MANGA CORPS** (CPM)
250 W. 57th St., Ste. 317
New York, NY 10107
212-977-7456
800-833-7456
Fax: 212-977-8709

CINEMACABRE VIDEO (CNM)
PO Box 10005-D
Baltimore, MD 21285-0005

**COLUMBIA TRISTAR HOME
VIDEO** (COL)
Sony Pictures Plaza
10202 W. Washington Blvd.
Culver City, CA 90232
310-280-8000
Fax: 310-280-2485

**CONGRESS ENTERTAINMENT,
LTD.** (CNG)
604 Route 611
PO Box 845
Tannersville, PA 18372-0845
717-620-9001
800-847-8273
Fax: 717-620-9278

**CRITICS' CHOICE VIDEO,
INC.** (CCB)
PO Box 749
Itasca, IL 60143-0749
708-775-3300
800-367-7765
Fax: 708-775-3355

**DISCOUNT VIDEO TAPES,
INC.** (DVT)
PO Box 7122
Burbank, CA 91510
818-843-3366
Fax: 818-843-3821

DRACULINA (DRA)
PO Box 587
Glen Carbon, IL 62034
618-659-1293
Fax: 618-659-1129

EI INDEPENDENT CINEMA
(EII)
PO Box 371
Glenwood, NJ 07418
201-509-9352
Fax: 201-746-6464

FACETS MULTIMEDIA, INC.
(FCT)
1517 W. Fullerton Ave.
Chicago, IL 60614
312-281-9075
800-331-6197
Fax: 312-929-5437

**FAMILY HOME ENTERTAIN-
MENT** (FHE)
c/o Live Home Video
15400 Sherman Way
PO Box 10124
Van Nuys, CA 91410-0124
818-908-0303
800-677-0789
Fax: 818-778-3259

FOXVIDEO (FXV)
2121 Avenue of the Stars, 25th Fl.
Los Angeles, CA 90067
310-369-3900
800-800-2FOX
Fax: 310-369-5811

FRIES HOME VIDEO (FRH)
6922 Hollywood Blvd., 12th Fl.
Hollywood, CA 90028
213-466-2266
Fax: 213-466-2126

FRIGHT VIDEO (FRG)
P.O. Box 277
North Billerica, MA 01862

FULL MOON HOME VIDEO
(FLL)
8721 Santa Monica Blvd., Ste.
526
W. Hollywood, CA 90069
213-341-5959

FUSION VIDEO (FUS)
100 Fusion Way
Country Club Hills, IL 60478
708-799-2073
Fax: 708-799-8375

**GERMAN LANGUAGE VIDEO
CENTER** (GLV)
7625 Pendleton Pike

Indianapolis, IN 46226-5298
317-547-1257
800-252-1957
Fax: 317-547-1263

GLENN VIDEO VISTAS, LTD.
(GVV)
6924 Canby Ave., Ste. 103
Reseda, CA 91335
818-881-8110
Fax: 818-981-5506

**GOODTIMES ENTERTAIN-
MENT** (GKK)
16 E. 40th St., 8th Fl.
New York, NY 10016-0113
212-951-3000
Fax: 212-213-9319

GRAPEVINE VIDEO (GPV)
PO Box 46161
Phoenix, AZ 85063
602-973-3661
Fax: 602-973-0060

**HALLMARK HOME ENTER-
TAINMENT** (HMK)
6100 Wilshire Blvd., Ste. 1400
Los Angeles, CA 90048
213-634-3000
Fax: 213-549-3760

HBO HOME VIDEO (HBO)
1100 6th Ave.
New York, NY 10036
212-512-7400
Fax: 212-512-7498

HEMDALE HOME VIDEO
(HMD)
7966 Beverly Blvd.
Los Angeles, CA 90048
213-966-3700
Fax: 213-653-5452

**HOLLYWOOD HOME THE-
ATRE** (HHT)
1540 N. Highland Ave., Ste. 110
Hollywood, CA 90028
213-466-0127

HOME VISION CINEMA
(HMV)
5547 N. Ravenswood Ave.
Chicago, IL 60640-1199
312-878-2600
800-826-3456

HORIZON ENTERTAINMENT
(HEG)
45030 Trevor Ave.
Lancaster, CA 93534
805-940-1040
800-323-2061
Fax: 805-940-8511

IMAGE ENTERTAINMENT
(IME)
9333 Oso Ave.
Chatsworth, CA 91311
818-407-9100

800-473-3475
Fax: 818-407-9111

**INGRAM INTERNATIONAL
FILMS** *(INJ)*
7900 Hickman Rd.
Des Moines, IA 50322
515-254-7000
800-621-1333
Fax: 515-254-7021

**INTERNATIONAL HISTORIC
FILMS, INC. (IHF)** *(IHF)*
PO Box 29035
Chicago, IL 60629
773-927-2900
Fax: 773-927-9211

JEF FILMS, INC. *(JEF)*
Film House
143 Hickory Hill Circle
Osterville, MA 02655-1322
508-428-7198
Fax: 508-428-7198

JUST FOR KIDS HOME VIDEO
(JFK)
22025 Ventura Blvd., Ste. 200
PO Box 4112
Woodland Hills, CA 91365-4112
818-595-0666
Fax: 818-716-0168

KAROL VIDEO *(KAR)*
PO Box 7600
350 N. Pennsylvania Ave.
Wilkes Barre, PA 18773
717-822-8899
Fax: 717-822-8226

KINO ON VIDEO *(KIV)*
333 W. 39th St., Ste. 503
New York, NY 10018
212-629-6880
800-562-3330
Fax: 212-714-0871

LIVE ENTERTAINMENT *(LIV)*
15400 Sherman Way
PO Box 10124
Van Nuys, CA 91410-0124
818-988-5060

LOONIC VIDEO *(LOO)*
2022 Taraval St., Ste. 6427
San Francisco, CA 94116
510-526-5681

LSVIDEO, INC. *(LSV)*
PO Box 415
Carmel, IN 46032

MADERA CINEVIDEO *(MAD)*
525 E. Yosemite Ave.
Madera, CA 93638
209-661-6000
Fax: 209-674-3650

**MEDIA HOME ENTERTAIN-
MENT** *(MED)*
510 W. 6th St., Ste. 1032

Los Angeles, CA 90014
213-236-1336
Fax: 213-236-1346

**MGM/UA HOME ENTERTAIN-
MENT** *(MGM)*
2500 Broadway
Santa Monica, CA 90404-6061
310-449-3000
Fax: 310-449-3100

MIKE LEBELL'S VIDEO *(MLB)*
75 Freemont Pl.
Los Angeles, CA 90005
213-938-3333
Fax: 213-938-3334

REX MILLER *(RXM)*
Rte. 1, Box 457-D
East Prairie, MO 63845
314-649-5048

**MODERN CURRICULUM
PRESS - MCP** *(LCA)*
PO Box 70935
108 Wilmot Rd.
Chicago, IL 60673-0933
800-777-8100

**MODERN SOUND PICTURES,
INC.** *(MSP)*
1402 Howard St.
Omaha, NE 68102
402-341-8476
800-228-9584
Fax: 402-341-8487

MONARICH GROUP, INC.
(MGI)
2550 Corporate Pl., Ste. C103
Monterey Park, CA 91754
213-268-2288
800-700-8998
Fax: 213-268-2233

**MONDAY/WEDNESDAY/FRI-
DAY VIDEO** *(MWF)*
123 Scribner Ave.
Staten Island, NY 10301
718-447-1347

MONTEREY HOME VIDEO
(MON)
28038 Dorothy Dr., Ste. 1
Agoura Hills, CA 91301
818-597-0047
800-424-2593
Fax: 818-597-0105

MOORE VIDEO *(MRV)*
PO Box 5703
Richmond, VA 23220
804-745-9785
Fax: 804-745-9785

MOVIES UNLIMITED *(MOV)*
3015 Darnell Rd.
Philadelphia, PA 19154
215-637-4444
800-466-8437
Fax: 215-637-2350

MPI HOME VIDEO *(MPI)*
16101 S. 108th Ave.
Orland Park, IL 60462
708-460-0555
Fax: 708-873-3177

MTI HOME VIDEO *(MTH)*
14216 SW 136th St.
Miami, FL 33186
305-255-8684
800-821-7461
Fax: 305-233-6943

**MUSIC VIDEO DISTRIBU-
TORS** *(MVD)*
O'Neill Industrial Center
1210 Standbridge St.
Norristown, PA 19401
610-272-7771
800-888-0486
Fax: 610-272-6074

**NEW HORIZONS HOME
VIDEO** *(NHO)*
2951 Flowers Rd., S., Ste. 237
Atlanta, GA 30341
404-458-3488
800-854-3323
Fax: 404-458-2679

NEW VIDEO GROUP *(NEW)*
126 5th Ave., 15th Fl.
New York, NY 10011
212-206-8600
800-423-1212
Fax: 212-206-9001

**NEW WORLD ENTERTAIN-
MENT** *(NWV)*
1440 S. Sepulveda Blvd.
Los Angeles, CA 90025
310-444-8100
Fax: 310-444-8101

NOSTALGIA FAMILY VIDEO
(NOS)
PO Box 606
Baker City, OR 97814
503-523-9034
800-784-8362
Fax: 503-523-7115

ORION HOME VIDEO *(ORI)*
1888 Century Park E.
Los Angeles, CA 90067
310-282-0550
Fax: 310-282-9902

OUTRE PRODUCTS *(OUP)*
PO Box 1900
Evanston, IL 60204

PARAMOUNT HOME VIDEO
(PAR)
Bluhdorn Bldg.
5555 Melrose Ave.
Los Angeles, CA 90038
213-956-3952

**Distributor
Guide**

POLYGRAM VIDEO (PV)
(PGV)
825 8th Ave.
New York, NY 10019
212-333-8000
800-825-7781
Fax: 212-603-7960

PRISM ENTERTAINMENT
(PSM)
1888 Century Park, E., Ste. 350
Los Angeles, CA 90067
310-277-3270
Fax: 310-203-8036

**PROFESSIONAL MEDIA SER-
VICE CORP.** *(PMS)*
19122 S. Vermont Ave.
Gardena, CA 90248
310-532-9024
800-223-7672
Fax: 800-253-8853

PYRAMID FILM & VIDEO
(PYR)
P.O. Box 1048 .
Santa Monica, CA 90406-1048
310-828-7577
800-421-2304
Fax: 310-453-9083

**REPUBLIC PICTURES HOME
VIDEO** *(REP)*
5700 Wilshire Blvd., Ste. 525
North
Los Angeles, CA 90036-3659
213-965-6900
Fax: 213-965-6963

RHINO HOME VIDEO *(RHI)*
10635 Santa Monica Blvd., 2nd
Fl.
Los Angeles, CA 90025-4900
310-828-1980
800-843-3670
Fax: 310-453-5529

**SHANACHIE ENTERTAIN-
MENT** *(SHR)*
13 Laight St.
New York, NY 10013
212-334-0284
Fax: 212-334-5207

SINISTER CINEMA *(SNC)*
PO Box 4369
Medford, OR 97501-0168
503-773-6860
Fax: 503-779-8650

SOMETHING WEIRD VIDEO
(SMW)
c/o Mike Vraney
PO Box 33664
Seattle, WA 98133
206-361-3759
Fax: 206-364-7526

STREAMLINE PICTURES *(STP)*
2908 Nebraska Avenue
Santa Monica, CA 90404-4109

310-998-0070
800-846-1453
Fax: 310-998-1145

**TAPEWORM VIDEO DISTRIB-
UTORS** *(TPV)*
27833 Hopkins Ave., Unit 6
Valencia, CA 91355
805-257-4904
Fax: 805-257-4820

**TELEVISION INTERNATION-
AL** *(CDV)*
c/o Jason Films
2825 Wilcrest, Ste. 407
Houston, TX 77042
713-266-3097
Fax: 713-266-3148

TEMPE VIDEO *(TEM)*
Box 6573
Akron, OH 44312
216-628-1950
Fax: 216-628-4316

**TIME-LIFE VIDEO AND TELE-
VISION** *(TLF)*
1450 E. Parham Rd.
Richmond, VA 23280
804-266-6330
800-621-7026

TIMELESS VIDEO INC. *(TIM)*
9943 Canoga Ave., Ste. B2
Chatsworth, CA 91311
818-773-0284
800-478-6734
Fax: 818-773-0176

**TRANS-WORLD ENTERTAIN-
MENT** *(TWE)*
8899 Beverly Blvd., 8th Fl.
Los Angeles, CA 90048-2412

**TRIBORO ENTERTAINMENT
GROUP** *(TRI)*
12 W. 27th St., 15th Fl.
New York, NY 10001
212-686-6116
Fax: 212-686-6178

**TURNER HOME ENTERTAIN-
MENT COMPANY** *(TTC)*
Box 105366
Atlanta, GA 35366
404-827-3066
800-523-0823
Fax: 404-827-3266

21ST GENESIS HOME VIDEO
(GNS)
15820 Arminta St.
Van Nuys, CA 91406

UAV CORPORATION *(UAV)*
PO Box 5497
Fort Mill, SC 29715
803-548-7300
800-486-6782
Fax: 803-548-3335

UNICORN VIDEO, INC. *(UNI)*
9025 Eton Ave., Ste. D.
Canoga Park, CA 91304
818-407-1333
800-528-4336
Fax: 818-407-8246

**UNIVERSAL STUDIOS HOME
VIDEO** *(USH)*
100 Universal City Plaza
Universal City, CA 91608-9955
818-777-1000
Fax: 818-866-1483

**VALENCIA ENTERTAINMENT
CORP.** *(VEC)*
45030 Trevor Ave.
Lancaster, CA 93534-2648
805-940-1040
800-323-2061
Fax: 805-940-8511

VCI HOME VIDEO *(VCI)*
11333 E. 60th Pl.
Tulsa, OK 74146
918-254-6337
800-331-4077
Fax: 918-254-6117

**VCII HOME ENTERTAIN-
MENT, INC.** *(VHE)*
13418 Wyandotte St.
North Hollywood, CA 91605
818-764-1777
800-350-1931
Fax: 818-764-0231

VESTRON VIDEO *(VES)*
c/o Live Home Video
15400 Sherman Way
PO Box 10124
Van Nuys, CA 91410-0124
818-988-0303
800-367-7765
Fax: 818-778-3194

**VIDEO CITY PRODUC-
TIONS/DISTRIBUTING**
(VCD)
4266 Broadway
Oakland, CA 94611
510-428-0202
Fax: 510-654-7802

VIDEO CONNECTION *(VCN)*
3123 W. Sylvania Ave.
Toledo, OH 43613
419-472-7727
800-365-0449
Fax: 419-472-2655

VIDEO DATA BANK *(VDB)*
School of the Art Institute of
Chicago
112 S. Michigan Ave.
Chicago, IL 60603
312-345-3550
800-634-8544
Fax: 312-541-8073

VIDEO DIMENSIONS *(VDM)*
322 8th Ave., 4th Fl.
New York, NY 10001
212-929-6135
Fax: 212-929-6135

VIDEO GEMS *(GEM)*
12228 Venice Blvd., No. 504
Los Angeles, CA 90066

VIDEO SEARCH OF MIAMI
(VSM)
PO Box 161917
Miami, FL 33116
305-279-9773
Fax: 305-598-2665

VIDEO YESTERYEAR *(VYY)*
Box C
Sandy Hook, CT 06482

203-426-2476
800-243-0987
Fax: 203-797-0819

VIDMARK ENTERTAINMENT
(VMK)
2644 30th St.
Santa Monica, CA 90405-3009
310-314-2000
Fax: 310-392-0252

WARNER HOME VIDEO, INC.
(WAR)
4000 Warner Blvd.
Burbank, CA 91522
818-954-6000

WESTERN MEDIA SYSTEMS
(WFV)
30941 W. Agoura Rd., Ste. 302

Westlake Village, CA 91361
818-889-7350
Fax: 818-889-7350

WOMEN MAKE MOVIES
(WMM)
462 Broadway, Ste. 501
New York, NY 10013
212-925-0606
Fax: 212-925-2052

WORLDVISION HOME
VIDEO, INC. *(WOV)*
1700 Broadway
New York, NY 10019-5905
212-261-2700
Fax: 212-261-2950

Distributor Guide